Guide to
Weekend
Getaways

Guide to
Weekend
Getaways

74 Mini-Vacations
Across America

NATIONAL
GEOGRAPHIC
WASHINGTON, D.C.

Contents

Map 6-7
About this Guide 8

Atlanta
Southern Comforts 10
Wild, Wild Georgia 14

Boston & Hartford
Blackstone River
Ramble 20
Coastal Massachusetts 24
Monadnock Madness 29
Festive Vermont 33
The Berkshires 37
A Shore Thing 41

Charlotte
Cradle of Forestry 46
Appalachian Crafts 51

**Chicago &
Indianapolis**
Architectural Chicago 56
Into the Heartland 60
Car Mania 65
Brown County 69

Cincinnati
Along the Ohio River 74
Bluegrass Furlough 78

Denver
A Brewery Crawl 84
The Front Range 88
Rocky Mountain High 92

Detroit
Motor City 98
Gateway to Freedom 103

**Houston &
San Antonio**
Galveston by
the Sea 108
Tejano Spirit 113
Texas Hill Country 117

Kansas City
On a Musical Note 122
Trails West 127

Las Vegas
American Excess 132

Los Angeles & San Diego
Hollywood 138
Ojai & Carpinteria 142
See-worthy Sights
by the Seashore 147
California Dreamin' 151
Faces of the Desert 154

Miami
Miami Nice 160
The Middle Keys 165
Captiva Audience 169

Minneapolis
Mississippi Meander 174

Nashville & Memphis
Country Music City 180
Digging
Underground 184
Noodling Down the
Natchez Trace 187
In Memphis, the Beat
Goes on 191
Arkansas Ozarks 195

New Orleans
Once Over Easy 200
Roamin' Oaks 205
Cajun Country 209

New York City
Gilded Age Castles 214
Quiet Times 218
The Litchfields 221

Philadelphia
Independence Days 226
Bucks County 231
Brandywine Valley 235

Phoenix
Desert Gardens 240
Getting Teed Off 245
The Mild Wild West 249

Pittsburgh
Rubbing Elbows with
Robber Barons 254
Laurel Highlands 258

Portland & Seattle
Garden Delights 264
Seaside Oregon 268
Columbia River
Gorge 273
On the Volcano
Trail 277
Mill Town Memories 281
Orcas Island 285
Pure Pacific
Northwest 289

St. Louis
Mark Twain Country 294
Missouri Rhineland 298

Salt Lake City
Powder Paradise 304
Jurassic Journeys 308
Bear River Range 312

San Francisco
City of Views 316
Russian River
Wineries 320
Monterey Bay 325
Gold Rush Days 329

Washington, D.C.
Around the Chesapeake
334
Blue Ridge Ramble 338
Presidential Palaces 342

Illustrations Credits 346
Index 347
Credits 352

Front cover: Lake Placid, New York *Page 1:* Barn and fall foliage, Bucks County, Pennsylvania
Pages 2-3: Golden Gate Bridge, San Francisco *Opposite:* Mansion Inn, New Hope, Pennsylvania

Seattle

WASHINGTON

Columbia

Portland

Columbia

OREGON

Coast Ranges

San
Francisco

CALIFORNIA

CANADA

Missouri

MONTANA

G
R
E
A
T

NORTH
DAKOTA

SOUTH
DAKOTA

R
O
C
K
Y

IDAHO

Snake

WYOMING

*Great
Basin*

Great
Salt
Lake

Salt Lake
City

NEVADA

UTAH

N. Platte

NEBRASKA

Platte

S. Platte

COLORADO

Denver

M
O
U
N
T
A
I
N
S

P
L
A
I
N
S

KANSA

Colorado

Lake
Powell

Arkansas

Las
Vegas

Lake
Mead

*Mojave
Desert*

ARIZONA

NEW MEXICO

OKLA

Los Angeles

Colorado

San Diego

Phoenix

Rio Grande

Re

0   200
Miles

MEXICO

T E X A

Brazos

San
Antonio

Rio Grande

MINNESOTA

Lake Superior

MICHIGAN

MAINE

Minneapolis

WISCONSIN

Mississippi

VT.

N.H.

Lake Michigan

Lake Huron

NEW YORK

MOUNTAINS

MASS. • Boston

Lake Ontario

CONN.

IOWA

Detroit

Lake Erie

Hartford

R.I.

Missouri

Chicago

OHIO

PENNSYLVANIA

New York

ILLINOIS INDIANA

Pittsburgh

N.J.

Philadelphia

Kansas City

Indianapolis

Cincinnati

MD.

DEL.

Washington, D.C.

St. Louis

Wabash

Ohio

W. VA.

MISSOURI

KENTUCKY

VIRGINIA

Nashville

APPALACHIAN

NORTH CAROLINA

TENNESSEE

Charlotte

Memphis

Tennessee

SOUTH CAROLINA

ARKANSAS

Atlanta

Savannah

S

MISSISSIPPI

ALABAMA

GEORGIA

MAP KEY

LOUISIANA

Mississippi

Red

• Chicago Getaway Hub

Houston

New Orleans

FLORIDA

Miami

About this Guide

THE NATIONAL GEOGRAPHIC GUIDE TO WEEKEND GETAWAYS
presents 74 easy-to-reach mini-vacations across the United States.
Thoroughly planned and tested by expert travel writers, these rejuvenating experiences are found in or near 24 major metropolitan areas.
You can enjoy them whether you live nearby or are passing through.
With up to seven getaways per hub, there are many different kinds of
adventures from which to choose.

Most of the weekends focus on a region—California's Russian
River Valley, Louisiana's Cajun Country, Pennsylvania's Bucks
County—though some are city destinations, including Las Vegas
and New Orleans. Each one focuses on a dominant theme, a special
feature, that makes them unique: Chicago's early skyscrapers, cowboys and dude ranches in the Texas Hills, Virginia's Blue Ridge
wineries, desert wildflowers around Phoenix, gilded age castles in
the Hudson River Valley.

The writers present each getaway as a relaxed two-, three-, or
four-day itinerary that reflects the best things to see and do in the
designated area, and recommend ways to spend your time. A Travelwise section accompanies each entry and includes visitor information, best seasons to visit, annual events, additional things to see and
do, as well as specially selected restaurants and hotels. Locator maps
help you find the getaway route.

All information has been checked and, to the best of our knowledge, is accurate as of press time. Since information can change,
however, it is advisable to phone ahead when possible. In addition to
the stated days of closure, many sites close on national holidays.

Most importantly, enjoy your getaway!

Price ranges for hotels and restaurants

Hotels

$	Under $100
$$	$100-$200
$$$	Over $200

Restaurants

$	0-$10
$$	$10-25
$$$	Over $25

Atlanta

Southern Comforts 10

Wild, Wild Georgia 14

The 1842 Inn's beckoning porch

Southern Comforts
A drive along the Antebellum Trail

GENERAL SHERMAN MAY HAVE BURNED his way from Atlanta to the sea, but he left untouched a number of fine houses. Today a 100-mile heritage trail links antebellum towns from Athens to Macon. Along the way, you can visit and stay in several gracious old houses, while a national forest and two lakes offer plenty of recreation.

Athens area

Start your weekend in **Athens,** home of the University of Georgia. In fact, the university—founded in 1785—came first, with the town growing up around it. Federal and then big Greek Revival-style homes, bordered by boxwood gardens, appeared throughout the town. Today Athens blends Old South charm with an up-to-date cultural savvy. When you arrive in town, check out the **welcome center** *(280 E. Dougherty St. 706-353-1820)* in the 1820 Church-Waddel-Brumby House. Believed to be Athens's oldest surviving residence, the house is furnished with period antiques.

From the welcome center, it's about a three-block walk down to the historic North Campus of the **University of Georgia** *(706-542-0842).* Enter through the Arch (ca 1858) at Broad Street and College Avenue into a magnolia- and oak-shaded green. A plaque here notes that in the War for Southern Independence most of UGA's students joined the Confederate Army. Several buildings on this part of campus were built in the early 1800s, including Phi Kappa Hall (1836), Old College (1806), and the Chapel (1832). Among the Dixie-related archives in the Main Library are the original handwritten Confederate Constitution (1861), as well as the papers of Georgia statesmen and of *Gone with the Wind* author Margaret Mitchell.

NOT TO BE MISSED
● **Houses along S. Liberty Street in Milledgeville** ● **The Hay House lit up at night**
● **Cocktails on the 1842 Inn's veranda**
● **Gardens in spring**

When it's time for a break, head back to **Broad Street** and its assortment of trendy shops, coffeehouses, and restaurants. Nationally famous bands such as R.E.M. and the B-52's started out in the clubs of downtown Athens. You might even catch a local band on its ascent to stardom.

A few of Athens's antebellum houses are open to the public on a

Hay House, Macon

somewhat regular basis, the **Taylor-Grady House** *(634 Prince Ave. 706-549-8688. Mon.-Fri. by appt.; adm. fee)* most prominent among them. To get there, head up College to Prince Street. Gen. Robert Taylor, a planter and merchant, built the Greek Revival mansion in the 1840s; between 1865 and 1868 it was the home of journalist and orator Henry W. Grady, who coined the term "New South" and urged reconciliation with the North.

Madison & Eatonton

Head south on US 129/441 through the rolling hills of the Piedmont, exiting the highway for several antebellum towns. In Watkinsville, the **Eagle Tavern** *(Main and 3rd Sts. 706-769-5197)* was built about 1801 as a stage stop for coaches traveling from Milledgeville to Athens; it now operates as a museum.

Continue south to **Madison**, a town spared by Sherman because a leading citizen opposed secession. With a population of 3,500, Madison today holds more than 25 houses and churches that pre-date the Civil War. Pick up a walking-tour brochure at the welcome center *(115 E. Jefferson St. 706-342-4454 or 800-709-7406)* and amble along shady streets, admiring the architecture. A block east of the welcome center, the **Rogers House** *(contact welcome center for tour information)*, built in plantation plain style about 1810, is one of the town's oldest houses.

If it's lunchtime, stop in **Ye Olde Colonial Restaurant** (see Travelwise), housed in a 19th-century bank building, for cafeteria-style classic southern fare: black-eyed peas, butter beans, corn bread, cobbler, country-style steak, and sweet tea.

Less than a half hour farther south you come to **Eatonton,** home to the **Uncle Remus Museum** *(Turner Park. 706-485-6856. Closed Tues. Sept.-May; adm. fee).* Shadow boxes, paintings, and mementos relating to the Uncle Remus tales by local author Joel Chandler Harris (1848-1908) are housed in two former slave cabins similar to one occupied by the fictional Remus.

To Milledgeville & Macon

If you find yourself in historic **Milledgeville** on Sunday morning, attend a service at **St. Stephen's** *(220 S. Wayne St. 478-452-2710),* an 1841 Episcopal church built in carpenter Gothic style. Afterward, stroll around the historic district, which holds more than a dozen national register properties, many adorned with double porticoes and fanlights, with gardens shaded by crape myrtle and dogwood out back.

Milledgeville served as the capital of Georgia between 1803 and 1868. In November 1864, General Sherman occupied the governor's mansion for two days; his 30,000 troops burned many government buildings but left most houses intact. Now called the **Old Governor's Mansion** *(120 S. Clarke St. 478-445-4545. Closed Mon.; adm. fee),* the 1838 building is a striking example of Greek Revival design.

Take US 129 southwest to **Macon.** Before you drive over the Ocmulgee River into town, stop by **Ocmulgee National Monument** *(off Emery Hwy. 478-752-8257)* to see some decidedly antebellum architecture—as in a thousand years before the Civil War. The Mississippian people who lived here about A.D. 900-1100 built tremendous flat-topped mounds that remain today. The funeral and temple mounds are similar to others in the Southeast, but the most fascinating thing here is an earth lodge reconstructed during a 1930s dig with the original thousand-year-old clay floor.

A prosperous river-and-rail town before and after the war, Macon holds dozens of well-preserved antebellum structures. The most impressive is the 18,000-square-foot **Hay House** *(934 Georgia Ave. 478-742-8155. Adm. fee),* an Italian Renaissance showplace built between 1855 and 1860. A tour gives insight into the lavish lifestyles of wealthy 19th-century Georgians. A block south, the 1853 Greek Revival **Cannonball House and Confederate Museum** *(856 Mulberry St. 478-745-5982. Closed Sun.; adm. fee)* holds the distinction of being the only house in town damaged during the Civil War; you can touch the cannonball that smashed through a window in 1864.

For a look at another side of antebellum life, visit the **Tubman African American Museum** *(340 Walnut St. 478-743-8544. Adm. fee),* dedicated to the spirit of Harriet Tubman. Fourteen galleries take you on a journey through black history, art, and culture, including a world-class collection of African art and an exhibit focusing on African and African-American cuisine. —*John M. Thompson*

Travelwise

GETTING THERE

The Antebellum Trail links the historic communities of Athens, Watkinsville, Madison, Eatonton, Milledgeville, and Macon via US 441, Ga. 22, and US 129. Athens lies 70 miles east of Atlanta via US 29; Macon is 80 miles south via I-75.

GENERAL INFORMATION

Contact the **Georgia Antebellum Trail Association** (P.O. Box 4088, Eatonton, GA 31024. 706-485-7701); **Athens Convention & Visitors Bureau** (300 N. Thomas St., Athens, GA 30601. 706-357-4430 or 800-653-0603. www.visitathensga.com); or the **Macon-Bibb County Convention & Visitors Bureau** (200 Cherry St., Macon, GA 31208. 478-743-3401 or 800-768-3401. www.maconga.org).

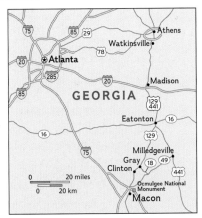

ANNUAL EVENTS

Holiday Tour of Homes (early Dec., Madison. Call Madison Chamber of Commerce, 706-342-4454) A chance to see several old houses in their holiday finery.

Spring Tours of Homes Athens and Eatonton offer tours in April, Madison in May; Macon has garden tours in May. Contact the local convention and visitors bureaus.

White Columns & Holly—Christmas in Macon (Thanksgiving-Dec., Macon. Call Macon-Bibb County Chamber of Commerce; see above) This citywide celebration features historic houses decorated for the holidays.

MORE THINGS TO SEE & DO

Jarrell Plantation State Historic Site (from Clinton, about 20 miles W on Ga. 18/Jarrell Plantation Rd., then N 3 miles. 478-986-5172. Closed Mon.; adm. fee) An 1847 plantation house with 20 historic buildings dating from between 1847 and 1945.

Old Clinton Historic District (1.5 miles SW of downtown Gray, just off US 129) Twelve buildings dating from 1808 to 1830 portray one of the Old South's fastest growing centers of trade and culture. Old Clinton War Days in May reenact the Federal occupation of Clinton during the Civil War.

LODGING

1842 Inn (353 College St., Macon. 478-741-1842. www.the1842inn.com. $$$) A Greek Revival mansion and adjoining Victorian house offer 21 luxurious rooms. Convenient to Macon's main attractions.

Antebellum Inn (200 N. Columbia St., Milledgeville. 478-454-5400. $) Antebellum in look and feel if not date, this circa 1890 Greek Revival home has five handsomely appointed rooms and a wraparound porch.

Nicholson House (6295 Jefferson Rd., Athens. 706-353-2200. $$) A 1947 Colonial Revival home built over an 1820s log house, this B&B sits on 34 acres. Six rooms, three suites.

DINING

Downtown Grill (562 Mulberry St., Macon. 912-742-5999. $$$) Southern specialties include cheese grits and pork loin in Vidalia onion barbecue sauce.

Harry Bissett's (279 E. Broad St., Athens. Closed lunch Mon. 706-353-7065. $$$) A New Orleans-style café serving turtle soup, oysters Bienville, and homemade desserts; try the Cajun martini made with pickled okra.

Weaver D's Delicious Fine Foods (1016 E. Broad St., Athens. 706-353-7797. $) This Athens soul-food landmark dishes up comforts such as buttermilk biscuits, corn muffins, squash casserole, fried chicken, and barbecue.

Ye Olde Colonial Restaurant (108 E. Washington St., Madison. 706-342-2211. Closed Sun. $$) Classic southern fare. See p. 11.

Wild, Wild Georgia
Hiking, fishing, & paddling in the southern Appalachians

A COUPLE OF HOURS NORTH of Atlanta, the southern end of the Appalachians offers a peaceful escape. Trekking up forested peaks, tossing a line in clear streams, canoeing down frothy rivers, and relaxing in quaint little mountain towns are a few of this area's refreshing pleasures. In one weekend you can hike the first part of the Appalachian Trail, drive to the top of Georgia's highest peak, see a handful of beautiful waterfalls, and treat yourself to fine southern food.

Dahlonega area

If you get away from the city in the morning, you can easily make it to Dahlonega (da-LON-eh-ga) in time for lunch; proceed straight to the **Smith House** (see Travelwise). Built in the 1880s, this comfortably rambling house has operated as an inn and restaurant since 1922, and it is now one of northern Georgia's most notable eateries. Patrons are served family style at big tables laden with about 15 different dishes: fried chicken, roast beef, collard greens, black-eyed peas, fried okra, yams, yeast rolls, and much more.

Afterward, a stroll around the square is in order. Dahlonega dates back to the 1828 gold rush that brought thousands of prospectors swarming to the hills of northeast Georgia. Local Cherokee were soon forced out by land-hungry settlers, and little towns such as Dahlonega sprang up. Around the square you can shop for mountain crafts and jewelry made with Georgia gold. **Quigley's Rare Books & Antiques** *(104 Public Sq. N. 706-864-0161)* is a fun place to hunt for used and rare books, including first editions of American classics. Don't overlook the **Dahlonega Gold Museum State Historic Site** *(Public Sq. 706-864-2257. Adm. fee)*, occupying the former Lumpkin County Courthouse (ca 1836). A film, gold nuggets, miners' tools, and exhibits on the history of local mining

Waterfall in Vogel State Park

and minting give you a worthwhile history lesson.

To get a better feel for what the mines were like, take a tour of the **Consolidated Gold Mines** *(Consolidated Gold Mine Rd. 706-864-8473. Adm. fee)* and learn more about local geology and historical mining techniques; you descend to 120 feet below ground. There's also an opportunity to pan for gold. The nearby **Crisson Gold Mine** *(2736 Morrison Moore Pkwy. 706-864-6363. Adm. fee)* is a fourth-generation hard-rock mine with a 117-year-old stamp mill for crushing ore; gold panning is available.

North of Dahlonega

Spend the morning driving up into the highlands, pausing for a hike when the call of the wild becomes irresistible. You'll be traveling through the **Chattahoochee National Forest,** a 750,000-acre spread carved by rocky defiles and hemlock-lined rivers. In spring the woods take on a dazzling array of delicate color, with pink dogwoods, yellow jasmine, and a full spectrum of wildflowers. Turkeys, hawks, deer, and bears are a few of the 500 animal species inhabiting the forest. Head north on US 19, then US 129; you'll shortly come to **DeSoto Falls Scenic Area.** The 2-mile **DeSoto Falls Trail** meanders to two picturesque waterfalls; you can fish for trout in the streams.

Farther on, the road twists up the mountain to Neels Gap, where it crosses the **Appalachian Trail,** the famous 2,167-mile footpath that links Georgia with Maine. Stock up on maps, snacks, and good advice at the conveniently located Walasi-Yi Center. From here you can make a day hike up to 4,458-foot **Blood Mountain,** gaining about 1,300 feet in elevation along with wonderful mountain views. The mountain was named for a legendary battle between the Creek and Cherokee; the fighting was said to have made the streams run red.

For a somewhat tamer outdoor experience, continue north on US 129 a few miles to **Vogel State Park** *(US 129, 11 miles S of Blairsville. 706-745-2628. Adm. fee).* Included in the 17-mile trail system is the 1-mile **Byron Herbert Reece Nature Trail,** with interpretive markers to help explain the natural order of an oak-hickory forest. In summer you'll likely see and hear scarlet tanagers, rose-breasted grosbeaks, warblers, vireos, bluebirds, and woodpeckers. You can also camp and fish here, and there's a lake for swimming.

In the afternoon, head north on US 129, then right on Ga. 180 and watch for the spur road up to **Brasstown Bald.** In a few zigzagging miles you'll come to a parking lot *(fee),* where you can get out and walk a steep half-mile trail through rhododendron and laurel thickets—or take a shuttle—to the top. At 4,784 feet, the bald is the highest point in the state. The **visitor center** *(closed winter. 706-896-2556)* has several interesting exhibits on the area's natural and cultural history, and the observation deck gives you a stunning panorama of the Appalachians.

West of Dahlonega

Head west from Dahlonega on Ga. 52, where more natural wonders await. In a few miles you cross the swift and narrow **Etowah River.** April through September, Appalachian Outfitters in Dahlonega *(706-864-7117)* offers canoe and kayak trips on an 8-mile section of the Middle Etowah, past rock cliffs, banks of mountain laurel, and Class I and II rapids. It makes for a nice half-day trip. For a shorter, gentler outing, you can try the **Chestatee River,** back near Dahlonega.

Continuing west about 20 miles brings you to **Amicalola Falls State Park** *(off Ga. 52. 706-265-4703. Adm. fee).* Amicalola is a Cherokee word meaning "tumbling waters," and these you'll find at the end of an easy footpath beneath oaks and maples. The falls, at 729 feet high, are among the highest in the East; their spray has nurtured lush fern gardens on the rock walls. The park is a popular gateway for backpackers heading out on the Appalachian Trail, which begins atop Springer Mountain 8 miles away.

Many through-hikers, as those who hike the entire Appalachian Trail are called, begin their several-month journey at Georgia's only backpacking inn, the **Len Foote Hike Inn** *(for reservations call 770-389-7275 or 800-864-7275).* It lies a moderate 5-mile walk from the park, through a wildflower-dotted woodland. You don't, however, have to be a hard-core hiker to enjoy this woodsy getaway. Dinner and breakfast are included with the night's lodging.

Before leaving the area, try to spend a little time on one of the many rivers that slice Georgia's mountains. Paddlers often take to the **Toccoa River** north of Blue Ridge; it feeds into the Ocoee in Tennessee, which was the site of the white-water events in the 1996 Summer Olympics. A number of outfitters offer rafting expeditions on a lively section of the Ocoee that boasts Class III and IV rapids. Southeast of Ellijay, the **Cartecay River** is a much gentler ride. A little farther west, anglers favor the **Conasauga River.**

—John M. Thompson

Travelwise

GETTING THERE

Dahlonega is 60 miles north of Atlanta via US 19.

GENERAL INFORMATION

Contact the **Dahlonega/Lumpkin County Chamber of Commerce** *(13 S. Park St., Dahlonega, GA 30533. 706-864-3711. www.dahlonega.org)* or the **Chattahoochee National Forest** *(1755 Cleveland Hwy., Gainesville, GA 30501. 770-297-3000. www.fs.fed.us/conf).*

SEASONS

Spring is the most spectacular season, heralded by the blushing blossoms of redbud and the tassels of maples, followed by white hawthorn, pink azalea, and a host of wildflowers. Summers can be hot, though relief generally comes at night. Fall colors are well worth coming for; winter days can vary from mild to cold.

ANNUAL EVENTS

Autumnfest *(3rd weekend in Sept., Dahlonega. Contact Dahlonega Chamber*

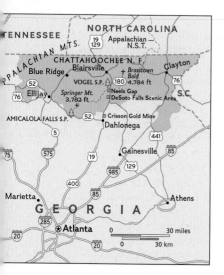

Holly Theatre *(69 W. Main St., Dahlonega. 706-864-3759)* This community theater presents popular plays from March to December.

Horseback riding Gold City Corral *(Forrest Hills Mountain Resort, E of Dahlonega. 706-867-9395. www.goldcitycorral.com)* offers trail rides lasting from one hour to overnight, plus dinner wagon rides; Sunny Farms North *(Dahlonega. 706-867-9167)* also gives lessons.

LODGING

Blueberry Inn & Gardens *(400 Blueberry Hill, Dahlonega. 706-219-4024 or 877-219-4024. $-$$)* A lovely hillside setting with gardens and flowering trees makes this 12-room inn a little getaway unto itself.

Len Foote Hike Inn *(770-389-7275 or 800-864-7275. $)* Backpacking inn near head to Appalachian Trail. See p. 17.

Misty Mountain Inn & Cottages *(3 miles S of Blairsville on US 19. 706-745-4786 or 888-647-8966. $)* This bed-and-breakfast features a farmhouse, cottages with loft bedrooms, in-room fireplaces, and whirlpools (in some rooms).

Smith House *(84 S. Chestatee St., Dahlonega. 706-867-7000 or 800-852-9577. www.smithhouse.com. $-$$)* Historic inn with 18 guest rooms and famous restaurant. See p. 14.

DINING

Caruso's Ristorante Italiano *(19B E. Main St., Dahlonega. 706-864-4664. $$)* A casual restaurant on the square offers pasta, pizzas, and other Italian specialties; local artwork graces the walls.

Forge Mill Crossing *(6 miles E of Blue Ridge on US 76. 706-374-5771. $$)* Regional specialties at this casual country restaurant include baby-back ribs and brandied apple pork chops.

Renee's Café & Wine Bar *(135 N. Chestatee St., Dahlonega. 706-864-6829. Closed Mon.-Tues. $$$)* Contemporary regional cuisine with Mediterranean flavors served in a restored 19th-century residence.

Smith House *(84 S. Chestatee St., Dahlonega. 706-867-7000 or 800-852-9577. $-$$)* Quintessential southern cooking. See p. 14.

of Commerce, 706-864-5543 or 800-231-5543)* Features hayrides, Appalachian music on the square, barbecue cook-off, sidewalk sale.

Bear on the Square Mountain Festival *(3rd weekend in April, Dahlonega. 706-867-6710)* Appalachian crafts, bluegrass music, jam sessions, children's activities.

Gold Rush Days Festival *(3rd weekend in Oct., Dahlonega. 706-864-7247)* More than 300 arts and crafts booths, hog calling, liar's contest, crosscut sawing, clogging, buck dancing, and bluegrass music.

Sorghum Festival *(2nd, 3rd, and 4th weekends in Oct., Blairsville. Contact Blairsville, GA–Union Co. Chamber of Commerce, 706-745-5789 or 877-745-5789)* This small-town event features cooking and jarring sorghum syrup from ground cane, arts and crafts, a biscuit-eating contest, and a parade.

MORE THINGS TO SEE & DO
Bicycling Explore the area's many bike trails by calling Mountain Adventures Cyclery *(Dahlonega. 706-864-8525)*, which offers rentals, maps, and guided tours. Chattahoochee National Forest has some of the best mountain biking in Georgia. Three trails originating near the Nimblewill area feature a range of difficulty and stunning scenery; obtain information from the Chattahoochee National Forest Visitors Center in the Wal-Mart Shopping Center in Dahlonega.

Boston & Hartford

Blackstone River Ramble 20

Coastal Massachusetts 24

Monadnock Madness 29

Festive Vermont 33

The Berkshires 37

A Shore Thing 41

Fishermen's Memorial Statue, Gloucester, Massachusetts

Blackstone River Ramble

Discovering our working heritage

IN 1793 INDUSTRIAL CAPITALIST SAMUEL SLATER built the country's first mechanized cotton mill in Pawtucket, Rhode Island. Powering it was the hard-working Blackstone River, which falls some 450 feet in its 46-mile run from Worcester, Massachusetts, to Pawtucket. For the next century, industrial development followed the Blackstone upstream, etching on this rural valley the historical leap from farms to factories—commemorated today in the 400,000-acre John H. Chafee Blackstone River Valley National Heritage Corridor. The modern Boston suburbs of Waltham, Lowell, and Lawrence were built as model mill towns in the 19th century. Old mills and remarkable museums still stretch from Pawtucket to Lowell, tracing a critical chapter of American history.

NOT TO BE MISSED

- Coffee shops and ethnic restaurants of downtown Lowell
- Hiking in Purgatory Chasm State Reservation
- Paddling Blackstone River between Plummer's Landing and River Bend Farm ● A stop for fish and chips in Market Square, Woonsocket

Blackstone River Valley

Begin your tour at the Blackstone Valley Tourism Council's visitor center (175 Main St. 401-724-2200) in Pawtucket; here you can obtain maps of the entire Blackstone River Valley National Heritage Corridor. Then cross the street to the **Slater Mill Historic Site** (67 Roosevelt Ave. 401-725-8638. Daily June–Labor Day, weekends rest of year; adm. fee). There, beside the Blackstone River, stands Samuel Slater's 1793 mill, the first successful fully mechanized mill in the nation (it turned out cotton yarn). Nearby is the **Wilkinson Mill,** built in 1810, which housed a machine shop. Join a 90-minute group tour of Slater Mill—now a museum—for an overview of the technological revolution that was spawned by early textile manufacturing. In the little **Sylvanus Brown House,** built in 1758, spinning and weaving are demonstrated the old-fashioned way—by hand.

Follow R.I. 122 up the east side of the river to **Woonsocket.** Stop

Power looms at Boott Cotton Mills Museum

at the Blackstone River Valley National Heritage Corridor headquarters, in the old railroad station at One Depot Square, for current information. Then visit the **Museum of Work and Culture** *(42 S. Main St. 401-769-9675. www.rihs.org/visitone.htm. Adm. fee)*. This interactive museum views industrialization through the lives of the workforce, with a special focus on the French-Canadian immigrants who left Quebec in droves for jobs in the Blackstone Valley.

You might want to picnic in adjoining **River Island Park.** To get a feel for the river, launch your own canoe or kayak at the park's free canoe ramp, or take a 45-minute tour aboard the ***Blackstone Valley Explorer*** *(for schedule call 401-724-2200)*—a 49-passenger canopied riverboat. The Woonsocket Landing is on River Street, near the Museum of Work and Culture.

Continue north on R.I. 122 to Blackstone, Massachusetts, and turn left on County Road, following the signs to **Blackstone Gorge.** Look down into the 80-foot gorge or walk beside the Blackstone's last wild stretch to glimpse the power of what was once "the hardest working river in America."

Return to Mass. 122 and continue north to the 1,000-acre **Blackstone River and Canal Heritage State Park** *(287 Oak St., Uxbridge. 508-278-7604)*. This natural area is a good place for hiking, birding, and paddling the river. You'll find the visitor center, with picnic areas and a canoe launch, at the old **River Bend Farm,** which dates from prerevolutionary times. Pick up a map and hike or bike the trails and towpath beside the 1828 **Blackstone Canal,** built to transport goods from Worcester to Providence. The view from **Lookout Rock**—over the valley and its meandering river—is a particularly fine one.

Boston area mills

The Blackstone heritage corridor ends near Worcester, but the history of industrial development continues on other rivers farther east. Follow I-90 E (Massachusetts Turnpike) to I-95/Mass. 128 N, then take exit 26 for **Waltham.** Here in 1814, on the Charles River just a few miles upstream from Harvard University, Boston entrepreneurs built the world's first fully mechanized mill complex, combining under one roof all the previously dispersed steps of manufacturing cloth. To "man" the machines, they hired young girls and installed them in boardinghouses, forging a model for later mills.

New mills were added here throughout the 19th century. The last, built in 1911, now houses the **Charles River Museum of Industry** *(154 Moody St. 781-893-5410. www.crmi.org. Closed Sun.; adm. fee),* which focuses on the history of the American industrial revolution and on the meaning of work. To park, cross the river, turn left at Pine Street, and follow the signs to the parking area. Use the footbridge over the river to reach the museum.

Your next stop—and perhaps your most important one—is **Lowell.** Return to I-95/Mass. 128 N. Take exit 32 onto US 3, then exit 30A onto the Lowell Connector. Get off at Thorndike Street (exit 5B) and follow the signs to **Lowell National Historical Park** *(978-970-5000. www.nps.gov/lowe).* The park stands on the Merrimack River where the same group of "Boston Associates" who built the mills at Waltham—the Appletons, the Cabots, the Lowells, the Lawrences, and the Jacksons—constructed a model city of mills and canals, solidified an economic and political empire, and forever changed the way Americans work and live.

Begin your immersion at the visitor center at Market Mills. From there you can set out on a self-guided tour or with a group by foot, free trolley *(March-Nov.),* or canal boat *(May-Oct.; fare)* to visit the **Boott Cotton Mills Museum;** the **Working People Exhibit,** which features a reconstructed boardinghouse for mill girls; the grounds and canals; the old town; and ethnic neighborhoods. Also worth a look is the nearby **American Textile History Museum** *(491 Dutton St. 978-441-0400. www.athm.org. Closed Mon.; adm. fee).*

To reach **Lawrence,** return via the Lowell Connector to I-495N and the Marston Street exit. Take the first left onto Canal Street; go straight through the lights and take the second right onto Jackson St. On the right you'll see the restored 1840s boardinghouse that serves as the visitor center and museum of **Lawrence Heritage State Park** *(1 Jackson St. 978-794-1655).* Exhibits focus on the history of Lawrence and the textile industry, as well as on the historic "Bread and Roses" strike that immigrant millworkers staged in 1912, when the

Lawrence Mills were the world's largest producer of worsted woolen cloth. Pick up a walking-tour guide and stroll the greenway beside the Merrimack River to the Great Stone Dam. Make your way to Lawrence Riverfront State Park to picnic, relax, or launch your canoe or kayak one last time before driving back to Boston. —*Ann Jones*

Travelwise

GETTING THERE
To travel through history in chronological order, begin in Pawtucket and proceed north to finish the tour in Lowell or Lawrence. To reach Pawtucket from Boston, take I-95 south 50 miles to exit 29. Bear right onto Fountain Street, then right onto Exchange Street. At the light, turn left onto Roosevelt Avenue. Waltham, Lowell, and Lawrence, Massachusetts lie east and northeast of Worcester. They are accessible by commuter train from Boston's North Station *(Massachusetts Bay Transportation Authority 800-392-6100).*

GENERAL INFORMATION
Contact the **John H. Chafee Blackstone River Valley National Heritage Corridor** *(1 Depot Sq., Woonsocket, RI 02895. 401-762-0250. www.nps.gov/blac);* the **Blackstone Valley Tourism Council** *(175 Main St., Pawtucket, RI 02860. 401-724-2200 or 800-454-2882. www.tourblackstone.com);* or the **Blackstone Valley Visitors Bureau** *(110 Church St., Whitensail, MA 01588. 800-841-0919).*For Waltham, Lowell, and Lawrence, call the national and state parks and museums.

SEASONS
Most of the museums can be visited year-round. Summertime into early fall is the best time to enjoy the rivers.

LODGING
For something truly different, call the **Blackstone Valley Tourism Council** *(401-724-2200)* to book B&B accommodations on board the *Samuel Slater,* a British-built canal boat afloat on the Blackstone River.

General's Quarters Bed & Breakfast *(881 Aldrich St., Uxbridge. 508-278-6927. www .uxbridgeonline.com/generalsquarters. $)* Colonial style house with 2 rooms.

Grafton Inn *(25 Central Sq., Grafton. 508-839-5931. $)* This lovely eight-room inn has

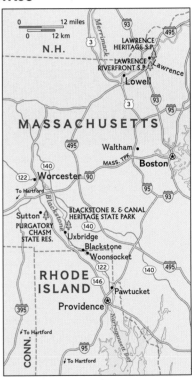

welcomed guests since 1805 on historic Grafton Common.

Morin's Victorian Hideaway Bed & Breakfast *(48 Mendon St., Blackstone. 508-883-7045. $)* Overlooks the Blackstone River. Five rooms.

DINING
Ye Olde English Fish & Chips *(25 S. Main St., Woonsocket. 401-762-3637. Closed Mon. $)* A Woonsocket institution since 1922. Also serves scallops, chowder, and stuffed quahogs.

Old Worthen House *(141 Worthen St., Lowell. 978-459-0300. $)* Oldest tavern in the area. Fantastic chowder.

Coastal Massachusetts
Down to the sea for the weekend

EARLY AMERICANS WERE BOUND TO THE SEA. Most arrived by ship, and many made their fortunes in the New World from maritime trade. Those fortunes built coastal cities and shaped American art and architecture for centuries afterward.

Just north and east of Boston, where the Atlantic carves a crenellated shore of rocky promontories, sheltered bays, and sandy beaches, this nautical history is visible in towns that began life as busy seaports, fishing villages, or shipbuilding stations. Here are mansions furnished centuries ago with exotic products of the China trade, wharves where fishermen still spread their nets, and salt marshes—and seafood restaurants—circled by seabirds.

Salem area
Begin your visit in historic Salem (founded in 1626) at the National Park Service visitor center of the **Salem Maritime National Historic Site** *(2 New Liberty St. 978-740-1650. www.nps.gov/sama)*. Watch the

Annisquam Lighthouse at Cape Ann

short film on the history of Salem and Essex County, then catch a tram at the nearby **Trolley Depot** *(191 Essex St. 978-745-3003. Daily April-Oct., weekends March and Nov.; fare)* for a one-hour tour of the town; after that, you can use the trolley to shuttle from one site to the next all day.

Most of the Salem historic site lies several blocks from the visitor center at the **Derby Street Waterfront.** Start at the Central Wharf Orientation Center with a short film on the Orient trade; check out the *Friendship,* a replica of a typical East Indiaman built in Salem in 1797; take a guided tour of the Custom House (where Nathaniel Hawthorne held his "day job"); and stroll to the lighthouse at the end of Derby Wharf for a fine view of the harbor.

Ride the trolley one stop to the Turner-Ingersoll Mansion, built on the harbor in 1668 and immortalized by Hawthorne in 1851 as the **House of the Seven Gables** *(54 Turner St. 978-744-0991. www.7gables.org. Adm. fee).* The seaside site includes Hawthorne's birthplace and other centuries-old houses plus a garden café.

Return to the vicinity of the visitor center for a quick circuit of the splendid **Peabody Essex Museum** *(East India Sq. 978-745-9500 or 800-745-4054. www.pem.org. Daily April-Nov., Nov.-March Tues.-Sun.; adm. fee).* Collections are being reorganized for the opening of a new wing in May 2003, but many gems are still on view. Don't miss the East India Marine Hall, the museum's first home, a historic building in its own right, displaying the figureheads of old vessels. The adjoining gallery re-creates the opulent saloon of America's first oceangoing yacht, the 1816 *Cleopatra's Barge.* The Asian Export Art

Wing, with its dazzling collection of China trade objects so beloved by America's upper crust, is a must. The museum grounds also encompass the Phillips Library neighborhood, an array of buildings representing three centuries of New England architecture, set in federal-style gardens.

Three blocks away lies the **McIntire Historic District** of federal mansions, all designed or influenced by Salem's fine architect Samuel McIntire (1757-1811) and built on the proceeds of silk from India and pepper from Sumatra. The spine of the district is Chestnut Street, a national historic landmark and possibly the most beautiful street in America. (Mathematician and astronomer Nathaniel Bowditch lived at 12 Chestnut St. shortly after publishing *The New American Practical Navigator* in 1802.) You will have passed through this area on the trolley, but you may want to return for a walking tour *(area guide available at visitor center)* or to visit the **Stephen Phillips Memorial Trust House** *(34 Chestnut St. 978-744-0440. www.phillips museum.org. Mem. Day–Nov. Mon.-Sat.; donation)*, a house museum showcasing the lives of five generations.

Five miles south and east of Salem *(via Mass. 114)* lies Marblehead, the unofficial yachting capital of America. In summer, more than 1,600 boats tie up in the sheltered harbor between Marblehead and Marblehead Neck; regattas and cup races fill the calendar from July through September. For landlubbers, Marblehead invites walking—on the harborside, the grounds of old Fort Sewall, or the narrow streets of Old Town, where prerevolutionary houses stand shoulder to shoulder. Among them is the **mansion** *(161 Washington St. 781-631-1768. June–mid-Oct. Tues.-Sat.; adm. fee)* built in 1768 by powerful colonial shipowner Jeremiah Lee.

Cape Ann

Mass. 127 winds along the coast north of Salem to **Gloucester,** the nation's oldest working seaport and the gateway to Cape Ann. Gloucester celebrates its salty heritage in a series of festivals: St. Peter's Fiesta and the Blessing of the Fleet *(June)*, the Waterfront Festival *(August)*, the Schooner Festival *(Labor Day weekend)*, and the Seafood Festival *(September)*.

Begin your visit at the visitor center *(Hough Ave.)* at **Stage Fort Park.** Pick up a guide to the **Gloucester Maritime Trail,** a series of approximately 1-mile walking tours of four historic areas: the fort and seafront, downtown, the working waterfront, and picturesque Rocky Neck. Among the highlights of these tours are the views of the city and harbor from the trail behind the monument

---

NOT TO BE MISSED

- The sights and smells of Gloucester's working docks ● The Chinese plates in the Peabody Essex Museum ● Fresh seafood ● Cycling around Cape Ann ● Purchasing a watercolor seascape in a Rockport gallery

rock at Stage Fort Park; the Jodrey State Fish Pier (8 acres of fishing-boat docks) in the inner harbor; and the 1926 fishing schooner *Adventure (978-281-8079. www.schooner-adventure.org)*, which is undergoing restoration at a downtown pier and is scheduled to reopen to the public in the fall of 2002.

The **Cape Ann Historical Museum** *(27 Pleasant St. 978-283-0455. www.cape-ann.com/historical-museum. Closed Sun.-Mon. and Feb.; adm. fee)*, housed in a historic sea captain's mansion, displays artifacts from Gloucester's fishing and sea-trading past. It also contains a fine collection of paintings by Fitz Hugh Lane (1804-1865), a Gloucester artist renowned for his seascapes; Lane's imposing granite house can be seen near Harbor Loop.

Drive around the harbor to **Rocky Neck,** a peninsula that forms the eastern gate of Gloucester's inner harbor. Off East Main Street lie the studios, galleries, shops, and houses of **Rocky Neck Art Colony,** the oldest colony of working artists in the country.

Many vessels offer deep-sea fishing or sailing trips in and around Gloucester Harbor. Sail into history aboard the 65-foot schooner *Thomas E. Lannon (Rogers St., Seven Seas Wharf. 978-281-6634. www.schooner.org. Mid-May–mid-Oct.; fare)*. Go lobstering with Cape Ann Cruises *(978-283-1979. www.capeanncruises.com. Mid-June– Labor Day, weekends May and Sept.; fare)*. Or head offshore to humpback feeding grounds with Cape Ann Whale Watch aboard the *Hurricane II (415 Main St., Rose's Wharf. 978-283-5110 or 800-877-5110. www.seethewhales.com. Mid-April–mid-Oct.; fare)*.

Rockport

Fans of *A Perfect Storm* (both book and movie were based in Gloucester) can take the "Perfect Tour" of the town's relevant sights on summer Sunday mornings with Gloucester Guided Tours *(978-283-4194. Mem. Day–mid-Oct. Reservations reqd.; fee)*.

Others can take Mass. 127A east along the rocky coast of Cape Ann to reach the village of **Rockport.** Here, on a spit of land called Bearskin Neck, old fishing shacks have been converted to art galleries, restaurants, and smart shops to make a promenade that is quintessentially quaint. One old red shanty on the wharf has been the subject of so many artists and photographers that it's known as **Motif #1.**

Rockport offers many small inns, such as the **Inn on Cove Hill** (see Travelwise) and the **Pleasant Street Inn** (see Travelwise), an 1893 Victorian. Either one makes a good staging area for visits to **Halibut Point State Park** *(978-546-2997. Parking fee)* to the north, where the Atlantic crashes against the granite headland at the northernmost tip of Cape Ann, or to the ocean beaches to the south *(accessible via Mass. 127A)*. **Long Beach** is especially beautiful, as are the less frequented **Cape Hedge Beach** and **Pebble Beach.** —*Ann Jones*

Travelwise

GETTING THERE

To reach Salem from Boston, take I-93 to exit 37A, then Mass. 128 north to exit 25A, and Mass. 114 east to Salem. There is commuter rail service from Boston's North Station and bus service from Haymarket Square. *(800-392-6100. www.mbta.com).*

For Gloucester, take Mass. 114 back to Mass. 128 north to the Grant Circle exit, then Mass. 127 south; or take a more leisurely drive north on Mass. 127A and 127. Mass. 127 allows you to drive a complete circuit of Cape Ann before returning to Boston via Mass. 128 and I-95 or US 1.

GENERAL INFORMATION

Contact **Destination Salem** *(59 Wharf St., Salem, MA 01970. 978-744-3663 or 877-725-3662. www.salem.org);* **Gloucester Visitor Center** *(22 Poplar St., Gloucester, MA 01930. 978-281-8865 or 800-649-6839. www.gloucesterma.com);* or **Cape Ann Chamber of Commerce** *(33 Commercial St., Gloucester, MA 01930. 978-283-1601 or 800-321-0133. www.capeannvacations.com).*

SEASONS

Most seaside venues stay open from Memorial Day to Labor Day. Many remain open through October. Both sea and sand are at their sunny best in July and August.

MORE THINGS TO SEE & DO

Deep-sea fishing and whale-watching boats leave from Rockport harbor. Contact **Rockport Whale Watch** *(Tuna Wharf. 978-546-3377. www.rockportwhalewatch.com)* or **Tuna**

Hunter Fishing Charters *(978-407-1351. Mid-April–Nov. www.tunahunter.com).* For an intimate glimpse of the coastline, rent a kayak at **North Shore Kayak Outdoor Center** *(9 Tuna Wharf. 978-546-5050. www.north shorekayak.com)* or join one of the center's guided kayak tours.

LODGING

Best Western Bass Rocks Ocean Inn *(107 Atlantic Rd., Gloucester. 978-283-7600 or 800-528-1234. www.bestwestern.com/bass rocksoceaninn. $-$$$)* All 48 rooms have an ocean view. Outdoor pool, rooftop observation deck, rental bikes.

Harbor Light Inn *(58 Washington St. 781-631-2186. www.harborlightinn.com. $-$$)*

Hawthorne Hotel *(18 Washington Sq. W., Salem. 978-744-4080 or 800-729-7829. www.hawthornehotel.com. $$-$$$)* A 1925 Federal-style hotel located on the common. Each of the 89 guest rooms is distinctive.

Inn on Cove Hill *(37 Mt. Pleasant St., Rockport. 978-546-2701 or 888-546-2701. www.innoncovehill.com. $-$$)* Think red rocking chairs, white picket fences, and pastel pink roses. See p. 27.

Ocean View Inn & Resort *(171 Atlantic Rd., Gloucester. 978-283-6200 or 800-315-7557. www.oceanviewinnandresort.com. $-$$$).* Seaside resort on 6 acres. 62 guest rooms.

Pleasant Street Inn *(17 Pleasant St., Rockport. 978-546-3915 or 800-541-3915. www.pleas antstreetinn.net. $-$$)* 1893 Victorian B&B. See p. 27.

DINING

Blackburn Tavern *(2 Main St., Gloucester. 978-282-1919. $$)* Good sandwiches and salads. Live entertainment on weekends.

Madfish Grill *(77 Rocky Neck Ave., Glouces- ter. 978-281-4554. Closed mid-Oct.–mid- April. $$)* Seafood restaurant. Also serves pasta and chicken dishes.

My Place By-the-Sea *(Rockport. 978-546- 9667. $$)* This spot, at the far end of Bearskin Neck, is a popular place for oceanfront dining.

Rudder Restaurant *(73 Rocky Neck Ave., Gloucester. 978-283-7967. Closed mid- Oct.–mid-April. $$)* Dining on the water.

Monadnock Madness
*Biking & hiking a hidden
corner of New Hampshire*

THINK COLONIAL FARMHOUSES set among rolling hills. Think lightly
traveled roads winding amid dairy farms and woodlots. Think
covered bridges spanning crystalline streams. Now imagine yourself cycling the serpentine byways that thread this corner of southwest New Hampshire. Finally, top off this mental image with a
lone, rugged giant—Monadnock Mountain—and you'll be close
to hearing (and heeding) the clarion call it sends out to hikers: On
a clear day, the view from its 3,165-foot-high summit takes in the
towering Presidential Range—and seemingly all of New England.

Jaffrey/Peterborough area

For a real mountain experience, camp in **Monadnock State Park**
(603-532-8862. Adm. fee), which offers 21 primitive tent sites year-
round *(for reservations call 603-271-3628. Fee).* For more creaturely
comforts, check into an old-fashioned New England inn within sight
of the mountain. In the **Jaffrey area,** the **Grand View Inn** is a 19th-
century mansion with nine suites and a wonderful
view of Monadnock from its base. Nearby are the
Benjamin Prescott Inn, an 1853 house amid a
500-acre dairy farm; the **Inn at Jaffrey Center,** a
rambling 1830s house with 11 guest rooms; and
the **Currier's House,** an 1810 colonial with three
guest rooms. (See Travelwise for all four inns.)

You may prefer to find lodgings in the larger
and lovely old town of **Peterborough;** said to
have been the model for Thornton Wilder's *Our
Town,* it lies not far to the north, on the banks of
the Contoocook River. There you'll find two
good bed-and-breakfasts: The **Peterborough
Manor** (see Travelwise) is a rambling, circa 1894
Victorian within walking distance of downtown shops and restaurants, while the **Apple Gate** (see Travelwise) is an 1832 colonial farmhouse set among apple orchards.

Bring your bike or rent one in Peterborough from Eclectic Bicycle
(109 Grove St. 603-924-9797. www.eclecticbicycle.com. Reservations

---

NOT TO BE MISSED

● **The bare granite bones
of Monadnock Mountain**

● **Fall foliage in crimson
and gold** ● **The Sharon
Arts Center** ● **The unique
New England Marionette
Opera in Peterborough**

recommended). This bike shop is a convenient place to seek out maps, guides, group rides, tours, and expert advice. Or head for that well-known Peterborough institution and social center, the **Toadstool Bookshop** *(12 Depot Sq. 603-924-3543)*, for a copy of Linda Chestney's *Bicycling Southern New Hampshire* (Nicolin Fields Pub., 2000); then, over coffee and a sandwich at Aesop's Tables in a corner of the store, you can map out your first ride. If you'd rather ride off road, try Specialists of Adventure Recreation in nearby Mount Vernon *(603-672-5272. www.soarnh.com)* for rentals, instruction, and tours.

An especially scenic bike ride (or drive, if you must) follows N.H. 101 west for 6 miles from Peterborough to **Dublin.** With its fine old homes and steepled white churches, Dublin is one of the area's most handsome villages. Stroll through town before turning off on New Harrisville Road to **Harrisville,** the nation's best preserved (and prettiest) 19th-century redbrick mill town. Under the management of Historic Harrisville, Inc. *(603-827-3722)*, the old mill buildings now house modern businesses. **Harrisville Designs** *(41 Main St. 603-827-3333 or 800-338-9415. www.harrisville.com)*, the last hurrah of the wool trade, offers weaving courses as well as its signature products—including yarns and hand-weaving looms—at its retail store. Stop in to buy a flier for a self-guided walking tour of the village.

You can return the way you came. If you get a second wind after visiting Harrisville, though, continue north and bear left at the Y onto Chesham Road. A series of left turns—check your map!—loops you back to N.H. 101 east, which then returns to Dublin and Peterborough. The entire trip covers about 26 miles. A less ambitious alternative is to drive to Dublin and bike the 14-mile Harrisville loop.

Monadnock Mountain

If you start from Peterborough, bike 6 miles south on US 202 to Jaffrey. Turn right on N.H. 124, pass through Jaffrey Center (2 miles), and soon you'll see the right turn for **Monadnock State Park** *(603-532-8862. Adm. fee)*. At the visitor center pick up a map of the park's 40 miles of trails, and plan your hike. Even though Monadnock is reported to be the most climbed mountain in the country, it's still no Sunday stroll in white sneakers. This is serious mountain terrain of folded metamorphic schist and granite, rugged and challenging; and although there are many trails to the top, every one has its steep stretches. For the shortest route—the 2-mile (one way) **White Dot Trail** from the visitor center—allow about four hours for the round-trip. The adjacent **White Cross Trail** is less steep but a little longer.

But why hurry up the mountain? As Henry David Thoreau (who camped near the summit of Monadnock in 1858 and 1860) lamented in his journal, "It is remarkable what haste the visitors make to get to the top of the mountain and then look away from it." He found greater pleasure on the mountain, and not merely in looking out from it. Taking a leaf from Thoreau's book, you can hike a beautiful ridge circuit through varying vegetation. Starting on the White Dot Trail, turn right on Cascade Link, then left on **Pumpelly Trail,** and carry on to the summit. Allow 3.5 hours for this hike of 3.75 miles. If you like, you can descend by either the shorter White Dot or White Cross Trails. Alternatively, pick up the 4.5-mile (one way) Pumpelly Trail at Dublin Pond *(off East Lake Rd. near Dublin)*.

By the time you've biked back to your lodgings, you'll be ready for (and deserving of!) dinner. In Peterborough, try the imaginative new American bistro cooking at the popular **Acqua Bistro** or the fresh seafood and Italian specialties at **R. A. Gatto's.** Closer to the mountain, try the updated bistro country fare at the lovely old **Inn at Jaffrey Center.** (See Travelwise for all three restaurants).

Swanzey area

Along the little Ashuelot River and its south branch, south of the city of **Keene,** five historic covered bridges are still in use. A leisurely 18-mile driving tour of the valley takes you over (and through) all of them. Better yet, drive to the village of **Swanzey** and leave your car.

A picnic lunch can be the payoff for scrabbling up Monadnock Mountain.

Consult your map to plan an inclusive route, then hop on your bike and head south on N.H. 32 to begin your meandering tour of the peaceful river valley. With minimal backtracking, you can take in the 60-foot **Carlton bridge** (1869)—the area's smallest covered bridge— as well as the **Coombs covered bridge** (1837), the **Slate covered bridge** (rebuilt in 2001 to replace the 1862 span burned in 1995), the **West Swanzey (or Thompson) covered bridge** (1832), and the 159-foot **Sawyers Crossing covered bridge,** a double-span rebuilt in 1859.

Time permitting, bike or drive to **Rhododendron State Park** *(Rhododendron Rd. off N.H. 119 near Fitzwilliam. 603-239-8153. Adm. fee).* The park's 16 acres of rhododendrons bloom around mid-July, creating a resplendent glen *(wheelchair accessible).*　　　—*Ann Jones*

Travelwise

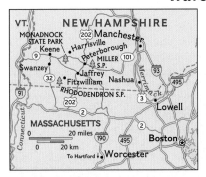

and the views from Monadnock Mountain even more spacious when the trees are bare. Monadnock State Park stays open for primitive winter camping and cross-country skiing.

GETTING THERE
From I-91, take the Keene (N.H. 9) exit. From I-93 or the F. E. Everett Turnpike, exit at Nashua for N.H. 101A. Peterborough is 75 miles northwest of Boston (1.75 hours) and 125 miles northeast of Hartford (2.5 to 3 hours).

GENERAL INFORMATION
Contact the **Monadnock Travel Council** *(603-355-8155 or 800-432-7864. www.monad nocktravel.com)* or the **Greater Peterborough Chamber of Commerce** *(603-924-7234. www.peterborough chamber.com).* The chamber dispenses information at the intersection of N.H. 101 and US 202 in Peterborough *(10 Wilton Rd.).*

SEASONS
The best seasons for biking and hiking are spring, summer, and the spectacularly flamboyant New England fall. But the New England winter, too, can be picture perfect

LODGING
Apple Gate *(199 Upland Farm Rd., Peterborough. 603-924-6543. $)* Charming two-story B&B with 4 guest rooms. See p. 29.

Benjamin Prescott Inn *(N.H. 124., Jaffrey. 603-532-6637 or 888-950-6637. www.ben jaminprescottinn.com. $-$$)* A lovely house with ten guest rooms. See p. 29.

Currier's House *(5 Harkness Rd., Jaffrey. 603-532-7670. www.thecurriershouse.com. $)* See p. 29.

Grand View Inn *(580 Mountain Rd., Jaffrey. 603-532-9880. www.thegrandviewinn.com. $$-$$$)* Resort/spa on 330 acres. See p. 29.

Inn at Jaffrey Center *(379 Main St., Jaffrey Center. 603-532-7800 or 877-510-7019. www.theinnatjaffreycenter.com. $-$$)* Known for its excellent restaurant *($$-$$$).* See p. 29.

Peterborough Manor *(50 Summer St., Peterborough. 603-924-9832. www.peterborough manor.com. $)* Six guest rooms. See p. 29.

DINING
Acqua Bistro *(18 Depot Sq., Peterborough. 603-924-9905. Closed Mon. $$-$$$)* Try the pan-seared black bass. See p. 31.

R. A. Gatto's *(6 School St., Peterborough. 603-924-5000. Closed Mon. $$-$$$)* Small, but popular. See p. 31.

Festive Vermont
A weekend celebration of the arts

THE BROAD, GREEN VALLEYS of southwest Vermont, where cows graze by red barns and churches lift white spires above tidy villages, make inviting summer stages for art, music, and theater festivals. On a leisurely drive from one picture-perfect town to the next, your biggest chore is to choose your entertainment.

Bennington area

Begin your visit in **Bennington,** founded in 1761. In the Old Bennington district you'll find the beautifully restored Four Chimneys Inn *(21 West Rd. 802-447-3500 or 800-649-3503. www.fourchimneys .com. $$-$$$)*, a good place to dine or stay. Take a turn through Old Bennington to the **Old First Church,** a fine Palladian edifice built in 1805. In the Old Burying Ground behind the church, you can pay your respects to Vermont's great farmer/poet, Robert Frost. His tombstone reads: "I had a lover's quarrel with the world."

Then visit the **Bennington Museum** *(W. Main St. 802-447-1571. www.benningtonmuseum.com. Adm. fee.)* to see the work of Anna Mary Robertson "Grandma" Moses (1860-1961), who lived and painted in this area. The museum also houses a collection of 18th- and 19th-century Bennington pottery. Make your next stop nearby **Potter's Yard** *(324 County St. 802-447-7531 or 800-205-8033. May-Nov.)*. Founded in 1950, it's the oldest art pottery in the country, hand-producing fine contemporary versions of the classic Bennington ceramic ware displayed in the museum.

At the **Bennington Center for the Arts** *(Vt. 9 and Gypsy Ln. 802-442-7158. www.vermontarts center.org. May-Nov.)* you'll find innovative exhibits housed in four galleries, events, and performances in spring, summer, and fall. The arts center is well known for its fine collection of Native American arts. In the evening, head to the center's intimate theater for a performance of the Oldcastle Theatre Company in residence *(802-447-0564. www.oldcastle.org. Mid-May– Nov.)*, a highly esteemed Equity company.

Call the box office in advance to reserve a discounted pretheater dinner at a nearby restaurant. Or try **Bennington Station** (see Trav-

NOT TO BE MISSED

- Browsing Northshire Book Store in Manchester
- Vermont cheddar cheese
- The Vermont Country Store in Weston for earmuffs, long johns, and stuff
- Canoeing the Batten Kill

Hildene's ornamental garden was designed by Robert Todd Lincoln's daughter, Jesse.

elwise): The town's historic blue marble train depot a century ago, it is now a popular restaurant serving steak, seafood, and pasta. Afterward, head next door to the red caboose (formerly of the Pennsylvania Railroad) for homemade maple ice cream.

Manchester area

Drive north along historic Vt. 7A to visit **Arlington,** a white clapboard town immortalized in the paintings of Norman Rockwell, who lived in Arlington from 1939 to 1953 and recruited friends and neighbors to pose for him. The **Norman Rockwell Exhibit** *(Vt. 7A. 802-375-6423 or 888-781-8357. www.normanrockwellexhibit.com. Adm. fee spring-fall)* showcases reproductions of the artist's work. Some of his former models even staff the exhibit!

Vt. 7A wends north along the swift-running Batten Kill river into the beautiful old village of **Manchester,** settled in 1761; from here the road leads seamlessly into the town of **Manchester Center.** Though small—the combined population is 2,675—Manchester and Manchester Center seem larger and more cosmopolitan, thanks to summer residents and winter skiers. In former days, the village's lovely setting drew prominent visitors to the colonnaded **Equinox Hotel** (see Travelwise). This facility, a good choice for Sunday brunch, was restored in 1985 and lavishly updated in the mid-1990s.

Manchester's many historic inns also include the **Inn at Ormsby**

Hill (see Travelwise), a restored manor house dating from 1764. Or you might select a charming bed-and-breakfast such as **River Meadow Farm** (see Travelwise); from roughly 1829 to 1945 this was a working farm owned by the town, with the bounty of its fields and gardens earmarked for feeding the poor.

If you want to devote the rest of the day to the arts, you'll find much to enjoy. Just opposite the Equinox, visit **Frog Hollow Vermont State Craft Center** *(802-362-3321)*, where the work of some of Vermont's finest craftspeople is available for purchase. Then visit the **Southern Vermont Arts Center** *(off West Rd. 802-362-1405. www.svac.org)*. This 407-acre site, which hugs the lower slope of Equinox Mountain, hosts a year-round arts festival that features a full calendar of exhibits, performances, and lectures. Ten galleries housed in a national historic trust mansion present classic and contemporary art, while the smart new Elizabeth de C. Wilson Museum houses the SVAC's 800-piece permanent collection and its traveling exhibits.

The SVAC is a lovely place to while away a summer afternoon. You may want to register in advance for a Saturday art class for adults or children; weeklong courses are available as well. You can also explore the arts center's hiking trails, sculpture garden, indoor-outdoor café, and its mile-long botany trail, which threads its way among the native plants and wildflowers growing on the premises. Every Thursday evening from mid-July to September, the **Manchester Music Festival** presents a concert in the SVAC's 400-seat Arkell Pavilion.

On Saturday evenings, head for **Hunter Park** *(802-362-0150 or 866-866-2086. www.hunterpark.com)* and its Riley Rink concert venue, where you may catch the **Vermont Symphony Orchestra** *(802-864-5741 or 800-876-9293. www.vso.org)* in concert, or visiting artists playing jazz, blues, or rock. Take a blanket and sit on the lawn to enjoy music under the stars. If you prefer theater, drive 5 miles north on Vt. 30 to the pretty little village of **Dorset.** Dine on traditional American "comfort fare" at the 1796 **Dorset Inn** (see Travelwise) on the village green before attending a play of the **Dorset Theatre Festival** *(802-867-5777. www.theatredirectories.com. Mid-June–mid-Sept.)*. Or attend a performance at the **Weston Playhouse** *(802-824-5288. www.westplay.com. June-Sept.)*, an old colonnaded theater on the village green in Weston, 20 miles north of Manchester via Vt. 11 and Vt. 100.

Cap off the weekend with a stop at **Hildene** *(Vt. 7A. 802-362-1788. www.hildene.org. Closed Dec.–mid-May; adm. fee, guided tours only)*, a 1904 summer home built by Robert Todd Lincoln. After touring the mansion, you can stroll through the gardens and grounds to the picnic area. Often under way is a special concert, a crafts show, an antiques fair, a garden party, or perhaps even a Saturday afternoon polo match (call for schedule).   —*Ann Jones*

Travelwise

GETTING THERE

The Bennington and Manchester areas lie 125 miles north of Hartford and 140 miles west of Boston. From Hartford, take I-91N, then Vt. 9 west to Bennington. To return, take Vt. 11 and 30 east from Manchester, then turn south on Vt. 30 to rejoin I-91S at Brattleboro. From Boston, take Mass. 2/US 202 west to I-91N and follow directions above.

GENERAL INFORMATION

Contact the **Bennington Area Chamber of Commerce** (Veterans Memorial Dr., Bennington, VT 05201. 802-447-3311 or 800-229-0252. www.bennington.com) or the **Manchester Chamber of Commerce** (5046 Main St., Manchester Center, VT 05255. 802-362-2100. www.manchestervermont.net).

SEASONS

Arts programs and performances run mid-May to mid-October. Ask the chambers of commerce for a listing of festivals and events.

ANNUAL EVENTS

Top equestrians compete throughout July in the five-week-long **Summer Vermont Festival** (Harold Beebe Farm, Vt. 7A, East Dorset. www.vt-summerfestival.com. Adm. fee). In addition to summer-long theater and music festivals, Bennington holds an annual **Mayfest craft fair** and a **Quiltfest** in September. Arlington has its **Harvest Festival** every October, while Manchester hosts several weekend arts and crafts festivals and antiques fairs.

MORE THINGS TO SEE & DO

Two of Vermont's finest ski and snowboarding mountains are **Bromley** (802-824-5522. www.bromley.com) and **Stratton** (800-787-2886. www.stratton.com). For cross-country skiing in Manchester, head to the **Equinox Ski Touring Center** (802-362-4700. www.equinoxresort.com), **Hildene** (802-362-1788. www.hildene.org), or Stratton Mountain. For indoor skating there's Manchester's Hunter Park.

The 5-mile **Equinox Sky Line Drive** (802-362-1114. www.equinoxmountain.com/skylinedrive. May-Oct.; toll) lies between Bennington and Manchester, off Vt. 7A. The road climbs 3,852-foot Equinox Mountain. Trails at the top offer vistas of valley and village.

LODGING

Equinox Hotel (3567 Main St., Manchester. 802-362-4700 or 800-362-4747. www.equinoxresort.com. $$-$$$) Luxury resort with 183 rooms. See p. 34.

Inn at Ormsby Hill (1842 Main St., Manchester Center. 802-362-1163 or 800-670-2841. www.ormsbyhill.com. $$-$$$) Ten rooms in a historic house. See pp. 34-35.

River Meadow Farm (Sugar House Ln., Manchester Center. 802-362-1602. $) A five-room bed-and-breakfast. See p. 35.

DINING

Bennington Station (150 Depot St., Bennington. 802-447-1080. $$) See pp. 33-34.

Dorset Inn (8 Church St. 802-867-5500 or 877-367-7389. $$$) Lamb chops, angus steaks, and baked eggplant crepes. See p. 35.

Four Columns Inn (21 West St., Newfane. 802-365-7713 or 800-787-6633. $$$) Renowned for its superb kitchen.

The Berkshires
Finding your muse in the mountains

THE WILD BEAUTY OF THE BERKSHIRES—a hilly, remote corner of western Massachusetts—has inspired writers and artists for more than a century. Herman Melville, Edith Wharton, and Norman Rockwell all became enchanted with the area's dreamy mountain vistas, pine-scented woods, and white-steepled villages full of Victorian charm. Visit the stomping grounds of these personalities, getting a glimpse of their quest for creative illumination—and discovering more than a few opportunities to ignite your own.

Monument Mountain & Stockbridge

On a summer day in 1850, local writers Nathaniel Hawthorne and Herman Melville climbed 1,750-foot **Monument Mountain** for a picnic. A sudden thunderstorm drove them into a cave and sparked a friendship that lasted a lifetime. You can follow in their footsteps along a quintessential New England trail—ambling beneath a mantle of hemlocks, white pines, and oaks—before summiting the mountain with magnificent views all around. Pity the writers for missing out on autumn's glory; the best time to visit is when the tulip poplars and maples explode in vibrant hues. Monument Mountain Reservation *(413-298-3239)* lies just off US 7 north of Great Barrington; from the parking lot, the longer, easier trail—the one the authors trod, perhaps?—branches off to the left, while the steeper approach heads right.

Nearby **Stockbridge** epitomizes New England charm. The village is probably best known as the longtime home of illustrator Norman Rockwell, who lived off Main Street from 1953 to 1978. His trademark painting, "Stockbridge Main Street at Christmas," shows the town center in snowy, festive splendor. You can visit the artist's museum (and see that particular painting; see p. 38) just west of town; before you do, take time to stroll the picturesque streets of Stockbridge and poke about in its antique shops.

Stockbridge's centerpiece is the historic **Red Lion Inn** (see Travelwise), unmissable at the corner of Main and US 7. To stay here is to step into a Rockwell painting. The inn's 1950s throwbacks include

NOT TO BE MISSED

- Hiking to the top of Monument Mountain at autumn's peak
- A literary tour of The Mount
- Sunrise from Mount Greylock's summit

flowery wallpaper, Staffordshire china, and an enormous veranda where people-watching is a venerable tradition. Begun in 1773 as a stagecoach stop on the road from Boston to Albany, the Red Lion also features a couple of restaurants with classic New England cuisine.

A short drive west into the countryside leads to the **Norman Rockwell Museum** *(0.6 mile S of jct. of Mass. 183 & 102. 413-298-4100 or 800-742-9450. www.nrm.org. Adm. fee),* home to more than 200 works by the prolific illustrator, including every single *Saturday Evening Post* cover, for which he is probably best known. A short stroll away stands his studio, an immaculate barn moved here from town.

Practically next door, sculptor Daniel Chester French purchased a country estate in 1896 and named it **Chesterwood** *(4 Williamsville Rd. 413-298-3579. www.chesterwood.net. Closed Nov.-April; adm. fee).* The setting was sufficiently scintillating to inspire the artist for the next 34 summers: French's home and studio commands, as he put it, "the best dry view" he had ever seen. Here he put the finishing touches on such masterpieces as the seated Abraham Lincoln (1922) for the memorial in Washington, D.C. The house is maintained in turn-of-the-century splendor. You can wander the woodland walks that wind through the gorgeous 122-acre grounds.

Lenox & Pittsfield

Embodying the cultural Berkshires, **Lenox,** about 8 miles north of Stockbridge, is the shining star of the Gilded Age. Here some of the world's finest writers—among them Nathaniel Hawthorne, Herman Melville, and Edith Wharton—retreated to be inspired by the cool, woodsy breezes. They joined New York's and Boston's genteel elite, whose summer "cottages" gave the area the feel of an inland Newport. The 1929 crash turned easy street into a dead end, but many of the mansions have been reborn as inns or bed-and-breakfasts.

Combining two old estates, **Tanglewood** (see Travelwise) has been the summer home of the Boston Symphony Orchestra since 1937. In addition to its splendid views over the hills, Tanglewood offers classical, jazz, and popular concerts by world-famous performers and musicians. If it's summer, don't miss a performance here.

Across the road from Tanglewood, seek out the reconstruction of Hawthorne's charming **little red house,** where the author wrote *The House of the Seven Gables* (1851). The view takes in a wide sweep of the Taconic Range, whose beauty so distracted Hawthorne that he had to move back to gritty Salem in order to get his writing done.

One of the region's most elegant mansions is **The Mount** *(2 Plunkett St. 413-637-1899 or 888-637-1902. www.edithwharton.org. Closed Nov.-April; adm. fee),* the former residence of social satirist Edith Wharton. The writer built her palatial "cottage" in 1902, where she wrote *The House of Mirth.* Overlooking exquisite Italian-style gardens, the baroque rooms seem to echo lazy afternoon conversations between Wharton and her sophisticated guests, including her close friend and mentor, Henry James. Tours give a literary slant.

Herman Melville lived in a more modest abode—an 18th-century farmhouse called **Arrowhead** *(780 Holmes Rd. 413-442-1793. www .mobydick.org. Closed Nov.-April; adm. fee)* that he bought in Pittsfield, a few miles north of Lenox, in 1850. From his second-floor study, while conjuring *Moby-Dick*, Melville stared out the window as he would "out of a porthole of a ship in the Atlantic." His view: Mount Greylock, a great white ridge that he likened to the whale that sent Ahab to his grave. The simple furnishings provide a sense of Melville's life and times. Melville's letters, books, and other memorabilia await at the **Herman Melville Memorial Room** *(Berkshire Athenaeum, 1 Wendell Ave. 413-499-9486. Closed Sun.)* in downtown Pittsfield.

In the evening, check whether a work by Wharton or one of her contemporaries is being performed by Shakespeare & Company at the **Founder's Theatre** *(70 Kemble St. www.shakespeare.org. 413-637-1199. May–mid-Nov.)* in Lenox. Nearby, an apt place to stay is the **Gables Inn** (see Travelwise); Wharton occupied this gracious Queen Anne "cottage" while waiting for The Mount to be built.

Mount Greylock

Rising high above the northern Berkshires' remote landscape, 3,487-foot **Mount Greylock** *(US 7 N to Lanesborough to N. Main St., follow signs. 413-499-4262)* is distinctive from all directions. Its stand-alone summit, which takes in five states, has been a moody muse for writ-

Reader atop Monument Mountain Reservation in the Berkshires

ers, artists, and romantics through the ages. Here's how Henry David Thoreau described a sunrise from the top: "The rosy fingers of dawn, and not a crevice through the clouds from which those trivial places of Massachusetts, Connecticut, and Vermont could be seen." **Bascom Lodge** (see Travelwise), which sits on the peak and offers simple rooms, is the best place to experience a Greylock dawn. Forty-five miles of hiking trails lace the reservation, offering you the chance to get lost in its untamed beauty—and perhaps find your own artistry.

—*Barbara A. Noe*

Travelwise

GETTING THERE

From Boston, the Berkshires lie 130 miles west via I-90. From Hartford, the Berkshires lie 75 miles northwest; take US 44 west and US 7 north, or I-91 north and I-90 west. US 7 is the region's main north-south artery.

GENERAL INFORMATION

Contact the **Berkshire Visitors Bureau** (*Berkshire Common, Plaza Level, Pittsfield, MA 01201. 413-443-9186 or 800-237-5747. www.berkshires.org*). The **Lenox Chamber of Commerce** (*Walker St., Lenox, MA 01240. 413-637-3646. www.lenox.org*) offers information on lodging, dining, shopping, and cultural attractions.

SEASONS

Summer is alive with cultural events, the most significant of which is Tanglewood. To miss the crowds but catch the leaves, come in fall.

ANNUAL EVENTS

Jacob's Pillow Dance Festival (*358 George Carter Rd., Becket. 413-243-0745. www.jacobspillow.org. Mid-June–late Aug.*) The world's finest dancers in a bucolic setting.

Tanglewood (*Concert line 888-266-1200. www.bso.org. Late June–Labor Day*)

LODGING

Berkshire/Folkstone Bed & Breakfast Homes (*413-268-7244 or 800-762-2751. www.berkshirebnbhomes.com*) A reservation service for more than 60 B&Bs and small inns.

Bascom Lodge (*atop Mount Greylock. 413-743-1591. www.naturesclassroom.org/bascom.html. Closed Nov.–mid-May*) 1930s lodge with 4 private rooms and 28 bunks. See this page.

Gables Inn (*81 Walker St., Lenox. 413-637-3416 or 800-382-9401. www.gableslenox.com. $$$*) 19 guest rooms. See p. 39.

Kemble Inn (*2 Kemble St., Lenox. 413-637-4113. www.kembleinn.com. $$-$$$*) An elegant cottage converted to an inn in the center of historic Lenox.

DINING

Candlelight Inn (*35 Walker St., Lenox. 413-637-1555 or 800-428-0580. www.candlelightinn-lenox.com*) American-Continental cuisine (*$$$*) in a historic and gracious inn (*$$*).

Church Street Café (*65 Church St., Lenox. 413-637-2745. $$*) Bistro featuring fresh pasta, grilled fish, and regional specialties.

Red Lion Inn (*30 Main St., Stockbridge. 413-298-5545. www.redlioninn.com*) Contemporary regional cuisine served in antique-filled dining room (*$$$*), tavern (*$$*), or courtyard. Comfortable guest rooms (*$$-$$$*). See p. 37.

A Shore Thing
Seeing seaside Connecticut

THE EUROPEANS WHO SETTLED the quiet bays and beaches of the Connecticut coast in the 17th century fished, farmed, and built fine houses on the ocean overlooking Long Island Sound. Today these old houses still stand sentinel beside quiet village greens, reminding visitors of that sturdy life re-created so well at Mystic Seaport. The U.S. Coast Guard Academy at New London and the U.S. Naval Submarine Base at Groton stand ready for defense.

Mystic

Start your maritime tour in picturesque Mystic, the highlight of the weekend. Settled in the 1650s, Mystic straddles the Mystic River, a saltwater estuary. Long famous as a shipbuilding center, Mystic celebrates its heritage in a premier maritime museum: **Mystic Seaport** *(75 Greenmanville Ave. 860-572-5315 or 888-973-2767. www.mystic seaport.org. Adm. fee).* You could spend the entire day exploring Seaport's 17 riverside acres. Visit the busy 19th-century seafaring village, tall ships in port, a working boatyard, or superb galleries presenting "Voyage to Freedom" (the story of the *Amistad)* and "Voyages: Stories of America and the Sea." Or take a river cruise on the 1908 steamboat *Sabino.*

Next, stop at the brilliant **Mystic Aquarium** *(55 Coogan Blvd. 860-572-5955. www.mystic aquarium.org. Adm. fee)* to scope out fish and marine invertebrates in their habitats, watch sea lions perform, or take part in a penguin or beluga whale contact program.

If time permits, visit **Stonington** and the Victorian mansion of Capt. Nathaniel B. Palmer *(40 Palmer St. 860-535-8445. May-Nov. closed Mon., closed rest of year; adm. fee),* who in 1820 sighted Antarctica from the deck of his Mystic-built sloop, the *Hero.* Visit the **Old Lighthouse Museum** *(7 Water St. 860-535-1440. Daily July-Aug., May-June and Sept.-Nov. closed Mon.; adm. fee),* and climb the lighthouse tower for a fine view of Long Island Sound.

> **NOT TO BE MISSED**
>
> ● **Wooden whaler *Charles W. Morgan,* Mystic Seaport**
> ● **Florence Griswold Museum in Old Lyme**
> ● **Monte Cristo Cottage (Eugene O'Neill's boyhood home), New London**
> ● **Mystic Pizza on Main St.**

New London & Groton

Head west on I-95 or Conn. 1 to **Groton** *(U.S. Naval Submarine Base.*

Windborne craft above and beside the wharf at Mystic, Connecticut

860-694-3174 or 800-343-0079. www.submarinemuseum.com), home
of the U.S.S. *Nautilus;* first of the nuclear-powered submarines, it was
launched in 1954. A tour of the *Nautilus* and the adjacent **Submarine
Force Museum** will immerse you in the history of submersibles.

To become a marine biologist overnight, take a three-hour hands-
on **study cruise** aboard an "Enviro-lab" vessel operated by the nonprofit Project Oceanology *(Avery Point. 860-445-9007 or 800-364-
8472. www.oceanology.org. June-Aug.; fare)*. Enviro-lab also offers
tours *(June-Aug. Tues., Thurs., Sat., and Sun. p.m.; fare)* of the historic
New London Ledge lighthouse, at the mouth of the Thames River.

Just across the Thames *(via I-95S)* stands **New London.** Its prime
location on the river, just upstream from the sound, dictated (and
dictates) its maritime preeminence. On the river north of the city
stands the **U.S. Coast Guard Academy.** Pick up a map and guide for
the self-guided walking tour of the grounds at the front gate *(Mohe-
gan Ave.)*. At the **Coast Guard Museum** *(Waesche Hall. 860-444-
8511)*, artifacts document Coast Guard history since 1790. At the
dock, the 295-foot training barque *Eagle,* a tall ship, is open for tours
when it's in port.

Top off your visit with a one-hour cruise up the Thames or down to Long Island Sound aboard the 36-foot lobster boat *SeaPony (15 Hillside Rd. 860-443-0795. www.seapony.com. Fare)*. Or stroll the sea-front boardwalk at New London's **Ocean Beach Park** *(860-447-3031 or 800-510-7263. Mem. Day–Labor Day; adm. fee)*. The park offers swimming in the sound or its Olympic pool.

Southern shore

A leisurely drive west lets you enjoy coastal beaches and villages. Ten miles west of New London on Conn. 156 is the long crescent beach of **Rocky Neck State Park** *(860-739-5471. Mem. Day–Labor Day, weekends April and Sept.; adm. fee)*, a good place to swim, fish, or picnic.

Next you'll pass through handsome **Old Lyme** before crossing the Connecticut River *(on I-95 west)* to **Old Saybrook village.** Make a southerly loop on Conn. 154 to view the wetlands along the mouth of the Connecticut River at **Saybrook Point. Fort Saybrook Monument Park** harbors the remains of an old fortified settlement.

Loop west on Conn. 154 to rejoin US 1 west. Just west of Clinton, at **Hammonasset Beach State Park** *(203-245-2785. April-Sept.; adm. fee)*, stretches a beautiful beach that is 2 miles long. The park has bathhouses, concession stands, a nature center with interpretive trails, a bike trail, and a cartop boat launch; it is popular with swimmers, fishermen, and bird-watchers.

A few miles west on US 1 is **Madison,** a colonial village with a fine public green and the 1785 **Allis-Bushnell House Museum** *(853 Boston Post Rd. 203-245-4567. May-Oct. Wed., Fri., and Sat. p.m., year-round by appt.)*. Its period furnishings include China Trade products and a model of the Civil War ironclad *Monitor;* homeowner Cornelius Bushnell was key to getting the craft's design accepted in 1861.

Five miles farther west, Conn. 146 leads to the beautifully aged coastal town of **Guilford.** Set in a 1639 stone building (New England's oldest), the **Henry Whitfield State Museum** *(248 Old Whitfield St. 203-453-2457. Feb.–mid-Dec. Wed.-Sun.; adm. fee)* features memorabilia of Native Americans, early settlers, and maritime history. The gift shop sells brochures for a walking tour of Guilford village.

Continue west on Conn. 146 to **Stony Creek.** From May to October, sight-seeing boats *(fare)* leave the dock for 45-minute tours of **The Thimbles,** 350 islands scattered offshore. Try Sea Mist Thimble Island Cruises *(203-488-8905)*, Volsunga Thimble Island Sightseeing *(203-488-9978)*, or Connecticut Sea Ventures *(203-397-3921)*.

Continue on Conn. 146 to **Branford** with its handsome village green, then take I-95 west to New Haven for a last look at the sound and harbor from the town's **Black Rock Fort** and adjacent **Fort Nathan Hale** *(Woodward Ave. 203-946-6970. Mem. Day–Labor Day. Grounds open to walkers year-round)*. Return to Hartford via I-91.

—*Ann Jones*

Travelwise

GETTING THERE
From Hartford take Conn. 9 south and I-95N through New London to Mystic. The New London/Groton area is one hour from Hartford. Amtrak and the Shore Line commuter rail service serve Connecticut's shore.

GENERAL INFORMATION
Contact the **Connecticut River Valley & Shoreline Visitors Council** (393 Main St., Middleton, CT 06457. 860-347-0028 or 800-486-3346. www.cttourism.org) or **Connecticut's Mystic & More Visitors Bureau** (860-444-2206 or 800-863-6569. www.mysticmore.com).

SEASONS
The shore is at its best from late spring through fall; prime beach time is July & Aug.

ANNUAL EVENTS
In July, New London holds Sailfest, a weekend of riverfront entertainment. Festivities at Mystic Seaport include Lobsterfest (May), Sea Music Festival (June), Antique & Classic Boat Rendezvous (July), and Chowderfest (Oct.).

MORE THINGS TO SEE & DO
Deep-sea fishing (Mataura Sportfishing, 255 Cedar Rd., Mystic. 860-536-6970 or 800-605-6265. www.mataurasportfishing.com)
Mashantucket Pequot Museum & Research Center (Conn. 2 and 214, 110 Pequot Trail, Mashantucket. 800-411-9671. www.mashantucket.com. Closed Tues. Labor Day–Mem.

Day; adm. fee) Presents the region's natural and Native American history.

LODGING
Bee and Thistle Inn (100 Lyme St., Old Lyme. 860-434-1667 or 800-622-4946. www.beeandthistleinn.com. $-$$$) Built as a judge's residence in 1756.
Deacon Timothy Pratt Bed & Breakfast (325 Main St., Old Saybrook. 860-395-1229. www.connecticut-bed-and-breakfast.com. $$-$$$) This charming 6-room house was built about 1746 and has many original details; seven fireplaces.
Griswold Inn (36 Main St., Essex. 860-767-1776. www.originalinns.com. $-$$) This 31-room inn dates from 1776.
Inn at Mystic (Conn. 1 and 27, Mystic. 860-536-9604 or 800-237-2415. www.innatmystic.com. Motor inn $$, mansion $$$) Situated on the harbor, with views of the sound.
Lighthouse Inn (6 Guthrie Pl., New London. 860-443-8411 or 888-443-8411. www.lighthouseinn-ct.com. $$) Overlooks the sound; once owned by steel magnate Charles Guthrie.
Pequot Hotel B&B (711 Cow Hill Rd., Mystic. 860-572-0390. www.pequothotelbandb.com. $$) Three-room 1840s Greek Revival home in Burnett's Corners historic district.
Randall's Ordinary Inn & Restaurant (41 Norwich-Westerly Rd., North Stonington. 860-599-4540 or 877-599-4540. www.randallsordinary.com. $$-$$$) Dates from 1685.
Steamboat Inn (73 Steamboat Wharf, Mystic. 860-536-8300. www.visitmystic.com/steamboat. $$$) Ten-room riverside inn downtown.

DINING
Bank Street Lobster House (194 Bank St., New London. 860-447-9398. Closed Sun.-Mon. Oct.-May. $$-$$$) Riverside dining.
Captain Scott's Lobster Dock (80 Hamilton St., New London. 860-439-1741. March-Oct. $-$$) Dine alfresco on fresh lobster.
Mystic Pizza (56 W. Main St., Mystic. 860-536-3700. $) Delicious pizza made famous by the movie of the same name.
Schooners (250 Pequot Ave., New London. 860-437-3801. $$-$$$) Steak and seafood with a water view.

Charlotte

Cradle of Forestry 46

Appalachian Crafts 51

Biltmore Estate and its gardens

Cradle of Forestry
Asheville & the Vanderbilt legacy

WHILE MANY PEOPLE KNOW ASHEVILLE as the home of the spectacular Biltmore Estate, few realize that the estate was the birthplace of American forestry. Upon arriving at Biltmore in 1891, conservationist Gifford Pinchot remarked that "there was not…a single acre of forest under forestry anywhere in the United States." Six years later, the Biltmore Forest School opened as the country's first school of forest management; some 78,000 acres of the estate became the nucleus of Pisgah National Forest. Now more than six times that size, the forest brims with high peaks and cool streams, all connected by the famous Blue Ridge Parkway.

Biltmore Estate

Most people will want to go directly to Asheville's main attraction, **Biltmore Estate** *(US 25 just N of I-40. 828-274-6333 or 800-543-2961. www.biltmore.com. Adm. fee).* In the last several years, Biltmore has gradually expanded its offerings to include a full day of activities. You could see the house and gardens in a half day, but if you want to have a leisurely lunch and visit the winery or take part in an outdoor activity, it's best to plan on taking the better part of a day.

NOT TO BE MISSED

- View of Biltmore's gardens from third floor
- Pumpkin walnut muffins at Malaprop's
- Rhododendron blooms everywhere in spring
- Top of Mount Mitchell

George Vanderbilt was so pleased with the mountains of North Carolina that he decided to build his mansion here. But his idea of a "mansion" was like nothing the locals had ever seen or heard of. Completed in 1895, Biltmore is a French Renaissance-style palace whose grandeur rivals the very mountains themselves. More than a thousand people labored five years on the project, which ran through most of Vanderbilt's five-million-dollar inheritance. Owned and operated by his descendants, Vanderbilt's 250-room limestone château remains the largest private residence in the United States. Its wealth of art and antiques alone would make it a stunning museum, but as a testament to the opulent lifestyles of the Gilded Age, it is unequaled.

The winding, 3-mile-long approach road from the gatehouse to the mansion was carefully landscaped by Frederick Law Olmsted to create a series of little surprises—a bank of rhododendrons, a

Slipping down Sliding Rock in Pisgah National Forest

stream, and canebrake—before finally opening out to a view of the house. As you piece together the story of the estate and its central role in founding Pisgah National Forest, keep in mind that the area was mostly played out farmland; Vanderbilt was not so much chopping down woods as restoring them from scratch.

The house holds four floors of breathtaking rooms for self-guided exploration (or you can reserve a guided tour). Among the highlights, the **library** was a favorite of Vanderbilt and his guests. Both grand and inviting, this is a room you could imagine relaxing in—on one of those plush red sofas, while a fire crackles in the massive fireplace and the butler selects a book for you from one of the gallery shelves. The 18th-century ceiling mural is by Pellegrini and the tapestry is from 17th-century France. On the opposite side of the house, the **banquet hall** is a king's dream of medieval splendor with a pipe organ and 70-foot-high ceiling.

After wandering around the formal **gardens,** you have a number of choices for lunch right on the estate. Afterward, treat yourself to the intoxicating aromas of the **winery,** open since 1985. And the 213-room **Inn on Biltmore Estate** (see Travelwise) provides luxury accommodations, along with a dining room, bar, outdoor pool, fitness room, and hiking trails; all that and an 8,000-acre estate almost makes you feel like a Vanderbilt.

Biltmore's new outdoor program is a further chance for exploring the estate and indulging your lord-of-the-manor fantasies. By horseback, carriage, or mountain bike, you can take many miles of trails through meadows, fields, and forests. At one time, Vanderbilt was able to boast that he owned everything he could see, and that included Mount Pisgah, 17 miles away.

Asheville's downtown

A day in Asheville will not only prep you for what you'll see in the forest, it will give you a relaxing look at western North Carolina's cultural and commercial center, a town consistently appearing on short lists of America's most-livable small cities.

To learn more about the area's native flora, start your morning at the **Botanical Gardens of Asheville** *(151 W.T. Weaver Blvd. 828-252-5190).* These 10 acres are filled with plants indigenous to the southern Appalachians. You might want to follow up this introduction by shooting across town (less than 15 minutes) to the **Western North Carolina Nature Center** *(75 Gashes Creek Rd. 828-298-5600. Adm. fee),* where you can bone up on both plants and animals. Among the live forest denizens on display are bears, snakes, otters, and deer. Take a good look, because other than deer you likely won't see many of these elusive creatures out in the woods.

For lunch, try one of the eateries downtown. Afterward, there are plenty of neat little shops that mix uptown sophistication and Appalachian charm, or you can check out one of the museums over on **Pack Place,** which is known for its graceful 1920s architecture.

The nearby **Thomas Wolfe Memorial State Historic Site** *(48 Spruce St. 828-253-8304. Closed Sun.-Mon.; adm. fee)* is a must-see for fans of North Carolina's greatest author. Though the rambling house is closed for restoration, you can see a film and exhibits in the new visitor center, at 52 North Market. The 12-story Renaissance Hotel just east blocks much of the hilly view Wolfe would have known, but the site is well worth a visit for its presentation of early Asheville and the town's most famous native.

Blue Ridge south

Plan to put in at least a full day exploring the forest south of Asheville. Begin with a visit to the **North Carolina Arboretum** *(N.C. 191 and Blue Ridge Pkwy. 828-665-2492),* a 426-acre spread within Pisgah National Forest. Originally part of Biltmore Estate, the arboretum has a variety of trails winding through themed settings that showcase regional heritage; for instance, a Blue Ridge Quilt Garden is planted in the shape of a quilt.

Now get on the **Blue Ridge Parkway** and head south, stopping as often as you like at overviews to admire the stunning vistas of mountains muscling up on both sides of the parkway. About 13 miles south of the arboretum, at Milepost 408.6, pull to the left for the **Mount Pisgah** parking area. For one of the greatest panoramas of the North Carolina mountains, you'll need to walk the 1.5-mile (one way) trail to the top of the 5,450-foot peak (the one with the radio towers on top). You gain 712 feet of elevation, but the effort is well worth it. In spring the rhododendrons and wildflowers are in bloom, and in fall the whole forest blazes in fiery color. Vanderbilt's holdings once extended all the way to Mount Pisgah, where he built a hunting lodge he could reach via a 17-mile trail from the mansion.

If you didn't bring a picnic, you can still have lunch with a view at the **Pisgah Inn** (see Travelwise), a modern facility that replaced its rustic 1919 predecessor. Then continue down the parkway a few miles, stopping at US 276 (Wagon Road Gap) for a look at 6,030-foot **Cold Mountain,** recently made famous by the best-selling Civil War–period novel of the same name.

Head south 4 miles on US 276 to the **Cradle of Forestry in America National Historic Site** *(US 276. 828-877-3130. Closed early Nov.–mid-April; adm. fee).* Situated on the grounds of the forestry school that operated here from 1898 to 1913, this site takes you back to the time when the country was just waking up to the fact that forests could not supply endless amounts of trees on demand. Wrote Biltmore's first forester, Gifford Pinchot: "Biltmore could be made to prove what America did not yet understand—that trees could be cut and the forest preserved." Two nature trails loop past reconstructed and original cabins, a sawmill, and a logging locomotive. The spiffy **visitor center** offers a simulated helicopter ride over a forest fire, a tunnel with animal burrows, and a walk-through forest canopy.

Just to the south, don't fail to turn right for **Sliding Rock Recreation Area** *(parking fee in summer),* where generations of kids and adults have enjoyed the gentle 60-foot natural slide down to a plunge pool of cool water. A bit farther down the road, you can see Looking Glass Creek making a dramatic 60-foot cascade at **Looking Glass Falls.** And hidden in the woods to the west but accessible by a trail from Forest Road 475 stands **Looking Glass Rock,** a spectacular granite dome—one of the largest in the South.

If you have an extra day, or even a few extra hours, by all means head north from Asheville on the Blue Ridge Parkway. Also part of Pisgah National Forest, **Craggy Gardens** *(18 miles NE of Asheville at Mile 365. 828-298-0495. Visitor center open May–Oct.)* is especially beautiful—and popular—during the mid-June rhododendron blossoming. Throughout the year, trails wend to breathtaking views. And if you're heading north, don't miss **Mount Mitchell State Park** *(Mile 355, then 5 miles up N.C. 128. 828-675-4611).* From the highest peak in the east (6,684 feet), you can't help but be awestruck by the endless ranks of blue mountains rolling in every direction. The chilly alpine environment lends a clarity to the air. Though it was never part of Biltmore Forest, Mount Mitchell lies within the Pisgah, and up here the words of Carl Schenck, founder of the Biltmore Forest School, seem especially appropriate: "If men should hold their peace, the trees would cry aloud: 'Honor and thanks to you, George W. Vanderbilt!'" —*John M. Thompson*

Travelwise

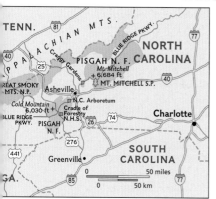

GETTING THERE
Asheville lies in western North Carolina, 115 miles west of Charlotte via I-85, US 74, and I-26.

GENERAL INFORMATION
Contact the **Asheville Area Chamber of Commerce** (*P.O. Box 1010, Asheville, NC 28802. 828-258-6101 or 800-257-1300. www.exploreasheville.com*).

SEASONS
Asheville's mountain setting promises cold and sometimes snowy winters; summers can vary from pleasant to hot, with highs in the 90s. The fall foliage and spring azalea and laurel blossoms are splendid.

ANNUAL EVENTS
Appalachian Spring Celebration (*late April-May, Cradle of Forestry. 828-877-3130*) Guided walks, bird-watching, wildflower workshops.

Bele Chere (*late July, Asheville. 828-258-6101. www.belechere.com*) Street festival with music, food, arts and crafts, and more.

Biltmore Estate's Candlelight Christmas

Evenings (*Nov.-Dec. 828-274-6333 or 800-543-2961. Fee*) Luminaria and glowing fireplaces re-create an old-fashioned Christmas.

MORE THINGS TO SEE & DO
Adventure sports Contact the Chamber about outfitters offering trips on the French Broad River, rock climbing, and mountain biking.

LODGING
Asheville Bed & Breakfast Association (*877-262-6867. $-$$$*) Information on 17 bed-and-breakfasts, from Victorians to mountain retreats.

Grove Park Inn Resort and Spa (*290 Macon Ave. 828-252-2711. $$$*) Renowned for its arts and crafts furnishings, the historic inn has hosted Presidents and celebrities. Features elegant restaurants with views. 510 rooms.

Inn on Biltmore Estate (*828-225-1660. $$$*) Luxury accommodations. See p. 47.

Richmond Hill Inn (*87 Richmond Hill Dr. 828-252-7313. $$-$$$*) Centered on an 1889 Queen Anne-style mansion overlooking the French Broad River, the inn offers 36 luxurious rooms and an elegant restaurant.

DINING
Laughing Seed Café (*40 Wall St. 828-252-3445. Closed Tues. $-$$*) Vegetarian fare, fruit drinks, and specialty pizzas.

Malaprop's Bookstore/Café (*55 Haywood St. 828-254-6734. $*) The place to browse for regional authors while sipping chai latte.

Market Place (*20 Wall St. 828-252-4162. Dinner only; closed Sun. and Mon.-Tues. Nov.-March. $$*) Sophisticated downtown establishment featuring local game and trout.

Pisgah Inn (*Milepost 408.6, Blue Ridge Pkwy. 828-235-8288. $*) Seafood, chicken, and beef entrées. See p. 49. You can also stay in the modern inn, with 52 rooms.

Appalachian Crafts
Hunting for handmade treasures in the Smokies

IN THE MOUNTAINS WEST OF CHARLOTTE, craftsmen and -women have been turning out beautifully executed works of art for centuries. The region now holds one of the largest concentrations of craftsmakers in the country, with over 160 studios, more than 100 galleries, scores of museums, and two well-established crafts schools. Spend a delightful weekend rambling the back roads, learning about handcrafts and contemporary crafts, and seeking out that perfect objet d'art.

North of Asheville
You could really start in anywhere and, in less than an hour, almost certainly come across a studio or gallery. Bear in mind that you're more likely these days to meet artisans who learned their trade somewhere else and then moved to western North Carolina. So while the old-time Appalachian whittlers and quilters are nearly extinct, the traditions—albeit greatly expanded—are still intact. Also be mindful that this is mountainous terrain; roads are twisty and it's often a long haul between sites. Pop in a CD of your favorite mountain group and enjoy the ride.

To hit some of the highlights, from northeast to southwest, start in the mountain town of **Boone,** home of Appalachian State University. Steep yourself in regional lore by visiting the **Appalachian Cultural Museum** *(University Hall, University Hall Dr. 828-262-3117. Closed Mon.; adm. fee),* which displays a number of antique fiddles, quilts, and other crafts. The 1913 **Mast General Store** *(630 W. King St. 828-262-0000)* is a fun place to shop for items your country cousins might have used.

A few miles south, the village of **Blowing Rock** lies just off the Blue Ridge Parkway, known for its inspiring views. At the **Bob Timberlake Gallery** *(946 Main St. 828-295-4855)* you'll find finely crafted furniture based on 18th-century designs, while **Bolick Pottery** *(3 miles S off US 321. 828-295-3862)* offers items made by fifth-generation potters.

NOT TO BE MISSED

● **View from Blowing Rock** ● **Watching master chairmaker Max Woody at work** ● **Special exhibits at the Folk Art Center** ● **Wooded trails around John C. Campbell Folk School**

About an hour south (halfway to Asheville), near Spruce Pine, visit the **Penland School of Crafts and the Penland Gallery** *(828-765-6211. Gallery closed Mon.)*. Dating from 1929, this mountaintop institution is one of the nation's oldest and largest crafts schools, providing instruction each year to some 1,200 students who seriously want to make a living with their hands. Instruction is given in clay, glass, iron, metals, textiles, wood, and printmaking, and, though the classes are not open to the public, you can take a campus tour on Tuesdays and Thursdays and wander over to the gallery. The staff can provide you with information on more than 75 studios in the area.

On the way back into Asheville, detour down to **Old Fort,** where you can find the rustic workshop of **Max Woody** *(3 miles E of Old Fort on US 70. 828-724-4158)*, who comes from a long line of chairmakers and storytellers. A custom-made maple or oak chair costs as little as $375, a walnut as much as $850, and the wait may be two years.

Asheville & south

Start the morning in Asheville. Among the many shops and galleries, you won't want to miss the **Folk Art Center** *(Milepost 382, Blue Ridge Pkwy. 828-298-7928)*. In the pioneer days, craftsmanship was geared toward what was needed for everyday life. Now objects such as cherry walking sticks, river-cane baskets, and cornshuck dolls are prized as much for their workmanship as their usefulness. At this fine facility—headquarters of the Southern Highland Craft Guild—you can watch craft demonstrations, learn about the many innovative ways mountain people have been using local forest materials for generations, and explore where the craft industry is going with contemporary arts. For example, you can see (and purchase) brooms made of cherry or alder found along the nearby French Broad River, or baskets woven with honeysuckle vines. Nearby, the **Grovewood Gallery** at the Homespun Shops *(111 Grovewood Rd. 828-253-7651. Closed Sun. Jan.-March)* was started more than 70 years ago by Mrs. George Vanderbilt as a training school for craftsmen; it specializes in wood products and woven wools.

South of Asheville, the resort town of **Brevard** has a number of craft studios and galleries, particularly along US 276 running south. Many shops carry crafts from all over; don't hesitate to inquire about the origins of a particular piece. If you want to visit a store that primarily sells local pottery, stop at **Mud Dabber's Pottery and Craft** *(4 miles S of Brevard. 828-884-5131)*.

Now follow the winding and highly scenic US 64 south and west through the little towns of Cashiers, Highlands, and Franklin. **Highlands** is especially busy with quaint craft and antique galleries, gift emporia, and high-priced inns. Just west of town are a number of lovely waterfalls worth pulling over for, including **Bridal Veil Falls, Dry Falls** (which you can walk behind), and **Cullasaja Falls.**

A blacksmith instructor demonstrates his trade at the Penland School.

From Franklin you can take a side excursion about 15 miles north via US 23/441 to the charming four-block hamlet of **Dillsboro,** which acts as an unofficial headquarters for a large number of area craftsmen. Among the scores of shops and galleries, don't miss **Dogwood Crafters** (*Webster St. 828-586-2248. Closed Jan.-Feb.*), a co-op of artisans plying their wares in a clutch of old log cabins. If you have time, go north another 15 miles to **Cherokee** and head straight for the **Qualla Arts and Crafts Mutual** (*US 441 and Drama Rd. 828-497-3103. Closed Sun. in winter*), which sells the region's only truly indigenous crafts—those made by Native Americans. Ceremonial masks, river-cane baskets, low-fire pottery, and wood carvings are among the choices. While in town, also visit the **Oconaluftee Indian Village** (*off US 441. 828-497-2315. Closed Nov.–mid-May; adm. fee*) to see how Cherokee crafted things in the 18th century.

West of Franklin, head deeper into the rolling countryside on US 64 until you come to the back-of-beyond village of **Brasstown.** Here the **John C. Campbell Folk School** (*off US 64, follow signs. 828-837-2775 or 800-365-5724*) was established in 1925. Instructors offer one-week classes in such folk arts as basketry, jewelrymaking, banjo playing, and storytelling. Since classes usually run Monday through Friday, there's not a lot going on during the weekends. But you're free to visit the little museum, peruse the craft shop, and get a feel for the easygoing back-to-nature essence of the place.

—*John M. Thompson*

Travelwise

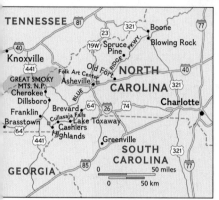

GETTING THERE

The Blue Ridge Parkway cuts through most of western North Carolina and is a good main artery on which to base your tour. Boone is located on US 321, 100 miles northwest of Charlotte (Milepost 291.9 off the parkway).

GENERAL INFORMATION

Contact the **Southern Highland Craft Guild** *(P.O. Box 9545, Asheville, NC 28815. 828-298-7928. www.southernhighland craftguild.org)* or **Handmade in America** *(P.O. Box 2089, Asheville, NC 28802. 828-252-0121. www.handmadeinamerica.org).*

SEASONS

A moderate four-season climate makes western North Carolina a delight just about anytime. Average February temperatures are 36°F; for July 77°F. Expect some snow in the the winter and chilly evenings fall through spring. The fall foliage and springtime blossoms are spectacular.

ANNUAL EVENTS

Art in the Park *(multiple weekends May-Oct., Blowing Rock. 800-295-7851)* Juried art and fine craft shows that have been held more than 40 years.

Craft Fair of the Southern Highlands *(mid-July and mid-Oct., Asheville Civic Center. 828-298-7928)* A gathering from nine states of premier crafters in various media.

Fall Festival *(Oct., John C. Campbell Folk School, Brasstown. 828-837-2775)*

A celebration of Appalachian heritage.

Sourwood Festival *(early Aug., Black Mountain. 800-669-2301. www.blackmountain p.org)* A craft festival with 150 exhibitors, a car show, and an 8K run.

MORE THINGS TO SEE & DO

Outdoor activities You can do anything from golf and hiking to skiing, horseback riding, and llama trekking. Inquire at local chambers of commerce or national forests in North Carolina *(160A Zillicoa St., Asheville, NC 28801. 828-257-4200).*

LODGING

See p. 50 for suggestions in Asheville.

Greystone Inn *(Greystone Ln., Lake Toxaway. 828-966-4700. $$$)* A restored 1915 Edwardian mansion with 33 rooms offers great lake and mountain views, water sports, restaurant.

Innisfree Victorian Inn *(108 Innisfree Dr., 6 miles N of Cashiers. 828-743-2946. $$-$$$)* An elegant ten-room bed-and-breakfast with gardens and mountain views.

Maple Lodge *(152 Sunset Dr., Blowing Rock. 828-295-3331. $$)* This cozy 11-room B&B off Main Street features full breakfast with homemade baked goods.

DINING

See p. 50 for suggestions in Asheville.

Falls Landing *(23 E. Main St., Brevard. 828-884-2835. $$)* Caribbean-accented mussels, clams, and other seafood top the menu.

Horacio's Restaurante *(US 64 and N.C. 107, just E of Cashiers. 828-743-2792. Dinner Mon.-Sat. $$)* An imaginative Italian restaurant with rustic atmosphere.

Speckled Trout Café & Oyster Bar *(Main St. and N.C. 221, Blowing Rock. 828-295-7851 or 828-295-9819. $$)* Mountain trout, seafood, and angus beef; homemade soups and sandwiches.

Vintners Restaurant & Wine Shoppe *(978 N. Main St., Blowing Rock. 828-295-9376. Seasonally closed Tues. $$)* A historic arts and crafts church provides the setting for lunch and dinner. The creative menu features high-country cuisine.

Chicago & Indianapolis

Architectural Chicago 56

Into the Heartland 60

Car Mania 65

Brown County 69

Spiral staircase in Chicago's Rookery Building

Architectural Chicago
First City of modern skyscrapers

WITH ITS MAGNIFICENT ARRAY of early and modern skyscrapers, Chicago is sometimes grandly referred to as the Paris on the Prairie and the Rival of Baroque Rome. Simply put, the city is a feast for the eyes, a vast open-air museum. But Chicago's architecture is not merely about size or looks: It's about innovation, a brand-new vision. For here, turn-of-the-century architects dared to go higher than ever before, using techniques untested heretofore. Exploring the lifeworks of some of the world's master builders, this getaway focuses on Chicago's unique collection of architectural treasures.

Inside the Loop

The Great Chicago Fire of 1871 destroyed a third of the city's buildings, leaving a grand opportunity for young architects—including Frank Lloyd Wright, Louis H. Sullivan, and Dankmar Adler. You'll find their handiwork clustered inside the Loop area, bounded by the El subway system. Wander as you wish, or perhaps take a walking tour, a delightful way to spend a morning. The Chicago Architecture Foundation *(224 S. Michigan Ave. 312-922-3432. www.architecture.org)* offers two-hour tours with several themes, including Historic Skyscrapers and Downtown Deco.

As you stroll, keep an eye out for the most famous buildings, including the 1888 **Rookery Building** *(209 S. LaSalle St.),* an important precursor to the skyscraper; it features a masonry base and terra-cotta ornamentation, and Wright designed the stunning atrium. The 1891 **Manhattan Building** *(431 S. Dearborn St.)* incorporates metal-frame construction, unique bay windows, and an upper brick facade. Revolutionary in its plain exterior, the 1889-1891 **Monadnock Building** *(53 E. Jackson Blvd.)* is the last skyscraper constructed using 6-foot-thick ground-floor walls, resting on an iron raft to support the weight of 16 floors. Adler and Sullivan first gained notoriety with their 1889 **Auditorium Building** *(430 S. Michigan Ave.),* showcasing an intricately designed interior and arched theater.

NOT TO BE MISSED

- Unity Temple's light and silence
- Cocktails at the top of the John Hancock Center ● Sunset swim in Lake Michigan
- Sunrise jog on Lakeshore Drive

Sky-high buildings crowd the Chicago River.

As the world's buildings grew taller, so did those in Chicago, the most famous of which, of course, is the 1973, 110-floor **Sears Tower** *(233 S. Wacker Dr. 312-875-9696. Adm. fee for observation deck)*, North America's tallest skyscraper; a viewing deck on the top floor is open to the public.

In the afternoon, head to nearby Michigan Avenue, also known as the **Magnificent Mile,** lined with exquisite shops. Leaving from Michigan Avenue at the Chicago River, architecture-oriented boat tours give a river perspective. The most enlightening are the Chicago Architecture Foundation's **Official Architecture River Cruises** *(312-922-3432),* which spotlight more than 50 noteworthy architectural sites.

After seeing the city from its streets and river, you may want to see it from up high. Climb to the 95th-floor observatory of Chicago's second tallest building, the 100-floor **John Hancock Center** *(875 N. Michigan Ave. 888-875-8439. Adm. fee for observation deck),* where you'll find a spectacular 360-degree view. From the restaurant/bar on the 94th floor, watch Lake Michigan darken and the city begin to sizzle with light.

Oak Park

You'll want to spend the whole day exploring this leafy residential neighborhood about 10 miles west of the Loop via I-290. Frank Lloyd Wright made his mark in **Oak Park** between 1889 and 1909, developing his signature prairie style of architecture in 25 buildings and houses—the world's largest collection of his work.

Start at the **Frank Lloyd Wright Home and Studio** *(951 Chicago Ave. 708-848-1976. Adm. fee)*, where you can tour the architect's own residence and work space and see for yourself how he emphasized large, open, free-flowing spaces. The house also contains Wright-designed furniture and decorative objects. Afterward, join one of the walking tours that depart from here several times a day to view some of his other masterpieces throughout the neighborhood. Or purchase an "Architectural Guide Map of Oak Park and River Forest" from the gift shop and take your own stroll.

Be sure to seek out **Unity Temple** *(875 Lake St. 708-383-8873. Closed for services; adm. fee)*, in continuous use since 1908 and arguably one of Wright's most important contributions to modern architecture. Dubbed "my little jewel box" by the architect, its unprecedented cubist design features the abundant use of concrete and an unusual receding flow of interior space.

The **Cheney House Bed & Breakfast** (see Travelwise), built by Wright in 1903 for a young couple (the wife later became his lover), offers the chance to sleep in an authentic prairie-school house. The owner collects furniture designed by Wright in 1955, and even the bedspreads in the rooms were designed by Wright.

The Ukrainian flair & more Frank Lloyd Wright

While Chicago is known for its skyscrapers and its Wright legacy, the city also boasts some intriguing Ukrainian architecture. Head about 5 miles west from downtown on Chicago Avenue, west of the Loop, to the **Ukrainian Village** neighborhood *(bound by Division, Damen, Western, and Chicago Sts.)*—the site of two unusual churches. The first, **St. Nicholas Ukrainian Catholic Cathedral** *(2238 W. Rice St.)*, is a copy of the Kiev cathedral in the Ukraine, a fine example of Russo-Byzantine architecture notable for its elaborate frescoes and mosaics. Ukrainian immigrants founded the parish in 1905, and the cathedral was built on the land they acquired between 1913 and 1915.

Nearby is the oldest Russian Orthodox church in Chicago, the Louis Sullivan–designed **Holy Trinity Cathedral** *(1121 N. Leavitt St.)*, built in 1903 in Russian Provincial style. Sullivan called this small, simple structure a "poetic building." The interior, however, is elaborate, with icons and many fine pieces of Slavic art.

Now head to Hyde Park, south of downtown, to visit another significant Frank Lloyd Wright building, the 1910 **Frederick C. Robie House** *(5757 S. Woodlawn Ave. 773-834-1847. Adm. fee)*. With its bold horizontal lines, big spaces, and magnificent art glass windows, this exquisite example of a prairie house was designated by Wright as the "cornerstone of American architecture." Built in

1910, it is a later example of his work. It's currently being meticulously restored; tours of the restoration work are offered.

From Hyde Park, find your way back to **Lake Shore Drive** and head north. Hugging Lake Michigan, this elegant boulevard gives you a breathtaking view of the city's skyscrapers. For an added delight, exit at Montrose and head east to the pier (keep turning right), and you'll be on a piece of land that juts out into the lake. An afternoon walk here is a fine way to view the skyline and, if it's summer, you may enjoy a swim in the lake with the magnificent urban vista as your backdrop.   —*Haas H. Mroue*

Travelwise

GENERAL INFORMATION
The premier source of information on Chicago's architecture is the **Chicago Architecture Foundation** *(224 S. Michigan Ave., Chicago IL 60602. 312-922-3432. www.architecture.org)*, which offers tours, an interpretive center, and two galleries. More information is available at the **Chicago Office of Tourism/Visitor Information Center** *(Chicago Cultural Center, 78 E. Washington St., 1st fl., Chicago, IL 60602. 312-744-2400 or 877-244-2246. www.877chicago.com)*. For Oak Park information contact the **Oak Park Visitor's Center** *(158 N. Forest Ave., Oak Park, IL 60302. 708-848-1500)* and the **Frank Lloyd Wright Preservation Trust** *(951 Chicago Ave., Oak Park, IL 60302)*.

SEASONS
Biting winds blow off the frozen lake in winter; spring and fall are mild, although sudden cold spells are not uncommon. July and August are hot, with high humidity.

MORE THINGS TO SEE & DO
Chicago Athenaeum: Museum of Architecture and Design *(190 S. Roselle St., Schaumburg. 847-895-3950. www.chi-athenaeum.org)* Dedicated to the importance of good architectural design, the museum showcases historical items relating to Chicago structures, including drawings and building fragments. The gift shop is at 307 N. Michigan Ave.

Chicago Cultural Center *(78 E. Washington St. 312-744-8032)* Built in 1897, this beaux arts–style, colonnaded building, once the Chicago Public Library, is a masterpiece of mosaic and glasswork.

Marshall Field's *(111 N. State St. 312-781-1000)* The flagship department store is an architectural masterpiece built between 1882 and 1907; note the Tiffany dome and the grand clock.

LODGING
Allerton Crowne Plaza *(701 N. Michigan Ave., Chicago. 312-440-1500. $$)* At 25 stories, this national historic landmark was Chicago's tallest building when constructed in 1924.

Cheney House Bed & Breakfast *(520 N. East Ave., Oak Park. 708-524-2067. $$)* Designed by Frank Lloyd Wright. See p. 58.

The Drake *(140 E. Walton Pl., Chicago. 312-787-2200. $$$)* This venerable hotel is an imposing structure at the head of the Magnificent Mile. Afternoon tea in the Palm Court is a Chicago tradition.

Hotel Burnham *(1 W. Washington St., Chicago. 312-782-1111. www.burnhamhotel.com. $$-$$$)* The former Reliance building dates back to 1894 and is now an elegant boutique hotel.

DINING
Atwood Café *(Hotel Burnham, 1 W. Washington St., Chicago. 312-368-1900. Also open Sun. brunch. $$$)* Euro-Midwest menu includes homemade pot pies and pasta with dried cherries and roasted duck.

Café Winberie *(151 N. Oak Park Ave., Oak Park. 708-386-2600. $-$$)* Eclectic dishes with a Mediterranean flair.

Cucina Paradiso *(814 North Blvd., Oak Park. 708-848-3434. $$)* Cozy restaurant offering fresh Italian dishes.

Into the Heartland
Simple pleasures & outdoor treasures

THERE'S A DISTINCT FEELING OF TIME standing still in the farm country of south-central Illinois. Golden fields and two-lane roads, forgotten towns and horses and buggies all seem from another era. Few city dwellers tread here, offering the visitor complete tranquility. In your wanderings, though, you'll find some surprises, including a magnificent estate park, where you can spend the night, a river for canoeing, and a thriving Amish community.

Allerton Park

Leaving Chicago on the Dan Ryan Expressway, take I-57 south to I-72, and head west 25 miles to Monticello. As the skyscrapers recede, you enter the state's fertile heartland—a realm of 78,000 farms and 1,500 different soil types. Corn, soybeans, and wheat are the main crops here.

Seemingly out of place next to the farmland is the magnificent, 1,500-acre **Robert Allerton Park** *(515 Old Timber Rd. 217-762-7011.www.conted.uiuc.edu/allerton)*, on the outskirts of Monticello, the most enchanting place to base yourself for a night or two. Art collector Robert Henry Allerton (1873-1964) donated his estate to the University of Illinois in 1946 for private use and education.

You have three different lodging options: the Evergreen Lodge, the Gate House, and the House in the Woods (eight bedrooms, with private baths), the most secluded choice. Note that the accommodations are fairly simple; most rooms come with private baths, but you should not expect luxurious amenities and should come prepared with extra blankets and other supplies.

More than 20 miles of trails, perfect for hiking and cross-country skiing, wind through this oasis, where more than 120 museum-quality statues and garden ornaments from around the world grace English landscaped gardens, upland and lowland forests, and restored prairie along the Sangamon River.

The park offers various educational programs focusing on nature, including birding and wildflower hikes, and tree identification talks.

NOT TO BE MISSED

- Strolling the Fu Dog garden at Allerton Park
- Seared Ahi tuna at The Heron restaurant, Danville
- Canoeing up the Middle Fork River
- Listening to woodpeckers at Kickapoo State Park

On the Middle Fork Vermilion River

The park's flora and fauna change throughout the year, each season played up to perfection. In winter, silence reigns, interrupted only by the wind rustling through bare trees. In spring, wildflowers pop up everywhere, while the gardens peak in summer. Come fall, the woods explode in brilliant reds and deep golds, the perfect time to take a quiet stroll.

Evenings are quiet; there is no food available in the park, so bring picnic supplies or make the drive to Monticello. If you're in the mood for a night out, drive 25 miles east from Monticello on I-72 to **Champaign/Urbana.** Kids enjoy the **William M. Staerkel Planetarium** *(2400 W. Bradley Ave., Champaign. 217-351-2568. Fri.-Sat. 7-9:30 p.m.; adm. fee),* where a Zeiss Star Projector casts 7,000 stars on a 50-foot overhead dome. The **Krannert Center for the Performing Arts** *(500 S. Goodwin Ave., Urbana. 217-333-6280)* offers an impressive menu of dance, theater, opera, and music on the University of Illinois campus.

Clinton Lake & Amish country

Breakfast at Allerton is a light affair. You might wish instead to drive up to Monticello, where homemade buttermilk biscuits await at **Montgomery's On The Square** (see Travelwise).

Then devote the morning to savoring the quiet. Practice your tai chi or meditate in the serenity of the **Fu Dog garden,** with its lapis-lazuli–blue ceramic Fu dogs. Stroll around the **sunken garden,** then walk to the estate's farthest end to find the enormous bronze sculpture by Carle Milles, "The Sun Singer." You may also hike along the Sangamon River or stretch out with a good book in one of the landscaped gardens.

In the afternoon, head west on Ill. 10 toward Clinton to cast a line at one of tranquil **Clinton Lake**'s many tributaries and hidden corners. The lake also offers camping, swimming, hiking, waterskiing, and sailing. To find the park office off Ill. 10, go north on County Road 14 toward De Witt.

Instead, you may wish to head south of Allerton about 25 miles to the farming communities of Arthur and Arcola, in the heart of Amish country. **Arcola,** just off I-57, is the slightly larger of the two, with a visitor center located in the old railroad depot. Shops purveying crafts, quilts, wood furniture, cheese, and sausage line Main Street. Also downtown, exhibits at the **Illinois Amish Interpretive Center** *(411 S. Locust St. 217-268-3599 or 888-452-6474. www.amish center.com)* explain the history and culture of the local Amish, whose 4,000-member community began as a small number of families in 1865. The center arranges tours and meals in Amish homes.

Nine miles west in Arthur, you'll find more shops selling Amish goods. A **farmers' market** takes place every Saturday morning July through September in the gazebo parking lot on Vine Street, where you can mingle with growers and find farm-fresh produce (as well as home-baked goods). A popular lunchtime stop is the **Dutch Oven** (see Travelwise), located behind the Wood Loft on Illinois Street, featuring Amish-style food.

Two-lane roads edged with trim white farmhouses crisscross the surrounding countryside, perfectly manicured with the help of slow-moving, hitched teams of six to eight horses. It's fun to wander, stopping at various cottage industries along the way—the perfect chance to pick up a quilt, fresh apple butter, baked goods, or furniture. You can obtain a map of local businesses from the Amish Country Visitor's Information Center (see Travelwise).

Rockome Gardens *(125 N. Cty. Rd. 425 E. 217-268-4106),* located off Ill. 133 between Arthur and Arcola, is a 14-acre complex showcasing Amish crafts and farming techniques. It includes gardens, a family-style restaurant, rides, and artisan workshops. Check the schedule of events throughout the summer; you may catch a quilt auction, a bluegrass festival, or horse-farming days.

East to Kickapoo

If you have an extra day, return east from Monticello past Champaign/Urbana and pick up I-74, heading farther east. The flat road is arrow straight, with nothing but soybeans and cornfields as far as the eye can see. This area is the nation's premier producer of ethanol, made from corn. Abraham Lincoln knew this region well, riding the circuit from Springfield to Danville between 1841 and 1861 to practice law.

Danville remains a quintessential small city, with its main street seemingly lost in time. When passing through town, Lincoln stayed with his friend, Dr. William Fithian; the Victorian mansion is now part of the **Vermilion County Museum** *(116 N. Gilbert St. 217-442-2922. Closed Mon.; adm. fee).* The Lincoln Room contains the canopied bed in which the future President slept.

Pick up a salad or sandwich for lunch from the **Java Hut** (see Travelwise) before heading out for a picnic at **Kickapoo State Recreation Area** *(10906 Kickapoo Park Rd., Oakwood. 217-442-4915),* just west of town via I-74. The highlight is the **Middle Fork Vermilion River,** the only national scenic river in Illinois. Especially popular among canoeists, the placid waterway winds through a forest of sycamore, sugar maple, beech, and dogwood—home to kingfishers and woodpeckers, plus the occasional turkey.

Spend the afternoon hiking, mountain biking, canoeing, or kayaking. Kickapoo Canoes *(2296-A Henning Rd., Danville. 217-354-2060)* rents boats by the hour or day and offers shuttles. Kickapoo is also one of the few state parks in Illinois to offer scuba diving.

—*Haas H. Mroue*

Travelwise

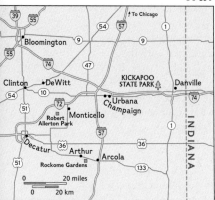

↑ To Chicago

GETTING THERE

Monticello is located about 130 miles south of Chicago via I-57 and I-72, a 2.5-hour drive. Danville is about 60 miles east of Monticello via I-72 and I-74.

GENERAL INFORMATION

Contact the **Champaign County Convention & Visitors Bureau** (1817 S. Neil St., Ste. 201, Champaign, IL 61820. 217-351-4133. www.cupartnership.org); the **Danville Area Convention & Visitors Bureau** (100 W. Main St., Ste. 146, Danville, IL 61832. 800-383-4386. www.danvillecvb.com), which offers a guide containing a good local map; or the **Amish Country Visitor's Information Center** (106 E. Progress St., Arthur, IL 61911. 800-722-6474. www.IllinoisAmishCountry.com), a must for a local map.

SEASONS

Spring and fall are best, when the weather is mild. The hot summer is ideal for water-related activities. Winters are bitingly cold, although snow may be elusive for weeks at a time.

ANNUAL EVENT

National Sweet Corn Festival (Labor Day weekend, McFerren Park, Hoopeston. 800-383-4386) Free locally grown sweet corn is distributed in this quintessential Illinois farming community. There's also a beauty pageant and a car show.

MORE THINGS TO SEE & DO

Heartland Spa (1237 E. 1600 North Rd., off I-57, Gilman. 800-545-4853. www.heartlandspa.com) Celebrities are among those who escape to this exquisite getaway, halfway between Chicago and Champaign/Urbana, for massages, honey mud facials, and sea salt body scrubs.

Lincoln Trail Homestead State Park (705 Spitler Park Dr., Mt. Zion. 217-864-3121) The site of Abraham Lincoln's first home in Illinois. Pleasant picnicking and hiking along the Sangamon River.

LODGING

Flower Patch (225 E. Jefferson St., Arcola. 217-268-4876. $) A homey Victorian set among gardens in the heart of Amish country.

Kickapoo State Recreation Area (10906 Kickapoo Park Rd., Oakwood. 217-442-4915. dnr.state.il.us/lands/Landmgt/PARKS/R3/KICK APOO.HTM. $) 217 tent & trailer sites. See p. 63.

Lamp Post Inn B & B (420 N. Gilbert St., Danville. 217-446-9458. $-$$) A restored turn-of-the-20th-century house with five rooms. The street outside can be noisy.

Robert Allerton Park (515 Old Timber Rd. 217-762-7011. www.conted.uiuc.edu/allerton. $) Simple accommodations in a serene setting; 24 rooms with private baths; no TVs or phones. See pp. 60-62.

DINING

Dutch Oven (116 E. Illinois St., Arthur. 217-543-2213. $) Homestyle Amish cooking. See p. 63.

The Heron (34 N. Vermilion St., Danville. 217-446-8330. Closed Sun.-Thurs. $$) The European-style menu features meat and fish prepared with the freshest ingredients.

Java Hut (13 N. Vermilion St, Danville. 217-443-6808. Closed Sun. $) Sandwiches and salads. See p. 63.

Montgomery's On The Square (108 S. Charter St. on the Main Sq., Monticello. 217-762-3833. $$) Eclectic American cuisine. See p. 62.

Radio Maria Restaurant (119 N. Walnut St., Champaign. 217-398-7729. $-$$) Seafood with Caribbean, Latin, and Asian flair.

Yoder's Kitchen (1195 E. Columbia St., Arthur. 217-543-2714. $) Popular homestyle Amish cooking.

Car Mania
Racing around Indianapolis & beyond

INDIANAPOLIS IS THE PERFECT GATEWAY to car-crazy Indiana, the birthplace of Studebakers and Duesenbergs, not to mention the venue for one of the world's most famous car races—the Indianapolis 500. For thrills you can zoom around a racetrack in an open-cockpit car after a short lesson at one of several racing schools. You can pay homage to the automobile at several fabulous museums. And, if you happen to be in Indianapolis during one of its many racing events, you may just spot some celebrity drivers. And their cars.

Fast cars in Indianapolis

Start your weekend with a visit to the **Indianapolis Motor Speedway** *(4790 W. 16th St. 317-484-6784)*. The 2.5-mile oval track is considered one of the world's most famous race courses, and, with 250,000 seats, it's the world's largest spectator sporting facility. The Indy 500 has been held here since 1911, with other big races including the Brickyard 400 (named after the thousands of bricks used to line the track) in early August, and the SAP U.S. Grand Prix in late September.

The speedway's **Hall of Fame Museum** *(317-484-6784. Adm. fee)* houses more than 75 antique and classic automobiles, plus 30 cars that have won the Indy 500 and a wealth of race memorabilia. For a small fee *(on non-race days)* you can take a lap around the track aboard a tour bus that leaves from the museum entrance.

Stop for lunch at the nearby **Union Jack** (see Travelwise), where racing people meet after a long day on the track for pizza and burgers, and the walls are lined with car memorabilia.

If you call ahead, you can spend the afternoon learning how to race a fast car. Contact either **No Limit Racing Adventure** *(317-885-8878. www.outrageousfun.com)* or **Track Attack Racing School** *(8740 E. 33rd St. 317-890-1519 or 888-722-3879. www.trackattack.com. Call for schedule),* both of which offer a variety of packages including high-speed driver training. Put your training to the test as you simulate "race day" with other students; if

> **NOT TO BE MISSED**
>
> ● **The fiery horseradish sauce at St. Elmo Steakhouse in Indianapolis**
> ● **Ogling a 1963 Studebaker Hawk at the Studebaker museum** ● **Kart racing at the Stefan Johansson Karting Center**

fast driving isn't your thing, you can copilot a car as a professional whips you around the track.

More than likely, your training will take place at the **Indianapolis Raceway Park** *(10267 E. US 136. 317-291-4090. www.irponline.com),* a motor-sports playground that also hosts more than 120 races between April and October each year; it's easier to get tickets for a race here than at the Speedway.

Another afternoon option is Kart racing at the **Stefan Johansson Karting Center** *(3649 Lafayette Rd. 317-297-5278. www.stefanjohans son.com. Reservations required),* named after the former Formula One driver who oversees this operation. After prerace driving instructions, you're off in your racing go-cart, speeding up to 40 miles an hour around the indoor track.

For dinner, try the **St. Elmo Steakhouse** (see Travelwise), a city landmark since 1902 and frequented by race-car champs. Racing photographs adorn the walls of this elegant restaurant.

Beyond Indianapolis

In the morning head for **Auburn,** the birthplace of the innovative and stylish Auburn and Cord motorcars built by the Auburn

Speeding around the Indy racetrack

Automobile Company from 1900 to 1937. The 145-mile trip north on I-69 takes about 2.5 hours. As he expanded his car empire, dynamic owner E. L. Cord bought out the Indianapolis-built Duesenberg in 1926. Duesenberg already had a reputation for making prestigious vehicles, but all standards changed when Cord introduced in 1928 the Duesenberg Model J. This sleek, ultra-expensive motorcar became the favorite of the very rich, monarchs, and movie stars, reigning as the queen of luxury through the twenties and thirties.

See some of these beauties first hand at Auburn's **Auburn Cord Duesenberg Museum** *(1600 S. Wayne St. 260-925-1444. Adm. fee).* Eight art-deco exhibit galleries, in the former showroom of the Auburn Automobile Company, house more than 110 classics. You'll also see Rolls-Royces, Cadillacs, Auburns, Cords, and Packards, plus carriages and sports cars.

To continue the auto pilgrimage, proceed to South Bend, via I-69 and I-80/90, where more car history awaits. In 1868 Henry and Clement Studebaker began the Studebaker Manufacturing Company. Eventually becoming the world's largest wagon manufacturer, Studebaker was also the only manufacturer to successfully switch from horse-drawn to gasoline-powered vehicles. The company closed its doors in 1963; abandoned factory buildings are still scattered about town.

Head to the excellent **Studebaker National Museum** *(525 S. Main St. 574-235-9714. Adm fee),* with cars ranging from settlers' carriages to 1960s station wagons. Celebrities include the carriage that in 1865 carried President Lincoln to Ford's Theatre the night he was assassinated; the bright yellow 1935 Commander Roadster used in the movie *The Color Purple;* and the postmodern Packard Predictor concept car designed in the mid-1950s.

You can dine in the 40-room mansion built in 1889 by Clement Studebaker, then president of the company. Local granite fieldstone covers the interior walls of the **Tippecanoe Place Restaurant** (see Travelwise), which is complemented with plenty of mahogany, decorative carvings, and 20 fireplaces. Dinner will transport you back to the turn-of-the-20th-century, when the Studebakers were the crème-de-la-crème of South Bend society and lavish parties were the norm. Try the delicious roasted Indiana duckling served with a sauce of raspberries and dried Bing cherries.

Head back 200 miles to Indianapolis on US 31. Along the way, break your trip in **Kokomo** with a stop at the **Automotive Heritage Museum** *(1500 N. Reed Rd. 765-454-9999. Adm. fee).* It was here in 1898 that Elwood Haynes (inventor of the first spark-ignition car) founded Indiana's first automobile factory, known worldwide as America's First Car until the company folded in 1925. More than 75 antique automobiles are on display. ——*Haas H. Mroue*

Travelwise

GETTING THERE

From Indianapolis, it's a 500-mile loop to Auburn and South Bend.

GENERAL INFORMATION

For information on racing-event tickets, contact the **Indianapolis Convention & Visitors Association** (1 RCA Dome, Ste. 100, Indianapolis, IN 46225. 317-639-4282 or 800-323-4639. www.indy.org).

SEASONS

Racing season is April to October. Make reservations many months in advance especially for Memorial Day and Labor Day weekends.

ANNUAL EVENTS

Auburn Cord Duesenberg Festival (Labor Day weekend, Auburn. 260-925-3600) More than 200 Auburn-built classic autos return home.

Ebay/Kruse International (Labor Day weekend, 5540 Cty. Rd.11A, Auburn. 800-968-4444) World's largest collector car auction.

Fairmount Museum Days: Remembering James Dean (last weekend in Sept., downtown Fairmount and Playacres Park, off I-69. 765-948-4555) More than 2,000 classic and custom autos in Dean's hometown.

MORE THINGS TO SEE & DO

Corvette Classics Museum (Pointe Inverness Way, Fort Wayne. 260-436-3444. Adm. fee) Fifty-two pristinely restored Corvettes.

Indy Racing Experience (317-243-7171 or 888-357-5002) This ride in an open-cockpit race car—from 0 to 100 mph in less than three seconds—is for the true racing enthusiast. Available a few days before and after Indy Racing League races.

National Automotive and Truck Museum of the United States (1000 Gordon M. Buehrig Pl., Auburn. 260-925-9100. Adm. fee) Post-World War II autos and trucks in two original Auburn Automotive Co. factory buildings.

LODGING

Auburn Inn (225 Touring Dr., Auburn. 260-925-6363. $$) Cozy, 53-room inn with a pool; near Auburn Cord Duesenberg Museum.

Canterbury Hotel (123 S. Illinois St., Indianapolis. 317-634-3000. $$) Traditional and luxurious, convenient to downtown, with 99 rooms.

Queen Anne Inn (420 W. Washington St., South Bend. 574-234-5959. $) Neoclassic mansion with wraparound porch. 6 rooms.

DINING

Auburn House Restaurant (131 W. 7th St., Auburn. 219-925-1102. $) Home-cooked meals; photos show the city's auto heritage.

St. Elmo Steakhouse (127 S. Illinois St., Indianapolis. 317-635-0636. $$-$$$) Elegant landmark restaurant, popular with race champions. See p. 66.

Tippecanoe Place Restaurant (620 W. Washington St., South Bend. 574-234-9077. $$) Fine dining in Studebaker's former home. See p. 67.

Union Jack (6225 W. 25th St. 317-243-3300. $-$$) Pizzas and burgers amid race-car memorabilia. See p. 65.

Brown County
An artist's—and outdoor lover's—natural haven

DRAWN TO ITS SPECTACULAR SCENERY, artists began flocking to Brown County in south-central Indiana at the turn of the 20th century. They formed an artist colony in Nashville and became known as the Hoosier group. Experimenting with light and color, these American impressionists—Theodore Clement Steele, Marie Goth, and Adolph Shulz among them—used the outdoors as their primary inspiration. Today this hilly corner, with its quiet woodlands, splashing streams, and farm-speckled pastures, remains virtually untouched, an inspiration to anyone who loves to hike, unwind, and get away from it all.

Artistry in Nashville

Leaving Indianapolis, drive south on Ind. 135 for about 60 miles to **Nashville,** in the heart of Brown County's thickly wooded ridges. You'll guess right away that you've stumbled across an artist's paradise. More than 200 shops and galleries selling handicrafts by locals—from braided rugs and quilts to stained and blown glass and oil paintings—cluster on the quaint main street. Stop by the **Brown County Art Gallery & Museum** *(1 Artist Dr. 812-988-4609)* to see the latest exhibit of local artists; it was established in 1926 by local Hoosier group painters. Another excellent gallery, the **Brown County Art Guild, Inc.** *(48 S. Van Buren St. 812-988-6185)* shows the works of more than 50 local and regional artists, including a collection of early Brown County residents. You might also wish to drive out to the **Schatz Studio & Gallery** *(2408 Gatesville Rd. 812-988-2897. Call ahead for appt. and directions)* to watch Greg Schatz at work on his unique wood-fired pottery and painted porcelains.

Join locals for lunch at **Hobnob Corner** (see Travelwise), housed in the old drugstore, Nashville's oldest commercial building (1868), complete with plank floor. Homemade soups are the

---

NOT TO BE MISSED

- **Hiking the trails around T. C. Steele's house**
- **Candlelight breakfast at the Olde Magnolia House**
- **Syrupy taste of local blackberry wine** ● **The scenic drive at dusk from Nashville to Story**

specialty, the bread pudding divine.

Then drive southwest on Ind. 46 about 3 miles to T. C. Steele Road, which brings you to the **T. C. Steele State Historic Site** *(4220 T. C. Steele Rd. 812-988-2785. Closed Mon.).* Like many artists, American impressionist Theodore Clement Steele fell in love with Brown County's undulating ridges, valleys, dells, and meadows. He and his wife, Selma, bought the 135-acre hilltop property in 1907 and transformed the hillside into a magnificent garden. They restored an abandoned farmhouse, called it the House of the Singing Winds, and summered here every year.

You can visit the house and "Large Studio," where more than 60 works by Steele hang, many depicting the garden and house. Stroll the grounds, through perennial gardens, past lily ponds and the cemetery, and along the half-mile **Trail of Silences,** filled with white oaks.

In the evening, attend a performance at the respected **Brown County Playhouse** *(70 S. Van Buren St., Nashville. 812-988-2123. June-Aug. and mid-Sept.–late Oct.),* known for its amusing productions of both classic and contemporary plays. The playhouse has been operating for more than 50 years and is the oldest professional theater in Indiana.

Outdoor enlightenment

Today you discover firsthand why the Hoosier group chose this land to settle, at **Brown County State Park** *(812-988-6406. www.brown countystatepark.com).* The artists often climbed these hills, perhaps along the very trails that you will walk, drinking in the same dreamy vistas. To reach the park, head 2 miles east of Nashville on Ind. 46 to the North Gate. Turn right onto the beautiful wood-covered bridge, built in 1838, and follow the signs.

If you wish to hike, the park offers more than 12 miles of trails through a splendid canopy of oak, hickory, sassafras, beech, and maple. A .75-mile nature trail explores Ogle Hollow Nature Preserve, its slopes covered with yellowwood trees. Or wander the 1.5-mile trail along the woodsy shores of Ogle Lake, popular among anglers who toss their lines for bluegill and bass.

For equestrians, about 70 miles of bridle trails meander through the park, providing another scenery-viewing option. Arrange for a guided ride at the **Brown County State Park Saddle Barn** *(812-988-8166),* near the visitor center. Kids love the pony rides offered here. Or take a leisurely drive along the park's quiet, shady roads, stopping to picnic atop **Weed Patch Hill,** the park's highest point.

Heading back to Nashville, stop at the **Brown County Winery** *(4520 State Rd. E. 46. 812-988-6144 or 888-298-2984. www.brown countywinery.com)* to taste some Indiana-made wines. The sweet wines are the specialty—especially blackberry and strawberry; be

sure also to sample the crisp white wine made from a mix of regionally grown Vidal and Vignoles grapes.

In the afternoon, and especially if you have kids in tow, check
out the show at Nashville's **Melchior Marionette Theater** (*W side
of S. Van Buren St. 317-535-4853 or 800-849-4853. June-July and
Sept.-Oct. Sat.-Sun., shows at 1 p.m. and 3 p.m.; adm. fee),* with its
handcrafted, half-life-size dancing marionettes.

At dinnertime, drive 12 miles southeast on Ind. 46 and 135
to the tiny town of **Story** (population: 7). The **Story Inn** (see
Travelwise), the county's finest restaurant, hides away in what
used to be the general store, complete with pot-bellied stove. Fresh
local produce and garden-grown herbs enhance such favorite
dishes as artichoke Romano dip and pork medallions with rose-
mary sauce. To avoid the winding drive back to Nashville, consider
spending the night in one of the inn's 14 bed-and-breakfast units,
full of rustic charm. If you're lucky, you'll be treated to the inn's
famous banana-walnut pancakes in the morning.

—Haas H. Mroue

Bean Blossom Bridge

Travelwise

GETTING THERE
Nashville, in Brown County, is located about 60 miles south of Indianapolis via Ind. 135.

GENERAL INFORMATION
Contact the **Brown County Convention & Visitors Bureau** *(Main and Van Buren Sts., P.O. Box 840, Nashville, IN 47448. 812-988-7303 or 800-753-3255. www.browncounty.com).*

SEASONS
Fall is when most visitors flock to Brown County, lured by brilliant fall foliage. The area's beauty, however, is evident year-round.

ANNUAL EVENTS
Bean Blossom Blues Festival *(mid-Sept., Bill Monroe Memorial Music Park and Campground, Bean Blossom. 800-783-7996)* Blues lovers congregate to hear renowned musicians.

Brown County Old Settlers Reunion *(1st Sat. in Sept., Bean Blossom. 812-988-2626 or 800-753-3255)* This annual event has featured dance groups, country music, an auction, and grandstand programs for more than 125 years.

MORE THINGS TO SEE & DO
Brown County Historical Society Museum *(Old School Way and Gould St., Nashville.*

812-988-7238. May-Oct. Sat.-Sun.; donation) Historical log structures and furnishings; living history demonstrations.

Little Nashville Opry *(1 mile W of Nashville on Ind. 46. 812-988-2235)* Local talent and country music stars perform Saturdays at 6 and 9 p.m. at this 2,000-seat venue.

LODGING
Artists Colony Inn *(Franklin and Van Buren Sts., Nashville. 812-988-0600. $-$$)* Charming 19th-century-style inn with hardwood floors and four-poster beds. 20 rooms, restaurant.

Brown County State Park *(off Ind. 46, 2 miles S of Nashville. 812-988-6406, lodge 877-265-6343)* Stay at the **Abe Martin Lodge** *($-$$)*, with 84 comfortable rooms and a scattering of cabins, or pitch a tent at one of the 650 year-round campsites *($)*.

Cornerstone Inn *(54 E. Franklin St., Nashville. 812-988-0300. $$)* Small inn with 20 plush rooms, just off Main St.

Hidden Valley Inn *(Ind. 135 N. at Mound St., Nashville. 812-988-9000. www.hiddenvalley-inn.com. $-$$$)* New 19-unit hotel with condominium-style suites.

Olde Magnolia House B&B *(213 S. Jefferson St., Nashville. 812-988-2434. $-$$)* Cozy inn with four comfortable guest rooms. Special candlelight breakfast and home-baked cakes.

Story Inn *(6404 S. State Rd. 135, Story. 812-988-2273 or 800-881-1183. Closed Mon. $)* B&B housed in old general store. See p. 71.

DINING
Artists Colony Inn *(Franklin and Van Buren Sts., Nashville. 812-988-0600. $-$$)* The inn's snug dining room has a large stone fireplace and beamed ceilings; the perfect place to enjoy a hearty soup or large salad.

Hobnob Corner *(17 W. Main St., Nashville. 812-988-4114. $)* Light fare. See p. 69.

Nashville House *(corner of Main and Van Buren Sts., Nashville. 812-988-4554. $$)* Established in 1859, this is Brown County's most popular restaurant; famous fried chicken with biscuits and baked apple butter.

Story Inn *(6404 S. State Rd. 135, Story. 812-988-2273 or 800-881-1183. Closed Mon. $$-$$$)* Gourmet dining. See p. 71.

Cincinnati

Along the Ohio River 74

Bluegrass Furlough 78

At Kentucky Horse Park, near Lexington

Along the Ohio River
Stern-wheelers & river towns

THE RIVER BROUGHT LIFE to the heartland in the late 1700s, when settlers arrived by boat from the East. Fleeing slaves later faced its daunting cold waters as they crossed to freedom. Rich with history and natural beauty, the sleepy towns that dot the Ohio's banks west of Cincinnati offer a simple way of life to recharge the weary traveler and revitalize the harried soul. Like the river, you'll find this is a land in which to meander.

Cincinnati's riverfront

Start your weekend with a leisurely walk along **Cincinnati's Central Riverfront,** a mile-long linear park that stretches from just south of downtown (at Broadway's eastern end) to the west. This has been the focal point of the city since 1788, when the first white settlers arrived on flatboats from Virginia and Pennsylvania. Now you'll find exquisitely landscaped gardens sprinkled with sculptures as well as fountains, an open-air concert hall, and wide paths for joggers and strollers. In summer, kids often cannot resist the temptation to wade in the huge shallow pool with its cascading waterfall. Nearby stands the **statue of Cincinnatus** (the city is named for the Revolutionary War Officers' Society of Cincinnatus, which in turned was named after the Roman soldier Cincinnatus).

At the western end of the park lies the training center for the U.S. Rowing Team; above it, one of Cincinnati's best loved restaurants, **Montgomery Inn Boathouse** (see Travelwise), overlooks the river; order the barbecued ribs and watch riverboats float peacefully by.

Retrace your steps back toward downtown and cross the river on the dedicated pedestrian walkway of the beautiful Roebling suspension bridge. You're now in **Covington,** Kentucky. To the west of the bridge awaits BB Riverboats (*1 Madison Ave., Covington Landing. 859-261-8500*), where you can catch a one-hour sight-seeing cruise along the river. Of course your transport is a three-deck stern-wheeler in late 1800s style—either the *River Queen* or the *Mark*

NOT TO BE MISSED

● **A moonlit walk on Cincinnati's suspension bridge** ● **Learning how a harp is made in Rising Sun** ● **Shopping at Vevay's historic Danner Hardware Store** ● **Early-morning fog low over the river**

Twilight on the Ohio River at Cincinnati, Ohio

Twain. If you'd prefer a lunch, dinner, or full-day cruise, ask for *The Belle of Cincinnati.*

Cincinnati boasts seven hills overlooking the river; it's worth tackling the climb to the top of Mount Adams for a visit to historic **Eden Park** and its collection of museums. Among them, the **Krohn Conservatory** *(1501 Eden Park Dr. 513-421-4086),* virtually a rain forest under a glass roof, showcases more than 5,000 varieties of tropical plants including orchids.

Atop Mount Adams you'll also find Cincinnati's hippest neighborhood, simply referred to as **Mount Adams.** During the 1800s, Catawba grapes that grew all over this hillside were made into the champagne known as Golden Wedding. Now the neighborhood is elegant and eclectic, with its windy and narrow streets lined with art galleries, quaint shops, cafés, and restaurants. The finest restaurant up here is **Celestial Restaurant & Incline Lounge** (see Travelwise), known for its classic French cuisine, impressive wine list, and views over the river. More casual places can be found throughout the neighborhood.

West along US 50

Drive west along the Ohio River on scenic US 50. In about 22 miles you'll arrive in **Lawrenceburg,** Dearborn County, one of Indiana's oldest counties. In 1669 René Robert Cavelier, sieur de La Salle, claimed this land for the French empire and, after losing it first to the British then to the new republic of the United States, settlers began arriving here in the early 1790s.

In the town of **Aurora,** farther southwest, a good place to sample a bit of local heritage is at **Hillforest Mansion** *(top of Main St. 812-926-0087. Call for tour hours; adm. fee),* occupying the highest point in town. Built in 1855 for industrialist and riverboat owner Thomas Gaff, the exquisitely restored mansion combines Italian Renaissance architecture with the elegance of a grand paddlewheeler. The "steamboat" verandas and balconies overlook the Ohio River. Tours showcase original furnishings.

Take Ind. 56 alongside the river for 12 miles until you reach **Rising Sun.** Legend has it that the first European settlers named the settlement in 1798, when on their first morning by the riverside someone cried: "Behold the rising sun!" Today you'll find a charming, slow-paced town, its historic downtown filled with federal and Greek Revival houses on tree-lined streets.

As you enter town, a left turn on Main Street will bring you to Front Street and the river, where benches provide quiet places for contemplation. The town's oldest surviving structure is the former **First Presbyterian Church** *(Main St. bet. Poplar and Walnut),* built in 1830 in the Romanesque Revival style. Next door at **Harps On Main** *(222 Main St. 812-438-3032. Closed Sun.),* you can watch members of the Rees family make harps by hand; informal tours take in the workshop and gallery. More and more art galleries are opening each year, fueled by the efforts of the **Pendleton Art Center** *(201 Main St. 812-438-9900)* to encourage up-and-coming artists.

If it's dinnertime, you may want to enjoy the gardens by the river at the **Courtyard Café** (see Travelwise), which also features live entertainment on select nights, or have a picnic on the riverbank.

Your destination for the night is a 21-mile drive west to **Vevay** (pronounced vee-VEE). Call ahead to reserve a river-view room at the **Rosemont Inn** (see Travelwise), and you'll have windows facing the water in this antique-filled 1881 house. Later in the evening, catch a play at the historic **Hoosier Theater** *(209 Ferry St. 812-427-2319. Adm. fee).* Built in 1837, it's one of the oldest commercial structures in Vevay; the theater was originally a warehouse that supplied the flatboats on the river.

A morning in Vevay

The scenes of the river change by the hour, especially in the morning when mist hangs low over the water. After breakfast, a walking tour of town is a good way to see Vevay's many 19th-century buildings— over 300 of them—built by Swiss settlers who made this county their home (thus its name, Switzerland County). Or stroll down to the 37-acre **Riverfront Park,** where you'll find a fishing pier and walking trails.

Before leaving town, make sure to stop at the **Danner Hardware Store** *(323 Ferry St. 812-427-3535),* which has museum-quality cash registers and an accounting system dating back to the Civil War.

On your way back to Cincinnati, a detour off US 50 for wine tasting and a good meal is a great way to break up the two-hour drive. From Lawrenceburg, head about 20 minutes north on Ind. 1 to the **Château Pomije Winery & Restaurant** *(25043 Jacobs Rd., Guilford. 812-623-3332).* A wide selection of grapes, ranging from Foch and Steuben to Pinot Noir and Chardonnay, stripe hills overlooking the Ohio River, providing yet another view of this classically beautiful river. —*Haas H. Mroue*

Travelwise

GETTING THERE
From Cincinnati, the town of Vevay, Indiana, is about 80 miles west via US 50.

GENERAL INFORMATION
Contact the **Greater Cincinnati Convention & Visitors Bureau** *(300 W. 6th St., Cincinnati, OH 45202. 513-621-2142. www.cincy usa.com);* **Dearborn County Chamber of Commerce & Visitors Bureau** *(555 Eads Pkwy. E., Lawrenceburg, IN 47025. 812-537-0814 or 800-322-8198);* or **Switzerland County Welcome Center** *(105 West Pike St., Vevay, IN, 47043. 812-427-3237 or 800-433-5688).*

SEASONS
Spring, summer, and fall are the best times to visit, when you can spend ample time outdoors along the river.

ANNUAL EVENT
Swiss Wine Festival *(4th weekend in Aug., Riverfront Park, Vevay. 800-435-5688)* Wine tastings and a grape-stomping contest, riverboat cruises, fireworks, and more.

MORE THINGS TO SEE & DO
Showboat Majestic *(Public Landing, on river at foot of Broadway, Cincinnati. 513-241-6550)* This floating theater offers matinees, evening musicals, and dramas.

LODGING
Amos Shinkle Townhouse Bed & Breakfast *(215 Garrard St., Covington. 859-431-2118 or 800-972-7012. www.amosshinkle.net. $-$$)* Steps from the river, this 1854 brick town house offers seven guest rooms in an opulent setting.

Cincinnatian Hotel *(601 Vine St., Cincinnati. 513-381-3000. www.cincinnatianhotel.com. $$$)* A few minutes' walk from the river, this is the city's most luxurious hotel, with 147 elegant rooms.

Rosemont Inn *(806 W. Market St., Vevay. 812-427-3050. Rosemont-inn.com. $-$$)* Five rooms, river views. See p. 76.

Schenck Mansion Bed & Breakfast Inn *(206 West Turnpike, Vevay. 812-427-2787. $$)* Built high on a hill, this Italianate mansion, with six guest rooms, was built in 1874.

DINING
Celestial Restaurant & Incline Lounge *(1071 Celestial St., Cincinnati. 513-241-4455. Closed Sun.-Mon. $$$)* French cuisine. See p. 75.

Courtyard Café *(135 N. Front St., Rising Sun. 812-438-3447. $-$$)* Steaks, seafood, burgers, homemade soups. See p. 76.

Montgomery Inn Boathouse *(925 Eastern Ave., Cincinnati. 513-721-7427. $$)* See p. 74.

Scalea's Ristorante & Italian Market Deli *(320 Greenup St., Covington. 859-491-3334. Restaurant closed Sun. $$-$$$)* This excellent restaurant has served fine Italian cuisine since 1925. The adjacent deli is a perfect place to pick up goodies for your picnic basket.

Bluegrass Furlough
Horsing around in Kentucky

SURROUNDING SOPHISTICATED LEXINGTON, the region's cultural and commercial heart for more than 200 years, the Bluegrass region is a magical place of rolling green hills and seemingly endless horse farms separated by white or black fences. Tiny lanes meander past palatial estates, grand barns, and regal horses grazing serenely in open pastures, the grass shimmering a brilliant blue-tinted green (thus the area's name). For horse fanciers, amateur and expert alike, there's no place quite like the Bluegrass.

West of Lexington
Leaving Cincinnati, head south on I-75 for 80 miles to the Lexington area. Make the **Kentucky Horse Park** *(4 miles N of Lexington, exit 120 off I-75, at 4089 Iron Works Pkwy. 800-678-8813. www.kyhorsepark .com. Closed Mon.-Tues. Nov.-March; adm. fee)* your first stop, where

Thoroughbreds graze the bluegrass.

nearly one million visitors flock each year. Think of this place as the Sea World of horses. From its fantastic **International Museum of the Horse** to the highly educating **Parade of Breeds** (a good introduction to different Thoroughbreds if you are a novice), you learn virtually everything there is to know about horses in an entertaining manner. Kids especially enjoy the **Breeds Barn,** where horses are groomed. Plan to spend at least half the day at the park, since different shows are held every hour and there's so much to see. For lunch, the **Clubhouse Restaurant** offers a wide selection of dishes.

After leaving the horse park, head for the **Thoroughbred Center** *(3380 Paris Pike. 859-293-1853. Closed Sun.),* home to a thousand horses, for a behind-the-scenes look at a working Thoroughbred training facility. Or call ahead to one of many private horse farms offering tours by appointment only (you see them on the side of almost every road—farm after farm). A good choice is **Three Chimneys Farm** *(Old Frankfort Pike, near jct. of I-64 and US 62. 859-873-7053),* former residence of the 1977 Triple Crown winner, Seattle Slew (the champion died on May 7, 2002, 25 years to the day after his victory in the Kentucky Derby). This farm has bred scores of Derby stars.

You are in the most scenic area of the Bluegrass here, between the charming towns of **Midway** and **Versailles,** both worth a peek for their quaint architecture and myriad antique shops. Travel along

US 62, the main road between the two, through a patchwork quilt of farm-studded, green-carpeted swells divided by parallel white fences. For the pure essence of Bluegrass beauty, follow quiet, tree-shaded **Old Frankfort Pike;** drifting past crumbling limestone fences, fields of flowers, and tobacco fields, you'll come across several horse farms along the way.

Historic Bluegrass towns

After a leisurely breakfast, head out to **Keeneland Race Course** *(4201 Versailles Rd. 859-254-3412)*, started shortly after the Depression by legendary horse trainer John Oliver Keene. Graced by limestone buildings dating back to 1875, Keeneland is one of the country's most beautiful racetracks. The grounds are open all day, but live Thoroughbred racing takes place only during a couple of weeks in April and October. Even if racing isn't going on, you're bound to see horses out for their morning workout, pounding around the track.

It's no coincidence that Kentucky, in addition to Thoroughbred breeding, is also famous for its bourbon distilling, since both benefit from the same natural element: limestone water. The Bluegrass sits on an enormous limestone aquifer that's rich in calcium, good for strong bones in horses and for clear, smooth bourbon.

You'll find one of America's oldest operating distilleries (and its smallest) nestled amid miles of horse farms near Versailles. **Labrot & Graham** *(7855 McCracken Pike, Versailles. 859-879-1812. Closed Sun. year-round, and Mon. Nov.-March)*, famous for its Woodford Reserve Bourbon, provides an intriguing overview of how the whiskey is made. Tours take in the distilling room, with its rare copper-pot stills, and the distillery's only surviving stone-aging warehouse, filled with barrels of bourbon maturing to perfection. The historic limestone buildings themselves are worth the trip.

NOT TO BE MISSED

● **Old Frankfort Pike at sunset** ● **The horses' morning workout at Keeneland**

● **The serene Carriage House at Historic Scottwood Inn**

Now head into the southwesternmost corner of the Bluegrass, via US 127 south for about 25 miles, to the little town of **Danville,** the birthplace of Kentucky statehood in 1792. **Constitution Square** still possesses its frontier look: The original log courthouse, where the negotiations and debates for statehood took place, sits beside the old meetinghouse, schoolhouse, and stockade-type jail. All are open and filled with interesting relics of the past. Keep in mind that Danville's **Pioneer Playhouse** *(840 Stanford Rd. 859-236-2747. Closed Sun.-Mon.)*, Kentucky's oldest outdoor dinner theater, is a fun way to spend an evening.

West of Danville via US 150 lies **Perryville,** another historic town. Along its main street, known as **Merchant's Row,** buildings that have stood here since before the Civil War now house galleries, restaurants, and shops. On Oct. 8, 1862, one of the Civil War's fiercest battles raged just west of town, on land now preserved as the **Perryville Battlefield State Historic Site** *(1825 Battlefield Rd., Perryville. 859-332-8631)*. At the end of that day, more than 6,000 soldiers were dead, dying, or missing after the South's last attempt to take Kentucky. Battle relics are displayed in the museum, while nature trails wander the serene battlefield. A battle reenactment takes place every October.

For an interesting place to spend the night, head northeast on US 68. About 7 miles east of Harrodsburg you'll find the **Shaker Village of Pleasant Hill** *(3501 Lexington Rd. 859-734-5411. www.shakervillageky.org. Adm. fee)*, a restored community and living museum that provides a veritable step back in time. The Shakers, known for "shaking off their sins" and their trembling movements during worship, occupied this farmland between 1805 and 1923. Some 2,800 acres of their lush Bluegrass land have been preserved, along with 33 structures—15 of which offer Zenlike overnight accommodations. The Shakers withdrew from the world, and here you'll have a chance to do the same. For dinner, the peaceful restaurant known as the **Trustees' Office** is a perfect place to enjoy a candlelit dinner of simple Shaker specialties: baked chicken or fish, corn bread, coleslaw, and locally grown vegetables.

Spending the day at Pleasant Hill

After breakfast you'll want to spend some time exploring Pleasant Hill. A self-guided tour takes in 18 meticulously preserved dwellings and workshops. You can wander around most of their simple interiors, discovering how the Shakers lived in groups as brothers and sisters—all sworn to celibacy. The highlight is the 40-room **Centre Family Dwelling,** with its exquisite collection of Shaker furniture, designs now being replicated by big-city designers. In the workshops, craftspeople make brooms, carve wood, spin, and weave, just like in the olden days.

An enjoyable afternoon can be spent wandering the settlement's acreage, by foot or on horseback. Among the scenic trails don't miss the **Shawnee Run Trail,** a 6-mile loop through fields and forests; and the 1-mile **Palisades Trail,** which follows the Kentucky River in the shadow of the massive Kentucky River Palisades. For a different perspective, head to nearby Shaker Landing for a cruise aboard the ***Dixie Belle*** *(859-734-5411. Fare)*. Floating on the placid water, you are treated to a wild landscape that looks much as it did 150 years ago.

When it's time to return to the present, wind northeast on Harrodsburg Rd./US 68 through a wooded canyon back to Lexington. Here, rejoin I-75 north for your drive back to Cincinnati.

—*Haas H. Mroue*

Travelwise

when the days are warm and nights cool. Summer can be hot and humid and winter cold but sunny.

ANNUAL EVENT
Kentucky Derby Simulcast *(1st Sat. in May. Keeneland Race Course, 4201 Versailles Rd., Lexington. 800-456-3412)* The second best place to be on Derby day if you're not in Louisville.

LODGING
Gratz Park Inn *(120 W. 2nd St., Lexington. 859-231-1777. www.gratzparkinn.com. $$-$$$)* Historic hotel in downtown Lexington with 44 rooms boasting four-poster beds.

Historic Scottwood *(US 421/Leestown Pike, near Midway. 859-846-5037. $-$$)* Sitting on five acres bordering horse farms, this cozy B&B was built of brick in 1795. Three rooms.

Shaker Village of Pleasant Hill *(3501 Lexington Rd., near Harrodsburg. 859-734-5411. $-$$)* Simple, peaceful accommodations. 81 rooms. See p. 81.

DINING
Beaumont Inn *(638 Beaumont Inn Dr., Harrodsburg. 859-734-3381. $$)* Famous two-year-old cured Kentucky ham and southern fried chicken.

Dudley's *(380 South Mill St., Lexington. 859-252-1010. $$-$$$)* Located in a restored 19th-century schoolhouse, this fine restaurant serves an eclectic menu, including braised lamb shanks, pesto pizza, and ahi tuna.

Elmwood Inn *(205 E. 4th St., Perryville. 859-332-2400. www.elmwoodinn.com. Tea served 1 and 3 p.m. $$)* English tea at this beautiful Greek Revival mansion is truly reminiscent of another era.

Holly Hill Inn *(426 N. Winter St., Midway. 859-846-4732. No dinner Sun. $$$)* Award-winning three-course meals in a 19th-century house featuring Kentucky arts and crafts. Fresh ingredients are the secret behind the ever changing selection of creative dishes.

Trustee's Office *(Shaker Village of Pleasant Hill, 3501 Lexington Rd., near Harrodsburg. 859-734-5411. $)* Shaker specialties by candlelight. See p. 81.

GETTING THERE
The Bluegrass surrounds the historic city of Lexington, in the heart of Kentucky. From Cincinnati, drive 80 miles south via I-75.

GENERAL INFORMATION
Contact the **Lexington Convention & Visitors Bureau** *(301 E. Vine St., Lexington, KY 40507. 859-233-1221 or 800-845-3959. www.visitlex.com)* for maps, brochures, and detailed Thoroughbred farm tour information.

SEASONS
Spring and fall are the best times to visit,

Denver

A Brewery Crawl 84

The Front Range 88

Rocky Mountain High 92

Mountain biking near Mount Princeton

A Brewery Crawl
Microbrews of Denver & beyond

COLORADO IS A HOTBED OF HEARTY BEERS. Maybe it's the mountain water, or perhaps it stems back to Prussian emigrant Adolph Coors, who, after landing in Colorado in the early 1870s, opened his Golden Brewery. Whereas Coors's creation was destined to evolve into the single largest brewery in the world, dozens of younger Colorado breweries are far more intimate. As you explore a handful of them, stay overnight in Denver and Boulder to minimize the on-duty time required of your designated driver.

Downtown Denver

Kick off your ramblings at Denver's 16th Street Mall, where you'll find the **Rock Bottom Restaurant & Brewery** (see Travelwise). The chain restaurant's lunch offerings are delectable, and this Denver brewery won a silver medal at the 2001 Great American Beer Festival for its Molly's Titanic Brown Ale.

To explore the lore of that ale's namesake, stroll a few blocks southeast—passing the **Denver Art Museum** (*13th Ave. and Acoma St. 720-865-5000. Adm. fee*) and the **Colorado History Museum** (*1300 Broadway. 303-866-3682. Adm. fee*)—to the **Molly Brown House Museum** (*1340 Pennsylvania St. 303-832-4092. Adm. fee*). Brown's rags-to-riches life was filled with adventure and drama. Best known for surviving the sinking of the Titanic, she was a pillar of Denver's nouveau riche society—her husband struck it rich in the Leadville gold mines; she was also a philanthropist and a publicity hound. When her cousin once inquired why she continued letting the newspapers tell a story that simply wasn't true, Molly reportedly said, "I don't care what the newspapers say about me, just so they say something."

As the afternoon wears on, return to the 16th Street Mall, then walk several blocks north to the **Wynkoop Brewing Company** (see Travelwise). Denver's first modern brew pub was opened late in 1988 by a laid-off oil geologist and home-brewer, John Hickenlooper, and his partners. Hickenlooper's renovation of the 1899 J. S. Brown

NOT TO BE MISSED

● A properly pulled Guinness Stout at Denver's Fado Irish Pub ● Live blues and jazz at Linden's Brewing Company, Old Town Fort Collins ● Claymore Scotch Ale at Mountain Sun Pub & Brewery

The Wynkoop Brewing Co., Denver

Mercantile Building was one of the pioneer attempts at preserving a historic structure in Denver's rapidly deteriorating Lower Downtown (LoDo), and his work helped spur others to action. Today, LoDo is a popular, polished part of the city.

To experience just how different various brews can taste, consider sharing a sampler tray containing small glasses of all the Wynkoop beers on tap. Begin with the lightest, Boxcar Kolsch, working up to the robust Sagebrush Stout, practically a meal in itself. After supper, head up the stairs to people-watch or to shoot eight ball in one of Denver's preeminent billiard halls.

Fort Collins & Boulder

Head north to **Fort Collins** to tour the innovative **New Belgium Brewing Company** *(500 Linden St. 970-221-0524. www.newbelgium .com. Closed Sun.).* Starting out about a decade ago in their basement, the husband-and-wife team of Jeff Lebesch and Kim Jordan now employ well over 150 people in their stunning, 70,000-squarefoot building. The juice to run the environmentally conscious enterprise comes from wind power generated in Wyoming. Another clean machine, the bicycle, is a recurring theme at New Belgium: Lebesch committed to the idea of starting a brewery while bike touring in Belgium, and the wildly popular Fat Tire Amber Ale is largely responsible for the brewery's success. So, it seems fitting that each employee is presented with a fat-tire cruiser bicycle after a year of service.

For lunch, visit the attractive **CooperSmith's Pub & Brewing** (see Travelwise) featuring at least ten handcrafted beers on tap at any given time. Then stroll the surrounding **Old Town Fort Collins historic district,** where galleries and boutiques occupy renovated Victorians built in the 1880s and '90s. Alternatively, drive northwest from town up the canyon of the **Cache la Poudre River,** where high granite walls provide a dramatic setting for a hike or for casting a line for brown and rainbow trout *(call Rocky Mountain Adventures 970-493-4005).* The canyon may well have served as the inspiration for Cutthroat Porter and Colorado Stream Lager, a pair of the beers brewed at another Fort Collins establishment, **Odell Brewing Company** *(800 E. Lincoln Ave. 888-887-2797. www.odells.com).*

Follow US 287 south to Longmont, then Colo. 119 southwest toward **Boulder,** a university city alive with fitness enthusiasts and magnificently situated at the foot of the Rockies. Just before getting into the heart of town, go left onto Jay Road to find **Celestial Seasonings** *(4600 Sleepytime Dr. 303-581-1202. www.celestialseasonings .com),* where on a guided tour you learn about an altogether different sort of "brew." The company's origins date from 1969, when 19-year-old Mo Siegel was prowling the canyons and high country of Colorado for herbs to use in home-brewed teas. His first commercial product, Mo's 36 Herb Tea, started something big: Today Celestial Seasonings is the largest herbal-tea company in North America, providing the bags for more than a billion cups poured yearly.

Before checking into your hotel, visit a fledgling enterprise that— who knows?—may one day rival Celestial Seasonings in its scope: the **Redstone Meadery** *(4700 Pearl St., #2A. 720-406-1215. www.redstone meadery.com. Closed Sun.-Tues., afternoon tours only).* Owner and meadmaker David Myers possesses an enthusiasm for his honey-wine product that borders on fanaticism. He also comes from entrepreneurial stock—his grandfather "Izzy" Myers founded the London Fog apparel company. After years as a home-brewer of beer and mead, David says, "I decided to shed my amateur status and go pro." Redstone cut the ribbon in September 2000 and began producing a relatively low-alcohol nectar flavored with fruit, and a more traditional, 12-percent-alcohol Mountain Honey Wine, which has no fruit added. Somewhere between beer and wine in cost and consistency, mead is widely regarded as the world's oldest alcoholic beverage, dating back at least 4,000 years.

You thought the days of peace and love were long gone? Not in Boulder. Entering **Mountain Sun Pub & Brewery** (see Travelwise) is like flashing back to a psychedelic Pearl Street of 30 years ago. Batik and beads are everywhere, old concert posters embellish the walls, and the scent of patchouli hangs heavy in the air. They make good beer, too, such as the rich Annapurna Amber.

Today, the heart of Pearl Street is a busy pedestrian mall teeming with street musicians and outside art, and lined with bookstores, coffee shops, and upscale clothiers. When evening arrives, walk a few blocks west and south to the **Oasis Restaurant and Brewery** (see Travelwise). The brew pub has a bit of Las Vegas kitsch to it, with an immense interior featuring an Egyptian-theme decor that echoes its beer titles; the two biggest award winners are Zoser Oatmeal Stout and Capstone E.S.B., an English-style extra-special bitter. The eclectic dinner menu features items such as a lip-smacking potato parmesan soup and "Pharaoh's Favorites," which include green-chili-stuffed blue-corn enchiladas with spicy rice, black beans, and guacamole.

—*Michael McCoy*

Travelwise

GETTING THERE
From Denver, Fort Collins is 65 miles north via I-25; Boulder is 25 miles north via US 36.

GENERAL INFORMATION
Contact the **Boulder Convention & Visitors Bureau** *(2440 Pearl St., Boulder, CO 80302. 303-442-2911. www.bouldercoloradousa .com);* **Denver Metro Convention & Visitors Bureau** *(1555 California St., Denver, CO 80202. 303-892-1112 or 800-233-6837. www.denver.org);* or **Fort Collins Convention & Visitors Bureau** *(3745 E. Prospect Rd., #200, Fort Collins, CO 80525. 970-491-3388. www.ftcollins.com).*

ANNUAL EVENT
Great American Beer Festival *(late Sept.– early Oct., Denver. 303-447-0816. www.gabf .org. Adm. fee)* Around 400 companies, serving nearly 2,000 brews, vie for the most prestigious honors in the microbrewery business.

MORE THINGS TO SEE & DO
Coors Brewery *(13th and Ford Sts., Golden. 303-277-2337. www.coors.com. Closed Sun.)* Guided tours of the brewery offered.

LODGING
Hotel Boulderado *(2115 13th St., Boulder. 303-442-4344. www.boulderado.com. $$- $$$)* A broad staircase climbs above a lobby and tile-ceilinged mezzanine to three floors of rooms decorated with Victorian touches.

Hotel Teatro *(1100 14th St., Denver. 303-228- 1100. www.hotelteatro.com. $$-$$$)* Luxury 111-room hotel in the heart of downtown.

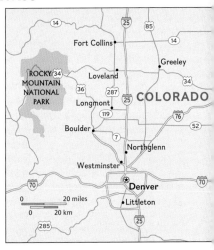

DINING
CooperSmith's Pub & Brewing *(5 Old Town Sq., Fort Collins. 970-498-0483. www.coop ersmithspub.com. $-$$)* See p. 86.

Mountain Sun Pub & Brewery *(1535 Pearl St., Boulder. 303-546-0886. $)* See p. 86.

Oasis Restaurant and Brewery *(1095 Canyon Blvd., Boulder. 303-449-0363. www.oasis brewery.com. $-$$)* See p. 87.

Rock Bottom Restaurant & Brewery *(1001 16th St., Denver. 303-534-7616. www.rock bottom.com. $$)* See p. 84.

Wynkoop Brewing Company *(1634 18th St., Denver. 303-297-2700. www.wynkoop.com. $-$$)* See pp. 84-85.

The Front Range
Discovering nature's secrets

THE COLORADO FRONT RANGE is home to a concentration of museums, federal agencies, and university laboratories involved in matters such as the weather, astronomy, and earth sciences. During this adventure you'll delve into some of those complex, yet fascinating subjects while enjoying a few of the extraordinary dining and lodging opportunities found in the area.

Golden & around

Make a requisite advance reservation for a weekday midafternoon lecture and tour at the U.S. Geological Survey's **National Earthquake Information Center** *(1711 Illinois St., Golden. 303-273-8500. http://neic.usgs.gov. Closed Fri.-Mon.)*. Located on the campus of the Colorado School of Mines, the NEIC is the national data center for earthquake-related information. Here you'll learn how and why the center monitors earthquakes across the globe; find out about research aimed at better understanding the dynamics of crustal shaking and breaking; and discover where in the world current earthquake activity is taking place.

From Golden, drive back east on US 6, then go west on I-70 and take the Colo. 470 exit. Leave Colo. 470 after about 4 miles and drive west toward Morrison, turning right at the eastern outskirts of town onto County Road 93. Immediately on your left you'll see the venerable **Cliff House Lodge** (see Travelwise), a wonderful place to overnight, with its six intimate cottages, each boasting a private hot tub.

For supper, consider moseying back to the Wild West of 150 years ago at **The Fort** (see Travelwise), an adobe-brick re-creation of Bent's Old Fort in southeastern Colorado. You can feast on buffalo ribs or elk steaks, after—if you've got the nerve—sampling appetizers such as Texas diamondback rattlesnake cakes, Rocky Mountain oysters, and bison tongue. Waitstaff, decked out as Native American and mountain men or women, are said to occasionally accept beaver pelts in lieu of cash.

NOT TO BE MISSED

- Egyptian Mummies wing, Denver Museum of Nature & Science • The view of Denver at night from The Fort • Walter Orr Roberts Weather Trail, NCAR • Cajun catfish with jambalaya vegetables at Wolfgang Puck's

National Center for Atmospheric Research, Boulder

Morrison area

Continue uphill past the Cliff House Lodge on County Road 93. After 2 miles, turn right onto Colo. 26, switchbacking around the high hogback, then arriving at the **Dinosaur Ridge National Natural Landmark Visitor Center** *(303-697-3466. www.dinoridge.org)*. You can take either a self-guided tour of the ridge or one led by a trained guide *(reserve a week in advance)*.

On the ridge's west side, fossil bones of *Stegosaurus, Diplodocus,* and other late Jurassic dinosaur species are exposed in Morrison sandstones, while on the east side, in younger Cretaceous period Dakota Group sandstones, several hundred tracks of ancient birds, crocodiles, and dinosaurs can be inspected. These Dakota sediments are near the known northern extent of the "Dinosaur Freeway," which has been traced intermittently all the way to New Mexico. Many believe it may outline a migration route following what was a several-hundred-mile stretch of coastline.

On the way back to Morrison, take the short detour to **Red Rocks Park** *(303-640-7334. www.redrocksonline.com)*, a stunning, acoustically acclaimed natural amphitheater. The star-studded list of those who've performed at the 9,000-seat outdoor venue during the past 60 years includes Igor Stravinsky (1948), the Beatles (1963), and the Grateful Dead (two dozen times between 1978 and 1987). The 1.4-mile Trading Post trail loops through spectacular rock formations, valleys, and a meadow; you might spot mule deer along the way.

Return to Golden, then drive north 20 miles to Boulder on Colo. 93, past large parcels of open space webbed with hiking trails. On the outskirts of Boulder, where the highway becomes Broadway, notice the isolated building sitting high on a mesa to your left: That's where you're headed. Turn left off Broadway onto Table Mesa Drive, climbing through open pine savanna, with the dramatic Flatirons erupting at steep angles immediately ahead.

Soon you'll drive onto the 400-acre grounds of the **National Center for Atmospheric Research** *(1850 Table Mesa Dr. 303-497-1174. www.ucar.edu)*. Its gorgeous headquarters, the Mesa Laboratory, was built in the 1960s by the renowned architect I. M. Pei, who drew inspiration from Stonehenge and Mesa Verde. NCAR is a consortium involving more than five-dozen universities, with research underwritten largely by the National Science Foundation. On a guided tour of the facility *(noon)*, you'll learn how researchers are studying the big picture of climate change by monitoring air, ozone and smog levels, weather, the ice pack, and ecosystems throughout the world.

While away the rest of the afternoon by touring scenic Boulder Canyon or wandering the city's attractive downtown pedestrian mall. After supper, head for the **Fiske Planetarium** *(Regent Dr., University of Colorado campus. 303-492-5002. www.colorado.edu/fiske)*. Inside the theater of the big geodesic dome you can enjoy a Friday evening star show *(call for start times; adm. fee)* such as "Mars Quest," "Searching for Distant Worlds," or "Cosmic Collisions." Afterward, wander over to the adjacent **Sommers-Bausch Observatory** *(303-492-2020. Fri. only; weather permitting)* for a session of stargazing through observation-deck-mounted telescopes, hosted by a graduate student or professor. Finally, return to the planetarium for an electrifying, late evening laser show *(Fri.-Sat.; adm. fee)* featuring the compositions of musicians such as Pink Floyd, the Red Hot Chili Peppers…or Mozart.

Denver

Return to Denver and spend a few hours at the **Denver Museum of Nature & Science** *(2001 Colorado Blvd. 303-322-7009. www.dmns.org)*. The outstanding Prehistoric Journey exhibit takes you from the time of Earth's creation 4.5 billion years ago to the present. Stops along the way include the Devonian period, when creatures began crawling from sea to land; the days of the dinosaurs; and the Rocky Mountains of 50 million years ago, when a tropical climate supported rain forests and tree-swinging primates.

Finally, drive to the **Tattered Cover** *(2955 E. 1st Ave. 303-322-7727 or 800-833-9327. www.tatteredcover.com)*, one of America's great bookstores. Grab a cup of coffee, a sofa, and a book—maybe something lighter than atmospheric sciences—and kick back for a while, resting up for a Saturday night in Denver's vibrant LoDo (Lower Downtown) District. —*Michael McCoy*

Travelwise

GETTING THERE

To reach the first site, the NEIC in Golden, head west 10 miles from Denver on US 6.

GENERAL INFORMATION

Contact the **Boulder Convention & Visitors Bureau** *(2440 Pearl St., Boulder, CO 80302. 303-442-2911. www.bouldercoloradousa .com)* or the **Denver Metro Convention & Visitors Bureau** *(1555 California St., Denver, CO 80202. 303-892-1112 or 800-233-6837. www.denver.org).*

MORE THINGS TO SEE & DO

National Institute of Standards and Technology *(325 Broadway, Boulder. 303-497-5500. www.boulder.nist.gov. Closed Sat.-Sun., call to arrange a tour)* NIST physicists conduct research on subjects such as radio frequency and electromagnetic technology, quantum physics, and material reliability. But the facility is best known for housing the atomic clock that maintains the U.S. primary standard of time. It's reportedly accurate to one second in 26 million years. *(Note: As of press time the NIST is indefinitely closed to the public.)*

National Oceanic and Atmospheric Administration *(325 Broadway, Boulder. 303-497-6286. www.boulder.noaa.gov. Closed Sat.-Sun., call to arrange a tour)* Located on the same grounds as NIST, this NOAA office researches climate, drought, El Niño and La Niña, water in the West, ozone depletion, and air quality, and it collects information on tsunamis. At the Space Environment Center, gaze through big window panels and see huge computer screens showing the sun's active surface in real time. *(Note: As of press time the NOAA is indefinitely closed to the public.)*

National Renewable Energy Laboratory Visitor Center *(15013 Denver W. Pkwy., Golden. 303-384-6565. www.nrel.gov. Closed Sat.-Sun.)* Videos and displays explain solar energy, wind power, and other renewable energy source technologies.

LODGING

Alexander Jameson House *(1704 Illinois St., Golden. 303-278-0200. www.jamesonhouse .com. $-$$)* A four-guest-room bed-and-

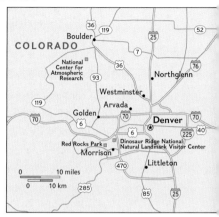

breakfast situated immediately across the street from the Colorado School of Mines.

Cliff House Lodge *(121 Stone St., Morrison. 303-697-9732. http://town.morrison.co.us /cliffhouselodge. $$-$$$)* See p. 88.

Queen Anne Bed & Breakfast *(2147 Tremont Pl., Denver. 303-296-6666 or 800-432-4667. www.queenannebnb.com. $-$$)* Two exquisite Victorian houses, located six blocks northeast of 16th Street Mall, feature 14 guest rooms and front Benedict Fountain Park.

University Inn *(1632 Broadway, Boulder. 303-442-3830 or 800-258-7917. www.u-inn.com. $-$$)* Within walking distance of downtown and the University of Colorado campus, this motel includes outdoor pool, Continental breakfast, and guest laundry.

DINING

The Fort *(19192 Colo. 8, outside Morrison. 303-697-4771. $$$)* See p. 88.

Greenbriar Inn *(8735 N. Foothills Hwy., N of Boulder. 303-440-7979. Closed Mon. $$-$$$)* Fine dining—lamb, game, seafood, beef, poultry—accompanied by an exceptional wine list.

Wolfgang Puck Café *(500 16th St., Denver. 303-595-9653. $$)* Located along the popular 16th Street Mall in the Denver Pavilions. The open kitchen—a controlled chaos of cooks, waiters, and bussers—is almost as fun to watch as the food is to eat (but not quite).

Rocky Mountain High
Lofty peaks & hot springs

THIS 300-MILE LOOP takes in a pack of the most spectacular peaks in all of Colorado. After leaving I-70, you'll wind through the upper Arkansas River Valley, where the crags of the Sawatch Range etch the loftiest skyline in the Rockies. There's nothing quite as exhilarating as setting foot on one of those 14,000-foot-plus peaks—unless it is the utter relaxation and bliss you will experience while soaking in one of nature's own hot tubs after making the exhausting hike.

Leadville

A late morning departure from Denver will deliver you to the shadowy canyon confines of Idaho Springs just in time for lunch at the **Tommyknocker Brewery** (see Travelwise). Named after mythical elf-like inhabitants of the early mines and housed in the 140-year-old Placer Inn, the brew pub dishes up goodies like beer-battered onion rings, buffalo-and-black-bean chili, and chicken-fried elk steak. Wash lunch down with a pint of Pick Axe Pale Ale or a nonalcoholic product, such as the scrumptious Key Lime Creme.

NOT TO BE MISSED

- **The scale model of Leadville's immense 1895-96 Ice Palace at the National Mining Hall of Fame** ● **The view from atop Mount Elbert**
- **Streamside soaking at Mount Princeton Hot Springs** ● **Tudor Rose's eggs Benedict**

After leaving the interstate near Copper Mountain, you'll crest 11,318-foot Fremont Pass and travel 12 miles into **Leadville,** a classic mining town settled late in the 19th century. Sitting at a lung-searing elevation of more than 10,000 feet, the town is closer to heaven than any other incorporated community in the United States, as your breathlessness and pounding heart will attest. Still, Mounts Elbert and Massive tower above town to the west, while the Mosquito Range looms to the east.

Wild West mining characters roam the sidewalks, and century-old redbrick buildings and rustic, false-fronted frame structures line the streets of downtown. Walk into the former hardware store at Harrison and West Fifth, now known as **Western Hardware Antiques Mall** *(431 Harrison Ave. 719-486-2213),* and you'll find that pair of old wooden skis to hang over the fireplace—

Historic Leadville

along with plenty of other items you didn't know you couldn't live without. Another must-visit in town: the **National Mining Hall of Fame & Museum** *(120 W. 9th St. 719-486-1229. www.leadville.com /miningmuseum. Adm. fee),* housed in the town's former high school and dedicated to the lore of ore. The colorful, sparkling Crystal Room alone is worth the price of admission. Another of many excellent exhibits focuses on how nearly everything we use, from cosmetics to concrete to car parts, begins with mining.

Before supper, visit the Leadville Ranger District office *(2015 N. Poplar St. 719-486-0749. Closed Sat.-Sun.)* to obtain detailed information on tomorrow's suggested hike up Mount Elbert, including directions to the trailhead. If you do not feel up to summiting a "fourteener," you can also inquire about shorter, less ambitious outings in the area.

Mount Elbert & Mount Princeton

At 14,433 feet, **Mount Elbert** is Colorado's highest peak; paradoxically, it's regarded as one of the easier fourteeners to surmount, owing to the relatively high elevations of the starting points. The **North Elbert Trail** begins at an elevation of more than 10,000 feet and gains the summit after a steep 4.5-mile ascent. The longer, though less strenuous and more popular, **South Elbert Trail** sets out at around 9,600 feet. "Less strenuous" is a relative phrase, obviously, and good fitness is needed to make this trip, along with common sense and careful planning; bring plenty of food, water, and sunscreen. Be aware of the symptoms of altitude sickness, and if they appear, as they can in even the most physically fit person, return to lower elevation at once. Finally, rise early for an alpine start, so that you'll be off the mountain before the common afternoon thunderheads build.

On returning to the trailhead after the long haul, head south on US 24 through the upper Arkansas Valley. At the colorful little tourist town of **Buena Vista**—"Buena" in localese—turn west onto paved County Road 306. In a little over 5 miles you'll come to the **Cottonwood Hot Springs Inn and Spa** (see Travelwise), a resort focusing on the purported healing properties of its hot waters, and also offering massage, herbal wraps, and various other therapies.

All in all, it's quite a menagerie, with a decidedly New Age/old hippie ambience. In addition to the 12-guest-room, two-story long box of a main lodge, four rustic log cabins are available for rent. A dormitory and tepee camping *(May-Sept.)* are also available. Boulders set in concrete form cabinside pools, sitting in the shade of beefy cottonwood trees alongside aptly named Cottonwood Creek. The resort's main pools vary in depth, their walls embellished with colorful underwater murals of mythical and mystical creatures.

To soak in different surroundings, find your way to the freshwater **Mount Princeton Hot Springs Resort** (see Travelwise). First, drive back toward Buena Vista for 4.5 miles, then turn south onto County Road 321 and continue for 8 miles to the resort. (After about 6.5 miles, County Road 322 goes west toward the trailhead for the hike up 14,197-foot **Mount Princeton**—should the allure of the rarified heights beckon you back tomorrow.)

Cliffside, poolside, and lodge rooms are all options for overnighting at the resort, which boasts a restaurant and a cozy bar with mounted moose and elk heads overhanging a big rock fireplace. Walk down beneath the main pool to recline in one of several small makeshift pools fashioned from big, polished boulders, particularly if it's later in the summer, after most of the high country snow has melted and the stream's flow has subsided. As you lie back in the hot waters, squint upstream into the low afternoon sun: The light sparkles off the bubbling waters of Chalk Creek as if liquid sunshine were tumbling down the streambed.

Around the high country

Enjoy an early morning breakfast ride at **Mount Princeton Riding Stables and Michael Martin Murphey's Singing Cowboy Ranch** *(719-395-6498. www.singingcowboyranch.com)*, a nearby chuck-wagon-and-cowboy camp where the well-known western singer sometimes performs. Return to US 285 by way of County Road 162. Check in your rearview mirrors as you drive for the pyramidal bulk of Mount Princeton, with its false summits and its forested ridges shooting downward. Next, travel 15 miles south to Poncha Springs, then 5 miles west on US 50 before making the left-hand turn dropping down to the **Mountain Spirit Winery** *(719-539-1175. Closed Sun. and Tues.-Wed.)*. The enterprise produces interesting wines made from traditional grapes and nontraditional fruits: blackberry Chardonnay and chokecherry dessert wine, to name a pair.

To gain a view from on high without having to expend much energy, go west from the winery on the frontage road until it re-meets US 50. Continue southwest several miles to Monarch Pass and the Continental Divide, elevation 11,312 feet, and pull in at the **Monarch Crest Scenic Tramway** *(719-539-4091. Closed mid-Sept.–mid-May)*. The tram whisks you on a 15-minute ride *(fare)* to an observation deck perched 700 vertical feet above the pass. You can enjoy close-up looks at gardens of tiny alpine wildflowers, and near and far views of big, bare peaks reaching high above timberline, including Pikes Peak, some 70 miles northeast.

As the afternoon wears on, drive east to **Salida,** an attractive community where the new and the old blend well. Consider staying at the **Tudor Rose** (see Travelwise), a comfortable bed-and-breakfast retreat atop a pinyon-studded tableland nestled above town but below the mountain foothills. The inn's 37-acre grounds abut federal lands, providing access for hiking, mountain biking, and horseback riding *(stabling available at inn)* on the heralded, 100-mile-long **Rainbow Trail.**

Before dinner, wander around Salida's historic downtown. You'll discover several galleries and the **Fabulous Finds Emporium** *(243 F St. 719-530-0544)*, packed with antiques and other goodies. And after supper? A soak, of course—at the popular and newly renovated **Salida Hot Springs Aquatic Center** *(410 W. Rainbow Blvd. 719-539-6738)*, whose warm lap pool and hot pools are filled with water pumped in several miles from the nearby mountains.

In the shadow of the Sangre de Cristos

The drive back *down* to the Mile High City on US 285, via Trout Creek, Red Hill, and Kenosha Passes, is about 140 miles. By now, though, you may have contracted a serious case of hot-spring fever; if so, and you're not in a rush, check out the **Joyful Journey Hot**

Springs Spa *(28640 Country Road 58EE, Moffat. 719-256-4328. www.joyfuljourneyhotsprings.com. Closed Wed.; fee).* This hot spring sits in the middle of a dry basin rather than in the forested mountains, but it offers outstanding panoramas of the Sangre de Cristo Mountains. To make the journey there, drive south from Poncha Springs on US 285 and south again on Colo. 17; watch for the sign pointing east. —*Michael McCoy*

Travelwise

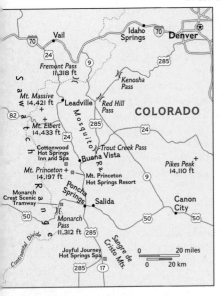

GETTING THERE
To begin, head west from Denver on I-70.

GENERAL INFORMATION
Contact the **Leadville Chamber of Commerce** *(P.O. Box 861, Leadville, CO 80461. 719-486-3900. www.leadvilleusa.com)* or the **Heart of the Rockies Chamber of Commerce** *(406 W. Hwy. 50, Salida, CO 81201. 719-539-2068 or 877-772-5432. www.salida chamber.org).* Recommended reading: *Colorado's Hot Springs,* by Deborah Frazier George, and *Colorado's Fourteeners,* by Gerry Roach.

SEASONS
Year-round. The high trails are typically snowed in until late June; some snowfields can persist into late summer.

LODGING
Cottonwood Hot Springs Inn and Spa *(18999 County Rd. 306, Buena Vista. 719-395-6434. www.cottonwood-hot-springs.com. $)* Lodge and cabins. See p. 94.

Leadville Country Inn *(127 E. 8th St., Leadville. 719-486-2354 or 800-748-2354. www.leadvillebednbreakfast.com. $-$$)* A purple Victorian beauty with five unique rooms in the main house and four in the carriage house.

Mount Princeton Hot Springs Resort *(15870 Cty. Rd. 162, Nathrop. 888-395-7799. www.mtprinceton.com. $)* Three separate lodging units with 47 rooms. See p. 94.

Tudor Rose *(6720 Cty. Rd. 104. 719-539-2002 or 800-379-0889. www.thetudorrose .com. $-$$)* A six-room stately inn on 37 acres. See p. 95.

DINING
Boomtown Brewpub *(115 E. 7th St., Leadville. 719-486-8297. $-$$)* Serves handcrafted English-style ales and hearty pub fare such as buffalo burgers.

Callaway's *(Delaware Hotel, 700 Harrison Ave., Leadville. 719-486-1418. $$)* A dining experience amid Victorian splendor.

First Street Café *(137 E. 1st St., Salida. 719-539-4759. Closed Sun. $-$$)* Scrumptious breakfasts; Mexican fare for lunch and dinner.

Laughing Ladies *(128 W. 1st St., Salida. 719-539-6209. Closed Tues.-Wed. $$)* Intimate restaurant with redbrick walls and pressed-tin ceiling. Outstanding dishes include goat-cheese and roasted-squash enchiladas, with black beans and avocado pico de gallo.

Tommyknocker Brewery *(1401 Miner St., Idaho Springs. 303-567-2688. $-$$)* Hearty sandwiches, soups, and salads. See p. 92.

Detroit

Motor City 98

Gateway to Freedom 103

Vintage roadster at the Henry Ford Museum, Dearborn, Michigan

Motor City
Discovering Detroit's auto legacy

IT'S HARD TO IMAGINE A SINGLE INDUSTRY shaping a city as thoroughly as the auto industry has shaped Detroit, Michigan; making cars has generated unfathomable fortunes, a melting-pot workforce, and hundreds of spin-off businesses that, in many ways, continue the cycle. Detroit remains proudly and inextricably linked to its automobile heritage, documenting its legacy with a wealth of excellent museums and well-preserved historic houses. Come to the Motor City on a three-day road trip devoted to—what else?—the Big Three.

Downtown & points east

Begin your weekend at Detroit's downtown landmark, the 73-story **Renaissance Center** *(Jefferson Ave. bet. Brush and Beaubien Sts.)*. The massive "Ren Cen" houses the world headquarters for General Motors Corp., along with shops, restaurants, a Marriott hotel, and the carmaker's multimedia visitor attraction, **GM World** *(100 Renaissance Center. 313-667-7151. Closed weekends)*. The showroom, as big as a football field, displays more than two dozen vehicles, from vintage Oldsmobiles to current concept cars.

NOT TO BE MISSED

- Old auto advertising displays at the Henry Ford Museum ● Meadow Brook Hall's secret spiral staircase ● The treasure trove of galleries at the Detroit Institute of Arts
- The wonderfully garish, vintage Fox Theatre

Woodward Avenue—America's first paved concrete highway—bisects the downtown, heading north through the Theater District and becoming the backbone of Detroit's Cultural Center near Wayne State University.

Auto fortunes funded what is considered one of the nation's most treasured fine-art collections at the **Detroit Institute of Arts** *(5200 Woodward Ave. 313-833-7900. www.dia.org. Closed Mon.-Tues.; adm. fee)*. Its most controversial installation in 1933 is now its most famous. Mexican muralist Diego Rivera spent months studying Ford Motor Company's Rouge plant before creating the "Detroit Industry" frescoes, four enormous murals depicting the gritty life on the automobile assembly line and industry's effects on society. City leaders were infuriated by Rivera's damning criticism of capitalism; ironically, a visionary Edsel Ford saved the work from being whitewashed.

Carphernalia at the Henry Ford Museum, Dearborn

Across the street at the **Detroit Historical Museum** *(5401 Wood-ward Ave. 313-833-1805. Closed Mon.; adm. fee)*, the "Motor City" exhibit explores intriguing aspects of the auto industry and its impact on the city, including race relations and the development of the United Auto Workers. The highlight for most is the dramatic "body drop." Taken from an old Cadillac plant, the two-story assembly line demonstrates how a car body was lowered onto a chassis and bolted in place. Today the work is done largely with robotics.

Henry Ford's only son, Edsel, built a grand Cotswold-style mansion east of downtown on the shores of Lake St. Clair. Tours of the 1929 **Edsel and Eleanor Ford House** *(1100 Lake Shore Dr., Grosse Pointe Shores. 313-884-4222. www.fordhouse.org. Closed Mon.; adm. fee)* showcase the couple's interest in art and British craftsmanship, down to the imported stone shingles split and laid by Cotswold artisans.

One of seven brothers who founded Fisher Auto Body, Lawrence Fisher was well known for his playboy lifestyle and rococo tastes—outrageously evident in the glitzy **Fisher Mansion** *(383 Lenox Ave., S of E. Jefferson Ave. and Dickerson St., Detroit. 313-331-6740. June-Aug. Fri.-Sun. and by appt.; adm. fee)*. More than 200 European craftsmen worked on the 1929 villa, a dizzying blend of hand-cut tile, marble, and gold and silver leaf. Today the estate houses a Krishna cultural center.

Dearborn

The father of the automobile assembly line, Henry Ford was born on a farm near **Dearborn** in 1863. He went on to create the Ford Motor Company, bringing the world the Model T in 1908. At the same time, Ford was interested in all American innovations and so began collecting a staggering array of artifacts—from the world's first single-rotor helicopter to Thomas Edison's actual laboratory. He opened the Henry Ford Museum in 1929 as a way to inspire people about the past. Dubbed "Ford's attic," this rare collection, an almost unabridged sampling of the inventions that shaped the 20th century, forms the centerpiece of the **Henry Ford Museum and Greenfield Village** (*20900 Oakwood Blvd. 313-271-1620. www.hfmgv.org. Adm. fee*).

The museum is huge, covering everything from agricultural equipment to toys, music, and household items. The "Automobile in American Life" exhibit displays dozens of rare vehicles representing the automobile's hundred-year evolution. Even more compelling is the examination of the car's influence on society. Under vintage fast-food signs and a 1960 "mo-tel" interior, the exhibit focuses on how the auto transformed America into a transient nation of family cars and family vacations, of highways and Holiday Inns.

Outside, the 81-acre **Greenfield Village** comprises an amalgamation of significant historic buildings—the actual cycle shop where the Wright brothers invented the airplane, the house where Noah Webster completed his dictionary, for example—brought here brick by brick and laid out in a tidy village within earshot of the Ford Motor Company test track.

You could easily while away a day or more here, but the Ford "campus" tempts you with even more. Next door, the **Automotive Hall of Fame** (*21400 Oakwood Blvd. 313-240-4000. Closed Mon. Nov.–Mem. Day; adm. fee*) honors pioneers of the auto industry, from Ransom E. Olds to Soichiro Honda.

Considering Ford's immense wealth, the nearby **Henry Ford Estate, Fair Lane** (*4901 Evergreen Rd. 313-593-5590. Closed Sat. Jan.-March; adm. fee*) can almost be considered modest. What makes Fair Lane remarkable is not its grandeur, but the engineering marvels tucked throughout the home and its brilliantly landscaped grounds. Ford and his mentor Thomas Edison designed the still intact powerhouse, which made the 1914 home completely self-sufficient for electricity, heat, light, and refrigeration. Fair Lane's pool room, with its original steam-heated benches and curved ceiling of skylights, now does duty serving lunch with delightful alfresco dining, weather permitting.

Allow ample time to wander the 72-acre grounds, designed by noted landscape architect Jens Jensen and considered one of the nation's finest examples of natural landscape art. Near the main entrance, Jensen crafted the view across the meadow so meticulously that the sun sets precisely between a notch in the distant trees at summer solstice. The **Ford Discovery Trail** winds along terraced paths down to a channel of the Rouge River, where Jensen created a natural-looking waterfall and grotto to attract birds. Ford so enjoyed bird-watching, he placed heated birdhouses around the property.

Northern suburbs

If you visit just one auto baron home, make it **Meadow Brook Hall** (*Adams Rd. and Walton Blvd., Oakland University campus, Rochester. 248-370-3140. www.meadowbrookhall.org. Tours daily at 1:30 p.m., additional tours July-Aug.; adm. fee*). Matilda Dodge Wilson, the young widow of Dodge Brothers Motor Cars cofounder John Dodge, was among the nation's wealthiest women in 1926, when she commissioned this lavish 80,000-square-foot Tudor Revival castle on a rolling farm estate north of Detroit.

Wilson proudly celebrated American craftsmanship in every inch of her home, from Tiffany art glass, Rookwood ceramic tile, and Stickley furniture to hand-carved plaster ceilings, 39 individually designed fireplaces, and custom switchplates and doorknobs for each of the 110 rooms. The estate included elaborate playhouses for both Dodge children—a log cabin with stone fireplace and electric railway for Daniel, and a six-room cottage with working kitchen, doll nursery, and miniature irons and other appliances for Frances, so she could learn the "art of housewifery." Completed in 1929, Meadow Brook cost an unthinkable four million dollars.

What makes this grand home especially fascinating is its time-capsule condition. Wilson lived at Meadow Brook most of her life, eventually donating it and two million dollars to found Oakland University. From its artifacts to its architectural detail, Meadow Brook is a true American treasure.

The nearby suburb of Auburn Hills is home to DaimlerChrysler (*I-75, Chrysler Dr. exit*) and the **Walter P. Chrysler Museum** (*next to the headquarters at 1 Chrysler Dr., near jct. of Featherstone and Squirrel Rds. 248-944-0001 or 888-456-1924. www.chryslerheritage.com. Closed Mon.; adm. fee*). Along with the expected assortment of vintage De-Sotos, Willys, Hudsons, and muscle cars from the Chrysler/Dodge/Plymouth line, this three-story museum does a good job of explaining the evolution of auto engineering and design, with a variety of hands-on displays about braking, aerodynamics, and other advancements. Don't miss the lighthearted look at styling innovations—including a 1941 steering wheel that featured a cigarette dispenser!

Perhaps most interesting are the insights into Walter Chrysler himself. A railroad mechanic, he began his love affair with cars at an auto show, where he was smitten with a $5,000 Locomobile, a car he couldn't afford and couldn't drive. He had it shipped to

Oelwein, Iowa, his home at the time, and immediately took it apart and reassembled it. Years later, still proud of his mechanic roots, Chrysler brought his toolbox with him to the executive offices of the Chrysler building in New York City.

A timeline in the museum illustrates the endless string of start-ups and mergers that define one part of the hundred-year-long history that still stars in the Motor City. —*Tina Lassen*

Travelwise

GETTING THERE
All of these attractions are found in the metropolitan Detroit area.

GENERAL INFORMATION
Contact the **Detroit Metro Convention & Visitors Bureau** (*211 W. Fort St., Ste. 1000, Detroit, MI 48226. 313-202-1800 or 800-337-7648. www.visitdetroit.com*).

ANNUAL EVENTS
Concours D'Elegance (*1st Sun. in Aug., Meadow Brook Hall, Rochester. 248-370-3140*) Vintage car displays and races draw collectors from around the country.

North American International Auto *Show* (*Mid-Jan., Cobo Hall, Detroit. 248-643-0250. Adm. fee*) Automakers unveil their newest production models and concept cars.

MORE THINGS TO SEE & DO
Flint The General Motors plant tours have been suspended, but GM's hometown offers other auto attractions, including the **Alfred P. Sloan Museum** (*1221 E. Kearsley St. 810-237-3450. Adm. fee*).

Motorsports Hall of Fame (*43700 Expo Center Dr., Novi. 313-349-7223 or 800-250-7223. Closed Mon.-Wed. Labor Day–Mem. Day; adm. fee*) From stock cars to powerboats, this museum honors the "heroes of horsepower."

LODGING
Dearborn Inn (*20301 Oakwood Blvd., Dearborn. 313-271-2700 or 800-228-9290. www.marriotthotels.com. $$*) Ford built this grand Georgian-style hotel to accommodate his business visitors. 227 rooms.

Hotel St. Regis (*3071 W. Grand Blvd., Detroit. 313-873-3055 or 800-848-4810. www.hotelstregisdetroit.com. $-$$*) Elegant hotel north of downtown, in New Center area. 223 rooms.

Wingate Inn (*2200 Featherstone Rd., Auburn Hills. 248-334-3324. $$*) Newer hotel near DaimlerChrysler headquarters and museum. 102 rooms.

DINING
Blue Nile (*508 Monroe St., Detroit. 313-964-6699. $$*) Located in Greektown, this spot caters to vegetarians and meat lovers with Ethiopian-style service.

Chuck Muer's Big Fish (*700 Town Center Dr., Dearborn. 313-336-6350. $$-$$$*) Popular seafood restaurant with lively outdoor patio.

Fishbone's Rhythm Kitchen Café (*400 Monroe St., Detroit. 313-965-4600. $$*) One of downtown's most popular restaurants, serving up seafood gumbo and other Creole specialties.

Gateway to Freedom
Last stops on the Underground Railroad

FOR ENSLAVED AFRICANS AND THEIR DESCENDANTS, the covert network of the Underground Railroad promised assistance on their dangerous journey north to "free soil" states and the safety of Canada. Near the end of the journey, just a river's width from Ontario, shone Detroit, dubbed the North Star, an active center of abolitionist activity. In Canada, fugitive slaves finally found safe haven in the towns of Windsor, Sandwich, and Amherstburg. This getaway explores the final stops on the Underground Railroad—historic sites and churches—as well as some intriguing museums that honor the Underground Railroad's place in history.

Downtown

Begin your weekend at the **Charles H. Wright Museum of African-American History** *(315 E. Warren St. 313-494-5800. www.maah -detroit.org. Closed Mon.-Tues.; adm. fee)*. This 120,000-square-foot facility ranks as the largest monument to African-American history in the world. Pass through the spectacular sunlit rotunda to the permanent exhibition, "Of the People: The African American Experience."

An actual size portion of a slaveship reproduction anchors the ambitious exhibit, which documents the horrors of slave capture and suggests how the disruption exposed the African continent to subsequent conquest and colonial exploitation. The museum continues on a chronological path, detailing the "imperfect union, race relations, and African-American contributions to art and science."

Displays about the Underground Railroad give harrowing accounts of escape and discuss the ingenious code that was developed to aid fugitives. Because the Big Dipper, or "drinking gourd," points to the North Star (Detroit), a gourd or dipper hung by a doorway signaled a safe house. Supporters identified themselves with broad-brimmed hats, full beards, and no mustaches. Though it is impossible to know exact numbers, tens of thousands of escaped slaves made their way to freedom along the Underground Railroad.

NOT TO BE MISSED

- **The mask above the entry to the Charles H. Wright Museum of African-American History**
- **Watching the freighters along the Detroit River**

Several **historical markers** dot the downtown, commemorating key events in abolitionist history. In the mid-19th century, Detroit's citizenry included a who's who of abolitionist leaders. In 1859 they gathered with prominent antislavery activists Frederick Douglass and John Brown at the home of William Webb, near the northeast corner of Congress and St. Antoine. The Detroit Metro Convention & Visitors Bureau has information on additional locations (though most sites have been torn down).

One historical site that survives—indeed, thrives—is the venerable **Second Baptist Church of Detroit** (441 Monroe St.). Michigan's oldest black church, it was organized in 1836 by determined blacks disheartened by discrimination at the First Baptist Church. It became a key "station" for the Underground Railroad, hiding slaves in the basement and working with a church in nearby Windsor, Ontario, to ferry them across the river to freedom.

Tours of the church are offered by the next door **Underground Railroad Reading Station Bookstore** (461 Monroe St. 313-961-0325. Church tours by appt. only Tues. and Thurs.-Sat.; fee for tours). The store carries an excellent selection of African-American biographies, novels, and historical accounts.

Belle Isle & across the river to Canada

Begin your day by enjoying some time along the **Detroit River,** which rolls past Detroit's south side. **Belle Isle Park** occupies a thousand-acre island in the river, accessible by a bridge 3 miles east of downtown. This urban oasis is a fine spot for walking, fishing, and watching the parade of freighters and pleasure boats that motor by on this busy waterway linking Lakes Huron and Erie. Belle Isle also is home to a number of attractions, including the superb **Dossin Great Lakes Museum** (100 Strand Dr. 313-852-4051. www.detroithistorical.org. Closed Mon.-Tues.; adm. fee) and the **Belle Isle Aquarium** (Inselruhe Ave. and Loiter Way. 248-398-0900. www.detroitzoo.org. Adm. fee), the nation's oldest freshwater aquarium.

Downtown, **Hart Plaza** (along the river, at the foot of Woodward St.) offers an expansive public space to enjoy the river. A memorial at river's edge offers a poignant reminder of the river's symbolism to those escaping from slavery. The **"Gateway to Freedom"** statue depicts George De Baptiste—a "conductor" on the Underground Railroad—beckoning eight figures forward as they gaze across the river to Canada and the promise of a free life.

Across the river in Windsor, Ontario, newcomers are welcomed by the **"Tower of Freedom,"** a companion monument in Dieppe Park (enter Canada via Ambassador Bridge or Windsor-Detroit tunnel. Toll). Stroll along the waterfront to explore Windsor's expansive sculpture garden and soak in the view of the Detroit skyline.

Eight miles east of downtown Windsor lies the **John Freeman**

Walls Historic Site and Underground Railroad Museum *(Hwy. 401 to Puce Rd. exit, then 1 mile N to 932 Puce Rd. 519-258-6253. Mid-May–mid-Oct. by appt. only; adm. fee).* The highlight of the complex is a restored 1846 log cabin—a joyous final stop on the Underground Railroad.

The suburb of **Sandwich,** part of today's Windsor, was another important terminal on the Underground Railroad, where the **First Baptist Church** *(3652 Peter St. 519-252-4917)* provided refuge for fugitives ever at risk of being caught by bounty hunters. The church's pastor stood facing the door at all times; if he thought he spied a suspicious character entering the church, he would break into song, signaling fugitives to slip to safety through a trapdoor in the floor.

Many fleeing slaves crossed into Canada at the Detroit River's narrowest point south of Windsor, at **Amherstburg**—making this city one of the largest Canadian terminals on the railroad. You'll find their stories at the **North American Black Historical Museum and Culture Centre** *(277 King St. 519-763-5433 or 800-713-6336. Closed Mon.-Tues.; adm. fee),* which depicts African life before, during, and after the slave trade. Chilling displays include shackles used to restrain slaves and posters offering bounties for escaped slaves, as well as farming equipment, musical instruments, and songbooks

Charles H. Wright Museum of African-American History

that represent the African way of life before slavery's end.

Here, too, is the **Nazrey African Methodist Episcopal Church National Historic Site,** a fieldstone structure completed in 1848 by a group of freed slaves. Small as it is, it was a huge beacon for fugitives seeking the end of the road. The church is named for Bishop Willis Nazrey, who led many African congregations into a new Canadian-based denomination so they could govern their own church.

—*Tina Lassen*

Travelwise

GETTING THERE
All of these attractions are in the Detroit, Michigan, and Windsor, Ontario, areas.

GENERAL INFORMATION
Contact the **Detroit Metro Convention & Visitors Bureau** *(211 W. Fort St., Ste. 1000, Detroit, MI 48226. 313-202-1800 or 800-337-7648. www.visitdetroit.com).* For southwest Ontario contact the **African Canadian Heritage Network** *(P.O. Box 15, Chatham, ON N7M 5K1. 519-354-7383).*

SEASONS
May through October offer the best weather for outdoor activities.

ANNUAL EVENTS
African World Festival *(3rd weekend in Aug., Hart Plaza. 313-494-5800)* Detroit's largest ethnic festival features an artists' market, international foods, and music.

Detroit International Jazz Festival *(Labor Day weekend, Hart Plaza. 313-963-7622)* Multiple stages host the greatest names in contemporary jazz.

MORE THINGS TO SEE & DO
Buxton Historic Site & Museum *(A. D. Shadd Rd./Cty. Rd. 6, North Buxton. 519-352-4799. April-Sept. Wed.-Sun.)* Rev. William King founded the Elgin Settlement here in 1849, which became a haven for some 2,000 fugitive slaves. The museum emphasizes the history of the original settlers.

Uncle Tom's Cabin Historic Site *(29251 Uncle Tom's Rd. at Park St., Dresden Site. 519-683-2978. Mid-May-Aug. Tues.-Sun.)* Josiah Henson, a fugitive slave from Maryland, lived in this cabin until his death in 1883 at age 94. His experiences inspired Harriet Beecher Stowe's controversial *Uncle*

Tom's Cabin, which Abraham Lincoln attributed to helping precipitate the Civil War. In addition to the cabin are five other historical structures, Henson's gravesite, and an interpretive center.

LODGING
Duffy's Restaurant & Motor Inn *(296 Dalhousie St., Amherstburg, ON. 519-736-4301. $)* Overlooks the Detroit River, in historic Amherstburg. 35 rooms.

Omni Detroit Hotel River Place *(1000 River Pl., Detroit. 313-259-9500 or 800-843-6664. www.omnihotels.com. $$)* Elegant, 108-room hotel on the Detroit River.

Shorecrest Motor Inn *(1316 E. Jefferson Ave. 313-568-3000 or 800-992-9616. www.shorecrestmi.com. $)* Family-owned motor inn that's a favorite of business travelers looking for a convenient downtown location. 54 rooms.

DINING
Beans & Cornbread *(29508 Northwestern Hwy., Southfield. 248-208-1680. $)* Expect a wait at this suburban soul food mecca, where pork chops with redeye gravy, sweet potato pie, and other down-home favorites are worth waiting for.

Gordon House 1798 *(268 Dalhousie St., Amherstburg, ON. 519-736-1133. $-$$)* Built in 1798, the Gordon House overlooks Kings Navy Yard Park and the Detroit River; it features a restaurant, tea room, and marine exhibit.

Harlequin Café *(8047 Agnes, Detroit. 313-331-0922. $$-$$$)* This romantic eatery in downtown's Indian Village neighborhood serves distinctive French-inspired cuisine. Live music.

Houston & San Antonio

Galveston by the Sea 108

Tejano Spirit 113

Texas Hill Country 117

Folk dancing in HemisFair Park

Galveston by the Sea

A Victorian romance

FUELED BY THE COTTON TRADE, GALVESTON REIGNED as Texas' largest city in the 19th century and the nation's second richest, its port the busiest in the entire Southwest. A devastating hurricane in 1900 for a time put a stop to its economic prowess, but the town rebuilt. Its legacy: a genteel island city filled with charming Victorian dwellings and edged with Gulf Coast beaches, with bird-filled havens hidden just around the corner.

To Galveston Island

On your way south from Houston on I-45, you'll pass **Space Center Houston** *(1601 NASA Rd. 1. 281-244-2100 or 800-972-0369. www.spacecenter.org. Adm. fee),* the official visitor center of NASA's Johnson Space Center. Here, among many other things, you can see Mercury, Gemini, and Apollo capsules; touch a moon rock; watch astronauts train for future space missions (and learn about current missions); and "land" the space shuttle with a computerized flight simulator. A range of interactive exhibits are specially aimed at kids, who can play astronaut in many ways, from commanding the space shuttle to experiencing the low gravity of the moon's surface.

> **NOT TO BE MISSED**
>
> ● The excitement of spring bird migration at High Island ● A sunset walk along a deserted beach on west Galveston Island ● Sweet treats from La King's Confectionery, at 2323 The Strand

Once you've crossed the causeway to **Galveston Island,** I-45 becomes Broadway. Follow signs to **The Strand,** known in its 19th-century heyday as the Wall Street of the Southwest for the businesses and financial institutions concentrated there. Preserved as the **Strand Historic District National Historic Landmark,** the area is full of renovated Victorian buildings that house shops, restaurants, museums, galleries, and entertainment facilities. Just beyond the historic district, the lavishly decorated **Grand 1894 Opera House** *(2020 Postoffice St. 409-765-1894. Adm. fee. Open daily for self-guided tours),* where such legendary performers as Sarah Bernhardt and Anna Pavlova performed, has been beautifully restored. More than 25 productions—dance, drama, musicals, and opera—are presented annually.

Galveston's glamour days abruptly ended on September 8, 1900,

The Richardsonian-Romanesque Moody Mansion, Galveston

when a powerful storm caught the city by surprise, taking 6,000 lives and destroying more than one-third of the city's structures. To learn more about this devastating event, amble over to the Port of Galveston waterfront and the Pier 21 Theater *(Harborside Dr. and Pier 21, 2nd fl. 409-763-8808. Adm. fee)* to see **"The Great Storm."** This 27-minute multimedia presentation recounts the events of that day, considered among the nation's worst natural disasters.

Also on Pier 21, the **Texas Seaport Museum** *(Harborside Dr. and 21st St. 409-763-1877. Adm. fee)* examines Galveston's role as a port and immigrants' entryway to the United States. Tour the 1877 sailing ship *Elissa,* beautifully restored and now a national historic landmark.

In the afternoon, the beaches beckon. Follow Broadway to its end on the island's south side, at Seawall Boulevard. The first thing you'll spot here is the 17-foot-high seawall, for which the boulevard is named. It parallels the beach westward as far as 85th Street, providing a promenade on which to stroll. Popular **Stewart Beach** *(409-765-5023. Daily March-Sept., weekends Oct.; parking fee)* lies right in front of you, across the boulevard, and is a perfect spot to throw a beach towel. Otherwise, turn right (west) and drive along Seawall Boulevard to find many other places where you can stroll, sunbathe, swim, fish, and surf.

Victoriana splendor

The "Broadway beauties," several enormous mansions along Broadway, preserve the opulence and glitz of Galveston's golden age. The amazing **Bishop's Palace** *(1402 Broadway. 409-762-2475. Adm. fee)* was originally called Gresham's Castle, for the wealthy businessman who built it in 1886. (The local Catholic diocese bought it in 1923 for the bishop's residence.) With an ornate exterior of limestone, sandstone, and granite (all from central Texas) and gorgeous woodwork and fireplaces inside, this house often has been listed among the most architecturally significant in America. Sixty-one craftsmen are said to have worked on the staircase—and when you see it, you'll believe it.

For more glamour, head to nearby **Ashton Villa** *(2328 Broadway. 409-762-3933. www.galvestonhistory.org. Adm. fee)*, built in 1859 by hardware magnate James Moreau Brown, one of Texas' wealthiest men. Filled with antiques, heirlooms, and art, it also contains many personal items belonging to Miss Bettie, Brown's daughter and a colorful Galveston character for many years. The guided tour highlights the mansion's connection to the 1900 storm and its aftermath.

Another Broadway beauty, the brick-and-stone **Moody Mansion** *(2618 Broadway. 409-762-7668. Adm. fee)* was built in 1895 and bought after the 1900 storm by a member of the Moody family, then and now highly influential in Texas business. Mary Moody Northen lived here for more than 40 years, and the house today displays many personal items and original furnishings among the intricately carved oak woodwork, stained glass, and plasterwork.

W. L. Moody and his wife, Libbie, created the Moody Foundation in 1942 to perpetuate their dedication to philanthropy. One of the foundation's biggest projects in the 1980s was the development of **Moody Gardens** *(1 Hope Blvd., off Jones Rd. 800-582-4673. Adm. fee)*, marked by three distinctive pyramids in the western part of the city. The ten-story-high Rainforest Pyramid contains 2,000 species of animals and plants, from birds, butterflies, and fish to tiny violets and tall palms. The nearby Aquarium Pyramid exhibits sea life from around the world: Penguins, sharks, groupers, and butterflyfish are among the thousands of species living in one of the country's largest aquariums. The Discovery Pyramid contains traveling interactive exhibits.

Galveston's natural side

Part of Galveston's allure is the natural beauty that embraces the island. Thanks to its diverse habitats and its location on key migration routes, this area ranks in the nation's top half dozen or so birding destinations. As you wander the beaches and parks, keep your eyes peeled for the many typical species of the coast, including herons, egrets, rail, plover, and sandpipers.

For a small sampling, drive west from the city on Farm-to-Market 3005. You'll find county "pocket parks" on the beach at 7-Mile Road, 9-Mile Road, and 11-Mile Road, where you can swim, beachcomb, look for shells, or just plop down on the sand and relax.

Farther west sprawls **Galveston Island State Park** *(14901 FM 3005, at 13-Mile Rd. 409-737-1222. Adm. fee)*, which encompasses the entire width of the island, from the Gulf of Mexico to West Galveston Bay. The park offers access to 1.6 miles of beach, plus 4 miles of nature trails winding through grassland and alongside wetlands.

For a grander experience, drive east from the city along Seawall Boulevard and turn north on Second Street, which will lead you to the free **Galveston Island Ferry** *(409-763-2386)* crossing Galveston Bay to the narrow strip of land called Bolivar Peninsula. Follow Tex. 87 through the town of Port Bolivar; 3.7 miles from the ferry terminal, take Rettilon Road south to the beach and drive west (being careful on the sand) to the posts marking the edge of **Bolivar Flats Shorebird Sanctuary.** The concentration of waterbirds here can be astounding. Even nonbirders will enjoy the mass of pelicans, ibises, spoonbills, avocets, sandpipers, gulls, and terns resting and feeding in the shallow Gulf water.

Continue east on Tex. 87, through beach communities and fishing villages. Twenty-two miles from Port Bolivar, drive north on Tex. 124 to **High Island,** one of America's most famous bird-watching sites. This small town, located not on an island but atop an underground salt dome that rises above the surrounding land, is dotted with oak woods that act as a magnet in spring for tired migrating birds. Turn east on Fifth Street to reach **Boy Scout Woods Bird Sanctuary** *(Adm. fee)*, where on any day in March through May you'll find birders looking for vireos, thrushes, warblers, orioles, and other species in the trees and shrubs. Fall also attracts birds, and birders, though not in the numbers of spring migration.

Return to Tex. 124 and drive north about 7 miles to Tex. 1985, which leads west to **Anahuac National Wildlife Refuge** *(off Tex. 1985. 409-267-3337)*. While High Island is exclusively a spring and fall birding site, 34,000-acre Anahuac offers a greater range of wildlife observation year-round. As you drive the gravel roads past grassland, marshes, and ponds, you may see alligators, armadillos, mink, muskrats, nutrias, bobcats, or swamp rabbits, in addition to birds such as snowy egrets, white ibises, least bitterns, common moorhens, and purple gallinules. In winter, great flocks of geese and ducks gather at the refuge. Stop at the visitor center at the refuge entrance to ask about the best locations for birding and other wildlife viewing.

—Mel White

Travelwise

GETTING THERE

Galveston is 50 miles southeast of Houston via I-45. To visit Space Center Houston along the way, take the Tex. 1 exit.

GENERAL INFORMATION

Contact the **Galveston Island Visitor Center** (*2428 Seawall Blvd. 409-763-4311 or 888-425-4753. www.galvestoncvb.com*).

SEASONS

Summer is the best season for beach fun. The birds are at their peak during spring migration.

ANNUAL EVENTS

Dickens on the Strand (*1st weekend in Dec., Strand Historic District NHL. 409-765-7834. www.dickensonthestrand.org*) Costumed participants depicting English Victorian-era characters, street entertainers, music, and parades.

Mardi Gras! Galveston (*Dates vary; ends Tues. before Ash Wednesday, Strand Historic District NHL. 409-763-4311 or 888-425-4753. www.mardigras galveston.com*) Parades, concerts, arts events, and a masked ball highlight Texas' largest Mardi Gras celebration.

MORE THINGS TO SEE AND DO

Galveston Island Trolley (*409-797-3900. Fare*) Trolleys offer a way to tour The Strand district and to travel from Pier 21 through downtown to Seawall Boulevard at 25th St.

Railroad Museum (*25th and The Strand. 409-765-5700. www.tamug.edu/rrmuseum. Closed Mon.-Tues. Jan.-Feb.; adm. fee*) The restored art-deco Santa Fe Union Depot is the center for exhibits including locomotives, rail cars, model trains, and city historical displays.

LODGING

Hotel Galvez (*2024 Seawall Blvd., Galveston. 409-765-7721. www.galveston.com /accom/galvez.html. $$-$$$*) A Galveston landmark since 1911, renovated and once again among the city's best hotels. Landscaped grounds, an excellent pool; across Seawall from the beach. 231 rooms.

The Mermaid and the Dolphin (*1103 33rd St., Galveston. 409-762-1561 or 888-922-1866. www.mermaidanddolphin.com. $$-$$$*) Eight rooms in an extensively restored 19th-century house, with a wealth of exotic plants in the garden; also an adjacent cottage. Owners cater to visiting birders.

Tremont House (*2300 Ship's Mechanic Row, Galveston. 409-763-0300. www.galveston .com/thetremonthouse. $$*) An 1879 warehouse and former newspaper office has been transformed into an elegant hotel in The Strand district, very near museums and other attractions. 117 rooms.

DINING

DiBella's (*1902 31st St., Galveston. 409-763-9036. $$*) This restaurant off the beaten path attracts a diverse crowd hungry for authentic Italian food and rib-eye steaks.

Mosquito Café (*628 14th St., Galveston. 409-763-1010. $*) This fun, casual spot in the historic East End attracts a young crowd from the nearby medical school.

Rudy and Paco (*2028 Postoffice St., Galveston. 409-762-3696. $$*) Near the Grand 1894 Opera House, this friendly restaurant offers seafood and steaks in South and Central American style. Paco has been called the unofficial mayor of Galveston.

Saltwater Grill (*2017 Postoffice St., Galveston. 409-762-3474. Closed weekends lunch. $$*) Great gumbo, steamed clams and mussels, red snapper, and other treats for seafood lovers.

Tejano Spirit
Celebrating San Antonio's diversity & history

SERENADING MARIACHI BANDS, spicy south-of-the-border cuisine, sultry temperatures, the buzz of Spanish mingling with English—you don't have to look far to immerse yourself in the vibrant Spanish and Latino culture that is San Antonio's heritage. Beloved for its colorful festivals and lively, danceable music, Mexican markets and tangy margaritas, this spirited city in the heart of Texas offers visitors a chance to delve into a fascinating cultural kaleidoscope, to experience a modern city rooted deep in the region's past.

Early San Antonio
The city dates back to a late 17th-century Indian village and successive Spanish missions established along the San Antonio River in the early 1700s. The first mission, San Antonio de Valero, built in 1718, served a different purpose in the next century under its better known name, the **Alamo** (*300 Alamo Plaza. 210-225-1391. www.the alamo.org).* On March 6, 1836, during Texas' fight for independence from Mexico, 189 Texan volunteers died heroes after a 13-day siege by Gen. Santa Anna's Mexican army, choosing to stay inside the Alamo's walls rather than surrender. Only the chapel and the long barracks remain from the original, much larger compound, but the spirit of those defenders—Jim Bowie and Davy Crockett among them—emanates throughout this sacred place. A museum tells the story of the fall of the Alamo; historical artifacts include items from Alamo defenders and from the 1836-1846 period when the Republic of Texas was an independent nation.

NOT TO BE MISSED

- **The mouth-watering aromas wafting from River Walk restaurants**
- **Breakfast at Mi Tierra Cafe and Bakery**
- **Cézanne's "Houses on the Hill" at the McNay Art Museum, 6000 N. New Braunfels**

To see what life was like before independence, visit the other missions south of town. Each was a combination church, educational center, and farm, where priests worked to convert the local Native Americans to Catholicism. These structures—Missions Concepción,

San José, San Juan, and Espada—are now part of **San Antonio Missions National Historical Park** *(210-534-8833. www.nps.gov/saan)*, which interprets this significant period in the development of the Southwest. The park visitor center is located at **Mission San José** *(6701 San José Dr. 210-932-1001)*, which, with its church, granary, living quarters, and walls, is the largest and most complete of the group. Here you can get information on visiting the other missions and see a film on their history. The missions are still part of active parishes.

To gain more insight into San Antonio's history, spend some time at the **Institute of Texan Cultures** *(801 S. Bowie St. 210-458-2300. www.texancultures.utsa.edu/public. Closed Mon.; adm. fee)* in Hemis-Fair Park. Exhibits recount the contributions of the various ethnic groups that have influenced Texas history. A multimedia show dramatizes important events in the Lone Star State's past—including, of course, the major contributions of Spanish and Latin American peoples, as well as Germans, African Americans, and many others.

As evening approaches, it's time to visit the city's justly celebrated **River Walk** (or **Paseo del Rio**), a festive, colorful 3-mile stretch of shops, restaurants, clubs, and hotels along a loop of the San Antonio River, 20 feet below street level. Palms, olive trees, and cottonwoods shade flower-bedecked, Mexican-style buildings, setting the mood for a romantic stroll or perhaps a margarita at one of the overflowing sidewalk cafés. Mexican restaurants are here in abundance, and sooner or later you'll pop into some place like **Rio Rio Cantina** (see Travelwise), a big, loud, crowded, fun spot, for enchiladas or burritos.

Consider taking a narrated boat cruise along the waterway; the jokes may be a little corny, but you'll discover lots of intriguing facts

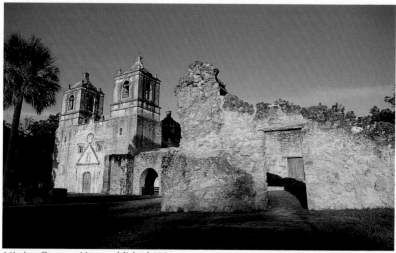

Mission Concepción, established 1731

about the city, the river, and the development of this splendid urban oasis. The **Arneson River Theatre,** an outdoor stage set right on the riverbank, is often the setting for music and dance performances.

More historical & cultural diversions

Start the morning at bustling **Market Square** *(514 W. Commerce St. 210-207-8600),* composed of restored 19th- and 20th-century structures, a courtyard promenade, and El Mercado—the largest Mexican market in the United States. Piñatas, woven blankets, colorful pottery, leather, jewelry, and fresh produce overflow from dozens of shops, while adjacent **Farmers Market Plaza** boasts even more stalls. There's always entertainment in the plaza, perhaps a Tejano band or graceful flamenco dancers, along with artists and photographers displaying and selling their works.

Nestled among the market's goings-on you'll find one of the city's longtime favorite restaurants, open 24 hours a day: **Mi Tierra Cafe and Bakery** (see Travelwise) attracts a diverse array of customers hungry for *chorizo* (spicy sausage), *huevos rancheros* (Mexican-style eggs), and enchiladas. Be sure to leave room for baked goods straight from the adjacent *panaderia.*

It's a short walk to the impressive **Spanish Governor's Palace** *(105 Plaza de Armas. 210-224-0601. Adm. fee),* headquarters for Spain's military officials in colonial times. The 1749 rock building contains period furnishings and historical exhibits; outside, a fountain graces a cobblestone courtyard. The Plaza de Armas, on which the palace is located, was the military parade ground for Spanish soldiers.

Not far southwest, **Casa Navarro State Historic Site** *(228 S. Laredo St. 210-226-4801. www.tpwd.state.tx.us/park/jose. Closed Mon.-Tues.; adm. fee)* interprets the Mexican history of Texas in three limestone-and-adobe structures built about 1848. The buildings, featuring period furnishings, were the home of José Navarro, an early Texas rancher, businessman, and political figure who worked for the rights of Hispanic citizens.

Return east a bit to wander through the historic area called **La Villita** *(S. Alamo and Nueva Sts. 210-207-8610).* The "little village" where the city began (Mexican soldiers stationed at San Antonio lived here with their families in the 18th century) is now a collection of artists' workshops, galleries, and restaurants, housed in restored adobe structures reflecting San Antonio's past. During Fiesta the city's diversity is celebrated with everything from German polkas to country two-stepping, from Cajun sausages to Chinese egg rolls.

From downtown, you'll need to catch a bus or drive north to the **San Antonio Museum of Art** *(200 W. Jones Ave. 210-978-8100. Closed Mon.; adm. fee).* The collection ranges from Greek and Roman antiquities to Asian art to John Singer Sargent and Andrew Wyeth. The museum also includes the **Nelson A. Rockefeller Center for Latin**

American Art; here you can see pre-Columbian and colonial-era works from Mexico and Central and South America, folk art, and contemporary art, all reflecting the breadth of Spanish and Latino experience in the New World.

To experience more Latin American-influenced art, check with the **Guadalupe Cultural Arts Center** *(1300 Guadalupe St. 210-271-3151. Adm. fee for events)*. This, the country's largest Hispanic arts organization, sponsors music, dance, theater, and cinema at its restored 1940 Guadalupe Theater, as well as exhibitions of paintings, sculpture, and other visual arts in various locations. —*Mel White*

Travelwise

GENERAL INFORMATION

Contact the **San Antonio Convention & Visitors Bureau** *(P.O. Box 2277, San Antonio, TX 78298. 210-207-6700 or 800-447-3372. www.sanantoniocvb.com)*. A **visitor information center** at 317 Alamo Plaza, across the street from the Alamo, provides brochures, city maps, and information on bus and trolley routes. VIA buses and trolleys *(210-362-2020. Fare)* access nearly all attractions.

SEASONS

San Antonio can be visited year-round, although summers can be very hot.

ANNUAL EVENTS

Fiesta San Antonio *(mid-April, various sites. 210-227-5191)* The city's major festival, held since 1891, includes parades, music, ethnic food, and fireworks.

Texas Folklife Festival *(2nd weekend in June, HemisFair Park. 210-458-2300)* A four-day event celebrating the varied cultures and ethnic groups that created Texas.

MORE THINGS TO SEE & DO

Buckhorn Saloon and Museum *(318 E. Houston St. 210-247-4000. www.buckhornmuseum.com. Adm. fee)* This popular complex includes an 1881 bar, a vast array of mounted animals from around the world, Texas wildlife displays, and a Hall of Texas History.

San Antonio Botanical Gardens and Conservatory *(555 Funston Pl. 210-207-3250. www.sabot.org. Adm. fee)* Striking glass-roofed structures house palms, ferns, cactuses, and other exotic plants, while 33 acres of grounds include a native Texas garden.

San Antonio Zoo *(3903 N. St. Mary's St., in Brackenridge Park. 210-734-7183. www.sazoo-aq.org. Adm. fee)* Among the nation's best zoos, it features more than 3,500 animals, including endangered whooping cranes, rhinos, and snow leopards. The extensive bird collection is renowned.

LODGING

La Mansion del Rio *(112 College St. 210-518-1000 or 800-292-7300. www.lamansion.com. $$$)* Located on the River Walk, this 337-room hotel features Spanish colonial architecture, in part utilizing a school built by priests in 1852.

Menger Hotel *(204 Alamo Plaza. 210-223-4361 or 800-345-9285. www.historicmenger.com. $$$)* Next to the Alamo, the 1859 Menger includes a famous bar modeled after an English pub. 318 rooms.

St. Anthony Hotel *(300 E. Travis St. 210-227-4392. $$-$$$)* A historic luxury 352-room hotel built in 1909; near the River Walk and other downtown attractions.

DINING

Boudro's *(421 E. Commerce St. 210-224-8484. $$)* Southwestern-style cooking and seafood.

Los Barrios *(4223 Blanco St. 210-732-6017. $)* Inexpensive and authentic Mexican food, plus southwestern and South American specialties.

Mi Tierra Cafe and Bakery *(218 Produce Row, Market Square. 210-225-1262. $)* Mexican. See p. 115.

Rio Rio Cantina *(421 E. Commerce St., River Walk. 210-226-8462. $$)* Mexican. See p. 114.

Zuni Grill *(511 River Walk. 210-227-0864. $$)* A standout among River Walk restaurants, this spot features southwestern regional dishes.

Texas Hill Country
A weekend on the range

GENERATIONS OF TEXANS have revered the place they call the Hill Country—known for wildflower meadows, oak-juniper woodlands, and clear, cool rivers. This rugged landscape northwest of San Antonio remains true to the spirit of the cowboys who've been jangling their spurs here for over a century, with enough ten-gallon hats, riding trails, and dude ranches to satisfy any traveler with a yearning for the Old West. The Hill Country was settled in part by Polish and German immigrants, and today its small towns offer a blend of Old World traditions and pure Texas cowboy heritage, adding up to a destination as full of delights as it is beautiful.

Bandera & its dude ranches

The town of **Bandera,** set on the Medina River northwest of San Antonio, calls itself the Cowboy Capital of the World—for more than one reason. It once was a center for cattle drives, and it still holds rodeos twice weekly through the warmer months, including a major professional competition on Memorial Day weekend. Usual rodeo nights are Tuesday and Friday, with occasional Saturday events as well. Even if you don't know bulldogging from barrel racing, you'll enjoy the sights and sounds of the arenas, at Mansfield Park, or the Twin Elm Guess Ranch, both west of town off Tex. 16.

Two spots in Bandera provide quick glimpses of its colorful history: A statue on the courthouse lawn *(Main and Pecan Sts.)* honors the eight world champion rodeo cowboys who hailed from these parts. A few blocks south stands the 1876 **St. Stanislaus Catholic Church** *(Cypress and 7th Sts.),* serving the country's second oldest Polish parish and testifying to the influence of Polish immigrants in Bandera's early days.

> ### NOT TO BE MISSED
>
> ● **A roadside field full of firewheel flowers**
> ● **Tex. 337 west of Medina—if you're not in a hurry** ● **The view from the top of Enchanted Rock**

For more on the town's past, take time to see the quirky **Frontier Times Museum** *(510 13th St. 830-796-3864. Adm. fee).* This homey, eccentric attraction is a repository of all sorts of historical artifacts and natural-history exhibits, from Asian temple bells to stuffed animals to saddles and branding irons.

Cattle ranches have long dominated the countryside around Bandera, but these days the town is known for a different kind of spread. Weekend cowboys come from around the world to enjoy Texas-style hospitality at the dozen or so local dude ranches, where guests can go on trail rides and hayrides, eat barbecue, swim in creeks, hike, or, in some cases, help with the chores on a working cattle ranch. Many places require a two-night minimum stay. All meals are usually included in rates, and most ranches provide so many activities that you may never need to leave the property for entertainment. If you do feel the urge to wander, though, you'll find plenty of places to visit on day trips from Bandera.

Dixie Dude Ranch (see Travelwise) has been taking in guests since 1937. Along with trail rides, Dixie offers riding lessons, fishing, cowboy breakfasts, games and sports, a swimming pool, and Western-style music on its 725 acres. The 350-acre **Mayan Ranch** (see Travelwise) is another well-established, family-run ranch along the Medina River; guests can swim, fish, or play tennis, in addition to hitting the trail on friendly and well-trained horses. The Bandera Convention & Visitors Bureau *(830-796-3045 or 800-364-3833)* can provide a list of other nearby guest ranches catering to a variety of tastes.

On the trail again

Several of the local ranches and outfitters take riders to **Hill Country State Natural Area** *(off Ranch Rd. 1077, 11 miles SW of Bandera. 830-796-4413. Closed Mon.-Thurs. Nov.-Jan.; adm. fee)*, but you should take time to see this picturesque park with or without a guide. The park's 5,400 acres have been left mostly undeveloped, with limited facilities intruding on its natural qualities.

Thirty-five miles of trails, highly popular with horseback riders, mountain-bike riders, and hikers, wind through the rolling hills and grassland. For a good short jaunt, take **Trails 1** and **5a** to a ridge between the prominent hills known as Twin Peaks, then continue to the westernmost peak, where you'll find wonderful views of the surrounding savanna-like terrain.

In the afternoon, take Tex. 16 northwest 13 miles to the small town of **Medina,** which calls itself the Apple Capital of Texas. Sample apple pie, apple butter, apple jelly, apple cider, and more fruit treats at **Love Creek Orchards Cider Mill and Country Store** *(Tex. 16. 830-589-2202 or 800-449-0882)*. Because this is Texas, you might even want to try their apple enchiladas.

It's worth continuing west from Medina on Tex. 337 and 187 to visit **Lost Maples State Natural Area** *(Tex. 187, 5 miles N of Vanderpool. 830-966-3413. Call ahead in Jan., closed some days for public hunt; adm. fee)*, one of the loveliest spots in a region known for its beauty. The "lost" trees are an isolated population of bigtooth maples. The 0.4-mile (one way) **Maple Trail** along the Sabinal River

Herding cattle at sunrise

is a popular walk, dotted with signs interpreting flora and fauna.

Saturday night is a good time to head back into Bandera to hang out with the locals in the compact downtown. Try some excellent Texas-style barbecue at **Busbee's Bar-B-Que** (see Travelwise), a long-time area favorite. Then drop in at one of the local saloons or dance halls for a little two-steppin'. **Cabaret Café & Dance Hall** *(803 Main St. 830-796-8166. Closed Mon.-Tues.; adm. fee)* features live music, often big-name acts. Or mosey on down to **Arkey Blue's Silver Dollar** *(308 Main St. 830-796-8826)* to see who's pickin' the night you're in town.

Kerrville & Fredericksburg

From Bandera follow Tex. 173 to **Kerrville,** stopping to visit the **National Center for American Western Art** *(1550 Bandera Hwy. 830-896-2553. Closed Mon. Sept.-May; adm. fee)*. Works by contemporary artists keep alive the tradition of Western realism pioneered by Frederic Remington and Charles Russell.

It's another 22 miles via Tex. 16 to **Fredericksburg,** a town in the heart of Hill Country renowned for its distinctive Old World heritage. Founded by German immigrants in 1846, Fredericksburg has maintained its strong cultural traditions, and German cooking, architecture, and customs are still apparent throughout the community—modified, of course, by a Texan spirit. Learn about the town's history at the **Pioneer Museum Complex** *(309 W. Main St. 830-997-2835. Adm. fee)*, a collection of significant structures including an 1849 general store, an 1880s log cabin, and a one-room school.

Don't miss the **Admiral Nimitz Museum State Historic**

Site/National Museum of the Pacific War (*340 E. Main St. and 305 E. Austin St. 830-997-4379. Adm. fee*), which combines several World War II-themed exhibits at various venues around town. One section honors Fredericksburg native Chester W. Nimitz, commander of U.S. Pacific naval forces in the war; it's located in a restored 1850s hotel once owned by Nimitz's grandfather. The nearby **National Museum of the Pacific War** uses realistic settings and authentic artifacts to depict the experiences of those who served in the campaign.
—*Mel White*

Travelwise

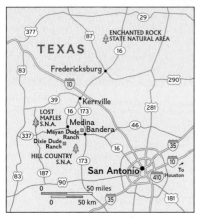

GETTING THERE
Bandera, the beginning of this weekend, is 40 miles northwest of San Antonio via Tex.16.

GENERAL INFORMATION
Contact the **Bandera County Convention & Visitors Bureau** (*P.O. Box 171, Bandera, TX 78003. 830-796-3045 or 800-364-3833. www.banderacowboycapital.com*) or the **Kerrville Convention & Visitors Bureau** (*2108 Sidney Baker, Kerrville, TX 78028. 830-792-3535 or 800-221-7958. www.kerrvilletexas.cc*).

ANNUAL EVENTS
Kerrville Folk Festival (*beginning Thurs. before Mem. Day. Quiet Valley Ranch, 9 miles S of Kerrville on Tex. 16. 830-257-3600. Adm. fee*) One of the country's largest and most important music festivals.

Oktoberfest (*1st weekend in Oct., downtown Fredericksburg. 830-997-4810. Adm. fee*) As

you'd expect, this German town celebrates Oktoberfest in a big way.

LODGING
Dixie Dude Ranch (*Ranch Road 1077, P.O. Box 548, Bandera. 800-375-9255. www.dixieduderanch.com. $$*) 725 acres on which to roam. See p. 118.

Flying L Guest Ranch (*566 Flying L Dr., Bandera. 800-292-5134. www.flyingl.com. $-$$*) Golf as well as horseback riding. 44 rooms.

Hill Country Equestrian Lodge (*1580 Hay Hollar Rd., Bandera. 830-796-7950. www.hillcountryequestlodge.com. $$*) Suites and large cabins on property adjoining Hill Country State Natural Area.

Mayan Ranch (*P.O. Box 577, Bandera, TX 78003. 830-796-3312. www.mayanranch.com. $$*) Family-run since 1937. See p. 118.

Running R Guest Ranch (*9059 Bandera Creek Rd., Bandera. 830-796-3984. www.rrranch.com. $$*) Fourteen cabins, with trail rides, lessons, campfire cookouts.

DINING
Busbee's Bar-B-Que (*319 Main St., Bandera. 830-796-3153. $*) See p. 119.

Der Lindenbaum (*312 E. Main St., Fredericksburg. 830-997-9126. $$*) German specialties such as schnitzel and sauerbraten.

Joe's Jefferson Street Cafe (*1001 Jefferson St., Kerrville. 830-257-2929. Closed Sun. $-$$*) Steaks, seafood, and Texas regional dishes in a restored Victorian-era house.

Po-Po Family Restaurant (*829 FM 289, Boerne. 830-537-4194. $$*) A longtime favorite spot famed for home-style cooking, including cobblers and chicken-fried steak.

Kansas City

On a Musical Note 122

Trails West 127

Eastern terminus of the Pony Express, St. Joseph, Missouri

On a Musical Note
Kansas City's jazz heritage

THOUGH JAZZ WASN'T BORN in Kansas City, it might be said that it came to maturity amid the high-spirited nightlife that abounded here in the 1920s and '30s. The legacy lives on in Kansas City clubs, concert halls, and a unique museum dedicated to this distinctively American sound. Listen to great music by night and explore the surprisingly diverse city by day. And spend a little time sampling another local tradition: barbecue. In Kansas City, it's esteemed as an art form in itself.

Around downtown

Even though Prohibition shut down most nightclubs nationwide in the 1920s, corrupt city boss Tom Pendergast kept liquor flowing and music playing in Kansas City. That, along with the community's large African-American population, attracted an extraordinary number of America's finest jazz musicians. Famed drummer Max Roach has called the clubs "classrooms" where jazz giants such as Benny Moten, Count Basie, Jay McShann, Mary Lou Williams, and Joe Turner learned from each other at regular gigs and in after-hours jam sessions. In fact, it's believed that the concept of these free-form improvisational and experimental musical gatherings was invented in Kansas City.

Many of the great jazz clubs—Havana Inn, Sunset, Blue Room, and Lucille's Paradise, to name a few—were located in the area of 12th and 18th Streets, the hub of African-American business and social life in the years before desegregation. Today the area is experiencing a modest rebirth: The **Museums at 18th and Vine** complex is dedicated to the cultural heritage of this historic neighborhood; the **Horace M. Peterson III Visitor Center** presents photos, exhibits, and a film on the district and its influence on Kansas City.

The excellent **American Jazz Museum** *(1616 E. 18th St. 816-474-8463. www.americanjazzmuseum.com. Closed Mon.; adm. fee)* honors many of the greatest jazz musicians, including influential saxophonist Charlie "Bird" Parker, born in Kansas City in 1920. (A huge

NOT TO BE MISSED

● **The time-capsule atmosphere of the Arabia Steamboat Museum**
● **Onion rings at Fiorella's Jack Stack Barbecue**
● **Nutcracker Ale, a Boulevard Brewing Co. seasonal specialty** ● **Live music in the Blue Room**

A lively night at the Phoenix Piano Bar and Grill

sculpture of Parker's head dominates the outdoor plaza behind the museum.) In this colorful, neon-lit room, hear recordings of jazz legends; learn about the evolution of straight jazz into swing, bebop, and "cool" jazz; and even play the role of studio engineer in blending instrumental tracks on a mixing board. Next door, a modern rein-carnation of the old **Blue Room** *(1600 E. 18th St. 816-474-2929)* brings the concepts of jazz theory and history to life, presenting live music Monday, Thursday, Friday, and Saturday nights.

The complex's other museum, the **Negro Leagues Baseball Museum** *(1616 E. 18th St. 816-221-1920. www.nlbm.com. Closed Mon.; adm. fee),* tells the story of African-American baseball in the era when racial prejudice kept black players from joining white major-league teams. Satchel Paige, "Cool Papa" Bell, and Josh Gibson were among the superb athletes who played in the Negro Leagues and are honored here. A film narrated by James Earl Jones makes a dramatic introduction to the museum, which features uniforms, photos, and the Field of Legends: life-size statues of Negro Leagues greats, posed around a small-scale baseball diamond.

Across the street, the restored 1912 **Gem Theater** *(1615 E. 18th St. 816-474-8463)*, part of the 18th and Vine complex, holds a series of jazz concerts called **"Jammin' at the Gem"** from October through May. The old-fashioned-looking storefronts on nearby Vine Street are courtesy of the Robert Altman movie *Kansas City,* which brought back the city's jazz milieu by re-creating a street scene of the 1920s.

Kansas City's monumental 1914 **Union Station** *(30 W. Pershing Rd.)* is the country's second largest train station (after New York's Grand Central). A 253-million-dollar renovation has turned it into a showplace containing shops, restaurants, and **Science City** *(816-460-2222. www.sciencecity.com. Adm. fee)*, an interactive science museum with exhibits on topics such as health, computers, media, and law enforcement. The station is worth a visit simply to admire the ornate stonework, 94-foot ceilings, and massive chandeliers. There's even a historical jazz link, if a sad one. In 1943, the great pianist-songwriter Thomas "Fats" Waller died of pneumonia on a train just before it pulled into the station.

Elevated walkways lead from Union Station to **Crown Center** *(2450 Grand Blvd. 816-274-8444. www.crowncenter.com)*, an eclectic complex of hotels, shops, theaters, and restaurants—one of the city's major entertainment meccas. It was developed by the Hall family, of Hallmark greetings cards; at the **Hallmark Visitors Center** *(816-274-3613. Closed Sun.)*, adjacent to the complex, you can see early cards, historical memorabilia, and original artwork, and watch greeting cards being designed and manufactured.

Head north to browse the **City Market** *(20 E. 5th St. 816-842-1271. www.kc-citymarket.com)*, which combines an expansive farmers' market with specialty shops and restaurants. After sampling the varied diversions, walk over to the amazing **Arabia Steamboat Museum** *(400 Grand Blvd. 816-471-4030. www.1856.com. Adm. fee)*. Inside, you'll find a sampling of the 200 tons of cargo recovered from the side-wheel steamboat *Arabia,* which sank in the Missouri River in 1856. Buried by mud and preserved until a 1988 excavation, the trove of goods includes clothing, tools, jewelry, glassware, guns, household items, and such oddities as bottled fruit pie fillings, perfume from France, coffee beans from South America, glass beads from Bohemia, and Wedgwood china from England.

To check out the night's jazz venues, find a copy of *Jam,* the magazine of the Kansas City Jazz Ambassadors; check their Web site as well *(www.jazzkc.org)*. The Kansas City Jazz Hotline *(816-753-5277)* also provides information about who's playing where. Some favorite destinations include **Majestic Steakhouse** *(931 Broadway. 816-471-8484)*, **New Point Grille** *(917 W. 44th St. 816-561-7600. Closed Sun.)*, and **Phoenix Piano Bar & Grill** *(301 W. 8th St. 816-472-0001. Closed Sun.)*, all of which regularly offer live jazz.

Midtown & beyond

For quiet contemplation, there's no better place than the **Nelson-Atkins Museum of Art** *(4525 Oak St. 816-751-1278. www.nelson-atkins.org. Closed Mon.; adm. fee).* This superb museum is most noted for its collection of Asian art, including porcelain, scroll paintings, sculpture, and T'ang dynasty tomb figures. European and American painters are also well represented, from Titian and Tiepolo to Georgia O'Keeffe, Willem de Kooning, and Missouri's own Thomas Hart Benton. Outside is a collection of bronze sculptures by Henry Moore, as well as four gigantic badminton shuttlecocks by Claes Oldenburg and Coosje van Bruggen. Plan on spending several hours here, enjoying the varied expressions of creativity from around the world.

Combine lunch and art at the **Kemper Museum of Contemporary Art** *(4420 Warwick Blvd. 816-753-5784. www.kemperart.org. Closed Mon.),* located south of downtown. Housing a permanent collection of modern works, as well as changing exhibitions, the striking building is guarded by an outsize and rather fearsome-looking spider—a Louis Bourgeois sculpture that has become a whimsical symbol of the museum. The museum's **Café Sebastienne** *(816-561-7740. Closed Mon. $-$$)* offers excellent dining for lunch (and dinner on Friday and Saturday).

Combine shopping with a bit of socioeconomic history on a visit to the landmark **Country Club Plaza** *(4745 Central St. 816-753-0100),* begun in the 1920s as the country's first suburban shopping center. With its Spanish-style architecture, impressive fountains and sculptures, and adjacent walking paths along Brush Creek, the plaza offers a more pleasant shopping experience than does a typical mall.

There's live jazz at the plaza most nights, and even a bit of jazz history: Charlie Parker played his first professional job here in 1938 at the restaurant that is now **210 at Fedora** *(210 W. 47th St. 816-561-6565).* This upscale restaurant's lounge features local musicians and regular Saturday-afternoon jam sessions, where you can sample some of the city's best players without waiting until the nightspots crank up later in the evening. Nearby, the **Club at Plaza III** *(4749 Pennsylvania Ave. 816-753-0000)* features a downstairs music club with regular jazz offerings, plus an excellent steakhouse above.

For more entertainment, consider wandering over to the **Westport** area, centered on Westport Road and Broadway, a laid-back area of specialty shops, bars, and eateries. Even funkier is the short stretch of **39th Street** east of State Line Road, just north of Westport, where ethnic restaurants and music clubs attract a diverse crowd of locals both young and old.

If you're adventurous and awake around midnight, head downtown to the 18th and Vine area to the venerable **Mutual Musicians Foundation** *(1823 Highland Ave. 816-471-5212).* This former union hall (on the National Register of Historic Places) hosts after-hours jam sessions on Saturdays, usually beginning a little before midnight and continuing as long as the musicians and the crowd are having a good time. The setting is completely informal, and the music continues a local tradition dating back decades.

—Mel White

Travelwise

GENERAL INFORMATION
Contact the **Convention & Visitors Bureau of Greater Kansas City** (1100 Main St., Kansas City, MO 64105. 816-221-5242 or 800-767-7700. www.visitkc.com).

SEASONS
Year-round; winter may have harsh weather.

ANNUAL EVENTS
American Royal BBQ Contest (1st full weekend in Oct., American Royal Center. 816-221-9800. www.americanroyal.com) Largest barbecue contest in the world; thousands of cooks compete in this two-day event.

Spirit Festival (weekend after Mem. Day, Penn Valley Park. 816-221-4444. www.spiritfest.org) Huge celebration including music, arts and crafts, food, children's activities, and varied exhibits.

MORE THINGS TO SEE & DO
Grand Emporium (3832 Main St. 816-531-1504. www.grandemporium.com) Nationally known blues, jazz, and zydeco musicians perform regularly at this popular restaurant and club.

Thomas Hart Benton Home and Studio State Historic Site (3616 Belleview St. 816-931-5722. www.mostateparks.com. Adm. fee) The Missouri-born artist lived here from 1939 until his death in 1975. His studio looks just as it did when he worked here and contains several of his paintings and sculptures.

Toy and Miniature Museum (5235 Oak St. 816-33-2055. Closed Mon.-Tues.; adm. fee) An extensive collection of dolls and doll houses, antique toys, and miniatures.

LODGING
Historic Suites of America (612 Central St. 816-842-6544 or 800-733-0612. www.historicsuites.com. $$) Three commercial buildings beautifully converted into studios, lofts, and two-bedroom suites.

LaFontaine Inn (4320 Oak St. 816-753-4434 or 888-832-6000. www.lafontainebb.com. $$) 1910 Georgian-style house with four guest rooms and a suite in the carriage house; near the Nelson-Atkins Museum of Art and Country Club Plaza.

Raphael Hotel (325 Ward Pkwy. 816-756-3800 or 800-821-5343. www.raphaelkc.com. $-$$$) This European-style hotel provides excellent service in a location convenient to many city attractions.

DINING
American Restaurant (201 E. 25th St. 816-426-1133. Closed Sun. $$-$$$) Elegant dining in the Crown Center, with a fabulous view of the downtown skyline.

Bryant's Barbecue (1727 Brooklyn St. 816-231-1123. $-$$) A cafeteria-style place where the sandwiches are huge and the sauce is savory.

Fiorella's Jack Stack Barbecue (101 W. 22nd St. 816-472-7427. $-$$) Great ribs, sandwiches, sausages, and beans.

Gates & Sons Bar-B-Q (1221 Brooklyn St. 816-483-3880. $) A local favorite serving spicy barbecue and ribs. Several other locations around the city.

Golden Ox (1600 Genessee St. 816-842-2866. $$-$$$) Located in the old stockyards area, this is perhaps the quintessential spot for a Kansas City steak.

Savoy Grill (219 W. 9th St. 816-842-3890. $$-$$$) The white-jacketed waiters tell stories of the celebrities, from Harry Truman to Paul Newman, who've eaten downtown at this traditional favorite steak and seafood restaurant; note the Santa Fe Trail murals overhead.

Trails West
Gateway towns to a new frontier

IN THE MID-19TH CENTURY, most of the wagon trains that made the arduous trip westward across prairies and mountains began their journeys in rough-and-ready Missouri River settlements. A visit to this region of northwestern Missouri encompasses an extraordinary breadth of history, from pioneers to Pony Express riders to legendary outlaws. And in a look at more recent history, you'll get to know one of our most outspoken and influential Presidents.

St. Joseph & Kearney

Trade and westward migration on the Santa Fe and Oregon Trails were already going strong when word spread that gold had been discovered in California in 1848, inducing even more people to pack up and leave their homes in the East. Many forty-niners departed from St. Joseph, a town founded as an Indian trading post in 1826. Wagonmakers, livestock sellers, grocers, and related businesses catered to the needs of the pioneers, as did guides promising safe passage.

Learn about those early days at the **St. Joseph Museum** *(1100 Charles St. 816-232-8471. www.stjosephmuseum.org. Adm. fee),* in the impressive **Hall Street Historic District.** Located in a castlelike Gothic 1879 mansion with gorgeous woodwork and stained-glass windows, it houses exhibits on regional natural history, the Lewis and Clark expedition of 1804-06, and the gold rush period. The collection of Native American artifacts is one of the Midwest's most important.

A few blocks south, the **Pony Express Museum** *(914 Penn St. 816-279-5059 or 800-530-5930. www.ponyexpress.org. Adm. fee)* honors the riders who carried the mail 2,000 miles between St. Joseph and Sacramento, California, braving mountains, deserts, and Indian attacks. Begun in April 1860, the service was made obsolete by the completion of a transcontinental telegraph line 18 months later; although short-lived, the service has long held a special place in the American imagination. Located in the 1858 building used as the eastern terminus stable, the museum includes displays on the riders and their horses, relay stations, the politics and economics of the service, and the

NOT TO BE MISSED

● **Hall Street Historic District in St. Joseph** ● **The sheer volume of stuff at the Patee House Museum** ● **The spirit of simplicity so manifest in the Truman home**

geography the riders had to cross. You'll see why the advertisements seeking riders specified young men "willing to risk death daily."

The Pony Express headquarters were down the street in an immense 1858 hotel, once one of the most luxurious in the region. The building now houses the **Patee House Museum** *(12th and Penn Sts. 816-232-8206. www.stjoseph.net/ponyexpress. Closed Mon.-Fri. Nov.-March; adm. fee),* which is filled with antique locomotives, fire engines, hearses, furniture, weapons, and even re-created 19th-century businesses—including the office of the legendary mail service.

Don't miss the **Jesse James Home** *(adm. fee),* which has been relocated to the grounds of the Patee House Museum and contains exhibits and artifacts relating to the notorious outlaw's life and times. In 1882, Jesse James was living in St. Joseph under the name Tom Howard; his life came to an ignominious end when he was shot in this house by a member of his own gang for the reward on his head.

For a look at Jesse James's start, rather than his bloody end, travel southeast via US 169 and Mo. 92 to **Kearney,** less than an hour's drive away. The **Jesse James Farm and Museum** *(21216 Jesse James Farm Rd. 816-628-6065. Adm. fee)* displays personal items of the celebrated outlaw and his brother and partner in crime, Frank. A film recounts their transition from Civil War guerillas to postwar bank and train robbers—and murderers. The house where Jesse was born in 1847, and where a younger half-brother was killed when Pinkerton detectives attacked the house in a futile attempt to capture the brothers, stands nearby. Frank led tours of the farm in his old age and died here in 1915, never having been convicted of any crime.

The Pony Express frozen in time

Independence

On the eastern side of Kansas City, **Independence** was another important departure point for westbound immigrants; "the streets were thronged with men, horses, and mules," an observer wrote in 1846. Relive that exciting era at the **National Frontier Trails Center** *(318 W. Pacific St. 816-325-7575. www.frontiertrailscenter.com. Adm. fee)*, a few blocks south of Independence Square. Maps, artifacts, illustrations, and firsthand accounts present the dreams, fears, hardships, and triumphs of overland migration; you'll see a Conestoga wagon, tools, trunks, guns, Bibles, and more. A short video provides an excellent overview of this epic period.

Across the street stands the **Bingham-Waggoner Estate** *(313 W. Pacific St. 816-461-3491. www.bwestate.org. Closed Nov. and Jan.-March; fee for tours)*. Originally a six-room house built in 1852, it was expanded in the 1890s to its present impressive size. Nineteenth-century travelers detoured off the main trail to reach a spring behind the house; their swales, or wagon-wheel ruts, are still visible. George Caleb Bingham, a notable painter of early Missouri life, lived here in the 1860s, and you can see two original portraits by him.

The Missouri-Kansas borderland saw a lot of bloodshed in the years surrounding the Civil War. Pro-Confederate guerilla leader William C. Quantrill was held for a time in what is now the **1859 Jail, Marshal's Home, and Museum** *(217 N. Main St. 816-252-1892. www.jchs.org. Closed Jan.-Feb.; adm. fee)*, just north of Independence Square. The house's rather spare rooms are furnished with period antiques; double metal doors kept prisoners inside the stark limestone cells in the rear. When Frank James temporarily resided here, his cell was reportedly furnished with unusual luxury, including carpets and paintings.

If it's hot, stop for an ice cream at **Clinton's Soda Fountain** *(100 W. Maple St. 816-833-2046)*, on the square's northeast corner. In the 1890s, when this business was a drugstore, a slight, bespectacled young man from an Independence family got his first job here. His name was Harry Truman—who succeeded to the Presidency on the death of Franklin D. Roosevelt in 1945. His memory remains vividly alive in the form of a larger-than-life statue on the square.

The **Truman Presidential Museum and Library** *(500 W. US 24. 816-833-1400 or 800-833-1225. www.trumanlibrary.org. Adm. fee)* is dedicated to America's 33rd President. A superb film and varied exhibits tell the story of Truman's rise from failed businessman to President, where he played a role in some of the 20th century's most important events: the end of World War II, the postwar economic boom, the birth of NATO and the United Nations, and the beginning of the Cold War. See a re-creation of Truman's White House Oval Office, a copy of the 1948 *Chicago Daily Tribune* with the famed "Dewey Defeats Truman" headline, a room dedicated to the use of the atomic bomb against Japan, and many other compelling displays. Harry Truman and his wife, Bess, are buried in the library courtyard.

Truman maintained strong ties to Independence. When he left the White House in 1953, he and Bess happily moved back to the 1885 Victorian house on North Delaware Street where they had previously lived. Their home is now part of the **Harry S. Truman National Historic Site** (*223 N. Main St. 816-254-9929. www.nps.gov/hstr. Closed Mon. Labor Day–Mem. Day; fee for house tour, tickets available on first-come first-served basis*). Incorporating stories and personal items, tours give visitors a real feeling for the Trumans' lives.

—Mel White

Travelwise

GETTING THERE
St. Joseph lies 55 miles north of Kansas City via I-29; Independence is just east of Kansas City via I-70.

GENERAL INFORMATION
Contact the **St. Joseph Convention & Visitors Bureau** (*P.O. Box 445, St. Joseph, MO 64502. 816-233-6688 or 800-785-0360. www.stjo mo.com*) or the **Independence Tourism Department** (*111 E. Maple St., Independence, MO 64050. 816-325-7111 or 800-748-7323. www.visitindependence.com*).

SEASONS
Year-round; winter may have harsh weather.

ANNUAL EVENT
Trails West (*3rd weekend in Aug., Civic Center Park, St. Joseph. 816-233-0231 or 800-216-7080*) The city's premier festival includes

drama performances, historical reenactments, music, arts exhibits, and food.

LODGING
Inn at Ophelia's (*201 N. Main St., Independence. 816-461-4525. www.ophelias.net. $-$$*) Seven rooms and a suite on historic Independence Square.

Shakespeare Château Bed and Breakfast (*809 Hall St., St. Joseph. 816-232-2667 or 888-414-4944. www.shakespearechateau .com. $$*) Seven rooms in a Queen Anne mansion located in the Hall Street district.

Woodson Guest House (*1604 W. Lexington Ave., Independence. 816-254-0551. www .woodsonguesthouse.com. $*) 1858 Italianate house set on 1 acre; two guest rooms and a suite.

DINING
Jerre Anne Cafeteria and Bakery (*2640 Mitchell Ave., St. Joseph. 816-232-6585. Closed Sun.-Mon. $*) Home-style cooking, pies, cakes, and bread make this informal spot a popular local tradition.

Old Hoof and Horn Steakhouse (*429 Illinois Ave., St. Joseph. 816-238-0742. Closed Sun. $-$$*) People drive long distances to enjoy the steaks and prime rib at this restaurant in an 1898 building in the St. Joseph stockyards.

Ophelia's (*201 N. Main St., Independence. 816-461-4525. $$*) Beef and seafood served in an upscale atmosphere.

Rheinland Restaurant (*208 N. Main St., Independence. 816-461-5383. Closed Mon. $$*) Fine German food at a longtime local favorite.

Las Vegas

American Excess 132

The bright lights of Las Vegas

American Excess
Kitsch, keno, & cabarets
in the ultimate tourist town

LAS VEGAS FIRST GAINED NOTORIETY in the mid-1900s as a desert
outpost of gambling and neon lights, a place run by East Coast
mobsters and ruled by Frank Sinatra's swingin' Rat Pack. In the
1990s, though, themed mega-resorts remade Sin City into a family-friendly, Disneyesque entertainment complex. (See an erupting
volcano! Ride a roller coaster!) Recently, Las Vegas has reinvented
itself again, building resorts that simulate the scenes and sophistication of Europe. Enjoy the best of nouveau Vegas on this weekend getaway, then ferret out what's left of the bad old days.

The new Vegas
Hit town at dusk, when Las Vegas turns on a gazillion kilowatts of
lights. (In harsh daylight the city looks homely, as plain as a showgirl
caught without her makeup on.) For an overview of the **Strip** (aka
Las Vegas Boulevard), head for **Paris Las Vegas** (*3655 S. Las Vegas
Blvd.*), whose half-scale **Eiffel Tower** is true to Gustave Eiffel's original
drawings (although three of its legs penetrate the casino). Ride the
glass elevator *(fee)* to the 46-story-high observation deck.

From aloft you see that the Strip starts in the south by McCarran
International Airport and runs in a river of light northward to the
1,149-foot-high **Stratosphere Tower** (*2000 S. Las Vegas Blvd. 702-
380-7777. www.stratlv.com. Adm. fee*), the tallest freestanding observation tower in the nation and another great viewpoint. Embodying
Las Vegas's new "entertainment architecture," the world's highest
roller coaster circles above the tower's observation pod—a hundred
stories off the ground.

More "Oh, wow!" architecture awaits at **New York-New York**
(*3790 S. Las Vegas Blvd.*), whose pop-art cityscape includes a facsim-
ile of the Empire State Building and a 150-foot-tall Statue of Liberty.
The casino's interior is themed as Central Park, complete with
autumn foliage and a pond; the cashiers' cages are in the Financial
District; the Greenwich Village food court features brownstone
buildings and steam-emitting manhole covers. Swooping around
(and through) the hotel, the hair-raising **Manhattan Express roller**

New York-New York's skyline, Las Vegas

coaster *(adm. fee)* actually simulates a barrel roll in a jet fighter.

Across the street from the New York skyline, a large golden statue of a lion keeps watch at the corner of Las Vegas Boulevard and Tropicana Avenue—the signature calling card of the enormous **MGM Grand** *(3799 S. Las Vegas Blvd.)*. This complex is perhaps best known for its entertainment venues, which play host to concerts, boxing matches, and stage acts.

Farther up the street rises a black pyramid guarded by a ten-story-tall Sphinx. (It makes no sense, but hey, this is Las Vegas!) Walk like an Egyptian into the **Luxor** *(3900 S. Las Vegas Blvd.)*, whose sides are sheathed in some 27,000 plates of smoked glass. The xenon light projected from the apex of the pyramid is the most powerful beam on Earth (equal to 40 billion candles) and can supposedly be seen from space. Inside, the Luxor displays a replica of King Tut's tomb with reproductions of his sarcophagus and other treasures, all hand-made in Egypt using historically accurate gold leaf, linen, pigments, and other materials.

Now wait a minute! Do we detect a dawning of high culture in…Las Vegas, of all places? For an answer, visit Lake Como-themed **Bellagio** *(3600 S. Las Vegas Blvd.)*, which boasts a colorful lobby canopy of Dale Chihuly art glass and the **Gallery of Fine Art** *(702-693-7722. Adm. fee)*, which stages impressive exhibitions.

Proceed to the **Venetian** *(3355 S. Las Vegas Blvd.)*, another resort that mimics Europe—in this case Venice, complete with a Doge's Palace and a Grand Canal where authentic gondolas glide. Here the **Guggenheim-Hermitage Museum** *(702-414-2440. Adm. fee)* brings in works such as Impressionist and early modernist paintings from its namesake American and Russian institutions. The larger **Guggenheim-Las Vegas** *(702-414-2440. Adm. fee)* imports exhibitions from its parent museum in New York.

You'll also find a new artistic approach in some of the Strip's big shows. Catch the edgy, funny performance art of **Blue Man Group** *(Luxor. Adm. fee)* or one of Cirque du Soleil's two spectacles: the dancing, music, and aerial bungee ballet of **Mystère** *(Treasure Island, 3300 S. Las Vegas Blvd. 702-894-7111. Adm. fee)* and the surreal aquatic wonders of **O** *(Bellagio. Adm. fee)*.

Of course, Las Vegas entertainment also dips lower on the cultural food chain. The Entertainment Capital of the World is famous for leggy showgirls wearing huge feathered headdresses and tiny costumes; try to catch a performance of the long-running **Folies Bergere** *(Tropicana, 3801 S. Las Vegas Blvd. 702-739-2411. Adm. fee)*. Vegas

NOT TO BE MISSED

• Watching people play craps with undiminished enthusiasm at 3:30 a.m.
• The outdoor "Neon Museum" around Fremont Street • Antique slot machines, "how to win" books, and personalized poker chips at the Gamblers General Store on Main Street

institutions **Siegfried and Roy** *(Mirage, 3400 S. Las Vegas Blvd. 702-791-7777. Adm. fee)* put on a glitzy (and expensive) magic show with white tigers and a mechanized dragon, but these days the stars pretty much phone in their performances. For pure, great conjuring, catch **Lance Burton: Master Magician** *(Monte Carlo, 3770 S. Las Vegas Blvd. 702-730-7160. Adm. fee)*, who performs both classical sleights of hand and big illusions, such as making a Corvette disappear.

The old Vegas

You'll find traces of Las Vegas's notorious past still thriving where the city itself started—**downtown.** As you head there, you'll note a down-market atmosphere creeping in: pawn shops, adult motels, and instant-marriage chapels ("Say I Do Wedding Drive-Thru"). Park near Main and Fremont Streets, where in 1905 a land auction launched what everyone hoped would be a railroad boomtown. Saloons and a red-light district duly appeared, and today the city's oldest hotel, the 1906 **Golden Gate,** still stands on this corner.

After casino gambling was legalized in 1931, the town's around-the-clock action and quickie marriages (and divorces) lured vice-versed visitors. The first few blocks of Fremont Street became **Glitter Gulch,** named for the flashing neon signs outside the gambling halls. Look for neon cowboy **"Vegas Vic,"** with his red bandanna and spurs, a character created in the 1940s for a chamber of commerce publicity campaign.

When tourists moved to the burgeoning Strip, downtown began a long run of hard luck. In order to revive its appeal, the city created in 1995 the **Fremont Street Experience** *(702-678-5600. www.vegas experience.com)*. It's a four-block-long canopy laced with 2.1 million lights choreographed with 540,000 watts of loudspeakers to produce sound-and-light shows overhead. You might see anything from bug-eyed tropical amphibians leapfrogging entire blocks to space stations whirling against a background of stars.

But more than glitz, downtown still offers the chance to see Las Vegas as it used to be—a place for adults to misbehave. Before the casinos renamed it "gaming," gambling was raucous, with a cast of Damon Runyonesque characters, bottle blondes, and tumbling dice. To sense those days, visit **Binion's Horseshoe** *(128 Fremont St. 702-382-1600. www.binions.com)*, where the decor (whorehouse/saloon) and $15,000-a-hand maximum bet (the highest limit in town) announce that this is a joint for gamblers. The casino puts on the **World Series of Poker** *(April-May)*, the world's richest card game, which sees top players bluff and battle for millions of dollars. You can watch from the sidelines or buy in and join the game, although it's not cheap. But then, Las Vegas was invented for high rollers who aren't afraid to take a walk on the wild side.

—*Jerry Camarillo Dunn, Jr.*

Travelwise

GETTING THERE
Las Vegas is 290 miles from Los Angeles via I-10 and I-15.

GENERAL INFORMATION
Contact the **Las Vegas Convention & Visitors Authority** (3150 S. Paradise Rd., Las Vegas, NV 89109. 702-892-7575. www.vegasfreedom.com. Closed Sun.) or the **Las Vegas Chamber of Commerce** (3720 Howard Hughes Pkwy., Las Vegas, NV 89109. 702-735-1616. www.lvchamber.com).

SEASONS
Spring and fall are the most pleasant. Summer is blazing hot; winter nights can be freezing.

MORE THINGS TO SEE & DO
Buccaneer Bay Sea Battle (Treasure Island at the Mirage, 3300 S. Las Vegas Blvd. 702-894-7111. www.treasureisland.com) Pirate battle with booming cannon and costumed actors. Every 90 minutes starting at 5:30 p.m.

Elvis-A-Rama Museum (3401 Industrial Rd. 702-309-7200. www.elvisarama.com. Adm. fee) Includes the King's '55 Cadillac concert limo, U.S. Army uniform, handwritten letters, and inevitable white jumpsuit.

Fountains of Bellagio (Bellagio, 3600 S. Las Vegas Blvd. 702-693-7111. www.bellagio .com) In the evening, more than a thousand water jets dance to music.

Gambling A cautionary note: Each year Nevada casinos win more than eight billion dollars from people like you.

Liberace Museum (1775 E. Tropicana Ave. 702-798-5595. www.liberace.org. Adm. fee) A mink cape lined with 40,000 rhinestones, a piano once played by Chopin, a Rolls-Royce clad in mirrors, a pair of red-white-and-blue hot pants—it all adds up to a celebration of "Mr. Showmanship."

Star Trek: The Experience (Las Vegas Hilton, 3000 Paradise Rd. 702-697-8700. www .startrekexp.com. Adm. fee) Costumes, props, and live actors on a mock-up bridge of the U.S.S. Enterprise.

Volcano (Mirage, 3400 S. Las Vegas Blvd. 702-791-7777. www.themirage.com) Flames and smoke erupt every 15 minutes from dusk to midnight.

Weddings Each year more than 100,000 people get married in Las Vegas. Wedding chapels include the Little Church of the West (where Mickey Rooney got married more than once) and facilities at major casino-hotels. Novelty weddings can include Elvis imitators, gondolas, you name it.

LODGING
The visitors authority Web site and www.veg as.com are good places to begin your search.

Bellagio (3600 S. Las Vegas Blvd. 702-693-7111 or 888-987-6667. www.bellagio.com. $$-$$$) 3,005 rooms; 316 suites. See p. 134.

Luxor (3900 S. Las Vegas Blvd. 702-262-4000 or 888-777-0188. www.luxor.com. $$-$$$) 4,000 rooms. See p. 134.

MGM Grand (3799 S. Las Vegas Blvd. 702-891-7777 or 877-880-0880. www.mgm grand.com. $$-$$$) 5,034 rooms and suites. See p. 134.

New York-New York (3790 S. Las Vegas Blvd. 702-740-6969 or 888-696-9887. www.nyny hotelcasino.com. $$-$$$) 2,023 rooms. See pp. 132-34.

Paris Las Vegas (3655 S. Las Vegas Blvd. 702-946-7000. www.parislasvegas.com. $$-$$$) 2,932 rooms. See p. 132.

Venetian (3355 S. Las Vegas Blvd. 702-414-1000 or 888-283-6423. www.venetian.com. $$-$$$) 3,000-plus suites. See p. 134.

DINING
Buffets Most casinos have all-you-can-eat, pay-one-price buffets for all three meals. The cheapest include Circus Circus, the Excalibur, and the Sahara; the better ones include Bellagio, the Luxor, Paris Las Vegas, and the Golden Nugget (downtown).

Fine Dining Las Vegas has become a major dining destination, with celebrity-chef establishments in the casino-hotels. Among the best are Bellagio's **Aqua** (3600 S. Las Vegas Blvd. 702-693-7223 or 877-793-7223. $$$) specializing in seafood; the Mirage's **Renoir** (3400 S. Las Vegas Blvd. 702-791-7353. Closed Mon. $$$) featuring southern French cuisine; and **Spago** at Caesar's Palace (3500 S. Las Vegas Blvd. 702-369-6300. $$$), which offers the chef's innovative California cuisine.

Los Angeles &
San Diego

Hollywood 138

Ojai & Carpinteria 142

See-worthy Sights by the Seashore 147

California Dreamin' 151

Faces of the Desert 154

Children's Pool, La Jolla

Hollywood

Searching for stars in Tinseltown

HOLLYWOOD IS LESS a geographical location than a state of mind. On this getaway you'll discover relics of Hollywood's golden era, see movie locations, explore new attractions, and maybe even glimpse some celebrities—by going where they go.

Hollywood Boulevard

Hollywood Boulevard epitomized glamour in the 1920s and '30s, when movie idols thronged nightclubs or attended premieres as searchlights crossed the sky. Today the area is rated SG (Shabby, Gritty) for its tacky souvenir shops, greasy cafés, tattoo parlors, and prostitutes. Revitalization is steadily elevating the area, however, and fans find Hollywood Boulevard as irresistible as popcorn at a movie.

Between La Brea Avenue and Gower Street, you can see some of the 2,000-plus stars in the **Walk of Fame.** Each bronze-trimmed, pink terrazzo star in the sidewalk cradles the name of an artist from movies, TV, radio, recording, or theater. Honorees range from Greta Garbo to Tom Cruise; you might see dedicated fans scrubbing scuff marks and gum off their idols' stars.

Step into the **Hollywood Entertainment Museum** *(7021 Hollywood Blvd. 323-465-7900. www.hollywoodmuseum.com. Closed Wed.; adm. fee),* to see a few treasures in its hodgepodge collection: the bar set from the sitcom *Cheers;* the bridge of the U.S.S. *Enterprise* (you can sit in the captain's chair) from *Star Trek: The Next Generation;* and pancake makeup and false eyelashes invented by Hollywood pioneer Max Factor.

The first Academy Awards were presented in 1929 at the **Hollywood Roosevelt Hotel** *(7000 Hollywood Blvd.).* Shirley Temple learned how to tap dance up the lobby stairs from Bill "Bojangles" Robinson. Marilyn Monroe posed for pictures at the swimming pool. The mezzanine displays photographs of Hollywood history.

World-famous **Mann's Chinese Theatre** *(6925 Hollywood Blvd.)*

NOT TO BE MISSED

● **The Capitol Records building on N. Vine Street shaped like a stack of records** ● **Purchasing an original movie poster at Larry Edmunds Bookshop on Hollywood Boulevard** ● **The shingled fairy-tale cottages and villas in the Hollywood Hills**

Mann's Chinese Theatre

looks like a movie set itself—a green-roofed pagoda guarded by a 30-foot-long dragon. Showman Sid Grauman opened it in 1927 with a premiere of Cecil B. DeMille's *King of Kings.* Immortalized in concrete in the forecourt are the handprints, footprints, and signatures of many Hollywood legends ("To Sid, may this cement our friendship"—Joan Crawford).

The nearby **Hollywood & Highland,** housing the Kodak Theatre, the new home of the Academy Awards, is an entertainment complex whose central Babylon Court was inspired by the mammoth set built for D. W. Griffith's 1916 silent epic, *Intolerance;* two gargantuan white elephants sit atop columns, and an arch with Egyptian inscriptions frames the distant **Hollywood Sign.** The 50-foot-high white letters atop Mount Lee originally spelled out Hollywoodland, the name of a real estate development, but in 1945 the last four letters were removed. In 1932 failed starlet Peg Entwistle revealed the dark side of the Hollywood dream when she jumped to her death from the "H."

Don't miss the **El Capitan Theatre** *(6838 Hollywood Blvd. 323-467-7674);* it's been restored to its art-deco glory and has an elaborate gilded ceiling. **Frederick's of Hollywood Lingerie Museum** *(6608 Hollywood Blvd. 323-957-5953. www.fredericks.com)* exhibits movieland lingerie, from an Ava Gardner garment to Madonna's black bustier—not to mention Tony Curtis's bra from *Some Like It Hot.*

Where did William Faulkner, F. Scott Fitzgerald, and other serious writers gather when they came to Hollywood to trade their talent for the studios' money at great cost to their souls? At Hollywood's oldest restaurant, right out of a Raymond Chandler detective story—the darkly paneled **Musso & Frank Grill** *(6667 Hollywood Blvd.)*. Slip into a red leather booth and order grilled chops or the famous seafood chiffonade salad from a red-jacketed waiter. Imagine gossip columnist Hedda Hopper interviewing stars or the Warner brothers clinching deals. Celebrities still enjoy the clubby Old Hollywood ambience; patrons have ranged from the Rolling Stones to Brad Pitt. Tim Burton filmed a scene here for *Ed Wood.*

North of the boulevard on Ivar Avenue, check out a few noteworthy places from Hollywood's past. The **Alto Nido** *(1851 N. Ivar Ave.)* is the Spanish-style apartment house where the failed screenwriter played by William Holden lived in *Sunset Boulevard.* At the **Parva-Sed** apartments *(1817 N. Ivar Ave.),* Nathanael West took inspiration from the neighbors in the bungalows across the street in writing his celebrated Hollywood novel, *Day of the Locust.* At the **Knickerbocker Hotel** *(1714 N. Ivar Ave.),* Faulkner wrote *Absalom! Absalom!* in his hours off from scriptwriting.

Spend the night on the trendy Sunset Strip at the French Normandy **Château Marmont** *(8221 Sunset Blvd.),* a Hollywood hideaway since 1929. Jim Morrison was portrayed by Val Kilmer in *The Doors* as he nearly fell drunkenly off the roof. In 1982 comic John Belushi died of a drug overdose in Bungalow 3. But most celebrities' stays have been happier; Paul Newman and Joanne Woodward fell in love here, and such figures as Howard Hughes, Jean Harlow, Errol Flynn, Dustin Hoffman, and Robert DeNiro have considered the hotel their home away from home.

Hollywood haunts

Begin a nostalgic tour of Tinseltown where many movie careers started, at **Paramount Studios** *(5555 Melrose Ave. 323-956-1777. www.paramount.com),* the last "major" still in Hollywood. Here Fred Astaire danced divinely, Cecil B. DeMille parted the Red Sea, and Elvis rocked onto celluloid. Paramount's wrought iron *gate (Marathon Ave. at Bronson Ave.)* has become a movieland icon; in the 1950 classic *Sunset Boulevard,* Gloria Swanson's limo sweeps through this Spanish-style portal. Television shows are often taped on Fridays.

Is fame eternal? Ponder the question at the adjacent **Hollywood Forever Cemetery** *(6000 Santa Monica Blvd. 323-469-1181),* which considerately provides a map and guidebook to the stars' graves. Marvel at Rudolph Valentino's crypt and Douglas Fairbanks's marble tomb and reflecting pool. Other Hollywood personages buried here include DeMille, cartoon voice Mel Blanc (epitaph: "That's All Folks"), and Alfalfa (Carl Switzer) from *Our Gang.*

Head to **Griffith Observatory** *(323-664-1191. www.griffithobs.org. Closed until 2005)* in Griffith Park to see where scenes with James Dean and Natalie Wood were shot for *Rebel Without a Cause.* The park has doubled for *King Kong*'s jungle and *Bonanza*'s Wild West.

Hungry? Drive west to the **Formosa Café** *(7156 Santa Monica Blvd.)*, whose walls are plastered with autographed photos of famous patrons. Clark Gable and Marilyn Monroe ate together while making *The Misfits*. A scene filmed here for *L.A. Confidential* has detectives mistaking Lana Turner for a prostitute. (The real Turner was a regular customer.) Nowadays you might spot Nicolas Cage or Jodie Foster, who come here for the Old Hollywood atmosphere.

It's time to survey the material rewards of stardom—i.e., shopping and dining—in **Beverly Hills.** Hit the designer shops along world-famous **Rodeo Drive** between Wilshire and Santa Monica Boulevards. Have lunch or dinner at a celebrity haunt such as Wolfgang Puck's **Spago** *(176 N. Canon Dr.)* or **Dan Tana's** *(9071 Santa Monica Blvd.)*, a movie and music-biz eatery popular with the likes of Bob Dylan, Drew Barrymore, and Jay Leno.

Finish your visit by peeking at the homes of the rich and famous. A guidebook such as Ken Schessler's *This Is Hollywood* or William A. Gordon's *The Ultimate Hollywood Tour Book* is recommended.

—Jerry Camarillo Dunn, Jr.

Travelwise

GETTING THERE
The featured area lies roughly between Santa Monica Blvd. and the Hollywood Freeway, and between Vine St. and La Brea Ave.

GENERAL INFORMATION
Contact the **LA Convention & Visitors Bureau** *(685 Figueroa St., Los Angeles, CA 90017. 800-228-2452. www.visitlanow.com).*

SEASONS
Generally mild and sunny year-round.

MORE THINGS TO SEE & DO
Universal Studios Hollywood *(Universal City. 818-622-3801. www.universalstudios.com. Adm. fee)* Movie studio with behind-the-scenes tour, theme park rides, live shows.

Warner Brothers Studios VIP Tour *(4000 Warner Blvd., Burbank. 818-846-1403. Closed Sat.-Sun.; adm. fee, reservations reqd.)* Soundstages, backlot sets, and museum.

LODGING
Beverly Hills Hotel *(9641 Sunset Blvd., Beverly Hills. 310-276-2251 or 800-283-8885. $$$)* Dealmakers and stars love the "Pink palace's" Polo Lounge and poolside cabanas.

Château Marmont *(8221 Sunset Blvd. 323-656-1010 or 800-242-8328. $$$)* See p. 140.

Hollywood Roosevelt Hotel *(7000 Hollywood Blvd. 323-466-7000. $$$)* See p. 138.

Hotel Bel-Air *(701 Stone Canyon Rd. 310-472-1211 or 800-648-4097. $$$)* Where stars get away; 92 hacienda-style suites and rooms.

Renaissance Hollywood Hotel *(1775 N. Highland Ave. 323-856-1200. $$)* 637-room high-rise hotel in heart of Hollywood. Pool.

DINING
Dan Tana's *(9071 Santa Monica Blvd., West Hollywood. 310-275-9444. $$$)* Pasta, steaks. See p. 141.

deep *(1707 N. Vine St. 323-462-1144. Closed Sun.-Wed. $$$)* Trendy restaurant; bar appeared in *Ocean's 11* remake.

Formosa Café *(7156 Santa Monica Blvd., West Hollywood. 323-850-9050. $$$)* Pan-Asian cuisine. See p. 141.

Musso & Frank Grill *(6667 Hollywood Blvd. 323-467-7788. Closed Sun.-Mon. $$$)* See p. 140.

Pig 'n Whistle *(6714 Hollywood Blvd. 323-463-0000. $$)* Restored 1927 haunt of Howard Hughes, Spencer Tracy. Bistro food.

Spago *(176 N. Canon Dr., Beverly Hills. 310-385-0880. $$$)* New American. See p. 141.

Ojai & Carpinteria
A respite from reality

THE RAREST THING IN MOBILE, MANIC southern California isn't a driver without a cell phone plastered to his ear. It's a moment of old-fashioned relaxation. Or a New Age experience of living in the "here and now." To find these treasures, visit Ojai, a mountain hideaway where spiritual life and spas both flourish, and Carpinteria, whose beaches and breezy good fun will straighten out your urban kinks. The towns are linked by another southern California rarity: a quiet two-lane road.

Ojai & spirituality

At ease beneath a clear sky and ringed by mountains, the Ojai Valley seems a little like the lost paradise of Shangri-la. (In fact, it doubled for that timeless place in Frank Capra's 1937 film, *Lost Horizon*.) Even the name Ojai (OH-hi) sounds welcoming. It is used for both the valley and the town tucked within it.

There's no doubt that Ojai has a special aura, an indefinable something that has long lured spiritual seekers and finders. Among those who have felt it was renowned Indian philosopher Jiddu Krishnamurti, who moved here in the 1920s. Calling Ojai one of the most extraordinary valleys he had ever seen, he perceived "a quietness in the mountains, a dignity…. The vast sense of permanency is there in them." Krishnamurti's teachings (which attracted such figures as Aldous Huxley and Anne Morrow Lindbergh) can be studied in books and videos at the **Krishnamurti Library** *(1070 McAndrew Rd. 805-646-4948. www.kfa.org. Closed Mon.-Tues.)* at the east end of the valley.

One of the first New Age centers, Ojai shelters numerous other spiritual and mystical groups, including devotees of Buddhism, transcendental meditation, the Science of Mind church, Sai Baba, Native American practices, and therapies from aroma- to psycho-.

At the valley's east end, Meditation Group, Inc., invites the public to **Meditation Mount** *(top of Reeves Rd. 805-646-5508. www.medita*

NOT TO BE MISSED

- The intoxicating scent of Ojai orange blossoms
- Browsing the Pink Crow and other Ojai Arcade shops ● Bodysurfing at Carpinteria's uncrowded Bates Beach
- Ground-shaking polo matches in Carpinteria

Meditating in a serene environment at Ojai Spa

tion.com), where the group holds meditations on spiritual principles in service to humanity; these are held just before the full moon, a time when the doors to the spiritual world are supposed to open wider. The view across the valley is inspirational any time.

The metaphysically curious may want to drive up a hill west of downtown to the **Krotona Institute of Theosophy and Library** *(2 Krotona Hill. 805-646-2653. www.theosophical.org/centers/krotona. Closed Mon.).* Blending the religions of East and West, theosophy seeks intuitive insight into God and the "unexplained laws of nature and our latent powers." The library's 10,000 books focus on esoteric wisdom, comparative religion, philosophy, and theosophy. They run the gamut from A to Z (i.e., astrology to Zen). With a beamed ceiling, the library is certainly conducive to Deep Thoughts. Outside, stroll around the rose gardens and lotus pond, and enjoy sights both intimate and vast—from cottontails rocketing around the hedges to a panorama of the mountain-girded valley.

From here you can observe that Ojai's mountains run east to west, a rarity in California. Around sunset this unusual geography regularly creates an ethereal vision: The 6,367-foot-high bluffs of Topa Topa Mountain are suffused with a radiant rose light. The whole town momentarily stops to admire this "**Pink Moment,**" and somehow it makes manifest the spiritual dimension so many people sense in Ojai.

Ojai & relaxation

Now for the mind-body connection! Head to one of Ojai's spas, of which the most luxurious (and expensive) is the world-class **Spa Ojai** *(Ojai Valley Inn and Spa, 905 Country Club Rd. 805-640-2000 or 888-772-6524. www.ojairesort.com)*. The complex looks like a village in Andalusia; there's even a plaza and a fountain, but this village is filled with steam rooms and fitness equipment. And it offers every sort of pampering—for example, having your skin dry-scrubbed with crushed rose petals.

The spa's signature treatment, the Kuyam, takes place in what appears to be a chamber in a Moorish palace, sheathed in blue tile. Soft light glows in star-shaped windows. New Age music plays as the room heats up and you spread organic mud over your naked body to cleanse and remineralize your skin. Then steam rises through an urn filled with lemongrass, for inhalation therapy. You rinse away the mud in a walk-through Swiss shower; then you're wrapped in a white robe and taken to a private terrace to sip mint tea and slowly reenter the world.

For another otherworldly experience, but one that costs nothing, hike the **Gridley Trail** *(upper end of Gridley Rd.)*, which climbs through the chaparral-covered foothills. From there you look down over the Ojai Valley—and understand why so many people consider this special place a Shangri-la.

Carpinteria

From Ojai, drive the winding, two-lane Calif. 150 over the Traverse Range. On reaching US 101, you'll be at the east end of **Carpinteria,** a coastal town that offers a breezy encounter with land, sand, and sea.

Heading south on US 101, check out the surf at **Rincon Park** *(Bates Rd. exit)*, a legendary point break where the waves are choice and surfers get stoked by the incredibly long rides. They (and nearby office workers) grab lunch north up the coast at **Surf Dog** (see Travelwise), a red wagon topped with a colossal hot dog; the lemonade's fresh, the food's cheap, and everything comes with a million-dollar view of the ocean.

From here you can walk right onto the **Bluffs** (officially, the **Carpinteria Bluffs Nature Preserve**), some 50 acres of unspoiled oceanfront that locals managed to save from developers. Meandering trails offer views of seabirds kiting on the breeze, as well as a panorama of the Santa Barbara Channel Islands.

Although it seems counterintuitive, you're looking south to the Pacific. (The coastline here runs east-west instead of California's usual north-south.) Walk the trail that leads westward along the bluff (be careful when crossing the railroad tracks) to the **Seal Sanctuary,** which protects a colony of harbor seals established more than a century ago. Adults and their pups haul out here by the hundreds. They're skittish about noise and commotion, so the beach is closed December through May, during pupping season. But from the bluff you can watch the seals bask on the sand, bark, and splash into the ocean to dive for fish or just to frolic.

If you'd like to behave like a seal, head downtown to the surf-and-sand playground called **Carpinteria City Bathing Beach** *(end of Linden Ave.),* which is so broad it appears to have been supersized. This beach ranks as one of the world's finest and safest; it has a southern exposure that makes it sunny all day, and its waters are free of undercurrents. Next door, **Carpinteria State Beach** *(805-684-2811, camping reservations 800-444-7275)* boasts the same ocean frontage, and you can also camp here—the cheapest accommodations in town, with sunsets and tide pools thrown in for free. (And here's some free advice: Wear beach sandals to keep tar off your feet.)

Spend a carefree day at the beach, and you'll be filled with the optimistic belief of a surfer on a sun-kissed wave: Life is an endless summer—or at least we should live that way.

—*Jerry Camarillo Dunn, Jr.*

Travelwise

GETTING THERE

Ojai is 65 miles north of Los Angeles; from US 101, take Calif. 33 inland at Ventura. Carpinteria is located on US 101, 80 miles north of Los Angeles.

GENERAL INFORMATION

Contact the **Ojai Valley Chamber of Commerce & Visitors Center** *(150 W. Ojai Ave., Ojai, CA 93023. 805-646-8126. www.the-ojai.org),* whose free *Ojai Valley Visitors Guide* includes a map; and the **Carpinteria Valley Chamber of Commerce** *(5285 Carpinteria Ave., Carpinteria, CA 93014. 805-684-5479 or 800-563-6900. www.carpchamber .org),* whose *Carpinteria Valley Magazine* contains a map and tourist information.

SEASONS

Ojai is characterized by mild spring and autumn weather; it has cool winters with some rain and summer temperatures reaching the 90s. Carpinteria has 60-to-80-degree temperatures year-round; typically there is some summer morning fog.

ANNUAL EVENTS

California Avocado Festival *(1st weekend in Oct., Carpinteria. 805-684-0038. www.avo fest.com.)* A weekend of food, music, and family fun in celebration of the avocado. The southern California region is the leading producer of avocados in the country.

Ojai Garden Tour *(May. 805-646-8126. Fee)* Self-guided tour of several thematically different gardens in the Ojai Valley.

Ojai Studio Artists Tour *(Oct. 805-646-8126. Fee)* This self-guided tour takes you to see the studios of working artists.

MORE THINGS TO SEE & DO

Cherubs (*321A E. Ojai Ave., Ojai. 805-646-7595*) This shop sells aromatherapy products and offers massage and aromatherapy.

Day Spa of Ojai (*1434 E. Ojai Ave., Ojai. 805-640-1100. www.thedayspa.com. Closed Sun.*) Intimate day spa in a century-old stone building; treatments with ocean algae (facials, body wraps, back stress management); massage with essential oils that have aromatherapy benefits. A staff clinical psychologist focuses on intimacy issues.

Heaven (*203 N. Signal St., Ojai. 805-640-8888*) Located in a cottage, Heaven specializes in hair care/coloring and facials (including microdermabrasion). It also offers massages and waxing services.

The Oaks at Ojai (*122 E. Ojai Ave., Ojai 805-646-5573 or 800-753-6257. www.oaksspa .com*) Reasonably priced residential health spa located downtown.

Ojai School of Massage (*619 W. El Roblar Dr., Ojai. 805-640-9798. www.ojaischoolof massage.com. Closed Fri.*) The school offers a variety of therapeutic massages, including Swedish, deep tissue, and reflexology. Professional and student practitioners.

Orchid Farm (*Gallup & Stribling, 3450 Via Real, Carpinteria. 805-684-9842*) Orchid-growing aids, "designer" hybrids at farm-direct prices.

LODGING

Carpinteria beach rentals (*Carpinteria Valley Chamber of Commerce 805-684-5479 or 800-563-6900. www.carpchamber.org. $$$*) By the week or month.

Moon's Nest Inn (*210 E. Matilija St., Ojai.*

805-646-6635. www.moonsnestinn.com. $-$$*) Historic downtown bed-and-breakfast inn with seven rooms; arty and antique furnishings.

Ojai Valley Inn & Spa (*905 Country Club Rd., Ojai. 805-646-5511 or 888-772-6524. www.ojairesort.com. $$$*) Beautiful 210-room inn with views, championship golf course, top spa. See p. 144.

Prufrock's (*600 Linden Ave., Carpinteria. 805-566-9696 or 877-837-6257. www .prufrocks.com. $-$$$*) Carpinteria's only bed-and-breakfast inn, occupying a circa 1904 bungalow a few blocks from the beach. Seven rooms.

Theodore Woolsey House (*1484 E. Ojai Ave., Ojai. 805-646-9779. www.theodorewoolsey house.com. $-$$*) Bed-and-breakfast in historic stone-and-clapboard house; five rooms, one cottage.

DINING

Bonnie Lu's (*328 E. Ojai Ave., Ojai. 805-646-0207. Closed Wed. $*) Homespun café serving "comfort food" breakfast and lunch; town's friendliest waitresses.

Cajun Kitchen (*865 Linden Ave., Carpinteria. 805-684-6010. $*) Popular for breakfast and Cajun dishes such as red beans and rice, jambalaya, and gumbo.

The Palms (*701 Linden Ave., Carpinteria. 805-684-3811. $-$$*) Local favorite for broil-your-own steaks; seafood.

Pisacali Grill (*585 W. El Roblar Dr., Ojai. 805-640-3726. Closed Mon. $$*) Sophisticated "Italiafornia" cuisine at down-home prices.

The Ranch House (*S. Lomita Ave., Ojai. 805-646-2360. Closed Mon.-Tues. $$$*) Peaceful garden setting, dishes with masterful use of homegrown herbs; world-class wine list.

Surf Dog (*jct. of Bailard and Carpinteria Aves. Carpinteria. $*) The best hot dog stand in town. See p. 144.

Suzanne's Cuisine (*502 W. Ojai Ave., Ojai. 805-640-1961. Closed Tues. $$$*) Fine contemporary European dishes; indoor and garden dining.

Zooker's (*5404 Casitas Pass Rd., Carpinteria. 805-684-8893. $$$*) Hearty, healthy California cuisine.

See-worthy Sights by the Seashore

Long Beach & Santa Catalina Island

ON THIS WEEKEND GETAWAY there's water, water, everywhere! Start in seaside Long Beach, visiting the fifth largest aquarium in the United States and spending the night aboard the 1930s ocean liner *Queen Mary*. Then it's off to Santa Catalina ("the island of romance"), whose whitewashed little port of Avalon looks more like southern France than southern California.

Long Beach

With indisputable logic, Long Beach took its name from the 5.5 miles of sand that stretch along its shore. But this is no laid-back beach town: It has 450,000 people, the most active container port on the West Coast, and a booming shoreline redevelopment area.

At the hub of the new waterfront, the **Aquarium of the Pacific** *(100 Aquarium Way. 562-590-3100. www.aquari umofpacific.org. Adm. fee)* displays 12,000 deni- zens of the world's largest body of water, all under a roof designed to resemble ocean waves. The sea creatures come mostly from three regions of the Pacific Ocean: southern California/Baja (sea tur- tles, rays you can pet, garden eels that anchor themselves tail first in the sand and look like Dr. Seuss drawings); the northern Pacific (playful sea otters, giant Japanese spider crabs); and the tropi- cal Pacific (fish in Day-Glo colors).

In the afternoon stroll or ride a bike along the **Shoreline Path** *(Shoreline Village shopping area S to Belmont Shore)*. Or indulge in a **Gon- dola Getaway** *(5437 E. Ocean Blvd. 562-433-9595. www.gondolagetawayinc.com. Fare)*, reclining in an authentic Venetian craft as it glides around Naples Island, where some of the streets are full of water and lined with million-dollar houses. (The canals were built by early 20th- century developers to evoke Venice, Italy.) As evening falls, your gondolier serenades you with "O Sole Mio" and streetlights twinkle on the water. Romantic, indeed: It is no wonder that so many

---

NOT TO BE MISSED

● Colorful lorikeets at the aquarium ● Small crabs scuttling around Avalon's seawall ● Fourth of July fireworks above Avalon Bay ● A sunset kayaking trip with an astronomer at Descanso Beach to see stars and planets

marriage proposals take place aboard these "love boats."

For an overnight stay that's nautical but nice, try the city's floating hotel—the legendary **Queen Mary** (see Travelwise) at the end of I-710 on Queens Highway. Permanently docked in Long Beach, the luxury liner was launched in 1936; it made 1,001 Atlantic crossings and even served as a World War II troop carrier (painted camouflage gray to deceive the enemy). Some staterooms are wood paneled and some have art deco designs.

Tour *(fee for nonguests)* the 1,019.5-foot-long ship, which has 12 decks and a maze of corridors. See the engine room's brass gauges and 40,000-horsepower steam turbines. (The vessel could travel only 13 feet on a gallon of fuel.) The Queen's Salon will transport you back to an elegant era when passengers such as Fred Astaire, the Duke and Duchess of Windsor, and Greta Garbo tinkled the ice in their cocktail glasses. A "Ghosts and Legends" tour leads to spots of reported supernatural doings—from voices heard in unused rooms to wet footprints found near the indoor pool, which has long been empty.

Santa Catalina Island

Boats leave for **Santa Catalina,** one of the largest Santa Barbara Channel Islands, from a dock near the *Queen Mary.* As you cross, playful dolphins may surf in your boat's wake. Soon the island's tawny mountains appear ahead, and the sky shines with a clear, crystalline light far different from the murky brown smog of the mainland. The boat docks at **Avalon,** a vest-pocket port of call (just over 2 square miles) where white sailboats reflect on azure water. Buildings and fountains along the waterfront are decorated with ceramic tiles of carnival colors, adding a wacky note of eccentricity to the town.

Catalina seems a world away from the everyday, especially around the water. The ocean is clear and calm on the island's leeward side, making Avalon a magnet for sailors, snorkelers, scuba divers, and fishermen. Even landlubbers enjoy taking a ride in a **glass-bottom boat** or a **semi-submersible,** a submarinelike craft whose below-the-waterline windows look out on undersea kelp gardens and vivid orange garibaldi (California's state marine fish), eels with needle teeth, and other sea creatures.

For big adventure, take a seat inside the watertight plastic bubble of a two-person submarine. Your pilot sits behind you in the water, breathing through an air mask, as he guides the sub as far as 40 feet down. In the evening, **flying fish cruises** go in search of unusual fish whose transparent fins act as wings to carry them as far as 50 feet across the water. Flying fish may sail right over the boat—or even land in your lap.

For a self-propelled outing, try kayaking, the island's fastest growing sport. You'll paddle through a floating world of kelp beds—the home of orange-and-black California sheephead, calico bass, and leopard sharks. In the distance you may spy gray whales passing along the California coast on their twice-yearly migrations. Gulls wheel above you, while comical pelicans dive-bomb for fish, hitting the water with a splash.

Check out the island's unspoiled west end by taking a bus to **Two Harbors** *(310-510-4205. www.catalina.com/twoharbors)*, an isthmus where the island narrows to just half a mile wide. You may recognize the coves here from classic films such as *Mutiny on the Bounty* and *Treasure Island*. Divers and yachties congregate around the outdoor patio bar at the **Harbor Reef Restaurant** (see Travelwise) for music, dancing, and a specialty called "buffalo milk," made with vodka, crème de cacao, crème de banane, milk, and whipped cream.

Two Harbors is a popular spot for scuba diving, as are other coves along the island's lee side. With visibility up to 80 feet, and underwater cliffs and caves to explore, the island ranks as one of North America's top dive destinations.

Right in Avalon you can dive at the **Avalon Underwater Dive Park,** next to the famous round **Casino** (a 1929 landmark built for dancing, not gambling). Marine plants range from electric green eel grass to red coral algae. Undulating forests of giant bladder kelp show off one of the world's fastest growing plants. Wrecks and artificial reefs attract plenty of sea life.

If you don't dive, try snorkeling at **Lover's Cove** in Avalon, an underwater preserve whose friendly fish appreciate it if you feed

Sailing the waters off Santa Catalina

them frozen peas. If you'd like to see the island's coves at water level, rent a paddleboard or zip around on a Jet Ski. For fishing, rent a boat on the green Pleasure Pier or board a charter boat heading out to deep water in pursuit of marlin and yellowtail.

In fact, if you like ocean activities, there's one terrific thing about an island—there's water, water, everywhere.

—Jerry Camarillo Dunn, Jr.

Travelwise

GETTING THERE
Long Beach is 25 miles south of Los Angeles via I-110. Santa Catalina Island is a one-hour boat trip from Long Beach *(Catalina Express 310-519-1212 or 800-805-9201).*

GENERAL INFORMATION
Contact the **Long Beach Area Convention & Visitors Bureau** *(1 World Trade Center, 3rd Fl., Long Beach, CA 90831. 562-436-3645 or 800-452-7829. www.visitlongbeach.com)* or the **Catalina Island Chamber of Commerce & Visitors Bureau** *(P.O. Box 217, Avalon, CA 90704. 310-510-1520. www.catalina.com).*

SEASONS
Sunny and pleasant year-round. Avalon is crowded on holidays and summer weekends.

ANNUAL EVENTS
International Sea Festival *(Aug., Long Beach. 562-570-8920)* Aquatic events, sand sculpture and volleyball competitions.

LODGING
Dockside Boat & Bed *(316 E. Shoreline Dr.,* Long Beach. 562-436-3111 or 800-436-2574. www.boatandbed.com. $$$) Stay on a private yacht near downtown.

Hotel Metropole *(Avalon, Catalina. 310-510-1884 or 800-300-8528. www.hotel-metro pole.com. $$-$$$)* Forty-eight spacious rooms on the bayfront; views, balconies.

Inn on Mt. Ada *(Avalon, Catalina. 310-510-2030. www.catalina.com/mtada. $$$)* Hilltop 1921 Georgian mansion; jaw-dropping views —and prices.

Queen Mary *(Queens Hwy., Long Beach. 562-435-3511 or 800-437-2934. www.queen mary.com. $$-$$$)* Luxurious staterooms aboard historic liner. See p. 148.

Zane Grey Pueblo *(Avalon, Catalina. 310-510-0966 or 800-378-3256. www.zanegrey hotel.com. $-$$)* "Hopi Pueblo" home of the Western novelist; 16 rooms, original furnishings, casual-to-funky decor, swimming pool.

DINING
Antonio's Pizzeria & Cabaret *(230 Crescent Ave., Catalina. 310-510-0008. $$)* Bay views, some outdoor tables; breakfast, pasta.

Avalon Seafood and Fish Market (Rosie's) *(Pleasure Pier. 310-510-0197. $)* Venerable spot for breakfast, burgers, fish-and-chips.

Descanso Beach Club *(Descanso Beach, Catalina. 310-510-7410. $-$$)* Beachside bar and grill, weekend barbecues.

Harbor Reef Restaurant *(Two Harbors, Catalina. 310-510-4233. $$$)* See p. 149.

Parkers' Lighthouse *(435 Shoreline Village Dr., Long Beach 562-432-6500. $$$)* Seafood served at a working lighthouse.

Ristorante Villa Portafino *(101 Crescent Ave., Catalina. 310-510-0508. $$$)* Fine regional Italian cuisine on bayfront street.

California Dreamin'
San Diego beach towns

ROLL THE WINDOWS DOWN, turn the radio up, and cruise to sunny towns out of a Beach Boys song. Start with Coronado's wide beach, then breeze northward through Mission and Pacific Beaches, La Jolla, and Torrey Pines State Reserve to Del Mar, with its racetrack and beaches. It's "Good Vibrations" all the way.

Coronado, Mission Beach, & La Jolla

Across the bay from San Diego, **Coronado's** sparkling white beach is crowned with the red-roofed turrets of the 1888 **Hotel Del Coronado** (see Travelwise). The white-shingled Victorian inspired L. Frank Baum's Emerald City of Oz. (Baum wrote several Oz books here and is credited with designing the Crown Room's chandeliers.) The wood-paneled lobby has welcomed royalty from Europe and Hollywood alike, including the stars of the 1959 comedy *Some Like It Hot.*

Farther north at **Mission Beach,** ride the 1925 wooden roller coaster at **Belmont Park,** or pedal a bike up the **Mission Beach Boardwalk,** checking out the beach scene. It's 2 miles to **Pacific Beach,** a hub for the young, hip, and surf-inclined, who get stoked at **Tourmaline Surfing Park** *(Tourmaline St. at La Jolla Blvd.).* Head north to **Windansea Beach** *(at Nautilus St.),* a legendary reef break where journalist Tom Wolfe met *The Pump House Gang*—surfers living the Endless Summer. Try to decipher their language: "Hey, dude! You fully torqued out that wave!"

La Jolla (lah-HOY-ah) brings to mind the French Riviera, with a pink hotel and a sea that glimmers like a mirror. In this town of old money and new glitz, women accessorize their sports clothes with diamonds. (Many believe La Jolla is a corruption of *la joya,* Spanish for "jewel.") Around Prospect Street and Girard Avenue, shops sell expensive, shiny things, and there are good galleries. Artsy La Jolla also boasts the **Museum of Contemporary Art, San Diego** *(700 Prospect St. 858-454-3541. www.mcasandiego.org. Closed Wed.; adm. fee),* which exhibits post-1950 minimalist, conceptual, and installation pieces.

Stroll to **La Jolla Cove** to watch the sea lions or snorkel among kelp

---

NOT TO BE MISSED

● Swimming at Silver Strand Beach, south of Coronado ● Exploring La Jolla's sea caves by kayak ● Eating your way from La Jolla to Del Mar, where local wealth means great restaurants

Crystal Pier at sunset, Pacific Beach

forests in an underwater park. Try tide-pooling at the cove or **Big Rock** *(off Camino de la Costa bet. Cortez Pl. and Via del Norte)*. You might spy tiny periwinkle shells or green anemones with tentacles waving in the water. **Ellen Browning Scripps Park** surrounding La Jolla Cove is popular for picnics and sunset-watching. Just north, descend into **Sunny Jim Cave** *(enter through La Jolla Cave Store, 1325 Coast Blvd. 858-459-0746. Adm. fee)*, a grotto with surging waves.

North of La Jolla

When locals hit the beach, they pick **La Jolla Shores** *(N of village, along Camino del Oro)* for its sloping white sand and jade waves. To view the Pacific from another perspective, visit nearby **Birch Aquarium at Scripps** *(2300 Expedition Way. 858-534-3474. www.aquarium .ucsd.edu. Adm. fee)*, where leopard sharks roam a kelp forest and tiny white jellies drift in their darkened tank like glowing moons.

As you drive to **Torrey Pines Gliderport** *(2800 Torrey Pines Scenic Dr. 858-452-9858. www.flytorrey.com)*, work up the nerve to take a paraglider flight. Harnessed with a pilot under a nylon "wing," you step off a bluff and catch the steady breeze like a gull. Below lies **Black's Beach,** where surfers ride huge winter waves and sunbathers consider clothing to be, well, optional.

Drive on to **Torrey Pines State Reserve** *(N. Torrey Pines Rd. 858-755-2063. www.torreypine.org. Adm. fee)*, a 1,750-acre preserve for the nation's rarest pine trees. Admire their wind-sculptured forms as you bike up the steep road, hike the cliffs, wander miles of unspoiled beach, or simply breathe in the aromas of salt spray and sage.

Ahead lies unhurried, glamorous **Del Mar,** famous for the **Del**

Mar Race Track *(2260 Jimmy Durante Blvd. 858-755-1141. www.del
marracing.com. Open July–mid-Sept.; adm. fee).* Bing Crosby and his
Hollywood pals established this Thoroughbred track in the 1930s.

The streets from 15th to 29th all lead to sand and sea, so join the
volleyball players, surfers, and swimmers. Head for the bluffs at 15th
Street around sunset for nature's fireworks show. It's the perfect way
to end your surfin' safari.   *—Jerry Camarillo Dunn, Jr.*

Travelwise

GETTING THERE
Del Mar, the town farthest north, is about 15
miles from San Diego via coastal roads or I-5.

GENERAL INFORMATION
Contact the **Del Mar Regional Chamber of
Commerce** *(1104 Camino del Mar, Del Mar,
CA 92014. 858-755-4844. www.delmar
chamber.org)* or the **La Jolla Town Council**
*(7734 Herschel Ave., Ste. F, La Jolla, CA
92037. 858-454-1444. www.lajollatc.org).*

SEASONS
The coast is pleasant year-round.

LODGING
Bed & Breakfast Inn at La Jolla *(7753 Draper
Ave., La Jolla. 858-456-2066 or 800-582-
2466. $$-$$$)* 1913 Cubist style inn designed
by architect Irving Gill; 15 rooms, country
antiques, gardens, near art museum.

Crystal Pier Hotel *(4500 Ocean Blvd., Pacific
Beach. 858-483-6983 or 800-748-5894. $$$)*
Cottage motel on pier; 29 rooms.

Hotel Del Coronado *(1500 Orange Ave.,
Coronado. 619-435-6611 or 800-468-3533.
$$$)* 688 rooms, beach, pool, fine dining.
See p. 151.

La Jolla Cove Suites *(1155 Coast Blvd., La
Jolla. 858-459-2621 or 888-525-6552. $$-
$$$)* Centrally located; 90 rooms with views.

L'Auberge Del Mar Resort & Spa *(1540
Camino Del Mar., Del Mar. 858-259-1515 or
800-553-1336. $$$)* Partial coastal views,
fireplaces, pools, spa.

DINING
Brockton Villa *(1235 Coast Blvd., La Jolla.
858-454-7393. $$-$$$)* Café in 1890s beach
cottage; popular breakfasts.

Café Japengo *(8960 University Center Ln., La
Jolla. 858-450-3355. $$$)* Contemporary

Japanese, Pacific Rim fusion; sushi bar.

Epazote *(1555 Camino Del Mar, Del Mar.
858-259-9966. $$)* Creative variations on
southwestern cooking, stylish crowd.

George's at the Cove *(1250 Prospect St., La
Jolla. 858-454-4244. $$$)* Splurge spot for
seafood, contemporary American dishes.

Il Fornaio *(1555 Camino Del Mar, Del Mar.
858-755-8876. $$$)* Northern Italian fare.

Faces of the Desert
San Diego's glorious
& inspiring backcountry

THE LANDSCAPE EXTENDING FROM San Diego's backcountry northward to Palm Springs may look as dry and dusty as a mummy, but this guise conceals various paradoxical personalities. Although Anza-Borrego Desert State Park appears gritty and stone-faced, it tenderly shelters many animals and plants. The oddly humanlike namesake of Joshua Tree National Park lends the desert unexpected personality. The lush playground of the Palm Springs region boasts not only irrigated golf courses and thousands of swimming pools but also a mysterious, sphinxlike desert landscape.

Anza-Borrego Desert State Park

Anza-Borrego *(760-767-4205. www.anzaborrego.statepark.org. Adm. fee)* is nearly as big as Rhode Island. Out here the lucid sky makes seeing into a new exploration. Every glistening grain of sand, every twig on a creosote bush stands out in the intense light. The world seems hyperreal.

- Sipping a date shake in the Coachella Valley
- Anza-Borrego abloom with prickly poppies and purple beavertail cactus flowers
- Inhaling the smoky scent of creosote bushes after a rain—the "smell of the desert"

Before exploring the park, fuel up your car (and yourself) in **Borrego Springs** *(Chamber of Commerce 760-767-5555 or 800-559-5524. www .borregosprings.com)*, a burg that's a balm for harried urbanites because it's the opposite of where they live: not noisy, crowded, or smoggy.

Then go to the **visitor center** *(200 Palm Canyon Dr., W of Cty. Rd. S22. Daily Oct.-May, weekends and holidays June-Sept.)*. That is, if you can find it: The facility is built underground for shelter from the desert heat, like a kangaroo rat's burrow. Exhibits cast their light backward through the tunnel of geologic time, revealing that 11 million years ago the region lay beneath an inland sea whose ancient floor now yields fossilized oysters. Later, it was a savanna roamed by saber-toothed tigers.

The desert appeared only yesterday on the geological calendar. You'll get a good introduction at nearby **Borrego Palm Canyon** *(W end of Borrego Palm Canyon Campground)*, an oasis of California

Camping at Indian Cove, Joshua Tree National Park

fan palms, which can grow 75 feet tall, weigh three tons, and live for 90 years. The canyon is also home to some of the park's 60 species of mammals, 225 birds, and 60 different reptiles and amphibians. Western yellow bats roost under the dead palm fronds that form protective skirts around the trees. Endangered desert bighorn sheep frequent the canyon, too—but you'll need luck to spy them, since they have undoubtedly already spotted *you.*

To further immerse yourself in the park, just choose your route. **Erosion Road** *(Cty. Rd. S22 E)* leads to viewpoints over geological features such as an alluvial fan—a semicircle of rocks and sand that rain has washed out of a canyon mouth. At the **Borrego Badlands** *(Font's Point Rd.)* ragged gullies and ridges were cut by storms and tinted pink, green, and yellow by chemical deposits. The sunset view is worth the trip.

Another route out of Borrego Springs *(Cty. Rd. S3 S to Calif. 78 W)* leads to two nature trails. On the 1-mile **Cactus Loop Trail** you'll see the barrel cactus, whose accordion pleats can expand after a rainfall until the plant is mostly water. Along the half-mile **Narrows**

Earth Trail, you can touch granitic rocks 100 million years old and see the ominous crack of a fault line.

For human rather than natural history, the **Southern Emigrant Trail** *(Cty. Rd. S2 S, off Calif. 78)* parallels a route used by explorers, missionaries, soldiers, sourdoughs, and settlers in the 1800s. A side trip to **Blair Valley** *(turnoff past Milepost 22)* visits the **Butterfield Overland Mail Route Historical Monument.** At steep Foot and Walker Pass, stagecoach passengers often had to get out and push their ungainly conveyance uphill. The nearby 2-mile **Pictograph Trail** leads to Native American rock art, now faded with time.

Back on County Road S2, the **Box Canyon Historical Monument** marks the spot where, in 1847, Mormon soldiers hacked away rock so their wagons could bypass a dead-end canyon. You can still discern this first wagon road into southern California.

Weary from exploring? Bunk overnight at **La Casa del Zorro Desert Resort** (see Travelwise), a classic luxury oasis where you'll find whitewashed casitas, spa facilities, and attentive hospitality.

Joshua Tree National Park

To learn to recognize two faces of the desert, head north to Joshua Tree National Park *(S entrance off I-10 near Chiriaco Summit; N entrances off Calif. 62 near Joshua Tree and Twentynine Palms. 760-367-5500. www.nps.gov/jotr. Adm. fee).* Here two deserts meld: The Colorado Desert (part of the larger Sonoran Desert) lies below 3,000 feet in the park's eastern half and is recognizable by its spiderlike ocotillos. To the west, the higher, slightly cooler Mojave Desert is characterized by Joshua trees.

These twisted, prickly trees—actually yuccas with dagger-shaped leaves—stand with their branching arms upraised, which explains why 19th-century Mormon pioneers named them after the heaven-supplicating prophet Joshua. Native Americans used fiber from the tree's tough leaves to make sandals. Later, cattle ranchers fenced corrals with their trunks and limbs. The park's largest Joshua tree, found in the Queen Valley forest, stands 40 feet high and is about three centuries old.

You'll enter the park from the south. **Cottonwood Spring** *(5 miles from entrance)* boasts many California fan palms, and there's a visitor center nearby. Take Pinto Basin Road north to the **Cholla Cactus Garden** to see teddy bear cactuses, whose spines may look fuzzy but are definitely sharp. Beyond eroded Arch Rock, the road crosses into the high desert. Turn west on Park Boulevard, soon passing some peculiar but natural granite sculptures: **Split Rock, Skull Rock,** and **Jumbo Rocks** (domes, balanced rocks, towers). Farther along, the 18-mile **Geology Tour Road** *(unpaved, 4WD recommended)* showcases desert washes, the remnant of a basalt volcano, and other geologic formations.

Continue to the turnoff for a side trip to **Keys View,** which encompasses 11,500-foot-high San Gorgonio Mountain and the infamous San Andreas Fault. Ahead on the main road lies the **Hidden Valley Nature Trail,** a 1-mile loop through a rock-ringed pocket valley dotted with desert shrubs and cactuses, where 19th-century rustlers used to hide horses.

Driving north, you leave the park near the town of Joshua Tree. Now head to the Palm Springs area to spend the night.

Palm Springs

In the Palm Springs resort area, winter temperatures stay in the 70s and statistics tell a tale of leisure: more than 100 golf courses, 600 tennis courts, and 30,000 swimming pools. Still, if all the green fairways and irrigated flowerbeds were to wither tomorrow, you feel that the desert's stony mountains and endless sand would endure forever.

For a stunning overview, go to the north edge of Palm Springs where the slowly rotating cars of the **Palm Springs Aerial Tramway** *(1 Tramway Rd. 760-325-1449 or 888-515-8726. www.pstramway.com. Adm. fee)* make a vertical climb of more than a mile from the desert floor up the side of Mount San Jacinto, from the haunt of rattlesnakes to the realm of deer. At the top explore the 13,000-acre **Mount San Jacinto State Park** *(760-323-3107. www.sanjac.statepark.org).* Hike a portion of its 54-mile trial network, or in winter go cross-country skiing. Eat lunch at Mountain Station, where the view takes in wooded peaks, the Coachella Valley, and the Salton Sea shining 40 miles to the east.

Adjacent to downtown Palm Springs, **Tahquitz Canyon Visitor Center** *(500 W. Mesquite Ave. 760-416-7044 or 800-790-3398. www .tahquitzcanyon.com. Adm. fee, guided tours only)* opens up a hidden world. A waterfall spills 60 feet into a pool edged with sycamore trees. Mortar holes for grinding seeds, worn into solid rock, are the legacy of early Cahuilla Indians, to whom the canyon was sacred. According to legend, the tribe's first shaman, Tah-kwish, who was banished for abusing his powers, still lives in the canyon, stealing people's souls and living on them. The legend is apparently alive and well: Some tribe members won't set foot here.

Just south of downtown lie three more **Indian Canyons** *(end of S. Palm Canyon Dr. 760-325-3400 or 800-790-3398. www.indian-canyons.com. Adm. fee).* Walking through this ancestral territory of the Cahuilla, imagine their stream-watered crops of melons, squash, and corn. Look for rock art in **Andreas Canyon;** admire a grove of California fan palms in **Palm Canyon;** and perhaps spy wild horses in less visited **Murray Canyon.**

You've just gazed at three more faces of the desert—a personality whose paradoxes, depth, and timeless beauty emerge only with study and patience.   *—Jerry Camarillo Dunn, Jr.*

Travelwise

GETTING THERE

Anza-Borrego SP is a two-hour drive east from San Diego via I-8, Calif. 79, and Calif. 78. Palm Springs is 2.5 hours from San Diego via I-15, I-215, I-10, and Calif. 111. Joshua Tree NP is east of Palm Springs via I-10 or Calif. 62.

GENERAL INFORMATION

Contact the **Palm Springs Desert Resorts Convention & Visitors Authority** (69-930 Hwy. 111, Ste. 201, Rancho Mirage, CA 92270. 760-770-9000 or 800-967-3767. www.PalmSpringsUSA.com).

SEASONS

Temperatures are pleasant in winter and hot in the summer. Best time to visit: Oct.-May.

ANNUAL EVENT

Peg Leg Liar's Contest (early April, Anza-Borrego Desert SP. 760-767-5555) Contestants tell whoppers around a campfire.

MORE THINGS TO SEE & DO

Desert Queen Ranch (Joshua Tree NP. 760-367-5555. Closed June-Sept.; adm. fee) Colorful prospector's family ranch.

Living Desert Zoo and Gardens (47-900 Portola Ave., Palm Desert. 760-346-5694. www.livingdesert.org. Adm. fee) Gardens, 150 species of the world's desert animals.

Wildflower viewing (Anza-Borrego Desert SP. 760-767-4684. Late Feb.–April) Desert flowers in often spectacular bloom.

LODGING

Borrego Valley Inn (405 Palm Canyon Dr., Borrego Springs. 800-333-5810. www.borregovalleyinn.com. $$) Bed-and-breakfast with 14 rooms, private patios, desert views.

Joshua Tree Inn (61259 Twentynine Palms Hwy., Joshua Tree. 760-366-1188 or 800-366-1444. www.joshuatreeinn.com. $-$$$) Hacienda-style rooms, cottages; pool.

La Casa del Zorro Desert Resort (3845 Yaqui Pass Rd., Borrego Springs. 760-767-5323 or 800-824-1884. www.lacasadelzorro.com. $$$) Casually elegant 77-room resort with pool, tennis courts, and spa. See p. 156.

La Quinta Resort & Club (49-499 Eisenhower Dr., La Quinta. 760-564-4111 or 800-598-3828. www.laquintaresort.com. $$$) Vast (800 rooms), upscale golf resort in the foothills.

Palm Canyon Resort (221 Palm Canyon Dr., Borrego Springs. 760-767-5341 or 800-242-0044. www.pcresort.com. $$) Frontier-style complex; 60 rooms, pool, fitness center.

29 Palms Inn (73950 Inn Ave., Twentynine Palms. 760-367-3505. www.29palmsinn .com. $$-$$$) Twenty spare, pleasant cabins of adobe or wood, fireplaces, pool.

Two Bunch Palms (67425 Two Bunch Palms Trail, Desert Hot Springs. 760-329-8791 or 800-472-4334. www.twobunchpalms.com. $$-$$$) Retro-bohemian spa and Hollywood hideaway; 45 rooms.

The Willows Historic Palm Springs Inn (412 W. Tahquitz Canyon Way, Palm Springs. 760-320-0771 or 800-966-9597. www.thewillowspalmsprings.com. $$$) Eight-room 1927 villa on hillside; antiques, pool, fine dining.

DINING

La Casa del Zorro Desert Resort (3845 Yaqui Pass Rd., Borrego Springs. 760-767-5323 or 800-824-1884. $$$) Relaxed breakfasts and gourmet dinners; old California atmosphere.

Louise's Pantry (44491 Town Center Way, Palm Desert. 760-346-9320. Breakfast and lunch only) Popular breakfasts, burgers, comfort-food lunches.

Miami

Miami Nice 160

The Middle Keys 165

Captiva Audience 169

Flying fish in Florida's Middle Keys

Miami Nice

A deco(rous) weekend for devotees of design

LOOK BEYOND THE STANDARD-ISSUE skyscrapers of downtown Miami and you'll find one of the country's richest collections of 20th-century buildings. The weekend outlined here—featuring art deco hotels, Mediterranean Revival fantasies, and an opulent Italian Renaissance villa—is for fans of fun architecture. As eye-popping now as they were in the 1920s, these vibrant buildings can be enjoyed inside and out. Come take a walk through subtropical architecture suited to sea breezes, warm sun, and moonlit nights.

Miami Beach

Pink stucco, flamingos, and neon went from kitsch to cool in the 1980s, transforming the formerly run-down **South Beach** area into paradise reclaimed. It also became the capital of all things deco— think 1920s glass brick, bas-relief, and vertical bands—but Miami added tropical motifs to create its own style. The country's largest deco district—the square mile of Miami Beach circumscribed by the Atlantic, Lenox Avenue, Sixth Street, and Dade Boulevard—encompasses more than 800 art deco and Mediterranean Revival structures.

Start with a visit to the **Art Deco Welcome Center** *(1001 Ocean Dr. 305-531-3484),* then strike out on a guided walk *(Thurs. and Sat.; fee)* or pick up a map and chart your own course. The center is located in the 1954 Oceanfront Auditorium; the adjoining building at the rear is the 1934 **Beach Patrol Station,** whose portholes and other ocean-liner stylings typified the "streamline moderne" look of the 1930s (which in turn grew out of deco and its rectilinear designs). Cafés line the main strip for deco, **Ocean Drive;** have a seat and take in the passing parade of the beautiful and the strange.

As you stroll Ocean Drive, scan the small hotels for such deco details as glass bricks, etched glass, and nautical motifs. Upon reaching its heyday in the late 1920s, the deco style was done in by the Depression and the ensuing construction slowdown in South Florida.

NOT TO BE MISSED

- **Ocean Drive on South Beach** ● **Vizcaya in late afternoon light** ● **Venetian Pool**
- **Views of Biscayne Bay and city skyline from Venetian Causeway**

Facades & fronds: Art deco hotels and palms on Ocean Drive, Miami Beach

Gradually, however, builders began picking up where they had left off. Catercorner from the auditorium, for example, you'll notice that the bold blue-and-yellow **Breakwater Hotel** boasts a neon sign and terrazzo floors; the building did not go up until 1939.

Three blocks west at Tenth Street and Washington Avenue, the **Wolfsonian Florida International University** *(1001 Washington Ave. 305-531-1001. Closed Wed.; adm. fee)* is housed in a Mediterranean-style former warehouse built in 1927 with a terra-cotta facade and a gold-leaf fountain. Miami native Mitchell Wolfson, Jr., drew on his huge collection of decorative arts, paintings, books, and prints to create this research center and museum of art and design. The Wolfsonian museum is the perfect place to learn more about the early 20th-century design aesthetic that produced the buildings outside.

Along Washington Avenue you'll find plenty of chic restaurants, as well as shops, delis, and avant-garde nightclubs.

Back on Ocean Drive, walk north a block to see the 1930 palazzo-style **Casa Casuarina** *(1116 Ocean Dr.),* home to designer Gianni Versace until July 1997, when he was shot to death on its front steps by suspected serial killer Andrew Cunanan. Two blocks north stand four hotels—the **Leslie,** the **Carlyle,** the **Cardozo,** and the **Cavalier**—that started the wave of restorations in South Beach. Singer Gloria Estefan owns the 1939 Cardozo, designed by noted architect Henry Hohauser.

You can do South Beach, including its museums, in a few hours, leaving your afternoon free to spread a towel on the beach and relax.

Coconut Grove

If you base yourself in Miami Beach, the Coconut Grove and Coral Gables enclaves are only 15 minutes away. Architecture fans should reserve at least part of a day for each of these adjoining classy neighborhoods. That will still give you time to bask in the sun.

Miami's oldest settlement, **Coconut Grove,** goes all the way back to the 1870s. The Grove has always attracted an enlightened cross section of society—wealthy industrialists, black Bahamians, hippies, intellectuals. Accordingly, the residential architecture often jumps without warning from simple modern homes to rustic bungalows to urbane mansions.

The oldest house in its original location in Dade County is the **Barnacle State Historic Site** *(3485 Main Hwy. 305-448-9445. Fri.- Mon., guided tour only; adm. fee),* built in 1891 by Ralph Middleton Munroe with lumber salvaged from shipwrecks. The two-story dwelling has a hip roof, cupola, and verandas positioned to funnel breezes through the house.

When it's time for a break, the Grove can be most accommodating. In the heart of town, check out **CocoWalk** *(Grand Ave. and Virginia St.),* a colorful, open-air horseshoe of cafés, bars, and funky boutiques, all harmonized with greenery. Just west of the walk, the **Coconut Grove Farmers' Market** *(Grand Ave. and Margaret St.)* takes place each Saturday from 10:30 a.m. to 5 p.m.

In the afternoon, drive along sparkling Biscayne Bay to **Vizcaya** *(3251 S. Miami Ave. 305-250-9133. www.vizcayamuseum.com. Adm. fee),* a splendid Italian Renaissance-style villa completed in 1916 that is one of the highlights of any trip to Miami. Paris-trained architect F. Burrall Hoffman was 29 years old when he designed this architectural gem for industrialist James Deering.

The building materials of the palatial home—stucco and limestone, the latter quarried from both Cuba and the Miami area—give the place a late 16th-century luster. Among its 34 decorated rooms are a trove of European treasures from the 16th to 19th centuries that Deering acquired on various shopping trips; these tapestries, hand-carved chairs, and rococo musical instruments convey a strong impression of one very sophisticated tractor maker.

Outside, 10 acres of formal gardens blend fountains, pools, ornamental urns, topiary, and other classical elements with native vegetation. The view of Biscayne Bay from the east terrace is unforgettable: A short distance out to sea, Deering erected a great stone barge that acts as a breakwater.

If you're not ready to head back to the beach, you can spend the afternoon wandering the lush side streets of Coconut Grove. Or browse one of its delightfully casual shopping areas, such as the Streets of Mayfair *(305-448-1700)* with its 50 shops and restaurants.

Come nightfall you'll find a number of good restaurants and hip clubs to cap the day.

Coral Gables

As if dreamed into being, **Coral Gables** sprang to life within just five years. One of the nation's first planned communities, it was built during the 1920s Florida land boom. The City Beautiful movement then sweeping the country called for wide, tree-lined avenues, fancy fountains, plazas, and green space galore. Thus did Coral Gables become a fantasy village of tropical pastels, rounded arches, coral-rock loggias, and red-tiled roofs, all set within a hot-house landscape of bougainvilleas, poincianas, hibiscus, and old vine-wrapped banyans.

Though it has mushroomed as a Miami suburb, Coral Gables retains its essential City Beautiful look (developers receive incentives to conform to the Mediterranean Revival style). If you approach on Coral Way from the east, you'll enter the city on its renovated **Miracle Mile**—actually half a mile of shops, bistros, and galleries stretching between Douglas and Le Jeune Roads. Just beyond on the left, look for the 1928 Spanish Renaissance-style **City Hall**.

Continuing west a few blocks brings you to the **Coral Gables Merrick House** *(907 Coral Way. 305-460-5361. Wed. and Sun.; adm. fee)*, a New England-style home built in the early 1900s by the pioneering parents of city founder George Merrick. Their forward-thinking oldest son saw the potential for an aesthetically designed city on his home turf, and his promotional skills made it a reality. He lost his shirt when the real estate boom collapsed, but the city he had dreamed up survived.

If you're too early for the Sunday afternoon tour of Merrick House, a few minutes away beckons the ornate 1926 **Biltmore Hotel** *(1200 Anastasia Ave. 305-445-1926. Tours Sun.)* and its iconic 16-story tower, inspired by the Giralda tower in the Spanish coastal city of Seville. Hollywood stars stayed here in the early days; thanks to restorations in the 1980s and '90s, the hotel has regained its former glory.

In the afternoon, save an hour for a swim in the lavish **Venetian Pool** *(2701 De Soto Blvd. 305-460-5356. www.venetianpool.com. Closed Mon. mid-Aug.–mid-June; adm. fee)*. Designed by Denman Fink (George Merrick's uncle) from an old coral rock quarry, this huge, spring-fed pool is an enchanted lagoon of grottoes, waterfalls, and Venetian-style architecture. Esther Williams and Johnny Weissmuller are just two of the celebrity swimmers who plied these waters in the past. If you're hungry after your swim, hit the snack bar.

Coral Gables has become a favored nightspot for cultural happenings. While South Beach has its glitzy clubs, Coral Gables is the place for poetry readings and live jazz. Just north of the Miracle Mile are several convivial cafés and bars.   *—John M. Thompson*

Travelwise

GETTING THERE

Miami, Miami Beach, Coconut Grove, and Coral Gables are all within a few miles of one another on a well-marked highway system.

GENERAL INFORMATION

Contact the **Greater Miami Convention & Visitors Bureau** (701 Brickell Ave., Ste. 2700, Miami 33131. 305-539-3000 or 800-933-8448. www.tropicoolmiami.com); **Coconut Grove Chamber of Commerce** (2820 McFarlane Rd., Coconut Grove 33133. 305-444-7270, www.coconutgrove.com); or **Coral Gables Chamber of Commerce** (2333 Ponce de Leon Blvd., Ste. 650, Coral Gables 33134. 305-446-1657. www.gableschamber.org).

SEASONS

With daytime highs in the mid-70s, winter is the most comfortable season for a visit. The summer climate is often sweltering, but that's also the time when hotel rates drop 20 to 35 percent. Always pack a hat and sunscreen. Summer thunderstorms are common.

ANNUAL EVENTS

Art Deco Weekend (January. South Beach. 305-672-2014) This celebration of the 1920s and '30s includes a street fair, lectures, a parade, and live entertainment.

Festival Miami (Late September–late October. University of Miami School of Music, Coral Gables. 305-284-4940) International festival of opera, jazz, and chamber music.

Miami-Bahamas Goombay Festival (1st weekend in June. Coconut Grove. 305-567-1399) Celebrate the area's Bahamian heritage with crafts, food, and street music.

LODGING

Biltmore Hotel (1200 Anastasia Ave. 305-445-1926. Tours Sun.) See p. 163.

Delano Hotel (1685 Collins Ave., Miami Beach. 305-672-2000 or 800-555-5001. $$$) A favorite of models and Hollywood types, this 208-room hotel built in 1947 features cool white decor, a rooftop bathhouse, and a swank restaurant.

Hotel Place St. Michel (162 Alcazar Ave., Coral Gables. 305-444-1666 or 800-848-4683. $$-$$$) The 27 rooms of this 1926 boutique hotel overflow with decorative touches, including ceiling fans and fresh flowers. Its restaurant is popular with locals.

Kent Hotel (1131 Collins Ave., Miami Beach. 305-604-5068. $$-$$$) This recently restored but affordable art deco beauty features a tropical garden patio.

Marlin (1200 Collins Ave., Miami Beach. 305-604-5063) Deluxe, all-suite hotel with Caribbean-inspired styling; attracts a celebrity and music-industry crowd.

The Park Central (640 Ocean Dr., Miami Beach. 305-538-1611. $$-$$$) Authentically restored to reflect the 1940s, this classic Hohauser hotel boasts wraparound corner windows and a beachfront location.

Wyndham Grand Bay Hotel (2669 S. Bayshore Dr., Coconut Grove. 305-858-9600. $$$) A 178-unit luxury hotel offering bay views, afternoon tea, and a restaurant.

DINING

Joe's Stone Crab (11 Washington Ave., Miami Beach. 305-673-0365. Mid-Oct.–mid-May) This popular landmark from the early days of South Beach serves reliably good stone crabs and Key lime pie. Expect long lines.

News Cafe (800 Ocean Dr., Miami Beach. 305-538-6397) This bustling 24-hour joint purveys sandwiches, bagels, pâté, and desserts; dine indoors or alfresco.

Norman's (21 Almeria Ave., Coral Gables. 305-446-6767) Diners flock to this restaurant, one of the city's finest, for the New World cuisine—a combination of Caribbean, Latin, Asian, and American influences—prepared by chef Norman Van Aken.

The Middle Keys
Palms, mangroves, crab cakes, & Key lime pie

MORE THAN LANDMARKS on the way to Key West, the Middle Keys are a destination in themselves. The 20-mile stretch from Grassy Key to Bahia Honda Key, known for its fishing and diving, also holds fine sites for delving into the Keys' environmental history. From swimming with dolphins to strolling subtropical hammocks, you'll find plenty of opportunities to explore. And when it's time to kick back, you can hit one of the best beaches in the Keys.

Southwest of Marathon

With long ribbons of bridge and causeway shooting out across breathtaking expanses of turquoise water, the Middle Keys are crucial stepping-stones in the 100-mile stretch from Key Largo to Key West. The audacious highway connecting the island chain started as a railroad in the early 1900s; **Marathon,** situated about halfway down, was named to honor the marathon effort required to complete the project. Now the commercial center of the Middle Keys, Marathon has a permanent resident population of about 10,000, making it the third largest town in the Keys (after Key West in first place and Key Largo in second).

With development eating away more and more of what little land there is in the Keys, places such as **Crane Point Hammock** (*Milepost 50.5, gulfside. 305-743-9100. www.cranepoint.org. Adm. fee*) have become extraordinarily valuable. You can spend the better part of a morning wandering this 63-acre site. Trails wind through palm and hardwood hammocks, into a mangrove forest, and past tidal lagoons. You'll see an osprey nest, golden orb spiders, and a wild bird rescue center that treats injured birds.

Also at Crane Point are two worthwhile museums. The **Museum of Natural History of the Florida Keys** has a simulated coral reef cave, exhibits on local fauna and geology, and a 600-year-old dugout canoe. In the **Children's Museum** you'll find a walk-on replica of a 17th-century pirate galleon, as well as shells and touch tanks. And don't miss one of the oldest houses around—the

NOT TO BE MISSED

- **Views from Seven-Mile Bridge** ● **Walking on Bahia Honda Bridge**
- **Nature trail at Bahia Honda State Park**
- **Deep-sea fishing for marlin and sailfish**

Bahamian-style **George Adderley House,** built in 1903 of tabby (a mixture of water, sand, and crushed shells).

A number of places to the north invite you to stop in for a bite to eat. These include the **Grassy Key Dairy Bar** (see Travelwise), a casual 1959 eatery that serves broiled and grilled fish specials and good homemade bread.

Afterward, drive a bit farther north to the **Dolphin Research Center** *(Mile 59, gulfside. 305-289-1121 or 305-289-0002. www.dolphins .org. Fee for programs, reservations reqd. for some programs).* Whether you take part in a swim-with-dolphins program or simply tour the facility, you'll come away with a renewed appreciation for the beauty and intelligence of marine mammals. More than half of the center's Atlantic bottlenose dolphins and California sea lions were born here.

Southwest of Marathon

Head southwest from Marathon to cross the **Seven-Mile Bridge,** with its stunning views of both the Atlantic Ocean and the Gulf of Mexico. To better appreciate those views, venture out onto the old Seven-Mile Bridge, which runs parallel to the new one; although it is closed to car

Catamaran near Bahia Honda State Park in the Florida Keys

traffic, 2.2 miles of it are open to pedestrians, cyclists, and fishermen.

Just beyond Marathon, you can reach **Pigeon Key** *(Mile 47, ocean-side. 305-289-0025. www.pigeonkey.org. Adm. fee)* by foot or by shuttle. Listed on the National Register of Historic Places, this 5-acre island served as a work camp for the crews that built the Florida East Coast Railway extension to Key West. After a 1935 hurricane destroyed parts of the railway, the railroad bridges were converted to a two-lane highway. As you meander through the museum (inside the former assistant bridge tender's house) and the wood-frame workers' buildings amid dense subtropical foliage, you get an idea of the early history of the Keys; when most of the nation was already settled, this area was still a frontier. From the dock on the north side of the island, you may see barracuda, grunts, snappers, and other fish.

If you're hungry, fresh grouper, shrimp bisque, and award-winning Key lime pie are all on the menu at the **7 Mile Grill** (see Travelwise); you'll find it on the other side of the highway from the entrance to Pigeon Key.

Motor across the Seven-Mile Bridge, slather on the sunscreen, and head for **Bahia Honda State Park** *(Mile 37, oceanside. 305-872-2353.*

Adm. fee). Because it juts into the ocean, the island of Bahia Honda catches more sand-carrying currents than the other Keys; for the same reason, it also boasts one of the best beaches. In addition to sunning and swimming, you can soak up some natural history on the **Silver Palm Nature Trail.** This is the place to look for such exotic flora as Jamaica morning glory and orange-flowering Geiger trees.

A concessionaire rents bikes and kayaks and operates snorkeling tours to the coral reef around **Looe Key.** If you don't have to hurry home, stay overnight in one of the park's rustic cabins or campsites (*reservations recommended*).   —*John M. Thompson*

Travelwise

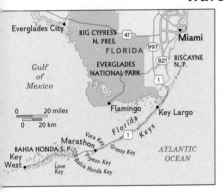

GETTING THERE
Marathon lies approximately 110 miles southwest of Miami via US 1.

GENERAL INFORMATION
Contact the **Marathon Chamber of Commerce** (*12222 Overseas Hwy., Marathon 33050. 305-743-5417 or 800-842-9580. www.floridakeysmarathon.com*).

SEASONS
From December through April, highs average in the mid-70s; in summer and fall the average rises to around 80. Frequent but brief summer thunderstorms bring some respite.

ANNUAL EVENT
Seven-Mile Bridge Run (*April. Marathon*) 1,500 runners compete in this race over the blue-green waters of the Gulf and ocean.

MORE THINGS TO SEE & DO
Marathon has outfitters for almost every sport. You can rent bikes, charter a fishing boat, go on a diving trip, or play nine holes of golf

(*800-842-9580*). The public **Sombrero Beach** (*Mile 50, oceanside*) has a grassy park with picnic shelters.

LODGING
Coral Lagoon Resort (*Mile 53.5, oceanside. 305-289-0121. www.corallagoonresort.com. $$*) Each cottage at this laid-back facility has a private deck and hammock. Snorkeling and fishing trips can be arranged.

Hawk's Cay Resort (*Mile 61, oceanside. 305-743-7000 or 800-432-2242. www.hawkscay.com. $$-$$$*) Restaurants, saltwater lagoon and pool, and activities including ecology tours and a Dolphin Discovery program.

Seascape Ocean Resort (*Mile 50.5, oceanside. 305-743-6455 or 800-332-7327. $-$$$*) A mellow nine-room retreat with freshwater pool swimming, kayaking, Continental breakfast, and evening wine and hors d'oeuvres.

DINING
Barracuda Grill (*Mile 49.5, gulfside. 305-743-3314. Dinner only; closed Sun. $$$*) Fresh fish and seafood specials, as well as beef, lamb, and a tasty Key lime cheesecake.

Grassy Key Dairy Bar (*Mile 58.5, oceanside. 305-743-3816. Closed Sun.-Mon.*) See p. 166.

Hurricane Grill (*Mile 49.5, gulfside. 305-743-2220. $$*) A little less expensive than the adjacent Barracuda, this spot features seafood, chicken, steaks, and live music.

Quay Marathon (*Mile 54, gulfside. 305-289-1810. $$-$$$*) Sample prime rib, swordfish, or alligator while savoring views of the Gulf.

7 Mile Grill (*Mile 47.5, gulfside. 305-743-4481*) See p. 167.

Captiva Audience
Back to nature on
Sanibel Island & beyond

FLORIDA'S QUIET SOUTHWEST COAST is the place to get back to the essence of the state. Among the lagoons, tidal flats, and mangrove forests of Sanibel and Captiva Islands, the natural world follows the age-old rhythms of sun and tide. Snowy egrets, crocodiles, and dolphins find sanctuary here; billboards, fast food, and stoplights do not. Life moves at the meditative pace of a beachcomber seeking that perfect shell, or a birder zooming in on that rare species.

Sanibel Island

Because **Sanibel Island** is famous for its seashells—more than 400 species of them—start your day with a visit to the **Bailey-Matthews Shell Museum** *(3075 Sanibel-Captiva Rd. 941-395-2233 or 888-679-6450. www.shellmuseum.org. Closed Mon.; adm. fee).* At this comprehensive museum of conchology, you can learn why Sanibel is a sheller's paradise. (The short answer: Its east-west orientation makes it a natural catchment for shells in the north-flowing Gulf Stream.) Exhibits outline the ecology of shells and their role in history and art; nearly a third of the world's 100,000 species are on display.

With bike paths running parallel to most island roadways, the best way to explore Sanibel is by two-wheeler. To rent one, head for nearby Bike Route *(2330 Palm Ridge Rd. 941-472-1955).*

Just west of the shell museum, you'll come to the **Sanibel-Captiva Conservation Foundation's Nature Center** *(3333 Sanibel-Captiva Rd.. 941-472-2329. Closed Sun. mid-Nov.–mid-April, closed Sat.-Sun. rest of year; adm. fee).* The nature center plays a big role in local land conservation, environmental education, and sea turtle research. In it you can learn more about the island's wetlands and native plants, visit a butterfly house, and handle sea creatures in a touch tank. Then stretch your legs on the 4-mile trail system; a 30-foot tower gets you above the forest canopy for views of the Sanibel River.

A bit farther west on Sanibel-Captiva Road, opposite the entrance

---

NOT TO BE MISSED

● "Ding" Darling refuge at dawn
● Shelling at the lighthouse ● Bailey-Matthews Shell Museum ● Lunch at Cabbage Key Inn

to the national wildlife refuge (see below), lies the **Clinic for the Rehabilitation of Wildlife,** or **CROW** *(3883 Sanibel-Captiva Rd. 941-472-3644. Mon.-Fri., one tour a day, call for schedule; donation).* More than 3,000 orphaned and injured creatures are treated here every year.

Now that you know how passionately Sanibel cares about its wildlife, you can heed the call of the wild yourself and hit the beach. Several quiet public beaches beckon with their wide swaths of powdery white sand. **Tarpon Bay Beach** *(S end of Tarpon Bay Rd.)* is centrally located and has plenty of parking. Here you can stretch out and recharge your batteries, or do the "Sanibel stoop" and hunt for shells. Common finds include lightning whelks, calico scallops, and turkey wings. Consider yourself lucky if you find a brown-speckled junonia or a tulip—the former might just get your picture in the newspaper. Shelling is best after a storm and just before low tide. Keep in mind that it's illegal to take a shell with a creature inside, whether it looks alive or not.

Dinner is a good reason to cross the causeway to **Captiva;** it's 3.5 miles to the end. The roads are narrower on this island, and the dense greenery—often veiling tony resorts or houses—makes it feel more confined. Furnished with an umbrella drink and a view of Pine Island Sound or the Gulf, however, you should be enviably content.

"Ding" Darling & more

Get up early—before sunrise, if possible—and head for the **J. N. "Ding" Darling National Wildlife Refuge** *(1 Wildlife Dr. 941-472-1100. Closed Fri.; adm. fee)* on Sanibel. A bicycle is the best way to appreciate the 5-mile **Wildlife Drive,** but a car makes an acceptable alternative as long as you drive slowly and stop frequently. Foot trails branching off the drive beckon you to get closer to nature (which in-

White ibis feeding at sunset, "Ding" Darling National Wildlife Refuge

cludes mosquitoes, so bring repellent). Named for conservationist Jay Norwood "Ding" Darling, the 6,300-acre refuge is home to bustling communities of herons, egrets, spoonbills, ibises, alligators, and more. If you time your visit to coincide with low tide, you'll see scores of waterbirds feeding on the exposed mudflats. By the time the visitor center opens at 9 a.m., you'll be ready to step inside and learn more about what you just saw.

To explore the refuge even further, go to the **Tarpon Bay Recreation Center** *(N end of Tarpon Bay Rd. 941-472-8900)* and sign up for a narrated tram tour or a guided kayak or canoe trek. If that sounds entirely too scripted, you can rent a kayak or canoe and explore the 6 miles of marked trails on your own.

If you got an early start this morning, you'll have time for a cruise to **Cayo Costa State Park** *(Captiva Cruises 941-472-5300. Nov.-May Tues.-Sat. Fee, reservations required)*. This 90-minute cruise takes you up the Intracoastal Waterway to the north tip of Cayo Costa Island, then allows you three hours to explore a wild beach, with dolphins and pelicans as your companions. There are also 5 miles of hiking and biking trails through a maritime forest. Pack a lunch.

For a slightly shorter cruise, book passage to **Cabbage Key** *(Captiva Cruises 941-472-5300. Fee, reservations required)*. This small island harks back to the Florida that was a barefoot paradise for drifters and the well-to-do alike. Have lunch at the 1930s **Cabbage Key Inn** *(941-283-2278)*. Its funky interior is decorated with 30,000 one-dollar bills, many of them signed by celebrities. A 30-foot water tower offers fine views of the sound and other islands, while a short trail penetrates the thickets of mangrove and strangler fig.

If the day's activities leave you energy in the evening, take in a comedy or drama at the **J. Howard Wood Theatre** *(2200 Periwinkle Way. 941-472-0006. www.thewoodtheatre.com. Closed Sun.)*, or check out the revue of light song and dance at the nearby **Old Schoolhouse Theater** *(1905 Periwinkle Way. 941-472-6862)*.

Lighthouse visits & views

Before saying good-bye to the beach, drive to the eastern end of Sanibel Island and park in the lot near the 1884 **Sanibel Lighthouse.** A boardwalk nature trail here investigates the local wetland and beach habitats; the strand itself is known for its exceptionally fine shelling. You can work up an appetite with a brisk stroll—stockpiling those final snapshots and mental images of pelicans planing over glassy breakers—then grab a coffee and a delicious homemade muffin at the **Lighthouse Café** *(362 Periwinkle Way. 941-472-0303)*.

On your way back to Miami, take the **Tamiami Trail** (US 41) to pass through Florida's largest remaining wilderness areas. With a couple of hours to spare you'll get only a glimpse of what's out there, but don't neglect to stop at the **visitor center** of **Big Cypress**

National Preserve *(17 miles E of Ochopee. 941-695-4111. www.nps .gov/bicy)* to take in its film and exhibits. Outside, you can walk a trail past canals where alligators live; to the south extend long views of wet prairies dotted with islands of cypress and pine. Flocks of white herons and ibises are common sights in these parts. The odds of seeing a Florida panther, by contrast, are extremely rare, but it's nice to know a few of the endangered cats may still roam out there.

Cap off the weekend with a stop at the **Shark Valley Visitor Center** *(305-221-8776. www.nps.gov/ever. Adm. fee)* on the north edge of **Everglades National Park.** Trails explore the tropical hardwood hammock and sawgrass marsh; a tram tour leads to an observation tower.　　　　　　　　　　　　　　　　　*—John M. Thompson*

....

Travelwise

GETTING THERE
Sanibel Island lies off Florida's Gulf Coast, 150 miles west of Miami via US 41 and I-75.

GENERAL INFORMATION
Contact the **Lee Island Coast Visitor & Convention Bureau** *(2180 W. 1st St., Fort Myers 33901. 941-338-3500 or 800-237-6444. www.leeislandcoast.com)* or **Sanibel Visitors Center** *(1159 Causeway Rd., Sanibel 33957. 941-472-1080).*

SEASONS
Winters are mild, with highs in the mid-70s; cool breezes and afternoon showers relieve the low 90s of summer. Water temperatures range from 66°F in winter to 87°F in summer.

ANNUAL EVENTS
Christmas Luminary Trail and Open House *(early Dec. 941-472-1080)* Thousands of candles line the streets of Sanibel and Captiva.

CROW's Taste of the Islands *(late April. Gulfside City Park, Sanibel. 941-472-3644)* Samples from area restaurants, waiter competitions, and live entertainment benefit the

Clinic for the Rehabilitation of Wildlife.
Sanibel Shell Fair *(early March, Sanibel Community House. 941-472-2155)* This celebration of the island's gifts from the sea features shell exhibits, rare shells, and shell art.

LODGING
Sanibel's Seaside Inn *(541 E. Gulf Dr. 941-472-1400 or 800-965-7772. $$$)* Quiet, family-oriented property; 32 beachside units and a pool. Shopping and restaurants nearby.

Shalimar Motel *(2823 W. Gulf Dr. 941-472-1353 or 800-995-1242. $$$ weekly)* Small, 33-unit gulfside facility with a pool.

South Seas Resort & Yacht Harbor *(N end Captiva. 941-472-5111 or 800-227-8482. $$$)* Exclusive resort offers golf, tennis, sailing, windsurfing, pools, and restaurants.

DINING
Bubble Room *(15001 Captiva Dr. 941-472-5558. $$$)* Eclectic decor features Christmas lights, Hollywood posters, and memorabilia from the 1930s, '40s, and '50s; generous portions of fresh fish, steak, and desserts.

Cabbage Key Inn *(941-283-2278)* See p. 171.

Jean-Paul's French Corner *(708 Tarpon Bay Rd. 941-472-1493. Dinner only; open seasonally, closed Sun. $$$)* Intimate spot offers snails, onion soup, veal, roast duckling, and chocolate mousse in a casual atmosphere.

Sunshine Café *(Captiva Village Sq., Captiva Dr. 941-472-6200. $$$)* Stylish eatery serving pizzas, salads, light entrées, and desserts.

Minneapolis

Mississippi Meander 174

Confluence of the Black and Mississippi Rivers, south of Trempealeau

Mississippi Meander
River towns & nature enclaves

ONE OF THE WORLD'S GREAT RIVERS, the mighty Mississippi may be at its grandest southeast of the Twin Cities, where it forms the Minnesota-Wisconsin border. It rolls smooth and strong between high, broad shoulders of limestone, occasionally bleeding through a labyrinth of islands, sloughs, and braided channels. Come join the Mississippi on its journey, past fiery autumn foliage and patches of native prairie, backwaters thick with bald eagles and blue herons, and dignified 19th-century river towns that invite you to slow to the pace of the waters rolling by.

Red Wing area
Redbrick buildings, proud and sturdy as the steamboats that once crowded its port, line block after block of **Red Wing,** Minnesota. Perched on the edge of the prairie and a placid bend in the river, Red Wing initially prospered from shipping grain and milling flour; lumbering, pottery, and shoe manufacturing soon followed.

Today tourism ranks as a key industry in this small town, which delights visitors with its buffed historic buildings and generous green spaces that seem to reach out and embrace the riverfront. Pick up a walking-tour brochure of the historic district at the Red Wing Area Chamber of Commerce *(420 Levee St. 651-388-4719),* housed in the 1905 pressed-brick railroad depot.

The Red Wing Shoe Company, one of the town's largest and oldest employers, restored much of Main Street, including the handsome Italianate **St. James Hotel** (see Travelwise *),* once again the city's finest lodging, and the **Riverfront Centre** *(314 Main St.),* an entire block of boxy mercantile buildings, home to shops and the Red Wing Shoe Museum. The fortunes of grain magnate Theodore Sheldon built one of the nation's first municipally owned playhouses, the exquisite **Sheldon Theatre** *(443 W. 3rd St. 651-385-3667),* its ceilings aglow in gold leaf and hand-painted murals. Sheldon's elaborate French Empire home *(805 W. 4th St. Private)* lies in the heart of the residential historic district.

NOT TO BE MISSED

- Listening to bluegrass music on the lawn of Trempealeau Hotel ● The eagle's-eye view from Wyalusing State Park
- Slipping a kayak into the Mississippi's backwaters
- Lock and Dam No. 9

Boathouses, Red Wing, Minnesota

At the west end of town, **Red Wing Stoneware** *(4909 Moundview Dr. 651-388-4610)* and **Red Wing Pottery** *(1920 W. Main St. 651-388-3562)* have revived one of the town's key 19th-century industries. Viewing windows let you watch artisans using traditional methods to throw vintage designs of utilitarian stoneware. The **Pottery Place Mall** *(1997 W. Main St.)* preserves one of the original sprawling brick pottery factories.

South of Red Wing, the Mississippi settles in across a wide basin, its natural flow choked by silt deposited at the mouth of Wisconsin's Chippewa River. The result is 22-mile-long **Lake Pepin.** Cross the river and pick up Wis. 35 to weave south along the Mississippi's curvy northeastern bank. Stop in **Maiden Rock** to browse through a growing array of galleries and antique shops, or follow the "Wildflower You Pick" signs to **Blossom Hill Wildflowers** *(W4084 120th Ave. 715-448-9221)* to create your own bouquets in the company of butterflies and twittering sparrows.

Lovely Lake Pepin was the childhood playground of Laura Ingalls Wilder, who chronicled her pioneer life in *Little House in the Big Woods* and subsequent children's books. Fans will enjoy the **Pepin Historical Museum** *(306 3rd St., Pepin. 715-442-3011. Mid-May–mid-Oct.; donation)* and the reconstructed log cabin at Wilder's **birthplace,** 7 miles northeast of town on County Road CC.

Continue 3 miles south on Wis. 35 to the **Tiffany State Wildlife Area** at the Chippewa's mouth. Bald eagles love to winter in the sloughs and about 20 pairs nest here year-round. To learn more, cross the river at Nelson to visit the **National Eagle Center** *(152 Main St. 651-565-4989. www.eaglecenter.org. Closed Mon.)* in Wabasha, Minnesota. You can have a "nose to beak experience" with two previously injured eagles no longer able to live in the wild. The nearby **Eagle-Watch Observation Deck** at the foot of Pembroke Avenue is open year-round; volunteers are on hand to answer questions on weekends from November through March.

Winona environs

From Wabasha, take US 61 south to Winona. Founded in 1851 by a steamboat captain, Winona quickly capitalized on the surrounding thick hardwood forests. Within a decade, its riverfront buzzed with sawmills, and more than 1,300 riverboats a year crowded its port. Winona flaunted its wealth and sophistication with lavish architecture, much of it detailed with exquisite stained-glass windows. The "Glorious Glass" brochure, available at the Winona Convention & Visitors Bureau *(67 Main St. 507-452-2272 or 800-657-4972)*, directs you to sites such as the 1916 Egyptian revival Winona National Bank, aglow in Tiffany Studios artistry.

At Levee Park *(Main St., at the Mississippi)*, the **Julius C. Wilkie Steamboat Center** *(507-454-1254. Mem. Day–Labor Day Tues.-Sun.; adm. fee)* features steamboat exhibits in a full-size replica steamboat, complete with second-floor Victorian grand salon. The **Winona Armory Museum** *(160 Johnson St. 507-454-2723)*, one of the state's largest historical museums, also recalls the town's vibrant past. A peaceful 5.5-mile bike path encircles **Lake Winona**—the original river channel—at the south end of town.

For a bird's-eye view of the Mississippi, head 20 miles south of Winona on US 61 and County Road 3 to **Great River Bluffs State Park** *(507-643-6849. Adm. fee)*. King's and Queen's Bluffs reach toward the river like outstretched fingers. Hike the trail atop King's Bluff, where coneflowers, black-eyed Susans, and other native prairie plants cling to hillsides steep enough to be dubbed "goat prairie."

As bird-watchers know, the Mississippi serves as a major migratory route; nearly 300 bird species have been spotted here. The vast **Upper Mississippi River National Wildlife and Fish Refuge** protects 261 miles of the Mississippi flyway from Wabasha, Minnesota, to near Rock Island, Illinois. It's headquarters are based in Winona *(51 E. 4th St. 507-452-4232)*; if you'd like to explore the refuge, staffers can suggest walks and observation points near Winona.

Cross the river at Winona to reach the Wisconsin shore, where **Trempealeau National Wildlife Refuge** *(Trempealeau. 608-539-2311)* protects even more shoreline. A series of dikes for 19th-century railroads isolated this 6,200-acre swath of Mississippi back-waters from siltation and pollution, preserving an extremely high-quality wetland. The 5-mile interpretive **Wildlife Drive** *(guide booklet available at entrance kiosk)* loops through sand prairie, marsh, and floodplain forest, where painted turtles sun on muddy banks and migratory birds rest and roost in the wetlands.

End your day with a stay at the **Trempealeau Hotel** (see Travel-wise). You'll feel like you've traveled through time at this classic 1871 hotel and saloon that anchors a simple, unspoiled little river town. The hotel hosts a lively roster of **"Stars Under the Stars"** summer concerts on its riverfront lawn.

La Crosse & south

River bluffs rise to frame lovely **La Crosse,** "a choice town," according to Mark Twain. Enjoy its attributes from the deck of the *Julia Belle Swain (jct. of Main and Front Sts. 608-784-4882 or 800-815-1005. Fare).* Hundreds of these steam-powered paddle wheelers plied the Mississippi a century ago; today, only a handful remain.

As part of your excursion, "lock through" one of the 29 locks and dams that span the Mississippi. The system transformed the river's natural loopy course of winding channels and scattered sandbars into an easily navigated waterway for commercial traffic. At **Genoa,** 12 miles south of La Crosse, **Lock and Dam No. 9** offers a good van-tage point for watching barge traffic. Stop for lunch at the **Big River Inn** (see Travelwise), where fresh local catfish often leads the list of specials. Ask about catfish cheeks—they're considered a delicacy.

Sixty miles south of La Crosse, French fur traders settled in Prairie du Chien. **Villa Louis** *(St. Feriole Island. 608-326-2721. Closed Nov.-April; adm. fee),* built with fur-trade fortunes, was the most opulent home in the upper Midwest in the mid-19th century. Today you can tour the meticulously restored home and fur-trade museum.

Just downriver, **Pikes Peak State Park** *(15316 Great River Rd., McGregor. 563-873-2341)* in Iowa and **Wyalusing State Park** *(13081 State Park Ln., Bagley. 608-996-2261. Adm. fee)* in Wisconsin face one another like bookends, each claiming a 500-foot-bluff above the confluence of the Mississippi and Wisconsin Rivers. Find a trail or well-placed bench to soak in the gorgeous blue-green jumble of waterways and waterlogged islands.

A natural trade route, this region was a vibrant Native American community for centuries. As early as 500 B.C., the Effigy Mound cul-ture built thousands of earthen mounds in the shape of birds and bears, archaeological wonders found predominantly only in the Mis-sissippi River Valley. Northwest of Prairie du Chien, in Iowa, **Effigy Mounds National Monument** *(151 Hwy. 76, Harpers Ferry. 563-873-3491. Adm. fee)* protects 191 known mounds. Humans, it seems, have forever been drawn to this lovely river valley.   —*Tina Lassen*

Travelwise

River City Days (1st weekend in Aug., Red Wing, MN. 651-388-4719 or 800-762-9516) Food booths, a parade, and concerts.

MORE THINGS TO SEE & DO

Biking The **Great River State Trail** (608-534-6409. Fee) wends along the Mississippi for more than 20 miles between Trempealeau and Onalaska, passing through a mix of prairies and bottomlands, and over several bridges spanning wetlands and tributaries.

LODGING

Anderson House (333 W. Main St., Wabasha, MN. 651-565-4524. www.theandersonhouse .com. $-$$) Minnesota's oldest hotel offers old-fashioned bed warmers: Call ahead to book one of the hotel's cats for your room.

Courtyard Marriott (500 Front St., La Crosse, WI. 608-782-1000. www.marriott.com. $-$$) Riverside full-service hotel in historic district.

Harbor Hill Inn (310 2nd St., Pepin, WI. 715-442-2002 or 877-475-6202. www .pepinsbest.com. $$) 1890 Queen Anne overlooking Lake Pepin.

St. James Hotel (406 Main St., Red Wing, MN. 651-388-2846 or 800-252-1875. www.st-james-hotel.com. $-$$$) This hotel boasts 61 distinctive guest rooms. See p. 174.

Trempealeau Hotel (150 Main St., Trempealeau, WI. 608-534-6898. www.trempealeau hotel.com. $-$$) A historic two-story hotel with 10 guest rooms. See p. 177.

DINING

Big River Inn (500 Main St., Genoa, WI. 608-689-2652. $-$$) See p. 177.

Burlington Hotel (809 N. Main, Alma, WI. 608-685-3636. $$$) This 1890s railway hotel in a historic river town is a good spot for hand-cut steaks and homemade soups.

Jefferson's Pub and Grill (58 Center St., Winona, MN. 507-452-2718. $-$$) Sandwiches and microbrews in an 1880s railroad freight house.

Piggy's (328 Front St., La Crosse, WI. 608-784-4877. $$) Award-winning barbecue on the banks of the Mississippi.

The Port (406 Main St., Red Wing, MN. 651-388-2846. $$) A sumptuous Sunday brunch.

GETTING THERE

Red Wing lies 50 miles southeast of Minneapolis. The sites in this getaway lie along a 120-mile stretch of the Mississippi south of Red Wing. Wis. 35 parallels the river's east bank; US 61 parallels its west bank.

GENERAL INFORMATION

Contact the **Minnesota Office of Tourism** (100 Metro Sq., 121 7th Pl. E., St. Paul, MN 55101. 651-296-5029 or 800-657-3700. www.exploreminnesota.com) or the **Wisconsin Department of Tourism** (201 W. Washington Ave., Madison, WI 53707. 800-372-2737. www.travelwisconsin.com).

SEASONS

Spring through fall. This getaway is lovely in October, when fiery autumn foliage lights up the bluffs.

ANNUAL EVENTS

AppleFest (3rd weekend in Sept., La Crescent, MN. 507-895-2800 or 800-926-9480) Apple foods and orchard tours celebrate the harvest.

Oktoberfest (late Sept.–early Oct., La Crosse, WI. 608-784-3378. www.oktoberfestusa .com) An immensely popular German festival with parades, ethnic entertainment and foods, and a rollicking beer garden.

Nashville &
Memphis

Country Music City 180

Digging Underground 184

Noodling Down the Natchez Trace 187

In Memphis, the Beat Goes on 191

Arkansas Ozarks 195

Performers take the stage in Nashville's Opry House.

Country Music City
Seeing stars & bars in Nashville

NASHVILLE IS THE CENTER OF country music, a uniquely American sound with origins in English and Irish ballads. The mecca of this genre is the Grand Ole Opry, a venue for legendary performers since 1925. Fiddles and guitars aside, downtown Nashville has come alive with new music clubs, restaurants, and sports arenas.

Nashville skyline

In the shadow of downtown skyscrapers is the **Country Music Hall of Fame and Museum** *(222 5th Ave. S. 615-416-2001 or 800-852-6437. www.countrymusichalloffame.com. Adm. fee),* where you can learn all about the Nashville sound, past and present. Relocated here in 2001, the museum offers recordings, interactive displays, and videos on the roots of country music and the recent boom in its popularity. If you're not watching a vintage television program or a recent interview with a country-music star, you can gawk at Webb Pierce's Pontiac convertible, studded with silver dollars and cowboy gear. In the **Songwriter's Theater,** composers discuss their work with audience members.

The **Hall of Fame** spotlights Thomas Hart Benton's last painting, "The Sources of Country Music." Plaques honoring country legends are displayed in a rotunda so that no performer gets top billing over another.

Walk north on Fourth Avenue, crossing Broadway to reach the fabled **Ryman Auditorium** *(116 5th Ave. N. 615-889-3060. www.ryman.com. Adm. fee).* The statue out front is of Thomas Ryman, a steamboat captain who built this brick structure as a place of worship in 1892; not until it hosted the Grand Ole Opry radio show (1943-1974) did it become the "Mother Church of Country Music." Though now on cable television as well as on radio, the Opry has stayed true to its format: Country's top stars perform in a casual setting that lets the audience get to know the performers.

On the rainy ides of March night in 1974, the Grand Ole Opry forsook the wood floors and uncomfortable church-pew seating of the venerable Ryman, decamping to a concrete palace with plush

NOT TO BE MISSED

● **Art deco details at Frist Center for the Visual Arts, 919 Broadway** ● **The scale (and incongruity) of the Parthenon in Centennial Park** ● **Christie's Cookies, a sinful local favorite** ● **Printmaking tradition at Hatch Show Print**

Dueling guitars

seats east of downtown. But the Ryman could not be silenced: It continues to host concerts by a wide range of musicians year-round. It also opens daily for self-guided tours; watch a short film on the building's history, check out Roy Acuff's fiddle, or have your picture taken on the same stage where Hank Williams, Patsy Cline, Johnny Cash, and countless other legends once stood and strummed.

Back at Fourth and Broadway, poke around in **Gruhn Guitars** *(400 Broadway. 615-256-2033. Closed Sun.),* where the walls are hung with new instruments and rare vintage guitars. The high guitar prices may leave you unstrung, but the immersion in musical history is worth the stop. Next, walk half a block east to **Hatch Show Print** *(316 Broadway. 615-256-2805. Closed Sun.).* This shop, founded in 1879, began making posters for the Grand Ole Opry in 1939; it still produces advertising posters by the centuries-old letterpress technique. Here you can watch craftspeople turning out posters for everyone from Bruce Springsteen to local bands playing in honky-tonks down the street.

Music clubs line the area called the **District,** on lower Broadway and Second Avenue. They bracket the spectrum from the relatively upscale **Wildhorse Saloon** *(120 2nd Ave. N. 615-902-8200. www .wildhorsesaloon.com)* to smoke-filled joints such as **Robert's Western World** *(416 Broadway. 615-244-9552).* Grand Ole Opry stars used to pop into **Tootsie's Orchid Lounge** *(422 Broadway. 615-726-0463. www.tootsies.net)* to wet their whistles between shows; the Ryman Auditorium's back door is just across the alley.

Friday night is a good time to visit the celebrated **Bluebird Café**

(4104 Hillsboro Rd. 615-383-1461. www.bluebirdcafe.com. Cover charge), where you can hear up-and-coming singer-songwriters in an informal setting—and often catch a headliner sitting in. A long list of stars (Garth Brooks, Mary Chapin Carpenter, Sweethearts of the Rodeo) got their start at the Bluebird. Call ahead for reservations—and don't even *dream* of talking while a set is in progress.

Pantry, Presley, Hickory, Opry

The likeliest time and place to spot a music star is probably during breakfast at **Pancake Pantry** (see Travelwise), a restaurant in the Vanderbilt University area just west of downtown. Its famous flapjacks and other morning goodies can make for long waits on the weekend.

Pancake Pantry draws its celebrity clientele from nearby **Music Row,** the stretch of 16th and 17th Avenues southwest of Demonbreun Street. Recording studios and music-company logos line the streets, but there's little else for the casual visitor to see. To get the lowdown on such country musicana as Elvis Presley's stormy early recording sessions, take a guided tour offered by the likes of **Johnny Walker Tours** *(615-834-8585 or 800-722-1524. www.johnnywalker tours.com)*.

For a historical intermission in the midst of your music tour, visit **The Hermitage** *(4580 Rachel's Ln., off Old Hickory Blvd. 615-889-2941. www.thehermitage.com. Adm. fee)*, President Andrew Jackson's plantation home from 1804 until his death in 1845. A short film and various exhibits introduce Jackson's life and times; you can then see the log house where Jackson and his wife, Rachel, lived from 1804 until they built a much larger house nearby in 1821. This mansion, remodeled and rebuilt after a fire, has been restored to its 1830s appearance. Original furnishings and personal items belonging to "Old Hickory," the hero of the 1815 Battle of New Orleans and President of the United States from 1829 to 1837, fill its rooms.

It's not far from the Hermitage to Opryland, USA, the new entertainment complex that has grown up around the Grand Ole Opry. The centerpiece of the vast **Gaylord Opryland Resort and Convention Center** *(2800 Opryland Dr. 615-889-1000. www.gaylordopryland .com)* is a quartet of glass-topped atria covering 9 acres; they encompass flowers, tropical plants, waterfalls, miniature lakes and a river, and several restaurants.

A short distance away is the **Opry House** *(2804 Opryland Dr. 615-871-6779. www.opry.com)*, home of the world's longest running radio show (since 1925, when it was called the *WSM Barn Dance)* and still the nation's premier showcase for country music. From late May to mid-August, the Opry presents one show on Friday night, two on Saturday, and one on Tuesday. It has even revived limited winter performances at the Ryman; check the schedule before making plans.

If you have time on your hands before a show, take in the free music on the plaza outside the Opry *(Fri.-Sat. evenings early June–mid-Aug.)* or tour the **Grand Ole Opry Museum** *(615-889-6779. www.opry.com. Closed Jan.-Feb.)* behind the Opry House. Other music-related enterprises in the area include **Nashville Palace** *(2400 Music Valley Dr. 615-885-1540. palace.citysearch.com. Adm. fee)*, one of the city's top venues for country artists, and the long-running *Ernest Tubb Midnite Jamboree* radio show, broadcast from the **Texas Troubadour Theatre** *(2416 Music Valley Dr. 615-889-2474. www.etrecord shop.com)* on Saturday nights after the Grand Ole Opry. Musicians who have finished their Opry gig start picking here around midnight and don't stop until they drop sometime in the early morning.

—*Mel White*

Travelwise

GENERAL INFORMATION
Contact the **Nashville Convention & Visitors Bureau** *(211 Commerce St., Ste. 100, Nashville, TN 37201. 615-259-4700 or 800-657-6910. www.nashvillecvb.com).*

MORE THINGS TO SEE & DO
Belle Meade Plantation *(5025 Harding Rd. 615-356-0501 or 800-270-3991. www.belle meadeplantation.com. Adm. fee)* This 1853 Greek Revival house features costumed guides, period furnishings, and a collection of antique carriages.

Belmont Mansion *(1900 Belmont Blvd. 615-460-5459. www.belmontmansion.com. Closed Sun.-Mon. Sept.-May; adm. fee)* Built circa 1850 and owned by one of America's wealthiest women, Belmont is filled with elegant furnishings and decorative objects.

Parthenon *(Centennial Park. 615-862-8431. www.parthenon.org. Closed Mon., and Sun. Oct.-March; adm. fee)* A full-scale replica of the ancient Greek temple, enclosing an art museum and a huge statue of Athena.

LODGING
Doubletree Hotel Nashville *(315 4th Ave. N. 615-244-8200 or 800-222-8733. $$)* A 338-room downtown hotel convenient to the District and other attractions.

Gaylord Opryland Resort and Convention Center *(2800 Opryland Dr. 615-889-1000 or 877-234-6779. $$)* 2,000 guest rooms, shops, and restaurants near the Grand Ole Opry and other attractions in Music Valley.

Union Station *(1001 Broadway. 615-726-1001 or 800-996-3426. $$-$$$)* A hotel set in a beautifully restored 1900 train station, with limestone towers, a magnificent lobby, 124 rooms, and one of the city's best upscale restaurants (Arthur's).

DINING
Arnold's Country Kitchen *(605 8th Ave. S. 615-256-4455. Breakfast and lunch only; closed Sat.-Sun. $)* An avatar of the Nashville "meat and three" lunch café.

Bound'ry *(911 20th Ave. S. 615-321-3043. $$)* This eclectic restaurant near Vanderbilt offers Asian, Caribbean, and Southern-style dishes with a highly imaginative twist.

Pancake Pantry *(1796 21st Ave. S. 615-383-9333)* See p. 182.

Sunset Grill *(2001 Belcourt Ave. 615-386-3663. www.sunsetgrill.com. $$$)* Contemporary American food near Music Row.

Digging Underground
Exploring caves & cubbyholes in Kentucky

RIDDLED WITH SINKHOLES, underground rivers, and caves, the limestone terrain of south-central Kentucky is known as a karst landscape. The awesome centerpiece of the region is Mammoth Cave National Park, which encompasses the world's largest known cave system. In addition to the variety of tours available at Mammoth, a weekend here can include hiking, history, and the exploration of a number of smaller but equally fascinating caves.

A well-named cavern

Located behind a storefront in the community of Horse Cave, the **American Cave Museum and Hidden River Cave** *(119 E. Main St. 270-786-1466. www.cavern.org. Adm. fee)* make a fine introduction to the Kentucky karst region. The excellent museum, run by a nonprofit cave-conservation group, examines local geology to explain why more than 800 caves exist in this five-county area. On a guided tour of Hidden River Cave, you'll learn how this cavern suffered from contamination for more than 50 years before recovery efforts restored its health.

A few miles back toward I-65 off Ky. 218, **Kentucky Down Under** *(270-786-2634 or 800-762-2869. www.kdu.com. Wildlife park closed Nov.-March; adm. fee)* combines two attractions: The first is an Australian-themed wildlife park that allows close looks at kangaroos, cockatoos, kookaburras, sugar gliders, and black swans. The second is **Kentucky Caverns,** where a short walk leads visitors to views of large columns, flowstones, and cave coral.

A short drive west on Ky. 70 delivers you to one of the continent's greatest natural wonders, **Mammoth Cave National Park** *(270-758-2328. www.nps.gov/maca. Fee for tours, reservations essential April-Oct.).* Both a World Heritage site and an international biosphere reserve, Mammoth encompasses more than 350 miles of passages; this makes it the longest cave anywhere in the world. Blessed with such an expanse of underground terrain, the national park is able to

---

NOT TO BE MISSED

- **The human history revealed in Mammoth Cave** ● **Walnut, cherry, and maple furniture at the Shaker Museum** ● **The beauty of Great Onyx Cave** ● **Kentucky Down Under's walk-in aviary**

Historical grafitti at Mammoth Cave

offer a wide variety of tours; research the options before arriving.

Sandstone ridges overlying much of Mammoth Cave limit the amount of water that enters the cave. As a result, large parts of Mammoth lack the elaborate stalactites, stalagmites, draperies, and other speleothems (cave formations) that many visitors expect. Tours of these sections—notably the **Historic Tour** and the **Discovery Tour**—emphasize Mammoth's fascinating human history, which includes extensive use by Native Americans. Other tours, such as **Frozen Niagara** and **Great Onyx,** visit parts of the cave bristling with beautiful formations. If you are physically fit, over 16, and don't mind crawling through tight passages off the main tour routes, you can also take the **Wild Cave Tour.** Other special tours include one designed for the physically impaired.

The 53,000 acres of Mammoth Cave National Park that lie *above* ground abound with recreational opportunities. The Green River flows through the park for 25 miles, offering fine, beginner-friendly canoeing. Check with local outfitters, including Barren River Canoe Rentals *(270-796-1979 or 888-680-6580),* for more information.

Spectacular spelunking

Plenty of dazzling formations sparkle deep inside **Diamond Caverns** *(270-749-2233. www.diamondcaverns.com. Adm. fee)* on Ky. 255, one mile west of I-65 near Park City. The half-mile cave tour showcases countless multicolored draperies and ornate stalactites and stalagmites. Having been a tour cave since 1859, Diamond Caverns reveals many instances of broken columns and other damage by early visitors.

On the outskirts of the city of Bowling Green, **Lost River Cave** *(2818 Nashville Rd. 270-393-0077 or 866-274-2283. www.lostrivercave .com. Adm. fee)* offers a different sort of subterranean experience: a boat ride on a buried river. Lost River itself emerges from the ground at a spot called Blue Hole. Here the stream flows through a wooded valley (actually a long-collapsed cave) for about 400 feet before returning to the bowels of the Earth via a cave in a large amphitheater-shaped opening. The boat ride ventures some 700 feet into this cavern, navigating spacious rooms decorated with large flowstones.

For a respite from all that spelunking, drive southwest from Bowling Green on US 68 to the **Shaker Museum at South Union** *(270-542-4167 or 800-811-8379. www.shakermuseum.com. Closed Dec.-Feb.; adm. fee)*. Once the center of a thriving religious community, the expansive 1824 Centre House displays wonderful examples of handmade furniture and other artifacts. —*Mel White*

Travelwise

GETTING THERE
Horse Cave is 100 miles north of Nashville via I-65.

GENERAL INFORMATION
Contact the **Kentucky Department of Travel** *(P.O. Box 2011, Frankfort, KY 40602. 502-564-4930 or 800-225-8747. www.kytourism.com)* or the **Bowling Green Area Convention & Visitors Bureau** *(352 Three Springs Rd., Bowling Green, KY 42101. 270-782-0800 or 800-326-7465. www.bg.ky.net/tourism)*.

SEASONS
Cave temperatures are in the 50s year-round. For other attractions, spring through fall is the best time to visit.

LODGING
1869 Homestead Bed & Breakfast *(212 Mizpah Rd., Bowling Green. 270-842-0510. www.bbonline.com/ky/1869homestead. $)* Two rooms and a suite on 55 acres. Listed in the National Register of Historic Places.

Mammoth Cave Hotel *(N. Entrance Rd. 270-758-2225. $)* A hotel, lodge, and cottages near Mammoth Cave's historic entrance.

Victorian House Bed and Breakfast *(110 N. Main St., Smiths Grove. 270-563-9403. www.bbonline.com/ky/victorian. $$)* Four guest rooms with private baths in a beautifully restored 1875 mansion.

DINING
440 Main *(440 E. Main Ave., Bowling Green. 270-793-0450. Closed Sun. $$)* Louisiana-style dishes; outdoor dining on the patio.

Brickyard Café *(1026 Chestnut St., Bowling Green. 270-843-6431. Closed Sun. $-$$)* Pasta and pizza; homemade breads and desserts.

Mariah's *(801 State St., Bowling Green. 270-842-6878. $$)* Located in the city's oldest brick house, this popular restaurant serves steaks, pasta, and seafood.

Noodling Down the Natchez Trace
A languid, leisurely drive

IT'S FAMED AS A SCENIC DRIVE, but the Natchez Trace Parkway offers much more than pretty views. Winding 444 miles from Nashville, Tennessee, to Natchez, Mississippi, the route follows a trail used by Native Americans, soldiers, and post riders, as well as by flatboatmen returning north after delivering their craft to New Orleans. Today, the northern half of this National Park Service road lets you experience history, culture, and nature as you wind through fields and wooded hills.

Nashville to Lawrenceburg

Get an early start so you can enjoy a delicious Nashville-area tradition: breakfast at **Loveless Cafe** *(8400 Tenn. 100. 615-646-9700).* Less than a mile from the northern terminus of the parkway, this small restaurant is regionally renowned for its down-home cooking, notably its country ham, biscuits, and gravy.

Enter the Natchez Trace Parkway from Tenn. 100 and you quickly get a sense of the essence of the drive: Low speed limits encourage leisurely travel through rolling terrain. Though agriculture becomes more apparent the farther south you go, this section through Tennessee—bordered by hillsides covered in beautiful oak and beech—is among the most natural looking of the entire drive. (Note: Mileposts sit on the east side of the road; they are numbered south to north.)

Although the modern road doesn't follow the exact route of the original Natchez Trace, it rarely strays more than two or three miles from it. At Milepost 426 is one of several places where you can park and walk a section of the Old Trace, ambling a woodland path under red and white oaks, sugar maples, beeches, and tulip magnolias. Evoking the historic use of the old Natchez Trace by both walkers and riders, this trail is popular with horseback riders as well.

At Mile 416, take Tenn. 7 east 17 miles to **Columbia,** a historic

---

NOT TO BE MISSED

- Biscuits and gravy at Loveless Cafe in Nashville
- The Old Trace Drive at Milepost 376
- Hiking in Tishomingo State Park
- Split-rail fences along parkway

town with an attractive courthouse square. Nearby stands the **James K. Polk Home** *(301 W. 7th St. 931-388-2354. www.jameskpolk.com. Adm. fee)*, the 1816 house where the future 11th President lived as a young man. The house contains personal items and historic artifacts, including White House china. Tours begin next door with a film in the visitor center—an 1820s house built for one of Polk's sisters.

The Columbia area is known for its restored 19th-century houses, several of them open for tours. Using the driving guide provided by the Middle Tennessee Visitors Bureau *(302 W. 7th St. 931-381-7176. www.visitplantations.com)*, spend a morning visiting such lovely antebellum homes as **Rattle & Snap** *(Tenn. 243, 6 miles SW of Columbia. 931-379-5861 or 800-258-3875. www.rattleandsnap.com. Closed Sun.; adm. fee)*, an 1845 Greek Revival residence filled with sumptuous furnishings. The mansion's name comes from the old-time gambling game in which the owner won this property.

Back on the parkway, near Milepost 386 you'll reach the site of a mysteriously tragic event. It was a dark and stormy night in October 1809, and Meriwether Lewis (of Lewis and Clark fame) had stopped over at rustic **Grinder's Inn** along the Old Trace. Sometime during the night, two gunshots were heard; in the morning the famed explorer was found dead. Though it's probable that the troubled Lewis committed suicide, many maintain that he met with foul play. A symbolic broken column rises over his grave in the **Pioneer Cemetery** here; only fragments of the inn's chimney remain.

At Mile 376, leave the main parkway for the one-way road (temporarily heading north) that follows the original Trace for 2.5 miles. This narrow ridgetop lane provides great views over valleys to the east, with pullouts to let you pause and enjoy the panoramas.

For pioneers on the Old Trace, sundown might have meant curling up in a blanket under the spreading branches of a beech tree. Though towns aren't plentiful along this stretch of the parkway, modern travelers will find lodgings much more comfortable than beech roots in Lawrenceburg, Tennessee, 16 miles east via US 64.

Lawrenceburg to Tombigbee

One of the nice things about navigating the Natchez Trace is the many nearby nature trails that bid you abandon your vehicle and embrace the great outdoors. Among the most pleasant is the short walk at **Rock Spring** *(Mile 330, in Alabama)*. The trail crosses Colbert Creek on stepping-stones, then leads to a pretty spot where a year-round spring creates a small pond full of lush vegetation.

One of the drive's most beautiful spots lies just over the Mississippi state line, near Mile 304. **Tishomingo State Park** *(662-438-6914. www.mdwfp.com/parks.asp. Adm. fee)* boasts 1,530 acres of sandstone bluffs and wooded hillsides, 13 miles of hiking trails, seasonal canoeing on Bear Creek, a campground, and rustic cabins.

Native American sites dot the Natchez Trace throughout Mississippi. At Mile 286 is striking **Pharr Mounds,** the largest and most significant archaeological site in the northern part of the state. Eight burial mounds more than 1,800 years old, the highest 18 feet tall, rise from a 90-acre clearing beside the road—reminders of the complex civilization that existed in these forests and grasslands long before the first Europeans arrived.

As you reach the city of Tupelo (birthplace of Elvis Presley), stop at the **parkway visitor center** at Mile 266. Here you'll find exhibits, a bookstore, video programs, a short nature trail, and interpreters to answer whatever questions you've amassed over the past 178 miles.

The **Chickasaw Village** exhibit, at Mile 262, marks the site of a Native American settlement that comprised several houses and a fort. You can see the tall grasses of a restored prairie here, and walk an interpretive trail describing the Indian use of such native plants as mulberry and plum.

Along the Natchez Trace Parkway, a split-rail fence evokes centuries past.

The parkway continues south through a region called the Black Belt: Its dark, fertile soil—the limestone-rich floor of an ancient ocean—makes it one of the South's top cotton-growing areas. Beyond this point, pines become more prominent among the roadside hardwoods. At Mile 247 you enter **Tombigbee National Forest** *(662-285-3264)*, where the trails at the **Witch Dance picnic area** *(Mile 233)* offer rewarding hiking. Dogwood, serviceberry, and redbud blossoms brighten the forest in spring.

The Natchez Trace Parkway meanders another 233 miles to the historic city of Natchez—too far to explore in a leisurely weekend. As you make your way back north, however, your newfound perspective will enhance the varied vistas; it may even inspire you to explore some of the trails and sites you missed on the way down. —*Mel White*

Travelwise

GETTING THERE
Pick up the parkway's north end on Tenn. 100, 15 miles southwest of downtown Nashville.

GENERAL INFORMATION
Contact the **Natchez Trace Parkway** *(2680 Natchez Trace Pkwy., Tupelo, MS 38804. 662-680-4025 or 800-305-7417. www.nps .gov/natr)*; the **Tennessee Department. of Tourist Development** *(320 6th Ave. N., Nashville, TN 37243. 615-741-2159 or 800-462-*

8366. www.tnvacation.com); or the **Mississippi Division of Tourism** *(P.O. Box 849, Jackson, MS 39205. 601-359-3297 or 800-927-6378. www.visitmississippi.org)*.

SEASONS
Drive the Trace in spring or fall; in summer it can be hot, humid, and highly trafficked.

MORE THINGS TO SEE & DO
Carter House *(1140 Columbia Ave., Franklin, TN. 615-791-1861. www.carter-house.org. Adm. fee)* A video and museum interpret the 1864 Battle of Franklin at this 1830 redbrick.

Elvis Presley Park *(306 Elvis Presley Dr., Tupelo, MS. 662-841-1245. Adm. fee)* Includes the two-room house where the King was born, plus a small museum and chapel.

LODGING
Magnolia House *(1317 Columbia Ave., Franklin, TN. 615-794-8178. $)* Four rooms with private baths in a 1905 house minutes from the northern terminus of the parkway.

Mockingbird Inn *(305 N. Gloster St., Tupelo, MS. 662-841-0286. $-$$)* B&B with seven rooms, each with an international decor.

DINING
Big John's Bar-B-Q *(904 N. Military Ave., Lawrenceburg, TN. 931-762-9596. $)* A local favorite for sandwiches, ribs, and chicken.

Gloster 205 *(205 N. Gloster St., Tupelo, MS. 662-842-7205. Closed Sun. $$)* Steaks, prime rib, seafood are sure bets at this upscale spot.

In Memphis, the Beat Goes on
Getting the blues & holding them close

ROCK-AND-ROLL WAS BORN AND BRED in Memphis, Tennessee. This weekend showcases the past and present of that music in the city's lively, revitalized downtown. Here you can visit fine museums and an entertainment district full of blues and rock clubs. Farther out there's Graceland, home of musical and cultural icon Elvis Presley.

Memphis as Mecca

Downtown **Memphis** perches on the east bank of the Mississippi River, directly across from Arkansas to the west and just a few miles north of Mississippi to the south. This was the merger site of three music styles—the country music of whites, the blues of Delta and urban blacks, and the gospel songs of both—which picked up a driving beat and became rock-and-roll.

The story of that fusion is told in riveting detail at the **Memphis Rock 'n' Soul Museum** *(145 Lt. George W. Lee Ave. 901-543-0800. www.memphisrocknsoul.org. Adm. fee)*. Researched and organized by the Smithsonian Institution, the museum's recordings and memorabilia present this cross-roads of music and culture as a theme. Don a headset and listen to dozens of historic recordings by musicians from country star Roy Acuff to bluesman Robert Johnson to soul legend Otis Redding. (Hearing them all would take hours, but you can pick your favorite tunes and listen to as much of each one as you like.) Among the exhibits are the guitar played on Elvis Presley's "Hound Dog" and instruments used at the city's Stax Records studio, where so many great soul tracks were laid down.

If you've ever lusted after *Lucille II*—the Gibson ES 335 guitar played by bluesman B. B. King—tour the **Gibson Guitar Factory** *(145 Lt. George W. Lee Ave. 901-543-0800. Adm. fee, reservations required)* on the floor just below the museum. Whether you're a lead guitarist or a listener, you'll enjoy this behind-the-scenes look at craftspeople assembling several different Gibson models.

> **NOT TO BE MISSED**
> ● **Listening to classic songs at the Memphis Rock 'n' Soul Museum**
> ● **Cocktails in the Peabody Hotel's lobby bar**
> ● **The River Walk on Mud Island** ● **The ribs at Rendezvous**

Beale Street, Memphis

To see the spot where early blues bands recorded rock-and-roll's first great hits, head for **Sun Studio** *(706 Union Ave. 901-521-0664. www.sunstudio.com. Fee for tours)*. Here in the 1950s, owner Sam Phillips produced recordings of Howlin' Wolf, Johnny Cash, and Roy Orbison. A young Memphis truck driver cut a record entitled "That's All Right" at Sun Studio in 1954, and the music world was never the same (his name was Elvis Presley). The Sun "tour" consists of little more than standing in the studio where hits such as "Great Balls of Fire" were made, learning about studio history, and listening to recordings. For true fans of rock-and-roll, however, that's plenty.

The appeal of Memphis music is not exclusively historical. The entertainment district around **Beale Street** encompasses several blocks of restaurants, shops, and rock and blues clubs showcasing the sort of talent that still flocks to the city. Stroll Beale Street on any night and you're bound to hear great music at spots such as **B. B. King's Blues Club** *(143 Beale St. 901-524-5464)*, **Isaac Hayes** *(150*

Peabody Pl. 901-529-9222), and **Rum Boogie Cafe** *(182 Beale St. 901-528-0150)*. B. B. King once worked as a disc jockey at Memphis radio station WDIA, where he was known as the "Beale Street Blues Boy" (hence his double initials). The legendary singer-guitarist appears at the club several times a year, with tickets selling out well in advance.

Heart & soul

Since long before 1912, when W. C. Handy's "Memphis Blues" became one of the first blues songs ever published, the city's sizable African-American community has played a key role in shaping both its musical and civic heritage. Joyous moments have been marred by tragic ones, notably the assassination of the Rev. Martin Luther King, Jr., in Memphis on April 4, 1968. The Lorraine Motel, where King was shot, has been transformed into the **National Civil Rights Museum** *(450 Mulberry St. 901-521-9699. www.civilrightsmuseum.org. Closed Tues.; adm. fee)*, where a timeline of poignant exhibits recalls milestones in the struggle for equal rights. Photographs, films, and artifacts examine such watershed events as the 1955 bus boycott in Montgomery, Alabama; the Freedom Rides of the early 1960s; and the 1965 Voting Rights Act. To honor Dr. King, the motel room where he was staying (he was in town to support striking sanitation workers) has been preserved as it was on the day he was slain.

After visiting this somber yet hopeful memorial, return to the healing spirit of music. Five miles from downtown, in an area known as **Soulsville, USA,** a new complex began to take shape in 2001. Its centerpiece, the **Stax Museum of American Soul Music** *(926 E. McLemore Ave. 901-946-2535. www.soulsvilleusa.com. Scheduled to open fall 2002; adm. fee)*, celebrates such Memphis-connected recording legends as Al Green, Booker T. and the MGs, Otis Redding, Sam and Dave, and Rufus Thomas. Located on the site of the demolished Stax recording studio, the museum uses video, artifacts, and audio recordings to recall the creation of soul classics: "Sittin' on the Dock of the Bay," "Walkin' the Dog," "Soul Man," "Green Onions."

Elvis lives!

On Elvis Presley Boulevard in southern Memphis stands one of America's most visited homes: **Graceland** *(3734 Elvis Presley Blvd. 901-332-3322 or 800-238-2000. www.elvis.com/graceland. Adm. fee)*, the white-columned 1930s mansion where Elvis lived for 20 years until his death there in 1977. The residence reflects Presley's unique taste in interior design: pleated fabric walls, three televisions playing simultaneously, white faux-fur bed, indoor waterfall. Personal memorabilia include Elvis's stage and movie costumes, his gold records (worldwide sales estimated at one billion), his jewelry, and his guns.

Additional Elvis attractions await across the street. An auto museum displays a Ferrari and his famed pink Cadillac, while the

"Sincerely Elvis" exhibit presents photos and mementos from his personal life. You can also tour one of the King's two customized jets.

If it's nearing 5 p.m., head back to the opulent lobby of the **Peabody Hotel** (see Travelwise) for a whimsical Memphis tradition: Each day at 11 a.m., the hotel's five resident ducks are led from the elevator along a red carpet to the lobby fountain, where they spend the day paddling about and looking cute. Precisely at 5 p.m., they march back to the elevator for a return ride to their rooftop sleeping quarters. So many flashbulbs document the procession you'd think Elvis had shown up for a beer in the hotel bar. —*Mel White*

Travelwise

GENERAL INFORMATION
Contact the **Memphis Convention & Visitors Bureau** *(47 Union Ave., Memphis, TN 38103. 901-543-5300 or 800-873-6282. www .memphistravel.com/leisure.asp).*

SEASONS
Memphis summers being hot and humid, spring and fall are the best times to visit.

ANNUAL EVENTS
Memphis in May International Festival *(May, Tom Lee Park and other locations. 901-525-4611. www.memphisinmay.org. Fee for some events)* This celebration salutes Memphis and a different country each year. It includes all sorts of musical performances, a barbecue-cooking contest, and other festivities.

MORE THINGS TO SEE & DO
Dixon Gallery and Gardens *(4339 Park Ave. 901-761-5250. www.dixon.org. Gallery closed Mon., but gardens open; adm. fee)* Impressionist paintings by Cézanne, Renoir, and Gauguin are among this museum's collection. Seventeen acres of landscaped gardens surround the gallery.

Memphis Brooks Museum of Art *(1934 Poplar Ave., Overton Park. 901-544-6200. www .brooksmuseum.org. Closed Mon.; adm. fee)* This highly respected museum displays Italian Renaissance and baroque works, English and American portraits, French Impressionist paintings, and contemporary works.

Peabody Place Museum *(119 S. Main St. 901-523-2787. www.belz.com/museum. Closed Mon.; adm. fee)* A breathtaking collection of Chinese works in jade, ivory, and cloisonné is the focus here. Painstaking craftsmanship

is evident in the carved boats, animals, and human figures.

LODGING
Hampton Inn & Suites at Peabody Place *(175 Peabody Pl. 901-260-4000 or 800-426-7866. $$-$$$)* A 144-room hotel with indoor pool near Beale Street and other attractions.

Peabody Hotel *(149 Union Ave. 901-529-4000 or 800-732-2639. www.peabodymem phis.com. $$$)* This historic 468-room hotel, one of the South's most famous, is centrally located downtown. Four fine restaurants.

Talbot Heirs Guesthouse *(99 S. 2nd St. 901-527-9772 or 800-955-3956. www.talbot house.com. $$-$$$)* This nine-room guesthouse features rooms with contemporary furnishings, kitchens, and other apartment-like amenities.

DINING
Automatic Slims Tonga Club *(83 S. 2nd St. 901-525-7948. Dinner only Sat.; closed Sun. $$-$$$)* A hip spot with Southwestern and Caribbean dishes and a popular bar.

Huey's Downtown *(77 S. 2nd St. 901-527-2700. $)* This downtown outpost of a Memphis mini-chain has fabulous burgers and a great beer selection.

McEwen's on Monroe *(122 Monroe St. 901-527-7085. Closed Sun. $$$)* Contemporary Southern dishes star at this downtown favorite.

Rendezvous *(52 S. 2nd St. 901-523-2746. Closed Sun.-Mon. $$)* This bustling restaurant (and Memphis legend) has been serving ribs spiced with secret seasonings since 1948.

Arkansas Ozarks
Down a lazy river & into the ground

A WORLD FAR REMOVED FROM freeways and urban frenetics lies just a few hours west of Memphis. In the rugged Ozark mountains of Arkansas, winding roads invite you to slow down and enjoy the highland scenery. Small towns bid you to stop, look around, and pause at the local café for a piece of pie and a cup of hot coffee. Here you'll find the first waterway in America to be designated a national river, a hidden sparkling cave, and a national forest with miles of back roads and crystal-clear streams to explore.

Homes in the hills

The flat farmland of eastern Arkansas dominates the view out the window as you drive north from Memphis on I-55, then west on Ark. 14. Once you cross the White River, however, the terrain becomes more rolling. Nearing **Mountain View,** the road climbs ridges and twists and turns down into hollows—"hollers," in local parlance.

You may want to poke around Mountain View's courthouse square, saying hello to passing strangers (expect responses) and looking into the shops. Antiques, musical instruments, and crafts are all on offer around the small downtown area.

Drive north 1 mile on Ark. 5/9/14 and take Jimmy Driftwood Parkway to **Ozark Folk Center State Park** *(870-269-3851. www.ozarkfolkcenter .com. Most attractions closed Nov.-March; adm. fee).* This unique facility was established in 1973 to keep alive the traditions of the self-reliant pioneers who settled these mountains. In the **Crafts Village,** artisans demonstrate blacksmithing, basketmaking, weaving, candlemaking, quilting, and other skills that may seem quaint today but were once the keys to survival in the remote Ozarks. Many of the finished products, from cornshuck dolls to mountain dulcimers, are for sale in the craft shops.

Don't hesitate to ask questions of the craftspeople as you watch them work; you'll find them eager to share their knowledge of these traditional pursuits. Then, after dinner at the folk center's **Skillet** restaurant or perhaps back in Mountain View, return for the enter-

NOT TO BE MISSED

- **Dogwoods and redbuds blooming in the early Ozark spring** ● **The old banjo tune "Soldier's Joy" being played on courthouse square** ● **A perfect swimming hole in a clear mountain stream**

tainment staged in the **Ozark Folk Center Theater.** Here, older musicians sharing their heritage—and younger ones learning from them in the process—perform songs generally written before 1942.

A-paddlin' & a-pickin'

From Mountain View, follow Ark. 14 west 49 miles to visit one of America's finest natural wonders, the **Buffalo National River** *(402 N. Walnut St., Harrison. 870-741-5443. www.nps.gov/buff).* This area, administered by the National Park Service, protects 135 miles of a free-flowing stream famed for its canoeing, swimming, fishing, and pristine scenery. Bluffs rise more than 400 feet above the water. Turn east on Ark. 268 to reach **Buffalo Point,** one of many recreation areas that stipple the riverbanks. Here you'll find swimming, camping, rustic cabins *(870-449-6206. March-Nov.),* and hiking paths. The easy **Overlook Trail** leads to a fine view of the river. The 3.5-mile **Indian Rockhouse Trail** takes its name from a bluff shelter used by Native Americans, perhaps as early as 10,000 years ago.

Return to Ark. 14, drive north 3 miles, and turn east to visit the **Rush Historic District** of Buffalo National River. A busy community existed here in the early 20th century, built around zinc mining. Today's ghost town includes an 1886 stone smelter and the remains of general stores, houses, and processing mills.

The sites profiled above furnish only a taste of the beauty and adventure available along the Buffalo River. To get out on the water, contact a local outfitter *(list of approved concessionaires available at park office)* and set up a canoe trip lasting anywhere from half a day to several. Sections of the river match paddling skills from tyro to expert. The lower river around Buffalo Point is primarily gentle, its rapids navigable by nearly everyone.

Back in Mountain View, local musicians gather at the courthouse square on weekend evenings in the warm months to play bluegrass, mountain, and country music—justifying the town's sobriquet of Folk Music Capital of the World. These informal concerts welcome anybody with a guitar, banjo, bass, fiddle, or mandolin; many listeners hop to their feet and dance a spontaneous jig or waltz. The character of these pickin' sessions varies from night to night, but when the music and the crowd are especially lively, the square captures the essential spirit of the Ozarks in joyous harmony.

Cave crawls & forest strolls

Don't even think about visiting the eastern Ozarks without taking in the varied beauty of **Blanchard Springs Caverns** *(off Ark. 14, 15 miles N of Mountain View. 870-757-2211 or 888-757-2246. www.fs.fed.us /oonf/ozark/recreation/bsc.html. Closed Mon.-Tues. Nov.-March; fee for tours).* Having enjoyed Forest Service protection since the early 1960s, Blanchard Springs has been spared the exploitation and damage that

The limpid waters and looming limestone caves of Buffalo National River

have befallen many commercial caves. Before opening the caverns to visitors, the Forest Service took steps to protect their "living" quality; as a result, speleothems (cave formations) are still active and growing, and native cave creatures such as bats and salamanders still find sanctuary here.

Blanchard Springs offers two main tours. The 0.7-mile **Dripstone Trail** passes a number of intriguing stalactites (they cling "tite" to the ceiling), stalagmites (they "mite" grow up one day), rock draperies, flowstones, and other speleothems. To illustrate the geologic processes of cave formation in the limestone underlying the Ozarks, the 1.2-mile **Discovery Trail** *(closed Labor Day–Mem. Day)* travels through a lower, younger part of the cave; for this reason, it features fewer colorful formations.

Ask about "wild cave" tours, in which visitors wear hard hats and crawl—with a guide—through undeveloped portions of the caverns. Reservations are required for wild cave tours; they are recommended for the other tours, especially in summer.

Blanchard Springs Caverns lies within the Sylamore Ranger District of the 1.2-million-acre **Ozark National Forest** *(P.O. Box 1279, Mountain View, AR 72560. 870-269-3228. www.fs.fed.us/oonf/ozark /welcome.html).* Next to the caverns, **Blanchard Springs Recreation Area** encompasses campgrounds, a picnic area, and—perhaps best of all—a section of North Sylamore Creek, a perfect swimming hole on a hot day. Take the short walk to **Blanchard Springs,** where the underground river that carved the caverns erupts from a bluff at about 7,000 gallons per minute, creating an impressive waterfall.

For a more intimate glimpse of the Ozark environment, walk part of the **North Sylamore Creek Trail,** which parallels the stream for 15 miles; you'll come to the recreation area about halfway along the route. Tall bluffs and wonderfully uncongested swimming holes dot this moderately strenuous path. You can pick up its western trailhead at the Barkshed Recreation Area and its eastern trailhead near the community of Allison.

—Mel White

Travelwise

GETTING THERE
Mountain View is 140 miles west of Memphis via I-55 and Ark. 14.

GENERAL INFORMATION
Contact the **Mountain View Area Chamber of Commerce** *(P.O. Box 133, Mountain View, AR 72560. 870-269-8068 or 888-679-2859. www.mountainviewcc.org).*

SEASONS
Spring and fall, when temperatures moderate and crowds thin out (except during Folk Festival weekend), are best. Fall foliage usually peaks in late October.

ANNUAL EVENT
Arkansas Folk Festival *(3rd weekend in April, Mountain View and Ozark Folk Center State Park. 888-679-2859 or 800-264-3655. www .mountainviewcc.org. Fee for some events)* Pro and amateur pickers come from all over to take part in jam sessions and impromptu concerts at this celebrated festival featuring bluegrass and traditional mountain music.

MORE THINGS TO SEE & DO
Arkansas Craft Gallery *(104 E. Main St., Mountain View. 870-269-4120. www .arkansascraftguild.org)* More than 250 artists display contemporary and traditional artwork and crafts at this cooperative gallery.

McSpadden Dulcimers *(Ark. 14 and Ark. 382, Mountain View. 870-269-4313. www.mcspad dendulcimers.com)* This shop has been making nationally renowned mountain dulcimers since 1962. Recordings, sheet music, and instructional materials are also available.

LODGING
Country Oaks Bed and Breakfast *(Ark. 9, 1 mile S of Mountain View. 870-269-2704 or 800-455-2704. www.countryoaksbb.com. $)*

Sited on 69 acres, this inn offers eight rooms filled with antiques in the main house and a separate carriage house. Stocked fishing lake.
The Inn at Mountain View *(Washington St., 1 block W of courthouse square, Mountain View. 870-269-4200 or 800-535-1301. www .innatmountainview.com. $)* Twelve rooms with private baths in 1880s Victorian house. Rocking chairs grace the large front porch.

Wildflower Bed and Breakfast *(Washington St., on courthouse square, Mountain View. 870-269-4383 or 800-591-4879. www.bbon line.com /ar/wildflower. $)* Six rooms and suites with private baths in a 1918 Craftsman-style house.

DINING
Gourmet Goose *(112 E. Main St., Mountain View. 870-269-8288. Lunch only; closed Sun.; closed Sat. Nov.–late April. $)* A converted gas station just east of the square, featuring pasta, soups, salads, and sandwiches.

Tommy's Famous *(W. Main and Carpenter Sts., Mountain View. 870-269-3278. $$)* A local favorite for pizza and calzones, as well as for barbecue and ribs.

New Orleans

Once Over Easy 200

Roamin' Oaks 205

Cajun Country 209

Parade floats under construction at Mardi Gras World

Once Over Easy
Rollin' 'round New Orleans

COLORFUL. FLAMBOYANT. UNIQUE. New Orleans conjures up a wide array of images and adjectives designed to capture its food, its music, and its famed revels such as Mardi Gras. But the place is also rich in lore: Spend a fascinating weekend exploring the French Quarter and beyond, learning how the "Big Easy" got its laid-back reputation. Great dining and music are never far away.

French Quarter orientation

Founded by the French in 1718 on swampy land along the Mississippi River, New Orleans would be largely under water if not for its surrounding levees. Stroll along the **Moon Walk** *(1 block S of Decatur and St. Peter Sts.)*, a promenade atop a riverside levee on the south edge of the French Quarter. Arrayed around you are the skyscrapers of the Central Business District (CBD to locals), the Crescent City Connection Bridge, the suburb of Algiers across the river, and the Mississippi itself, busy with barges and oceangoing ships.

Covering 90 square blocks to the north, the **French Quarter** (Vieux Carré) is where New Orleans began. Despite that "French" designation, the city was a Spanish possession until the late 18th century. Many buildings are of Spanish design—the result of fires that razed early French-built structures.

Consider taking a 90-minute walking tour of the French Quarter, led by a Park Service ranger. Each tour leaves from Jean Lafitte National Historical Park and Preserve, French Quarter Visitor Center *(419 Decatur St. 504-589-2133. www.nps.gov/jela. Daily at 9:30 a.m.)*. Space is limited; free tickets are available starting at 9 a.m.

In **Jackson Square,** across Decatur Street from the Moon Walk, gruesome public executions were conducted in the city's rebellious early days. The equestrian statue in the center of the flower-bright square honors Gen. Andrew Jackson, hero of the 1815 Battle of New Orleans. Dominating the square's north side (across Chartres Street) is **St. Louis Cathedral;** the country's oldest active cathedral, it was built in 1794 and remodeled in 1851.

NOT TO BE MISSED

- The laissez-faire spirit pervading New Orleans
- Buttered pecan pie at Mr. B's Bistro • A nightcap at Napoleon House
- Rocking, rattling history in motion on the St. Charles streetcar

A trumpeter serenades the street in Pirates Alley, New Orleans.

To the church's west stands the 1799 building called the **Cabildo** *(701 Chartres St. 504-568-6968. Closed Mon.; adm. fee)*, part of the **Louisiana State Museum** *(lsm.crt.state.la.us/)*, which comprises eight units in the city and around the state. The Cabildo contains an excellent time line retracing state history. This is the place to learn about the blend of cultures—European, African, Caribbean—that make up the societal gumbo that is today's New Orleans.

On the other side of the cathedral stands the **Presbytère** *(751 Chartres St. 504-568-6968. Closed Mon.; adm. fee)*, built in the 1790s as a priests' residence but never used for that purpose. It holds an entertaining exhibit on Mardi Gras, the raunchy "Fat Tuesday" pre-Lenten celebration that is central to the French Quarter mystique.

Make your way past the fortune-tellers, street artists, and mimes around Jackson Square to St. Ann Street. Facing each other across the square, the **Pontalba Buildings** (with their distinctively New Orleans cast-iron balconies) were built from 1840 to 1851 as luxury apartments and shops. In the "lower" Pontalba Building, the **1850 House** *(523 St. Ann St. 504-568-6968. Closed Mon.; adm. fee)* has been restored to represent antebellum New Orleans family life.

At the southeast corner of Jackson Square, the arcades of the **French Market,** built in the 19th century as an open-air shopping area, run along Decatur Street and then North Peters Street. Among the shops, galleries, and restaurants here, the most famous is **Café du Monde** (see Travelwise), which serves untold thousands of beignets (doughnut-like pastries) and cups of café au lait (chicory coffee with milk) every year. This city landmark, open 24 hours a day, is a great place for people-watching or late-night noshing.

Walk east on Decatur six blocks to reach the **Old U.S. Mint** *(400 Esplanade St. 504-568-6968. Closed Mon.; adm. fee),* an imposing 1835 structure that minted coins for both the federal government and the Confederacy. Its exhibit on jazz history ranges from the "spasm" bands of street boys to ragtime to such pioneers as New Orleans-born Louis Armstrong, whose first cornet is displayed here.

To experience such traditional jazz yourself, end your day at **Preservation Hall** *(726 St. Peter St. 504-522-2841. www.preservationhall.com. Adm. fee),* where devoted musicians play nightly in a bare-bones setting. This taste of New Orleans heritage is worth the wait in line.

Historic homes & hot beignets

The low-lying geography of New Orleans once meant aboveground burials in elaborate tombs. The resulting cemeteries, often called "cities of the dead," have appeared in films such as *Easy Rider,* as well as in numerous books. To guarantee entry, it's wisest to visit these evocative places (including Lafayette, in the Garden District west of the quarter, and St. Louis No. 1 and No. 2, north of the quarter) on a guided tour. Contact the visitors bureau (see Travelwise) for a list of tour companies.

Back in the very-much-alive French Quarter, restored historic homes offer a glimpse into early lifestyles. The **Hermann-Grima Historic House** *(820 St. Louis St. 504-525-5661. Closed weekends; adm. fee),* a federal-style brick building dating from 1831, is known for the only working outdoor kitchen remaining in the quarter. Its elegant interior depicts a wealthy family's home in the years 1830 to 1860. The 1857 **Gallier House** *(1118-1132 Royal St. 504-525-5661. Closed Sun.; adm. fee),* home of a prominent city architect, incorporated in its design Egyptian marble fireplaces, ornate plasterwork and wallpaper, and innovations such as hot water and a skylight.

Just around the corner from the Gallier House, **Croissant d'Or** (see Travelwise) offers sandwiches, soups, and wonderful pastries to boost your energy for more French Quarter exploration. Down the block stands the **Old Ursuline Convent** (*1100 Chartres St. 504-529-3040. www.accesscom.net/ursuline. Closed Mon.; fee for tours*), one of the few structures in the Quarter to have survived the great fires of the late 18th century. Built in 1745 as a girls' school and convent for French Ursuline nuns, it has been beautifully restored, as has the 1845 **St. Mary's Church** adjacent.

Across the street, the impressive **Beauregard-Keyes House** (*1113 Chartres St. 504-523-7257. Closed Sun.; adm. fee*) was built in 1826 in the style known as Raised American Cottage. Broke and looking for a job, Confederate Gen. Pierre Gustave Toutant Beauregard lived in a room in a courtyard building here after the Civil War. The house contains some of his personal items, including a rosewood bed. In 1948 the structure was purchased by 63-year-old Frances Parkinson Keyes, author of *Dinner at Antoine's*—a murder mystery set in New Orleans on the eve of Mardi Gras. Many of the novelist's books, manuscripts, and personal items are displayed in the house.

Walk north two blocks on Ursulines Avenue to famous (or is it in-famous?) **Bourbon Street,** home of tacky tourist traps, raucous bars, and a big helping of New Orleans fun. Even if you do it only once, take the time to saunter west along one of the best known streets in the country. At the corner of St. Philip Street, check out the ancient-looking bar dubbed **Lafitte's Blacksmith Shop** (*941 Bourbon St. 504-522-9377*). Dating from 1772 and perhaps earlier, this building is rumored to have belonged to the notorious pirate Jean Lafitte.

As you approach the western end of Bourbon (at Canal Street), among the decidedly non-tacky places you'll see will be the **Redfish Grill** (see Travelwise). Here you'll find some of the best oysters, shrimp, redfish, and other seafood in a town renowned for the stuff.

A streetcar to gumbo & jazz

From the corner of Carondelet and Canal Streets, take the famous and much beloved **St. Charles Streetcar** (*504-248-3900. Fare*) west along St. Charles Avenue. Itself a national historic landmark, the streetcar trundles through another national historic landmark, the famed **Garden District.** From the mid-19th century until today, this neighborhood of mansions and gardens south of St. Charles Avenue has been among the most fashionable areas of New Orleans. Here, wealthy English-speaking residents lived apart from the francophones of the Vieux Carré. Leave the streetcar at Washington Avenue and walk St. Charles Avenue and Prytania Street to see some of the great antebellum houses. Guided tours of the Garden District (*list of companies available at visitors bureau*) are safer than solo peregrinations.

Just two blocks south of St. Charles, you'll find one of the city's most famous (and priciest) restaurants, **Commander's Palace** (see Travelwise). Both the Creole dishes and the weekend jazz brunches (with live music) are legendary here, making reservations essential.

—*Mel White*

Travelwise

GETTING THERE
To reach the French Quarter, take Poydras Street south from I-10.

GENERAL INFORMATION
Contact the **New Orleans Metropolitan Convention & Visitors Bureau** (*1500 Sugar Bowl Dr., New Orleans 70112. 504-566-5003 or 800-672-6124. www.neworleanscvb.com*).

SEASONS
Fall through spring is the best time to visit. Summers can be hot and very humid.

ANNUAL EVENTS
Mardi Gras (*Date varies; official parades begin 2nd Fri. before Ash Wednesday, various sites. 504-566-5003 or 800-672-6124. www.neworleanscvb.com*) Parades with music, revelers in wild costumes, and partying galore. French Quarter festivities are decidedly raunchy, but elsewhere there's more family-friendly fun.

New Orleans Jazz and Heritage Festival (*Begins last Fri. of April. New Orleans Fair Grounds Race Course and other sites. 504-410-4100. www.nojazzfest.com. Adm. fee*) Concerts by world-famous performers, plus food, arts and crafts, and cultural exhibits.

MORE THINGS TO SEE & DO
Audubon Aquarium of the Americas (*1 Canal St. 504-565-3033 or 800-774-7394. www.auduboninstitute.org. Adm. fee*) Sharks, jellyfish, penguins, and a walk-through Caribbean reef are features of this fine aquarium. Be sure to see the celebrated white alligators.

Audubon Zoo (*6500 Magazine St. 504-581-4629 or 800-774-7394. www.auduboninstitute.org. Adm. fee*) Don't miss the World of Primates, the Asian Domain (with white tigers), and a patch of Louisiana swamp.

National D-Day Museum (*945 Magazine St. 504-527-6012. www.ddaymuseum.org. Adm. fee*) "Higgins boats" landing craft were built in New Orleans; a rare model is here.

New Orleans Jazz National Historical Park (*916 N. Peters St. 504-589-4841 or 877-529-*9677. www.nps.gov/neor. Closed Mon.-Tues.*) Jazz-oriented concerts, workshops, programs. Jazz history walking tour of French Quarter.

LODGING
International House (*221 Camp St. 504-553-9550. www.ihhotel.com. $$-$$$*) Luxurious digs two blocks from the French Quarter, with a fine French-Vietnamese restaurant.

Le Richelieu (*1234 Chartres St. 504-529-2492 or 800-535-9653. www.lerichelieuhotel.com. $-$$*) Fine service and good value near the eastern edge of the French Quarter.

Soniat House Hotel (*1133 Chartres St. 504-522-0570 or 800-544-8808. www.soniathouse.com. $$-$$$*) Small hotel with lovely courtyard near French Quarter historic homes.

DINING
Bayona (*430 Rue Dauphine. 504-525-4455. www.bayona.com. $$-$$$*) Susan Spicer's cooking earns this spot a national reputation.

Café du Monde (*800 Decatur St. 504-581-2914. www.cafedumonde.com*) See p. 202.

Commander's Palace (*1403 Washington Ave. 504-899-8221. www.commanderspalace.com. $$$*). See p. 204.

Croissant d'Or (*617 Ursulines Ave. 504-524-4663*) See p. 203.

Mother's (*401 Poydras St. 504-523-9656. $-$$*) Join the locals in line for red beans and rice and po'boy sandwiches at this slightly funky favorite in the Central Business District.

Mr. B's Bistro (*201 Royal St. 504-523-2078. www.mrbsbistro.com. $$*) This friendly spot in the quarter has excellent food (try the Gumbo Ya-Ya appetizer) and a Sunday jazz brunch.

Napoleon House Bar and Café (*500 Chartres St. 504-524-9752. www.napoleonhouse.com. $-$$*) A quintessential New Orleans restaurant-bar, great for people-watching.

Redfish Grill (*115 Bourbon St. 504-598-1200. www.redfishgrill.com*) See p. 203.

Roamin' Oaks
A Mississippi plantation meander

ANTEBELLUM PLANTATION OWNERS built dozens of showplace mansions on the lower Mississippi, the watery Main Street linking their lands. Several surviving structures can be toured today. Some have been restored to glittering splendor. Others are more historic than elegant. All provide a peek inside a vanished era.

Magical history tour

From Baton Rouge to New Orleans, the Mississippi twists in broad curves between tall levees. Fine plantation houses preside here, reachable via the parallel highways collectively known as the River Road.

About 15 minutes from New Orleans's airport stands **Destrehan Plantation** *(13034 La. 48, Destrehan. 985-764-9315. www.Destrehan Plantation.org. Adm. fee)*, the oldest documented plantation house in the lower Mississippi Valley. Built in 1787, it once anchored the nation's largest sugar-producing estate. Tours offer fascinating tidbits about daily life in early 19th-century Louisiana: Costumed guides make candles, dye cloth with indigo, and ply other bygone crafts.

For a rewarding history tour, cross to the south bank of the Mississippi on I-310 and head upstream (west) on La. 18. The 1805 main house of **Laura: A Creole Plantation** *(2247 La. 18, Vacherie. 225-265-7690 or 888-799-7690. www.lauraplantation.com. Adm. fee)*, distinguished by its yellow exterior, green shutters, and red roof, was owned for 190 years by just two families. Guides draw on 5,000 pages of family and business records, as well as the evocative memoirs of Laura Locoul Gore (1861-1962), a plantation owner who lived to be almost 102. Though many plantation tours ignore the lives of the slaves who worked the cane fields and made this ostentatious lifestyle possible, Laura presents their stories.

Far fancier than Laura is grand **Oak Alley** *(3645 La. 18, Vacherie. 225-265-2151 or 800-442-5539. www.oakalleyplantation.com. Adm. fee)*; its ancient live oaks interlace in a quarter-mile archway to the house. Built in 1839 by a sugar planter for his bride, the mansion displays furnishings evoking the two decades before the Civil War. You can have breakfast or lunch at the restaurant here or stay in a century-old cottage on the grounds.

NOT TO BE MISSED

- White-chocolate bread pudding at Grapevine Market and Café, Donaldsonville
- River Road African American Museum
- Ornate interiors at San Francisco Plantation
- Nottoway Plantation

Double rows of live oaks interlock limbs overhead to form a grande allée *to Oak Alley.*

Donaldsonville

That mainstay of Louisiana conversation—"Where'd y'all eat last night?"—will elicit a detailed reply once you visit Donaldsonville. In a renovated 1859 house, **Lafitte's Landing at Bittersweet Plantation** (see Travelwise) features the local cooking of celebrated chef John Folse. Among the temptations: turtle soup, potato-wrapped shrimp, and a dish called "Death by Gumbo." Just down the street, **Grapevine Market and Café** (see Travelwise) offers Cajun-style seafood and other dishes in an open, airy room hung with local artwork. Try the barbecued shrimp Pont Breaux-style.

The brick storefronts of Donaldsonville, once a key commercial center (and state capital from 1830 to 1831), reflect African, Italian, Jewish, and Lebanese influences. The **Historic Donaldsonville Museum** *(318 Mississippi St. 225-746-0004. Wed., Fri., and Sat.),* housed in a former department store, recaptures the town's colorful past.

A short drive northwest is spectacular **Nottoway Plantation** *(30970 La. 405, White Castle. 225-545-2730. www.nottoway.com. Adm. fee)*. With 64 rooms totaling 53,000 square feet, this white-columned monument boasted such novelties as gas lights, hot water, and coal-burning fireplaces when it was completed in 1859. Nottoway suffered only minor damage during the Civil War; original furnishings and authentic colors grace its ornate rooms today. The plantation's **Randolph Hall Restaurant** serves Cajun food, while its antique-filled bedrooms make for a relaxing overnight stay.

To Baton Rouge & back

Not all River Road residents were wealthy planters or impoverished slaves. For an eye-opening look at everyday lives, drive north to Baton Rouge and the **Louisiana State University Rural Life Museum** *(4600 Essen Ln. 225-765-2437. rurallife.lsu.edu. Adm. fee)*. A pioneer cabin, a dogtrot house, a shotgun house, and a country church typify folk architecture of the period, while a barn full of artifacts shows how rural Louisianans made a living and dealt with the environment.

Heading back southeast on I-10, stop in Sorrento at **Cajun Village** *(6470 La. 22. 225-675-5572. www.thecajunvillage.com)*, where galleries housed in 19th-century cabins display paintings, pottery, and Native American art. The Ascension Parish Tourist Center (see Travelwise) offers advice on other local attractions. A worthwhile stop nearby is **The Cabin** restaurant (see Travelwise); it serves crawfish, shrimp, and red beans and rice from a former slave cabin.

Not far away is **Tezcuco Plantation Home** *(3138 La. 44. 225-562-3929. www.tezcuco.com. Adm. fee)*, an 1855 house that melds Greek Revival style with the locally popular design known as Raised American Cottage. The restored interior features false graining—woodwork painted to resemble more expensive lumber. Outbuildings on the Tezcuco grounds include a chapel and a Civil War museum. Bed-and-breakfast cottages *($-$$)* make a comfortable place to overnight.

At the rear of the site is the **River Road African American Museum and Gallery** *(225-562-7703. www.africanamericanmuseum.org. Closed Mon.-Tues.; donation)*. Small but emotionally affecting, this museum-in-progress vividly unveils the lives of African slaves forced to cut sugarcane in the fields or work in the plantation house to maintain the rich lifestyle of antebellum planters. Exhibits show leg chains and other chilling artifacts of the era; they also illuminate African influences on the cooking, music, and language of Louisiana.

A few miles west of Tezcuco stands **Houmas House Plantation and Gardens** *(40136 La. 942, Darrow. 225-473-7841 or 888-323-8314. www.houmashouse.com. Adm. fee)*, a splendid mansion whose extensive cane fields earned owner John Burnside the nickname "prince of sugar." Preserved behind the 1840 main house is the original structure, a four-room house from the late 18th century. For a relaxed view of the Mississippi, cross La. 942 and walk to the top of the levee.

Following La. 44 back to New Orleans, you'll see the industrial results of decades of petrochemical development. Two miles east of Convent, enjoy a view (from the road) of the private **Manresa Retreat House** *(5858 La. 44),* an 1831 Greek Revival structure that served as a college for the sons of local planters. About 20 minutes farther east is **San Francisco Plantation House** *(2646 La. 44, Garyville. 985-535-2341 or 888-322-1756. www.sanfranciscoplantation.org. Adm. fee),* a strikingly restored 1856 house. Painted doors and ceilings, cast-iron gallery railings, ornamental columns, and gilded moldings make this tour an apt capstone to your plantation weekend.

—*Mel White*

Travelwise

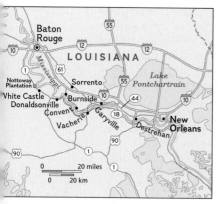

GETTING THERE

Drive west from New Orleans on I-10 for 15 miles, then turn south on I-310.

GENERAL INFORMATION

Contact the **Ascension Parish Tourist Commission** *(6470 La. 22, Sorrento, LA 70778. 225-675-6550 or 888-775-7990. www.ascensiontourism.com);* the **St. Charles Parish Tourist Information Center** *(13825 River Rd., Luling, LA 70057. 985-783-5145. www.parish.st-charles.la.us);* or the **Donaldsonville Area Chamber of Commerce** *(714 Railroad Ave., Donaldsonville, LA 70346. 225-473-4814. www.dvillecoc.org).*

SEASONS

Spring and fall are the best times to visit New Orleans; summer can be very hot and humid.

LODGING

Bay Tree Plantation Bed & Breakfast *(3785 La. 18, Vacherie. 225-265-2109 or 800-895-2109. www.baytree.net. $-$$)* Next to Oak Alley, this fine B&B offers rooms with private baths, some in an 1850 French Creole cottage. Separate cabin has kitchen, whirlpool.

Lafitte's Landing at Bittersweet Plantation *(404 Claiborne Ave., Donaldsonville. 225-473-1232. www.jfolse.com. $$-$$$)* Renowned restaurant; B&B accommodations upstairs and in house adjacent. See p. 206.

DINING

B&C Seafood Market & Cajun Restaurant *(2155 La. 18, Vacherie. 225-265-8356. Closed Sun. $-$$)* Po'boy sandwiches, gumbo, seafood, and specialties such as alligator.

The Cabin *(jct. of La. 22 & La. 44, Burnside. 225-473-3007. www.thecabinrestaurant .com. $-$$)* See p. 207.

Grapevine Market and Café *(211 Railroad Ave. 225-473-8463. Closed Mon. $$)* See p. 206.

Hymel's *(8740 La. 44, Convent. 225-562-9910. Closed Mon. $-$$)* Informal spot favored by locals; shrimp, oysters, crawfish, crabs, catfish, frog legs.

Lafitte's Landing *(404 Claiborne Ave. 225-473-1232. www.jfolse.com. Closed Mon. $$-$$$)* See p. 206.

Randolph Hall Restaurant *(Nottoway Plantation, 30970 La. 405, White Castle. 225-545-2730. www.nottoway.com. Adm. fee. $$)* See p. 207.

Cajun Country
Crawfish & culture down on the bayou

INFECTIOUS MUSIC, SPICY FOOD, and a rich history are the leitmotifs of Cajun country, the part of southern Louisiana settled by French speakers whose unique culture endures today in language, customs, and the smell of crawfish étouffée. The winding bayous may flow languidly beneath live oaks, but there's nothing lazy about the way you feel when a fiddle scrapes a rollicking Cajun tune.

Learning the past of a people

When names such as Hebert, Boudreaux, Breaux, Fontenot, and Guidry begin popping up on signs around **Lafayette,** the self-proclaimed "capital of French Louisiana," you know you're in Cajun country. Stop first at the **Acadian Cultural Center** *(501 Fisher Rd., just E of US 90. 337-232-0789. www.nps.gov/jela),* a unit of **Jean Lafitte National Historical Park and Preserve.** A film and exhibits tell the story of the *Grand Dérangement,* or Great Upheaval, the 1755 ouster of francophones from Acadie, their homeland in eastern Canada, by the ruling British. Several thousand Acadians—today's Cajuns—followed the Atlantic and Gulf coasts to settle in Louisiana.

The Acadian immigrants established communities in remote areas, where they kept their traditions alive. For years, Louisiana law barred French from being spoken in schools; pupils who spoke their native language were punished for it. Since the mid-1950s, however, resurgent pride in Cajun culture has sparked interest in everything from Cajun history classes to Cajun cooking schools to preserving the Cajun dialect.

Learn more about this unique world at **Vermilionville** *(300 Fisher Rd. 337-233-4077 or 866-992-2968. www.vermilionville.org. Closed Mon.; adm. fee),* a re-creation of southern Louisiana village life from 1765 to 1890. Interpreters demonstrate cooking, blacksmithing, woodcarving, and other frontier skills among restored buildings, including a barn, a school, a chapel, and several houses. The Performance Center hosts frequent concerts of Cajun music, while the restaurant serves traditional dishes such as jambalaya, shrimp Creole, and bread pudding.

For lunch, head to the **Olde Tyme Grocery** (see Travelwise) near

NOT TO BE MISSED

● **Early morning walk at Lake Martin** ● **Dancing to Chubby Carrier's zydeco band at Antlers in Lafayette** ● **Pastries from Poupart's Bakery, Pinhook Road, Lafayette** ● **"Signature door" at Shadows-on-the-Teche, New Iberia**

the University of Louisiana at Lafayette; the informal dining room serves legendary po'boy sandwiches.

In southwest Lafayette, **Acadian Village** *(200 Greenleaf Rd. 337-981-2364 or 800-962-9133. www.acadianvillage.org. Adm. fee)* comprises a restored blacksmith shop, a chapel, a village store, and many homes filled with antiques, household items, and other 19th-century artifacts. Time permitting, visit the **Alexandre Mouton House/Lafayette Museum** *(1122 Lafayette St. 337-234-2208. Closed Mon.; adm. fee),* once the home of Louisiana's first democratically elected governor. Exhibits include flamboyant Mardi Gras costumes.

After this immersion in the past, you'll be ready to drop by **Randol's Restaurant and Cajun Dance Hall** (see Travelwise) to dig into a plate of crawfish and listen to a Cajun band. The boiled seafood is good, but the main draw is the roomy dance floor and nightly music.

From A(cadia) to Z(ydeco)

Head to **Breaux Bridge,** a few minutes east of Lafayette on I-10 or La. 94, for the Saturday breakfast at **Café des Amis** (see Travelwise). The driving beat of live zydeco—related to traditional Cajun music, but showing the influence of African-American rhythm and blues—will get your day off to a rousing start.

Half an hour south on La. 31 is **St. Martinville,** a town with Cajun connections both real and mythical. The **Longfellow-Evangeline State Historic Site** *(1200 N. Main St. 337-394-3754 or 888-677-2900. www.crt.state.la.us/parks/longfell/longfell.htm)* includes fine exhibits on Creoles (settlers of French descent) and the Acadians, who arrived after the Creoles had formed a community dubbed Petit Paris. An 1815 plantation house and a rustic Cajun cabin show the settlers' varied existences.

In 1847, Henry Wadsworth Longfellow addressed the Acadians' expulsion from Nova Scotia (symbolized by the forced separation of two lovers, Gabriel and Evangeline) in his epic poem *Evangeline: A Tale of Acadie.* The poem's popularity bred the apocryphal belief that the story was true—and that St. Martinville was among its settings. Today there's an "Evangeline Oak" on the bank of Bayou Teche. A statue of the eternally waiting girl—donated (and posed for) by the actress Delores del Rio, who starred in a 1929 movie based on the poem—stands beside St. Martin de Tours Catholic Church.

At the nearby **Acadian Memorial** *(121 S. New Market St. 337-394-2258. www.acadianmemorial.org. Donation),* a 30-foot mural depicts the group's arrival in Louisiana. Artist Robert Dafford tracked down descendants of early Acadian settlers and used them as models.

Continue south to New Iberia and **Shadows on-the-Teche** *(317 E. Main St. 337-369-6446. www.shadowsontheteche.org. Adm. fee),* an 1834 white-columned mansion on the banks of pretty Bayou Teche. Nearly 40 trunks of family records and belongings in the attic

Harvesting hot peppers on Avery Island, Louisiana

conveyed with the home when it was willed to the National Register in 1958, making the house tour an especially fascinating one.

Head northwest to Eunice for the Cajun history on display at the **Prairie Acadian Cultural Center** *(250 W. Park Ave. 337-457-8499. www.nps.gov/jela)*. Exhibits illustrate the distinctive culture of prairie Cajuns—those who put down roots in the Gulf coastal grasslands, where they raised cattle and grew rice. The center holds demonstrations of crafts and cooking; a theater stages Cajun music concerts.

Hit Eunice on a Saturday evening and you can take in a live broadcast of its **"Rendez-Vous des Cajuns"** radio show, airing at 6 p.m. from the Liberty Center for the Performing Arts *(200 W. Park Ave. 337-457-7389. Adm. fee)*. The informal proceedings feature great Cajun and zydeco music, with commentary mostly in French.

If it's early and you feel like dancing, head back to **Mulate's** (see Travelwise) in Breaux Bridge, where Cajun bands play every night and the food is *formidable!*

Backwaters abounding

South Louisiana bayous have shaped regional culture. Cajun hunters piloted small boats called pirogues into the swamps and fed their families on the bass, crappie, crawfish, ducks, and even alligator (a menu item at many local restaurants) they found there. Several companies offer tours of the **Atchafalaya Basin,** a wonderland of wading birds, water tupelo, bald cypress, gators, and tannin-dark water. **Mc-Gee's Landing** *(1337 Henderson Levee Rd., Breaux Bridge. 337-228-2384 or 800-445-6681. Fee for tours)* guides visitors into the swamp—a venture often rewarded by glimpses of turtles, otters, and eagles.

A solid-ground alternative is **Lake Martin** *(from La. 31, 3 miles S of Breaux Bridge, take Lake Martin Rd. west)*, a preserve full of herons, egrets, and alligators. A trail around the lake lets you view the wildlife, most active at dawn and dusk. Time spent in this idyll reveals the hoot of a barred owl to be as melodic as an old-time Cajun waltz.

—*Mel White*

Travelwise

GETTING THERE
Drive 130 miles west of New Orleans on I-10.

GENERAL INFORMATION
Contact the **Lafayette Convention & Visitors Commission** *(337-232-3737 or 800-346-1958. www.lafayettetravel.com)*; **Bayou Teche (Breaux Bridge) Visitor Center** *(337-332-8500 or 888-565-5939. www.breaux bridgelive.com)*; or **Iberia Parish Convention & Visitors Bureau** *(337-365-1540 or 888-942-3742. www.iberiaparish.com)*.

SEASONS
Spring and fall are best; summers can be hot.

ANNUAL EVENTS
Festivals Acadiens *(3rd weekend in Sept., Lafayette. 337-232-3737 or 800-346-1958. www.lafayettetravel.com)* Cajun culture events include the Bayou Food Festival, a crafts show, kids' activities, and Cajun music.

Festival International de Louisiane *(late April, downtown Lafayette. 337-232-8086. www.festivalinternational.com)* Six-day cultural fete features musicians from around the world, plus dance, theater, and food galore.

LODGING
Aaah! T'Frere's House *(1905 Verot School Rd., Lafayette. 337-984-9347 or 800-984-9347. www.tfreres.com. $)* Excellent food in an eight-room bed-and-breakfast.

Bois des Chênes Bed and Breakfast *(338 N. Sterling St., Lafayette. 337-233-7816. $-$$)* Rooms in an 1820 plantation house; boat tours of Atchafalaya Swamp.

Maison des Amis *(111 Washington St., Breaux Bridge. 337-507-3399. www.cafedes amis.com. $-$$)* Antique-filled rooms in a Creole-Caribbean building on Bayou Teche.

DINING
Café des Amis *(140 E. Bridge St. 337-332-5273. www.cafedesamis.com. Closed Mon.-Tues.)* See p. 210.

Café Vermilionville *(1304 W. Pinhook Rd., Lafayette. 337-237-0100. $$$)* Try the turkey and andouille gumbo, or any seafood entree.

Catahoula's *(234 King Dr., Grand Coteau. 337-662-2275 or 888-547-2275. Closed Mon.)* Converted country store serves unique versions of seafood and other Creole dishes.

Charley G's Seafood Grill *(3809 Ambassador Caffery Pkwy., Lafayette. 337-981-0108. www.charlygs.com)* Casual restaurant offering local specialties: mahi-mahi, crab cakes, sausage, shrimp, and (of course!) crawfish.

Mulate's *(325 Mills Ave. 337-332-4648 or 800-422-2586)* See p. 211.

Olde Tyme Grocery *(218 W. St. Mary Blvd. 337-235-8165. Closed Sun.)* See p. 210.

Randol's Restaurant *(2320 Kaliste Saloom Rd. 337-981-7080 or 800-962-2586. www .randols.com)* See pp. 209-210.

New York City

Gilded Age Castles 214

Quiet Times 218

The Litchfields 221

Washington Irving's Sunnyside, Tarrytown

Gilded Age Castles
A journey up the Hudson River Valley

AT THE TURN OF THE 20TH CENTURY, just as the Gilded Age was in full swing, New York City's patricians and industrial barons built grandiose country estates upriver. The quiet Hudson River Valley became the center of romantic art and architecture at its most beautiful—and ostentatious. Today as you wander among stone-walled meadows, gnarled forests, and picturesque riverside towns, you—like the Vanderbilts of old—can stop to call at any grand mansion you choose.

Sleepy Hollow region

The best historic mansions line two stretches of the river's eastern bank. You can settle in for the weekend at Tarrytown (on the lower Hudson) or Rhinebeck (mid-Hudson) and visit the surrounding estates. Or you can travel the whole route, visiting only the historic houses that catch your fancy.

Either way, your first stop should be **Sunnyside** *(off US 9 on W. Sunnyside Ln., Tarrytown. 914-591-8763. April-Dec. Wed.-Mon., March Sat.-Sun.; adm. fee)*. This wisteria-covered Dutch-style cottage was the home of Washington Irving from 1835 until his death in 1859. Ichabod Crane and Rip Van Winkle haunt the half-hour tour.

North of Sunnyside on US 9—you can walk the half mile or so on the **Croton Aqueduct Trail**—stands magnificent **Lyndhurst** *(635 S. Broadway/US 9. 914-631-4481. www.lyndhurst .org. Mid-April–Oct. Tues.-Sun., Nov–mid-April Sat.-Sun.; adm. fee)*, one of the country's finest examples of 19th-century Gothic Revival architecture. Tour with a guide, audiotour, or self-guided brochure, and stroll the parklike 67-acre grounds overlooking the Hudson. You can get lunch or a carryout picnic on-site at the **Carriage House Café** (see Travelwise).

Proceed north to **Sleepy Hollow** (also known as North Tarrytown) and the **Philipsburg Manor** *(US 9. 914-631-3992. April-Dec. Wed.-Mon.; adm. fee)*. The big farming, milling, and trading complex, founded in the late 17th century by Dutch entrepreneur Frederick

---

NOT TO BE MISSED

● **Hiking at Hudson Highlands SP** ● **Strolling along the Hudson on the Hyde Park Trail** ● **Riding the scenic Metro North train downriver at dusk**

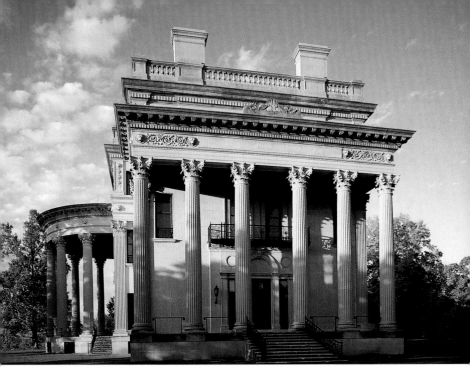

Vanderbilt Mansion

Philipse, was powered by slave labor. Today it's a living history museum of the 18th century, staffed by guides in period costume. Across the road you'll find the **Old Dutch Church,** once part of the estate, and **Sleepy Hollow Cemetery,** where Washington Irving lies buried.

A shuttle from the Philipsburg Manor Visitor Center carries you to nearby **Kykuit** *(914-631-9491. Closed mid-Nov.–late April; adm. fee).* Set amid grandly terraced gardens overlooking the river, Kykuit was home to four generations of Rockefellers, including former Gov. Nelson A. Rockefeller, whose collection of modern sculpture— Moore, Picasso, Calder, and others—ornaments the grounds. At the nearby **Union Church in Pocantico Hills** *(Bedford Rd. 914-631-8200. Closed Tues.),* see splendid stained-glass windows by Matisse and Chagall, commissioned by the Rockefellers.

Continue north on US 9 to **Van Cortlandt Manor** *(S. Riverside Ave., Croton-on-Hudson. 914-271-8981. April-Oct. Wed.-Mon., Nov.- Dec. Sat.-Sun.; adm. fee).* The 18th-century stone manor features original Georgian and federal furnishings, and its 200-year-old gardens occupy a particularly beautiful spot overlooking the Croton River.

Hyde Park to Rhinebeck

A few miles north of Poughkeepsie, on a commercialized stretch of US 9 in Hyde Park, stands the **Franklin D. Roosevelt National Historic Site** *(845-229-9115. Adm. fee),* which encompasses part of the family estate known as Springwood. Unpretentious in looks, the colonial revival house where Roosevelt was born in 1882 takes its weight from history. The grounds also contain a presidential library and a museum. A shuttle *(fare)* carries visitors to FDR's hilltop retreat **Top Cottage** *(May-Oct. Thurs.-Mon.)*.

Two miles east of Hyde Park, off N.Y. 9G, awaits the **Eleanor Roosevelt National Historic Site,** or Val-Kill *(845-229-9115. Daily May-Oct., Thurs.-Mon. Nov.-April; fee for tour),* Mrs. Roosevelt's modest rural getaway from 1925, and her home from 1945 until her death in 1962.

Two miles north of the Roosevelt site on US 9 is the **Vanderbilt Mansion National Historic Site** *(845-229-9115. Adm. fee for tour).* The 54-room classical limestone creation of Charles McKim—built between 1895 and 1908, lavishly decorated largely by Stanford White, and set in a park with stunning river views—was Frederick Vanderbilt's version of a weekend cottage.

Three miles north stands **Staatsburg,** formerly the Mills Mansion *(Old Post Rd., Staatsburg. 845-889-8851. Closed Mon.-Tues. and Nov.-March; adm. fee).* Take a tour of the beaux arts mansion, ambitiously remodeled by 1896 to 65 rooms, and roam the stately grounds.

Neighbor Robert Suckley in 1888 transformed his father's riverfront villa into a lavishly decorated, turreted Queen Anne fantasy: **Wilderstein** *(off US 9 at 330 Morton Rd., Rhinebeck. 845-876-4818. May-Oct. Thurs.-Sun. p.m.; adm. fee).* Take the guided tour, and walk a wooded trail to the river.

Rhinebeck area

Pretty **Rhinebeck** has strollable streets lined with shops, good restaurants, and cafés—a good place to relax and perhaps spend the night. Travelers have been stopping by the **Beekman Arms** (see Travelwise) for supper and a bed since 1766.

Just beyond the village, take N.Y. 9A along the river to **Montgomery Place** *(River Rd., Annandale-on-Hudson. 845-758-5461. April-Oct. Wed.-Mon., Nov.-mid-Dec. Sat.-Sun.; adm. fee),* an impeccably restored neoclassic mansion. Stroll to the river and pick your own apples on the exceptionally beautiful grounds.

Continue north on N.Y. 9G to **Clermont** *(off Woods Rd. 518-537-4240. April-Oct. Tues.-Sun., Nov.–mid-Dec. Sat.-Sun.; adm. fee),* home to seven generations of the politically prominent Livingston family. The lovely Georgian house replaces the early 18th-century manor burned by the British during the American Revolution.

Frederic Edwin Church, celebrated member of the Hudson River school of landscape painters, built his fanciful Persian palace high above the river in the 1870s, now called the **Olana State Historic Site** *(5720 N.Y. 9G, Hudson. 518-828-0135. April–mid-Oct. Wed.-Sun.; adm. fee).* Nearly every window frames a dazzling view of the great river and the Catskill Mountains beyond. Church's paintings, and others, are on view.   —*Ann Jones*

Travelwise

GETTING THERE

The Hudson River Valley runs due north from Manhattan between the Catskill Mountains on the west and the Taconic Highlands on the east. US 9, and farther north N.Y. 9G and 9J, winds along the river's east side, accessing the majority of sites. New York Waterway *(800-533-3779. May-Nov. Sat.-Sun.; fare)* offers ferry service to Tarrytown plus tour packages.

GENERAL INFORMATION

Historic Hudson Valley *(914-631-8200 or 800-448-4007. www.hudsonvalley.org)* maintains Sunnyside, Philipsburg Manor, Kykuit, Van Cortlandt Manor, and Montgomery Place. Also contact **Dutchess County Tourism** *(800-445-3131. www.dutchesstourism.com).*

SEASONS

River and valley are radiant May into Oct.

ANNUAL EVENTS

Holiday Celebration *(Dec., Dutchess County Tourism 800-445-3131)* Lavish decorations gild the great estates.

Pinkster Festival *(mid-May, Philipsburg Manor. 914-631-3992)* Celebrates the site's early 18th-century African and Dutch heritage.

MORE THINGS TO SEE & DO

American history sites Washington's headquarters at **Newburgh** *(Hasbrouck House, 84 Liberty St. 845-562-1195. Adm. fee)* and New York's first capital at **Kingston** *(www.ci.kingston.ny.us)* feature prominently.

U. S. Military Academy *(West Point exit off N.Y. 9W and follow signs. Visitor center 845-938-2638)* Historic training grounds of Grant, Lee, MacArthur, Patton, and Eisenhower.

LODGING

Alexander Hamilton House *(49 Van Wyck St., Croton-on-Hudson. 914-271-6737. www.alexanderhamiltonhouse.com. $$-$$$)* An 1889 Victorian B&B with 8 guest rooms and a swimming pool.

Beekman Arms *(6387 Mill St., Rhinebeck. 845-876-7077. www.beekmanarms.com. $-$$)* Romantic country inn that began as a coach stop in 1766; 63 rooms. The Traphagen Restaurant serves breakfast, lunch, and dinner. See p. 216.

Belvedere Mansion *(10 Old Rte. 9, Staatsburg. 845-889-8000. www.belvedereman-*

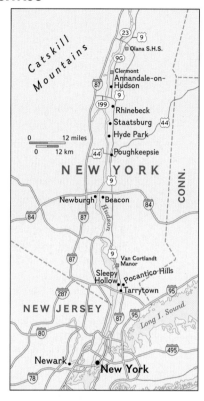

sion.com. $-$$$) Gilded age elegance in a circa 1900 neoclassic home; 16 rooms.

Castle at Tarrytown *(400 Benedict Ave., Tarrytown. 914-631-1980 or 800-616-4487. www.castleattarrytown.com. $$$)* Regal, luxurious, hundred-year-old Norman-style dwelling with 31 rooms and suites. Fine dining at the Equus restaurant.

DINING

Carriage House Café *(Lyndhurst grounds, Tarrytown. Lunch only; May-Oct. Wed.-Sun. 914-631-4481. $$)* Salads, soups, sandwiches. See p. 214.

Main Street Café *(24 Main St., Tarrytown. 914-332-9834. Closed Mon. $$)* American bistro cooking.

Stoney Creek *(76 Broadway, Tivoli. 845-757-4117. Closed Mon.-Tues. $$)* Down-home American seafood and game.

Quiet Times
Exploring Long Island's North Fork & Shelter Island

AT THE FAR NORTHERN END OF LONG ISLAND, away from the bustlings of the Hamptons and Montauk, the North Fork basks in an earlier century. Minutes away, in the quiet waters of Peconic Bay, lies Shelter Island, its coastline scalloped with bays, coves, and beaches. At any season, the North Fork and Shelter Island are sunny, sleepy places to poke around.

The North Fork

Where the main route from New York City ends at Riverhead, the North and South Forks begin. Traveling along N.Y. 25, the **North Fork**'s southern artery, you'll pass through fields, farms, and weathered villages where farmers and mariners have lived for 350 years.

The latest trend started in 1973 when vintners discovered that the area's glacial soils and moderating sea breezes made for world-class Cabernets, Chardonnays, Rieslings, and Merlots. **Paumanok Vineyards** *(1074 Main Rd., Aquebogue. 631-722-8800)* is one of the first you'll see of the North Fork's more than two dozen wineries. Follow the green Wine Trail signs from one winery to the next. Some wineries, such as **Gristina Galluccio Estate Vineyards** *(Main Rd., Cutchogue. 631-734-7089)*, welcome you to bring your own lunch to their vineyard picnic tables. Get a full list of wineries and a map from the Long Island Wine Council *(104 Edwards Ave., Calverton. 516-369-5887)*.

Look for roadside farm stands, too, all along the way. Farmers still produce and sell fruits, vegetables, and flowers of outstanding quality. Or pick your own berries, peas, tomatoes, or pumpkins in Mattituck at **Harbes Family Farm** *(247 Sound Ave. 631-298-9773. May–Oct.)* and in Cutchogue at **Wickham's Fruit Farm** *(Main Rd. 631-734-6441. May–Dec.)*.

To dip into history, stop at the village green in **Cutchogue** to see the 1649 **Old House** *(Main Rd. 631-734-7122. Late June–Labor Day Sat.-Mon.; adm. fee)*. In **Southold**, the **Southold Indian Museum** *(Main Bayview Rd. 631-765-5577. Adm. fee)* documents the lives of the area's first residents, and the **Southold Historical Society Museum**

NOT TO BE MISSED

- **Ogling shorebirds at Orient Point State Park**
- **Pumpkin ice cream at Scoops in Cutchogue**
- **The Blue Trail in Mashomack Preserve**

A North Fork dock

and Grounds *(Main Rd. at Maple Ln. 631-765-5500. July–mid-Sept. Sat.-Sun. and Wed.)* re-creates colonial life with historical houses.

Continue on N.Y. 25 to the fishing port of **Greenport,** a pleasant place to spend the night. Learn about Peconic Bay fishing at the **East End Seaport Maritime Museum** *(next to North Ferry Dock. 631-477-2100. Daily June-Aug., Sat.-Sun. May and Sept.-Dec.).* Dip into seafaring life past and present at **S. T. Preston & Son** *(102 Main St. 631-477-1990),* the country's oldest marine chandlery, where mariners can find every essential from rope to rudders. Join a leisurely sail aboard the 1906 schooner ***Mary E*** *(631-477-8966),* which leaves daily in summer from Preston's Dock.

Continue eastward on N.Y. 25 to the picture-perfect village of **Orient.** Stroll through the village and visit the museum buildings of the **Oysterponds Historical Society** *(Village Ln. 631-323-2480. Mem. Day–Labor Day Sat.-Sun. p.m.; adm. fee),* housing objects from three centuries of maritime and local history.

Head east again to road's end and **Orient Beach State Park** *(N. Country Rd./N.Y. 25. 631-323-2440),* a 342-acre peninsula bounded by unspoiled beaches and wetlands. It's a precious refuge for bird-watchers and beachcombers, just the place for a quiet walk in any season.

Shelter Island

Back in Greenport, catch the ferry for the 10-minute trip to **Shelter Island.** With a new seascape around every turn, the island is well worth exploring—by car, bike, foot, or kayak. You can rent a bike at Piccozzi's Bike Shop *(Bridge St. 631-749-0045)* on the island's north side. Rent a kayak or sign up for a guided tour at Shelter Island Kayak *(N. Ferry and Duvall Rds. 631-749-1990)*. You'll find good swimming beaches at **West Neck,** and beautiful biking on the road to Ram Head.

About one-third of the island has been set aside in a wild state as **Mashomack Preserve** *(79 S. Ferry Rd. 631-749-1001. Daily July-Aug., closed Tues. rest of year)*. To really get away from it all, pick up a map at the visitor center and set off on a walk. You're likely to encounter deer and abundant birdlife; some 200 bird species have been recorded, including ospreys, which nest here in unusually large numbers.

—*Ann Jones*

Travelwise

GETTING THERE
From New York City, take the Long Island Expressway (I-495) to Riverhead and pick up N.Y. 25, the North Fork's Main Road.

GENERAL INFORMATION
Contact the **North Fork Promotion Council** *(P.O. Box 1865, Southold, NY 11971. 631-298-5757. www.northfork.org)* or the **Shelter Island Chamber of Commerce** *(P.O. Box 598, Shelter Island, NY 11964. 516-749-0399. www.shelter-island.org)*.

SEASONS
Summer and fall are the most popular seasons on the North Fork; winter is more peaceful.

MORE THINGS TO SEE & DO
Antique shopping For a listing of shops, contact the North Fork Antique Dealers Association *(P.O. Box 40, Southold, NY 11971. www.northforkantiques.com)*.

Fishing Catch bluefish, cod, fluke, sea bass, tuna, and trophy striped bass. Go out from

Greenport with the 150-passenger **Peconic Star II** *(631-289-6899),* from Orient Point with the 49-passenger **Prime Time III** *(631-323-2618)*. The North Fork Captains Association *(Box 724, Southold, NY 11971. www.northforkcaptains.com)* offers charters.

LODGING
Bartlett House *(503 Front St., Greenport. 631-477-0371. $$-$$$)* Handsome, 10-room, turn-of-the-20th-century inn.

Belle Crest Inn *(163 N. Ferry Rd., Shelter Island. 631-749-2041. $$$)* Grand old Victorian with 10 guest rooms.

Chequit Inn *(23 Grand Ave., Shelter Island. 631-749-0018. www.shelterislandinns.com. $$-$$$)* Charming Victorian country inn with 35 rooms.

Olde Country Inn *(11 Stearns Point Rd., Shelter Island. 631-749-1633. www.oldecountryinn.com. $$-$$$)* 1886 Victorian lodging house with 13 rooms.

Sound View Inn *(N.Y. 48, Greenport. 631-477-1910. $$-$$$)* Modern hotel with 49 rooms.

DINING
Claudio's *(111 Main St., Greenport. 631-477-0627. Mid-April–Dec. $$$)* Fresh fish on the waterfront. **Claudio's Crabby Jerry's** *(Main St. wharf. 631-477-8252. $$)* is more casual.

Seafood Barge *(Main Rd. and Port of Egypt Marina, Southold. 631-765-3010. $$$)* More fresh fish on the waterfront.

The Litchfields
An Early American sampler

PEACEFULLY TUCKED AWAY IN northwest Connecticut, the Litchfield
Hills prospered by way of Yankee ingenuity some 200 years ago.
In this sylvan cranny, pragmatic local inventors designed portable
clocks, burglar-proof locks, and mass-produced chairs, all con-
tributing to the birth of the industrial revolution. Passed over by
time, the Litchfields' hidden hollows, indigo-blue mountain
lakes, rolling farmland abutting thick maple and oak woods, and
white-steepled villages whisk visitors back to those earlier times.
Romantic old inns, top-notch restaurants, and plenty of activities
assure a pampered stay.

Lake Waramaug & Kent

The perfect base for a night or two is **Lake Waramaug,** set deep
among the forested hills about 4 miles north of New Preston. Three
grand hotels here provide lodging and exquisite dining: the **Hopkins
Inn,** a cozy 19th-century country house high on a hill with a lake
view; the elegant **Boulders Inn,** built in 1895 and
named for the fieldstone rocks used in its construction; and the **Birches Inn,** a woodsy lodge
complete with evening wine-and-cheese by a
roaring fire and a French-style gourmet breakfast
(see Travelwise for all three). An 8-mile road rings
the popular boating and swimming lake, making
for an idyllic drive, or bike ride, especially during
autumn glory. **Lake Waramaug State Park** *(860-
868-2592),* at the lake's northwestern tip, beckons
with waterside picnic tables and campsites.

> **NOT TO BE MISSED**
>
> ● **Rösti potatoes at
> Hopkins Inn restaurant**
> ● **An autumn run around
> Lake Waramaug**
> ● **Riverton's storybook
> setting** ● **Hiking the
> Appalachian Trail along
> the Housatonic**

West of the lake, follow maple-edged lanes to
the village of **Kent,** poised on the shores of the
boulder-strewn Housatonic River. Charming,
outdoorsy, intimately walkable, Kent is also artsy,
with bountiful galleries. Premier among them is **Paris New York
Kent Gallery** *(860-927-4152)* in Kent Station Square, filled with
nationally known names. You could easily spend an afternoon visiting
all the galleries, along with bookshops, clothing stores, outdoor outfitters, and antique shops. For the galleried-out, the **Housatonic River**

is a popular canoeing and kayaking venue, with favorite put-ins at **Macedonia Brook State Park** *(860-927-3238)*, near Kent, and **Housatonic Meadows State Park** *(860-927-3238)*, about 4 miles north of town near Cornwall Bridge. All along the river's cold, cool length, fly fishermen patiently work to lure trout and bass.

US 7 heads north of Kent, offering intertwining views of the river and thick hardwood forests. After a mile or so, watch on the left for the **Sloane-Stanley Museum** *(US 7. 860-566-3005 or 860-927-3849. Mid-May–Oct. Wed.-Sun.; adm. fee)*, which celebrates the lost art of handmade tools, a form mostly forgotten after the advent of mass production. Americana artist and author Eric Sloane (1905-1985) saw the simple beauty in preindustrial tools and so collected them— planes, irons, yokes, brooms, wagon wheels, some dating as far back as the 1700s. He personally arranged his collection in this rustic barn/museum, handwriting the descriptions and setting up the lights just so. His re-created studio is also on display.

Follow US 7 a couple of miles farther north to roadside **Kent Falls State Park** *(860-927-3029 or 860-927-3238)*, where an easy trail climbs alongside the falls to an idyllic picnic perch amid a hemlock grove. For a picnic with a view, simply spread a blanket on the expanse of grass below the falls. A few miles on, the adorable hamlet of **West Cornwall** is easily identifiable by its historic barn-red covered bridge conveying cars above the river to its cozy clutch of shops (including a local pottery), a restaurant or two, and a B&B.

East of Lake Waramaug

On the second day wander east of Lake Waramaug en route to Litchfield via a couple of worn but interesting towns intrinsic to the industrial age. At one time **Terryville** was known as the Lock Town of America, with some 40 lock companies operating here. As befitting such a designation, you'll find the **Lock Museum of America** *(230 Main St. 860-589-6359. www.lockmuseum.com. May-Oct. Tues.-Sun. p.m.; adm. fee)* just across the street from the former site of the Eagle Lock Company (now a shopping center). Locks have been around since Egyptian times, but it took a local man, Linus Yale, Jr., to move them into the modern era. He introduced the combination lock as well as the pin-tumbler cylinder lock, which he based on an Egyptian concept; examples of both can be seen at the museum, along with some 20,000 other locks, keys, and Victorian hardware.

In nearby **Bristol**, the **American Clock & Watch Museum** *(100 Maple St., off US 6. 860-583-6070. www.clockmuseum.org. Closed Dec.-March; adm. fee)* belies the city's clockmaking legacy. Determined to come up with a clock that was affordable and transportable, area resident Eli Terry perfected in 1814 a wooden clock with interchangeable parts. By 1830 many clock factories in town were producing the famous Terry clock. Filled with more than 1,500 timepieces,

Dreamy Lake Waramaug

including punch clocks, Early American grandfathers, and several Terry classics, the museum is at its best (albeit noisiest) at noon.

A detour north of Bristol to **Riverton,** about 30 miles on Conn. 8 and 20, reveals another example of Yankee ingenuity. In this charming, flower-filled village, Lambert Hitchcock set out in 1818 to mass-produce chairs and other furniture; a decade later he was churning out 15,000 chairs a year in his streamside factory, each one hand-stenciled with colorful designs. Now the structure holds a factory store overflowing with brand-new Hitchcock wares *(Conn. 20. 860-379-4826).* To see some beautiful originals, stroll down the street to the **John Tarrant Kenney Hitchcock Museum** *(Conn. 20. 860-738-4950. April-Dec. Thurs.-Sun. p.m.),* housed in an 1829 gray-hued church. If you have time, be sure to take a walk along the picturesque river; you can stock up for a waterside picnic at the general store, located on Main Street before you come to the river.

Now it's on to stately **Litchfield,** deemed by many to be the most quintessential colonial town in America—offering the chance to glimpse preindustrial America. Prim clapboards clustering around a shaded green include the birthplace of Harriet Beecher Stowe and the 1760 **Sheldon's Tavern,** where George Washington slept on a visit here. The 1829 **Litchfield First Congregational Church,** with its soaring steeple and Greek Revival architecture, is one of the most photographed churches in New England.

Believed to be the country's first law school, the **Tapping Reeve**

House and Law School (*South St. 860-567-4501. May-Oct. Tues.-Sun.; adm. fee*) is found just around the corner from the green. Begun in 1774, its graduates include such prominent politicians as John C. Calhoun and Aaron Burr. Part of the **Litchfield History Museum,** it comprises two little white buildings filled with period antiques. Be sure to peek into the history museum as well, at the corner of East and South Streets, showcasing Early American paintings, furniture, and other artifacts that recall a simpler time.   —*Barbara A. Noe*

Travelwise

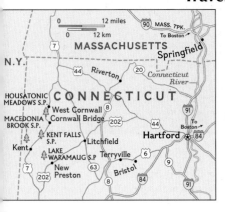

GETTING THERE
The Litchfields are found 100 miles northeast of New York City via I-95 and I-84; and 115 miles southwest of Boston via I-90 and I-84.

GENERAL INFORMATION
Contact the **Litchfield Hills Visitors Bureau** (*P.O. Box 968, Litchfield, CT 06759. 860-567-4506. www.litchfieldhills.com*). For information on galleries, shops, activities, and musical happenings: *www.cthills.com.*

SEASONS
The Litchfields are at their finest in fall, when the maples and oaks flash brilliant color. Summer is busy with vacationers. Many businesses close between late Oct. and spring.

MORE THINGS TO SEE & DO
Boating For guided rafting trips on the Housatonic, as well as kayak and canoe rentals, contact Clarke's Outdoors (*US 7, West Cornwall. 860-672-6365*).
Sharon Audubon Center (*Conn. 4, Sharon. 860-364-0520*) Nature center and wildlife sanctuary with more than 11 miles of hiking trails through forests, meadows, and wetlands.
White Memorial Conservation Center (*80 Whitehall Rd., Litchfield. 860-567-0857*) 4,000 acres include a nature center, picnic areas, camping, and hiking.

LODGING & DINING
Birches Inn (*233 W. Shore Rd., New Preston. 860-868-1735. www.thebirchesinn.com*) Five rooms in the main lodge and two cabins (*$$-$$$*). French-New American cuisine with a romantic flair (*$$$*). See p. 221.

Boulders Inn (*East Shore Rd./Conn. 45, New Preston. 860-868-0541 or 800-552-6853. www.bouldersinn.com*) Seventeen guest rooms in the main house and scattered around secluded grounds (*$$$*). Acclaimed New American cuisine (*daily June-Oct., Thurs.-Sun. Nov.-May. $$$*). See p. 221.

Fife 'n Drum Restaurant and Inn (*53 N. Main St., Kent. 860-927-3509. Closed Tues.*) Family-owned restaurant serving Continental cuisine, including rack of lamb and filet mignon au poivre (*$$$*). Eight guest rooms (*$$*).

Hopkins Inn (*Hopkins Rd., New Preston. 860-868-7295. www.thehopkinsinn.com. Restaurant closed Jan.-March*) Eleven simple, cozy guest rooms and two apartments (*$-$$*). Austrian cuisine (*$$$*). See p. 221.

Old Riverton Inn (*Conn. 20, Riverton. 860-379-8678. Closed Mon.-Tues.*) Opened as a stagecoach stop in 1796, this small, friendly hotel with 12 rooms sits on the Farmington River (*$-$$*). Contemporary American cuisine in a colonial atmosphere (*$$$*).

Village Pub and Restaurant (*25 West St., on the green, Litchfield. 860-567-8307. $$*) Casual restaurant serving steaks, seafood, and pasta.

Philadelphia

Independence Days 226

Bucks County 231

Brandywine Valley 235

Autumn in the Brandywine Valley

Independence Days
Seeing where America was born

As George Washington presided over the 1787 Constitutional Convention in Philadelphia, a curious carving of the sun on his chair back peeked over his head. After months of debate ended with the signing of the Constitution, a relieved Benjamin Franklin exclaimed: "I have the happiness to know that it is a rising and not a setting sun." To see where the sun rose on America, explore the history of the Revolutionary War in Philadelphia, from the sites of great debates in the historic downtown to nearby battlefields and barracks—places where soldiers and statesmen alike wrought bold new ideas into a hard-won reality.

Downtown Philadelphia's historic district

Begin your foray in downtown Philadelphia's historic district, most of which is part of **Independence National Historical Park** *(215-965-2305. www.nps.gov/inde).*

Pick up a map at the city's new Independence Visitor Center *(6th and Market Sts. 215-925-7676. www.independence visitorcenter.com).* The **Liberty Bell Pavilion,** with a long line to see the famous icon, sits across the street. If you're pressed for time, walk past it down Sixth Street to **Independence Hall** *(Chestnut St., bet. 5th and 6th Sts. Tours every quarter hour; timed ticket required)* on Chestnut Street. Both the Declaration of Independence and the Constitution were signed inside this former state house, and Congress met here from 1790 to 1800. On a tour of the meeting chambers, with their wooden writing desks and colonial decor, you can practically hear the Founding Fathers squabbling over the details of the young republic.

NOT TO BE MISSED

- **Reenactment of Washington's army crossing the Delaware** • **Stained-glass windows of the Washington Memorial Chapel** • **18th-century medical demonstration at the Old Barracks Museum**

The city's colonial past thrives among the many Revolutionary-era buildings on Chestnut Street. Step inside **Carpenters' Hall** *(320 Chestnut St.),* where the First Continental Congress met in 1774. Duck down the alley leading to **Franklin Court.** Benjamin Franklin's house is long gone, but a steel outline shows where it stood; the foundations, and a section of the privy, are still visible.

Reenactors take aim and fire at Washington Crossing Historic Park.

An underground museum provides a multimedia introduction to the city's favorite resident, but the highlight is the row of restored brick buildings along Market Street. Built by Franklin as rental properties, today they include a post office, a printshop, and a newspaper office. For a taste of domestic life in colonial Philadelphia, visit the **Todd House** *(adm. fee)* at the corner of Fourth and Walnut Streets.

Walk north along Second Street to **Christ Church** *(2nd and Market Sts. 215-922-1695. Donation)*, where notables such as Washington, Franklin, and Betsy Ross worshiped when the steeple was a city landmark. Then snoop around **Elfreth's Alley** *(2nd bet. Race and Arch Sts.)*, a shaded cobblestone remnant of an 18th-century neighborhood. Lovingly tended gardens are proof that people still live in most of the narrow houses, so respect their privacy, but step into the museum at No. 126 *(215-574-0560. www.elfrethsalley.org. Closed Mon.; adm. fee)* for a peek at photos and collections depicting the architecture and lifestyles of the 18th and early 19th centuries.

Walk west on Arch Street to call on Elizabeth Grishom—better known as Betsy Ross. At the **Betsy Ross House** *(239 Arch St. 215-686-1252. www.ushistory.org/betsy. Donation)*, the widowed seamstress sewed the first Stars and Stripes in 1776. The house, with its twisting staircases and modest decor, makes this Revolutionary icon accessible and human; pay your respects at her tomb in the courtyard.

Continue west on Arch Street past the Christ Church burial

ground; you can see Franklin's tomb through the iron fence. Hang a left and you're back at the visitor center—and no doubt hungry. Enjoy dinner just a few blocks away at the delightful **City Tavern** (see Travelwise). Such auspicious clientele as Washington, John Adams, and Thomas Jefferson supped at the original tavern on this site, and you'd never know that the current building is actually a reconstruction. The ambience, including costumed staff, is charming; relax with a mug of George Washington Ale.

Trenton & Princeton

On the next day, follow the path of George Washington during the "ten crucial days"—December 25, 1776, to January 3, 1777—when he reinspired the flagging American Revolution. Drive north on Pa. 532 to **Washington Crossing Historic Park** *(Washington Crossing, PA. 215-493-4076. www.tencrucialdays.com. Adm. fee).* On Christmas night 1776, Washington's sleet-stung army crossed the Delaware River here, intent on capturing Trenton. Today you can see replicas of the Durham boats that ferried the soldiers across the Delaware, the historic McConkey's Ferry Inn, and other later buildings.

On the New Jersey side, across a narrow steel bridge, is the 1,399-acre **Washington Crossing State Park** *(N.J. 29, 355 Washington Crossing-Pennington Rd., Titusville. 609-737-0623. www.njparksand forests.org).* The Continental Army landed here, and among the historic buildings is the Johnson Ferry House, where Washington finalized the strategy for his Trenton attack.

Next, prepare for battle. Drive 9 miles south on N.J. 29 to Memorial Drive in downtown **Trenton** to see where the Revolutionary tide turned: the **Old Barracks Museum** *(Barracks St. 609-396-1776. www .barracks.org. Adm. fee).* This remarkable 1758 fieldstone structure housed Hessian mercenaries until Washington's forces trounced them. Costumed interpreters step right out of history to share their meticulous knowledge with visitors—especially during a frank demonstration of 18th-century medical procedures.

After Trenton, Washington's forces clashed with the British just up the road in **Princeton.** Take the Princeton Pike (N.J. 583) to **Princeton Battlefield State Park** *(500 Mercer St. 609-921-0074. www.njparks andforests.org).* The battle centered on the front yard of the Thomas Clarke House; exhibits in the house and informative panels make the park well worth a stop. The battle devastated Princeton, but today its downtown is packed with boutiques and restaurants. On the south side of Nassau Street, the main drag, lies the gorgeous campus of **Princeton University** *(609-258-3000. www.princeton.edu),* which includes **Nassau Hall,** where British forces made a desperate stand in 1777. It's also where the Continental Congress, meeting there in 1783, learned that the treaty securing independence had been signed.

Recuperate at the **Nassau Inn** (see Travelwise), as countless weary travelers have since 1756. The inn is still an important local meeting place, and just as bustling as it was 250 years ago. On any given night you'll navigate a euphoric mélange of celebrations, business dinners, and wedding parties.

Valley Forge

In the morning, journey northwest of Philadelphia to **Valley Forge National Historical Park** *(Valley Forge. 610-783-1077. www.nps.gov /vafo)*. Washington's Continental Army camped on this vast plateau during the winter of 1777, enduring harsh weather, poor nutrition, and disease. The park is too large to walk; pick up a map at the visitor center and drive along the slopes and hills. Replicated huts and exhibits explain 18th-century military defenses; statues and a grand memorial arch honor the 12,000 troops who camped on these sprawling grounds for six months. Step into the stone house that served as **Washington's Headquarters** *(adm. fee)*, now staffed by gregarious interpreters.

Washington was something of a secular saint after the war, as demonstrated by the glorious **Washington Memorial Chapel** *(inside park on Pa. 23. 610-783-0120)*. Dim lights shine on stained-glass windows that depict Revolutionary War heroes.

From Valley Forge, take US 422 west to Pa. 363 and follow it north for about 10 miles to Center Point. Turn right on Pa. 73 then left on Shearer Road to the **Peter Wentz Farmstead** *(Shearer Rd., Worcester. 610-584-5104. Closed Mon.; donation)*. Pennsylvania doesn't lack for restored colonial homes, but this one is special. Not only is it a demonstration farm, but its interior—featuring a dramatic Germanic paint motif of dots, cross-hatching, and crescent marks—has also been meticulously restored to its original appearance.

Washington stayed at the Wentz house before the Battle of Germantown in October 1777. Drive south on the Germantown Pike into northwest Philadelphia to see where it all happened. When the cobblestones of the pretty Chestnut Hill neighborhood give way to the grittier Germantown, you're near **Cliveden** *(6401 Germantown Ave. 215-848-1777. www.cliveden.org. Thurs.-Sun. April-Dec., afternoons only; adm. fee)*, the solid, spacious mansion that served as a British bunker. The tour emphasizes the furniture collection, but historical paintings make it easy to picture anxious redcoats in the entry hall, holding out against Washington's artillery.

Germantown boasts a variety of interesting colonial-era homes. Drop by the Germantown Historical Society and Visitor Center *(5501 Germantown Ave. 215-844-0514. www.libertynet.org/ghs)* for a guide. Afterward, drive north for dinner in picturesque **Chestnut Hill**—out of the Revolutionary era, and into the world that Washington and his colleagues helped set in motion.

—Jeff Sypeck

Travelwise

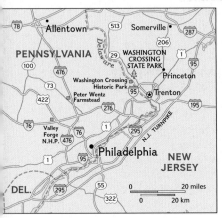

All locations are in Pennsylvania unless otherwise noted.

GETTING THERE
Philadelphia is accessible via I-95. Philadelphia International Airport is located south of town along I-95. Most attractions outside the city's downtown historic district are only reachable by car.

GENERAL INFORMATION
Contact the **Independence Visitor Center** (1 N. Independence Mall W., Philadelphia, PA 19106. 215-925-6101 or 800-537-7676. www.independencevisitorcenter.com).

SEASONS
Year-round; summer is humid.

ANNUAL EVENTS
Annual reenactments (weekend bet. Christmas and New Year's, Washington Crossing, PA, and Trenton, NJ. 609-777-1770. www .tencrucialdays.com) The reenactments include Washington crossing the Delaware (on Christmas Day) and the Battle of Trenton.

Candlelight tour of Peter Wentz Farmstead (1st Sat. in Dec., Shearer Rd., Worcester. 610-584-5104).

MORE THINGS TO SEE & DO
Atwater Kent History Museum (15 S. 7th St., Philadelphia. 215-685-4830. Closed Tues.; adm. fee) Engaging museum that focuses on Philadelphia's history.

Fort Mifflin (Ft. Mifflin Rd., Philadelphia. 215-685-4192. www.fortmifflin.org. Wed.-Sun. April-Nov.; adm. fee) Bombarded by British ships in 1777, this fort was rebuilt and used until 1954.

LODGING
Best Western Independence Park Inn (235 Chestnut St., Philadelphia. 215-922-4443 or 800-528-1234. $$-$$$) This 36-room hotel offers generous Continental breakfasts in a neat, lower-level dining room.

General Lafayette Inn (646 Germantown Pike, Lafayette Hill. 610-941-0600. www.generallafayetteinn.com. $$) A five-room hotel close to Philadelphia; within walking distance of an Irish pub and a Persian restaurant.

Joseph Ambler Inn (1005 Horsham Rd., North Wales. 215-362-7500. www.joseph amblerinn.com. $$-$$$) This inn centered around a 1734 house offers 37 rooms.

Nassau Inn (10 Palmer Sq., Princeton, NJ. 609-921-7500 or 800-862-7728. www .nassauinn.com. $$$). Historic inn with 203 rooms located in downtown Princeton. Gracious hospitality and sophisticated elegance. See pp. 228-29.

Thomas Bond House Bed and Breakfast (129 S. 2nd St., Philadelphia. 215-923-8523 or 800-845-2663. $$) This 12-room bed-and-breakfast, conveniently located across the street from the City Tavern, is housed in a restored 1769 town house.

DINING
City Tavern (138 S. 2nd St., Philadelphia. 215-413-1443. $$-$$$) Exquisite cuisine inspired by dishes of colonial America. Beef, lamb, venison, and seafood. See p. 228.

Hoagie Haven (242 Nassau St., Princeton, NJ. 609-921-7723. $) Famed local favorite for cold and hot hoagies. No seating, but the food is cheap and fast.

William Penn Inn (US 202 and Sumneytown Pike, Gwynedd. 215-699-9272. $$$) This inn dating from 1714 offers Continental and American cuisine in three restaurant venues. Enjoy the exquisite Sunday brunch in the Tavern dining room.

Bucks County
Pastoral perambulations

CREATIVITY IS A WAY OF LIFE in Bucks County. Attracted by picturesque country lanes, green hillsides, charming old bridges, and
remnants of rural tradition, countless painters, writers, and craftsmakers have sought inspiration in this farm-dappled county along
the Delaware River just north of Philadelphia. After a weekend in
central Bucks, it's easy to see why.

Doylestown

Doylestown is a beautiful small town whose intimate downtown
resembles the set of a grand old movie; its bookstores and small
shops are a charming place to start exploring Bucks County.

On the outskirts of town lies **Fonthill** *(E. Court St. 215-348-9461.
www.fonthillmuseum.org. Adm. fee, reservation required)*, a modern
concrete masterpiece and the dream home of Henry Mercer. A
locally born, Harvard-educated lawyer, the relentlessly inquisitive
Mercer abandoned the legal profession to pursue archaeology,
anthropology, and a passion for world-renowned arts and crafts.

Completed in 1912, Mercer's castle home is one of a kind: 44
unique rooms connected by a disorienting maze of serpentine
staircases and claustrophobic passageways. Painted
tiles (from his own tile works and from around the
world) cluster along walls and pillars, cling to the
ceiling, and encircle the windows. Tools and other
craft-related objects fill what space remains on
ledges and in shadowy nooks. Fonthill is a wonderfully garish introduction to one Bucks County
resident's vision, as well as his monumental com-
mitment to the world of crafts.

Head next door to the **Moravian Pottery and
Tile Works** *(130 Swamp Rd. 215-345-6722. www
.buckscounty.org/departments/tileworks. Adm.fee)* to
see where many of Fonthill's tiles were fashioned.
Here in this cloistered, mission-style building, Mercer developed his fascination for pottery- and tilemaking into a
famed—and highly profitable—business until his death in 1930.
Many of Mercer's distinctive painted tiles, fired from local clay,
depict historical scenes and document the tools and methods of
rural workers. Tour the quiet, cavelike workshop, with its incredible

NOT TO BE MISSED

● **The Pennsylvania
impressionists collection
at the Michener Museum**
● **French pastries on a
riverside terrace in New
Hope** ● **Tubing on the
Delaware River**

tile mantelpiece, and the musty basement where clay is still stored for use by on-site artisans.

In 1916 Henry Mercer built his second concrete castle, the **Mercer Museum** *(84 S. Pine St. 215-345-0210. www.mercermuseum.org. Adm. fee)*, to house his overwhelming collection of folk art and everyday objects, including more than 50,000 early American tools. The museum is literally bursting with wonders: Look up to see a garden of wooden furniture disconcertingly dangling from the atrium ceiling.

Across the street, the **James A. Michener Art Museum** *(138 S. Pine St. 215-340-9800. www.michenerartmuseum.org. Adm. fee)* is housed in the former county prison. Founded around the collection of the famously prolific author, the museum features many local paintings that demonstrate the importance of impressionism in Pennsylvania art, yet a breathtaking Japanese-style room also highlights the region's artistic diversity. Another gallery demonstrates the local connections of various American figures, including actor Claude Rains, author Dorothy Parker, and lyricist Oscar Hammerstein II. One intriguing room re-creates Michener's office, highlighting his careers in politics and philanthropy and debunking the popular myth that someone else wrote his many best-sellers.

Eight miles northwest of Doylestown is the **Pearl S. Buck Historic Site** *(520 Dublin Rd., Perkasie. 215-249-0100. www.pearlsbuck.org. Closed Jan.-Feb.; adm. fee)*. Buck, recipient of the Pulitzer Prize and the first American woman to win a Nobel Prize for literature, wrote *The Good Earth* in the stone farmhouse on this 60-acre estate. Tour the house and see her collection of Asian furniture and the desk where she crafted her writing. A passionate activist, Buck was deeply concerned for the plight of the world's children; today a renovated barn houses a cultural center that continues her humanitarian efforts.

New Hope & Lambertville

Bucks County still thrives on arts and crafts. Art galleries, craft shops, and boutiques in converted old houses line the streets of **New Hope,** a small riverside town 12 miles northeast of Doylestown. Stroll into the **J&W Gallery** *(3 and 20 W. Bridge St. 215-862-5119)* or the **Lachman Gallery** *(39 N. Main St. 215-862-6620)* and you'll find that impressionism is still the favored school. For a change of pace, the **Gallery of Stars** at **Image Makers Art, Inc.** *(12 W. Mechanic St. 215-862-4858)* specializes in prints by actors and musicians, including lithographs by Jerry Garcia.

Most shops in New Hope cater to the potpourri and peasant-dress set: Check out **Heart of the Home** *(28 S. Main St. 215-862-1880)* for unique home and garden goods; then sneak a look at the lovely backyard that abuts the river. Grab an ice-cream cone at **Gerenser's** *(22 S. Main St. 215-862-2050)* or savor sweet French pastries on the riverfront terrace at **C'est La Vie** *(20 S. Main St. 215-862-1956)*.

Looking for a life-size cardboard Elvis, or a 1960s Barbie? At New Hope's main intersection, the improbably named **Love Saves the Day** *(1 S. Main St. 215-862-1399)* serves up collectible toys, costumes, and more in a gloomy old drugstore. The incense-drenched **Now and Then Shop** *(15 E. Bridge St. 215-862-5777)* is a psychedelic paradise for anyone who wants to relive 1974.

From New Hope, it's just a short walk across the Delaware River to **Lambertville,** New Jersey. Check out the **Hrefna Jonsdottir Gallery** *(24 Bridge St. 609-397-3274),* where the bright landscapes of Pennsylvania artist Brian Keeler stand out. Down the street at the **Haas Gallery** *(71 Bridge St. 609-397-7988),* Gordon Haas combines French Impressionism and the glazing techniques of the Dutch masters to create renderings of local scenes; his prints are tempting and affordable. Local antique shops are pricey, but **Park Place** *(6 Bridge St. 609-397-0102),* specializing in gorgeous antique jewelry, is a must-see.

The countryside

The best way to see Bucks County's natural beauty is to parallel the Delaware on Pa. 32 (River Rd.)—one of the Northeast's prettiest riverside drives. North of New Hope, you'll find a rolling road dotted with inns, old bridges, and shadowed, narrow side roads that beckon.

If the river itself beckons, stop some 10 miles north of New Hope; when you see a series of stone pylons without a bridge, you know you're at **Bucks County River Country** *(Walters Ln., Point Pleasant. 215-297-5000. www.rivercountry.net), the* place to push off from the river's edge in a rented canoe, kayak, raft, or tube.

Dusk falls on Doylestown's State Street.

For a drier day spent outdoors, drive 2.5 miles south of New Hope and wander the shady trails at **Bowman's Hill Wildflower Preserve** *(Pa. 32. 215-862-2924. www.bhwp.org).* For much of the year, these 100 leafy acres are spangled with brilliant colors. Take in a final view of Bucks County from the top of Bowman's Hill. Fields and farms spread out below you in a colorful panorama worthy of a painter's canvas. Don't leave without recording your own artistic impression.

—*Jeff Sypeck*

Travelwise

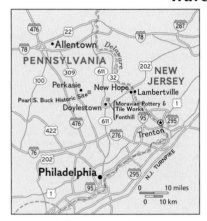

All locations are in Pennsylvania unless otherwise noted.

GETTING THERE
To reach Doylestown from Philadelphia, take Pa. 611 and then Pa. 263.

GENERAL INFORMATION
Contact the **Bucks County Conference & Visitors Bureau** *(3207 Street Rd., Ben Salem, PA 19020. 888-359-9110 or 800-836-2825. www.buckscountytourism.org).*

SEASONS
Year-round; inns are booked solid during the fall foliage season.

ANNUAL EVENTS
Lambertville-New Hope Winter Festival *(1st weekend in Feb., Lambertville, NJ. 215-862-2974. www.winterfestival.net)* Music performances, a chili cook-off, and ice sculptors.
Polish-American Festival *(Sept., Doylestown. 215-345-0600. www.polishshrine.com. Adm.*

fee) Rides, art, great food, and polka at the National Shrine of Our Lady of Czestochowa.

MORE THINGS TO SEE & DO
National Shrine of Our Lady of Czestochowa *(654 Ferry Rd., Doylestown. 215-345-0600. www.polishshrine.com)* A massive Catholic shrine and important Polish cultural center.

New Hope Canal Boat Company *(149 S. Main St., New Hope. 215-862-0758. April-Oct.; fare)* Offers barge rides peppered with local legends and folk songs.

LODGING
Barley Sheaf Farm *(US 202, Holicong. 215-794-5104. www.barleysheaf.com. $$-$$$)* An idyllic bed-and-breakfast with rooms in the main house, a cottage, and former barn; one-time residence of Pulitzer Prize-winning author George S. Kaufman.

Doylestown Inn *(18 W. State St., Doylestown. 215-345-6610. www.doylestowninn .com. $$)* Modernized but intimate downtown inn.

Inn at Lambertville Station *(11 Bridge St., Lambertville, NJ. 609-397-4400 or 800-524-1091. www.lambertvillestation.com. $$-$$$)* Beautiful river views; within walking distance of downtown New Hope and Lambertville.

DINING
Center Bridge Inn *(2998 N. River Rd., New Hope. 215-862-2048. $$)* This riverside colonial inn serves New American fare.

Horn and Hardart *(18 W. State St., Doylestown. 267-880-1901. $)* Hip coffee shop offering sandwiches, pastries, and wraps.

Logan Inn *(10 W. Ferry St., New Hope. 215-862-2300. $$-$$$)* Fine dining, whether indoors next to a stained-glass wall or outdoors on the porch. Try the chicken Valdostano.

Brandywine Valley
Idols of industry, idylls of art

AMBITIOUS AND RESOURCEFUL, the du Pont family established an industrial empire in this lush river valley along the Pennsylvania-Delaware border during the 19th century. The powder-mill smoke dissipated long ago, and today the Brandywine Valley offers a surprising wealth of art and architecture; artists have long sought inspiration here, including renowned illustrator Howard Pyle, his student N. C. Wyeth, and subsequent generations of Wyeths. The valley's estates, gardens, and museums attract both those who create beauty and those who admire it.

Wilmington, Delaware

The du Pont legacy is admirably explained at the **Hagley Museum and Library** (*Del. 141, Wilmington. 302-658-2400. www.hagley.org*). From 1802 until the early 20th century, these 240 acres along the Brandywine River were booming with powder mills—and explosions that sometimes shattered nearby windows; today, the site is serene, solemn, and utterly peaceful. Visit **Eleutherian Mills,** the first du Pont company headquarters and first American mansion, and the mill grounds—once a self-contained community. See the blacksmith's shop, workers' quarters, and ruined riverside mills. Don't overlook the restored steam engine; its operator takes true delight in his work.

Nearby sits the family home of later du Ponts: the **Nemours Mansion and Garden** (*1600 Rockland Rd. 302-651-6912. www.nemours.org. Tours Tues.-Sun. May-Dec.; adm. fee, reservations required*). Completed in 1910 by Alfred I. du Pont and named for his family's hometown in France, this impressive château boasts 102 rooms, including a billiard room and bowling alley. The two-hour tour also takes you through the stunning, manicured grounds—which certainly live up to the estate's claim that it has the finest French-style gardens in America.

And just a few miles to the northwest is another former du Pont estate: the magnificent **Winterthur Museum, Garden and Library**

NOT TO BE MISSED

- The romantic Italian Ruin Garden at the Hagley Museum
- Wyeth memorabilia at the Sanderson Museum
- The Silver Garden at Longwood Gardens

The East Conservatory at Longwood Gardens delights the senses.

(Del. 52. 302-888-4600 or 800-448-3883. www.winterthur.org. Adm. fee). Henry Francis du Pont, who died in 1969, created these natural-istic gardens adorning 966 acres of gentle hills; among the many distinctive areas is the Enchanted Woods designed specifically for children. Stroll through the wonderful museum, where numerous period rooms display a broad range of American antique furniture and other Americana—including a surprisingly interesting exhibi-tion of soup tureens.

The artistic heritage of the Brandywine region is on display at the **Delaware Art Museum** *(2301 Kentmere Pkwy. 302-571-9590. www.delart.org. Until spring 2004, collection is temporarily housed at First USA Riverfront Arts Center)* on the northern outskirts of Wil-mington. The museum was founded around the works of Howard Pyle and his art students; you'll recognize a surprising number of his influential book and magazine illustrations. The museum's collec-tion also includes work by other American artists and some alluring English Pre-Raphaelite paintings.

Check out the **First USA Riverfront Arts Center** *(800 S. Madison St. 302-425-3929. www.riverfrontwilmington.com. Adm. fee),* just off I-95, to enjoy more art. The new arts center opened to good reviews; a recent exhibition of Syrian treasures suggests a bright future.

Wilmington's new riverfront complex also includes a minor-league baseball stadium, outlet stores, and a European-style market.

Cap off your evening by taking in a performance at the **Grand Opera House** *(818 N. Market St. 302-652-5577. www.grandopera.org)*, a Victorian masterpiece in downtown Wilmington. The Delaware Symphony and Opera Delaware are regular performers, but the offerings are impressively diverse, and you may encounter anything from Chinese acrobats to Latin music.

Chadds Ford, Pennsylvania

Spend a day exploring **Chadds Ford,** just over the Pennsylvania border. After a satisfying breakfast at **Hank's Place** (see Travelwise), a lively diner with specialties such as homemade hash and grilled blueberry muffins, head across the street to the **Brandywine River Museum** *(Pa. 1. 610-388-2700. www.brandywinemuseum.org. Adm. fee).* This quaint old mill and its smooth modern addition feature the paintings of N. C. Wyeth, his son Andrew, and his grandson James—with an emphasis on Andrew's stark landscapes and portraits.

Between April and October you can enjoy a rare treat: a tour *(fee)* of the nearby **N. C. Wyeth House and Studio.** The studio is arrayed just as it was when Wyeth (died 1945) thrived as one of the country's top illustrators. Back at the museum, after seeing landscape paintings of the valley by other Brandywine artists, enjoy the soothing views of the river through the glass walls.

Next, drop into a little known attraction: the eclectic **Christian C. Sanderson Museum** *(Pa. 100, N of intersection with US 1. 610-388-6545).* Sanderson, who died in 1966, was a teacher, historian, nationally known square-dance caller, and all-around eccentric. Mementos of his friendship with the Wyeths, including sketches and paintings, appear throughout the house, yet even without the Wyeth connection, Sanderson would still merit his own museum. He collected everything from stamps and autographs to bizarre relics, including a strand of George Washington's hair and sawdust from a Billy Sunday tent revival. The collection is mind-boggling in its scope and randomness, but it's a glorious tribute to a unique local life; don't miss it if you want to get the full story of Brandywine Valley.

If there's a paradise on Earth, it's surely down the road at **Longwood Gardens** *(US 1, Kennett Square. 610-388-1000 or 800-737-5500. www.longwoodgardens.org. Adm. fee),* Pierre S. du Pont's living masterpiece. He purchased an arboretum on this site in 1906 and personally redesigned most of its 1,050 acres, creating a spectacular landscape that glows with his delight in nature. Every path offers up amazing sights, from sculptured topiary to a luminous indoor garden of silver plants. During the Christmas season, long lines form to scc the conscrvatory's interior decorations and a delightful outdoor fountain-and-light show.

If you're a bibliophile, drive six miles north of the town of Kennett Square to **Baldwin's Book Barn** *(865 Lenape Rd. 610-696-0816)* on the outskirts of West Chester. It's easy to get lost among the 300,000 books in this drafty, five-story maze, though you'll never forget you're in an 1822 barn: Listen for doves cooing in the upstairs rafters.

—*Jeff Sypeck*

Travelwise

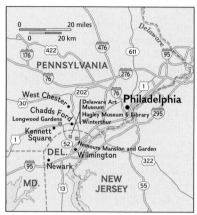

GETTING THERE

Brandywine Valley is about 40 miles south-west of Philadelphia between Chadds Ford, Pennsylvania, and Wilmington, Delaware. From Philadelphia, drive south on I-95 and exit at Del. 52. US 202 directly connects Wilmington and Chadds Ford; for a more leisurely drive between the two towns, take scenic Del. 52, or tiny, winding Del. 100.

GENERAL INFORMATION

Contact the **Chester County Conference & Visitor Center** *(300 Greenwood Rd., Kennett Square, PA 19348. 610-280-6145 or 800-228-9933. www.brandywinevalley.com)* for maps, brochures, and additional information.

SEASONS

Year-round; delightful in fall.

ANNUAL EVENTS

Check out the **Winterthur Point-to-Point Races** *(May)*, an old-fashioned steeplechase horse race; **Chadds Ford Days** *(early Sept.)*, a celebration of the town's heritage; the **Winterthur Craft Festival** *(Labor Day weekend)*;

the **Battle of Brandywine** reenactment *(late Sept.)*; and the **Christmas Display at Longwood Gardens** *(Dec.)*.

MORE THINGS TO SEE & DO

Brandywine Battlefield Park *(US 1, Chadds Ford. 610-459-3342. Closed Mon.)* A 1777 Revolutionary War battle site that includes a museum and two historic houses *(adm. fee)*.

LODGING

Brandywine River Hotel *(US 1 and Pa. 100, Chadds Ford. 610-388-1200. www.brandy wineriverhotel.com. $$)* An elegant 40-room hostelry in the heart of Chadds Ford, within walking distance of Hank's Place.

Inn at Montchanin Village *(Del. 100 and Kirk Rd., Montchanin, DE. 302-888-2133 or 800-269-2473. www.montchanin.com. $$-$$$)* This restored 19th-century millworkers' village midway between Chadds Ford and Wilmington is luxurious. The main building's lounge, with its vast fireplace and sumptuous leather gaming tables, redefines comfort.

DINING

Chadds Ford Inn *(US 1 and Pa. 100, Chadds Ford. 610-388-7361. $$)* Eighteenth-century inn and tavern with fine fare—and a thoughtful kids' menu.

Chadds Ford Tavern Restaurant *(US 1, across from Brandywine Battlefield Park, Chadds Ford. 610-459-8453. $$)* Good food and superb service, near Pa. 202.

Hank's Place *(US 1 and Pa. 100, Chadds Ford. 610-388-7061. $; cash only)* A Chadds Ford institution. Home-style cooking; breakfast served all day. See p. 237.

Krazy Kat's Restaurant *(Del. 100 and Kirk Rd., Montchanin, DE. 302-888-4200 or 800-269-2473. $$-$$$)* Acclaimed formal dining in a former blacksmith's shop at the luxurious Inn at Montchanin.

Phoenix

Desert Gardens 240

Getting Teed Off 245

The Mild Wild West 249

Poppies carpet a montane meadow below the Ajo Mountains in Arizona.

Desert Gardens
Bloomin' good fun in Phoenix

IT'S EASY TO FALL UNDER THE THRALL of the Sonoran Desert's beauty —and easier still to be captivated by its vitality. Plants burst into blossom with the first spring rains, creating a pointillist canvas before your eyes. The first blooms usually emerge in February, followed by a parade of color that unfolds through March and April.

In & around Phoenix

Despite **Phoenix's** sprawl, natural preserves thrive within its confines, reminding visitors that the city perches on the edge of the fertile Sonoran Desert. The best place to explore its beauty is the **Desert Botanical Garden** *(Papago Park, 1201 N. Galvin Pkwy. 480-941-1225. www.dbg.org. Adm. fee)*, a living history museum where themed paths wind among red boulders and thousands of species of cactuses, trees, flowers, and succulents. Come spring, the place explodes in waves of unimaginable color, making for intoxicating strolls along its five thematic trails.

The best displays are in the core garden as well as along the **Harriet K. Maxwell Wildflowers Trail,** whose star blooms include African daisies, desert lupine, aloes, bluebells, and rock daisies. To find out what's blossoming in advance, call the Wildflower Hotline (see Travelwise) for weekly updates.

Have lunch at the garden's outdoor **Patio Café,** which features dishes that incorporate plants and vegetables from desert regions; then take a scenic drive through **South Mountain Park** *(10919 S. Central Ave. 602-495-0222. www.ci.phoenix.az.us/PARKS/hikesoth.html. Adm. fee)*. The 16,500-acre preserve, on the southern fringe of Phoenix, is said to be the world's largest city park. Here you'll discover some of the region's most photogenic Sonoran landscapes, including magnificent clusters of cactus: barrel, hedgehog, jumping cholla, pincushion, and prickly pear. For one brief shining moment each spring, the scene is softened by acres and acres of orange poppies, yellow-dotted creosote bushes, and pungent desert lavender.

The main draw at South Mountain, however, is saguaros. The

NOT TO BE MISSED

- Foreign cactus collection at Boyce Thompson Arboretum
- A walk and a picnic in the Hassayampa River Preserve
- Sunday brunch at The Phoenician
- Viewing the sunset from Dobbins Lookout, South Mountain Park

Hiker at rest, desert in bloom north of Phoenix

most imposing specimens stand along the **Hidden Valley** trail; this 4-mile loop off the park's National Trail passes through a seemingly Old West set, with the old saguaros standing guard. The trailheads can be hard to find; consult a park map for their locations.

In the evening, head northeast from South Mountain Park for an alfresco Mexican feast at **Carlsbad Tavern** *(3313 N. Hayden Rd., bet. E. Earll Dr. and E. Osborn Rd., Scottsdale. 480-970-8164).* Follow the small boardwalk across the stream to reach the patio tables.

An urbane counterpoint to these outdoor escapades beckons in the form of the **Arizona Theatre Company** *(box office at 502 W. Roosevelt St. 602-256-6899 for information or 602-256-6995 for tickets. www.aztheatreco.org. Thurs.-Sun.).* A sophisticated playbill and a troupe of superb actors ensure a memorable evening.

Boyce Thompson Arboretum

Start southeast of downtown Phoenix, in Tempe, with a savory organic breakfast at the **Desert Greens Café** (see Travelwise). Expect hearty, tasty fare at this top-notch vegetarian eatery, whose specialties include the delectable "botanical burrito," stuffed with hot veggies and tofu. Sit outside even if it's hot; water sprayed from overhead misters cools the ambient air.

Head east 54 miles on US 60 to reach **Boyce Thompson Arboretum State Park** *(37615 US 60, Superior. 520-689-2723. arboretum.ag .arizona.edu. Adm. fee).* This 323-acre botanical garden, Arizona's oldest, was established in the 1920s by a visionary philanthropist intent on convincing the world of the beauty and practicality of desert plantings. Thompson's legacy, at the base of craggy 4,375-foot Picketpost Mountain, includes most species of Sonoran Desert flora, as well as thousands of plants from deserts worldwide.

A map in the **visitor center** previews arboretum trails, which are marked with interpretive information. The main attraction is the **Cactus Garden;** its 800 varieties include regal saguaros, prickly pears, and cute pincushions. Proving that outward appearances are deceiving, cactuses are responsible for some of the desert's most exquisite and delicate flowers. The blooms may last but a day, fading quickly to conserve limited water. For more wildflowers, stop by the **Demonstration Gardens,** which explode with the brilliant hues of verbena, primrose, purple aster, desert marigold, and other water-efficient plants that have managed to adapt to this "aqueously challenged" environment.

Returning to Phoenix via US 60, you can buy just about any desert plant you saw today at **Arizona Cactus Sales** *(US 87 S 8 miles to 1619 S. Arizona Ave., Chandler. 480-963-1061. www.arizonacactus sales.com. Closed Sun.).* The 2-acre nursery specializes in native Arizona flora and exotic, drought-tolerant varieties. Sizes range from potted sprouts to mature, "landscape-ready" trees.

Come evening, if you haven't wilted from the desert heat, check the playbill at the **Scottsdale Center for the Arts** *(7380 E. 2nd St., Scottsdale. 480-994-2787. www.scottsdalearts.org).* Its outdoor amphitheater hosts jazz and classical music concerts.

Desert oases, underground streams

No brunch spot in Phoenix can compare with the **Terrace Dining Room** (see Travelwise) at **The Phoenician,** a five-star resort amid 250 acres of rock-and-cactus Sonoran landscaping. Reserve a table on the patio overlooking the Phoenician's croquet lawn and desert garden.

Parks may be wonderful places to view desert wildflowers, but there's nothing like discovering their allure in their own natural setting. One highway that delves deep into the phenomenon of the explosive desert spring is Ariz. 74 (also known as the Carefree Highway), which heads north and then west from Phoenix. Along both sides of the road thrive acres and acres of brittlebush, lupine, scorpion weed, owl clover, rock daisies, Mexican poppies, and saguaros. If the surroundings seduce you into taking a stroll, take along a field guide to identify the many species of blooms. Turnouts are few, so pull far off the roadway.

Continuing north on US 60 from Ariz. 74 toward Wickenburg, you'll come across the Nature Conservancy's serene, oasislike **Hassayampa River Preserve** *(49614 US 60, near Milepost 114. 928-684-2772. www.tncarizona.org/preserves/hassay.asp. Mid-Sept.– mid-May Wed.-Sun., mid-May–mid-Sept. Fri.-Sun.; donation).* For most of its 100-mile length, the Hassayampa River runs underground between the Bradshaw Mountains and the Gila River. It emerges briefly from the Earth hereabouts, nurturing a rare riparian habitat in the middle of the desert.

Among the many self-guided trails that explore this marvel, don't miss the **River Ramble Trail** through willow, mesquite, and cottonwood trees thronged with a variety of resident creatures, including some 230 bird species. Another good walk is the **Lake Trail** around 4-acre **Palm Lake,** shaded by century-old fan palms and inhabited by grebes, ibises, coots, and herons. Don't be surprised—or alarmed—if you encounter a javelina or a coyote. Shaded picnic tables await near the late 19th-century visitor center building.

Cap off your immersion in the natural Southwest with a Southwestern dinner at **Richardson's** (see Travelwise), 7 miles north of downtown Phoenix. This spot is a well-regarded purveyor of authentic New Mexican cuisine, which uses varieties of chilis to create dishes of varying flavor and heat, such as fresh swordfish in a jalapeño hollandaise. From downtown, take Ariz. 51 north to the Bethany Home Road exit, then bear left at the ramp's fork and merge onto East Bethany Home Road. —*Mark Miller*

Travelwise

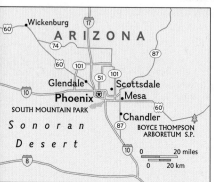

GETTING THERE
This getaway is centered in Phoenix. Each out-of-town excursion is 120 miles round-trip.

GENERAL INFORMATION
Contact the **Greater Phoenix Convention & Visitors Bureau** *(1 Arizona Center, 400 E. Van Buren St., Ste. 600, Phoenix 85004. 602-254-6500 or 877-225-5749. www.phoenixcvb .com. Closed Sat.-Sun.);* the **Desert Botanical Garden Wildflower Hotline** *(480-481-8134. March-April);* or the **Arizona State Parks info line** *(602-542-4988).*

SEASONS
Generally, good blooms follow winters of light rain. Warming in February and March triggers the event. Phoenix-area wildflowers bloom from late February into April. The season is over once temperatures reach the 90s.

MORE THINGS TO SEE & DO
McDowell Mountain Regional Park
(15 miles NE of Scottsdale; 15612 E. Palisades Dr., Fountain Hills. 480-471-0173. www.maricopa.gov/parks/mcdowell. Adm. fee) This 21,099-acre enclave is home to myriad wildflower species. More than 40 miles of park trails, ranging from half a mile to 15 miles.

South Mountain Park *(10919 S. Central Ave., Phoenix. 602-495-0222. www.ci.phoenix .az.us/PARKS/hikesoth.html. Adm. fee)* In season, the 1-mile **Kiwanis Trail** is bedecked with flowers. Enter the park via Central Avenue, turn left, and continue to the trailhead parking lot.

Valley Garden Center *(1809 N. 15th Ave., Phoenix. 602-252-2120)* The center's tree-shaded 3-acre grounds, northeast of the I-10/ I-17 junction, include a splendid rose garden and a koi pond. Visitors are welcome.

Wildflower drives In season the **Beeline Highway** (Ariz. 87), northeast of Fountain Hills, is flanked by dozens of signature Sonoran Desert plants, as is the **Carefree Highway** (Ariz. 74), west of I-17.

LODGING
Maricopa Manor B&B *(15 W. Pasadena Ave. 602-274-6302 or 800-292-6403. www.mari copamanor.com $-$$$)* 1928 Spanish-style manse, with spacious suites, palmy flower gardens, and a pool.

Royal Palms Hotel and Casitas *(5200 E. Camelback Rd. 602-840-3610 or 800-672-6011. www.royalpalmshotel.com. $$$)* 1920s Spanish-mission architecture at the foot of Camelback Mountain. Casitas and guest rooms feature antiques, tiles, artifacts.

DINING
Desert Greens Café *(234 W. University. 480-968-4831)* See p. 242.

Los Dos Molinos *(8646 S. Central Ave., Phoenix. 602-243-9113. Lunch and dinner Tues.-Sat. $$)* This restaurant housed in a hacienda is known for its fiery hot Mexican dishes.

The Farm at South Mountain *(6106 S. 32nd St., Phoenix. 602-276-6360. Breakfast and lunch Tues.-Sun., closed July-Aug. $$)* Picnic table dining in a pecan grove.

Los Picos *(1542 W. University Dr., Mesa. 480-833-4711. Breakfast, lunch, and dinner Sat.-Sun.; lunch and dinner Mon. and Wed.-Fri.; closed Tues. $)* A family eatery specializing in seafood from Mexico's Pacific coast.

Richardson's *(1582 E. Bethany Home Rd. 602-265-5886)* See p. 243.

Terrace Dining Room *(The Phoenician, 6000 E. Camelback Rd., Scottsdale. 480-423-2530)* See p. 243.

Wildflower Bread Company *(15640 N. Pima Rd., Scottsdale. 480-991-5180. $)* A good source of gourmet sandwiches and salads for picnics. Brews premium coffees.

Getting Teed Off
In Phoenix, 72 holes, 1 weekend

ON A CLEAR DAY—and there are more than 300 of them per year in
Phoenix, America's sunniest city—it's easy to see why this region
has become the golf capital of America: One out of seven Arizo-
nans play the game, and 180 of the state's 300 courses are scattered
through the area. The more progressive courses are evolving from
heavily watered eastern lookalikes to western designs that incorporate arid landscapes; some even qualify as wildlife habitats.

Adobe Course & Links Course

If your weekend companions include any potential golf widows,
widowers, or orphans, consider making your base of operations the
Arizona Biltmore Resort and Spa *(24th St. and Missouri Ave. 602-
955- 6600 or 800-950-0086. www.arizonabiltmore.com).* Its myriad diversions include eight swimming pools, a lawn dedicated to croquet,
and seven tennis courts. Nongolfing partners can also pamper themselves at the luxurious **Biltmore Spa** *(602-381-7632)* or stroll by
the brick walks, cafés, fountains, and facades of
the **Biltmore Fashion Park** *(Camelback Rd. and
24th St. 602-955-8400. www.shopbiltmore.com),*
which evoke the tony shopping districts of
London and Paris.

NOT TO BE MISSED

- **Sunrise tee time on the Stadium golf course** ● **Afternoon croquet on the Arizona Biltmore lawn** ● **Drinks and dinner at sunset on the patio of the Hermosa Inn** ● **Midnight tennis in summer**

The Biltmore owes its harmony with the surrounding desert to Albert Chase McArthur, a dis-
ciple of Frank Lloyd Wright's. Perforated blocks
—the hotel's trademark—allow light to filter indoors. Every U.S. President since Herbert Hoover
has stayed at the Biltmore, and most of them
have swung a club on its 18-hole **Adobe Course**
(for tee times call 602-955-9655), a parklike ar-
rangement of trees and pondish water hazards.

The 18-hole **Links Course** *(for tee times call
602-955-9655),* which opened in 1979, is more
difficult; its rolling fairways are fringed with pines, and its bunkered
greens demand well-placed shots.

Start with a healthy breakfast at **The Café,** the Biltmore's South-
western-style eatery, before heading out to the course. Be sure to take
plenty of drinking water with you; dehydration is just as much a haz-

ard in golf as it is in more aerobic activities such as cycling. If you play 18 holes or fewer per day, you can use your off-hours to sample such Phoenix attractions as the remarkable **Heard Museum** (see Travelwise), a treasury of Native Americana.

Come evening, drive 5 miles to east Phoenix for a rustic Mediterranean dinner at **T. Cook's** (see Travelwise), housed inside the Royal Palms Hotel. The Spanish mission–style estate was once the winter home of Cunard steamship mogul Delos Cooke. Inside you'll find beamed ceilings and redbrick walls with tiled murals. The fare features Old World meat, poultry, and pasta dishes prepared with a light New World touch.

For a musical nightcap, check out the live jazz *(Wed.-Sat.)* in the lounge of the **Different Pointe of View** restaurant *(11111 N. 7th St. 602-863-0912)* at the Pointe Hilton Tapatio Cliffs Resort. Take the Northern exit off Ariz. 51, turning left onto East Northern Avenue and then right onto North Seventh Street. The lounge overlooks the valley's brocade of night lights.

Seeking Sanctuary

The popular Scottsdale breakfast spot **First Watch** (see Travelwise) features heart-healthy fare along with more traditionally sclerotic offerings such as pancakes and egg dishes.

Use the morning to visit Frank Lloyd Wright's architectural legacy, **Taliesin West** *(12621 Frank Lloyd Wright Blvd. 480-860-2700. www.franklloydwright.org)*. Tours *(fee)* offer insights into Wright's work and the winter home he built in the late 1930s for family and apprentices. From Ariz. 51, follow Frank Lloyd Wright Boulevard southeast past Thompson Peak Parkway, the route to the Sanctuary course.

After Taliesin, nongolfers may backtrack to **Westworld Equestrian Center** *(16601 N. Pima Rd. 480-312-6810),* a city park where desert trail rides are available at **Trail Horse Adventures** *(800-723-3538)*. Golfers should head for the valley's most intriguing new course, the par 71 **Sanctuary Golf Course at Westworld** *(10690 E. Sheena Dr. 480-502-8200. www.sanctuarygolf.com)*. Opened in 1999 in the foothills of the brush-tufted McDowell Mountains, this is the first golf course in the region (and the 17th worldwide) to be designated an Audubon International Institute Signature Course—an honor awarded to links that protect and enhance wildlife habitats. Play in the late afternoon, when the surrounding hills reach their most vivid hues.

Having spent the day exploring Sonoran landscapes, why not end it with an investigation of Sonoran cuisine? **Aunt Chilada's** (see Travelwise) at **Pointe South Mountain Resort,** a family place in Phoenix just west of I-10 off Baseline Road, offers a menu that's an encyclopedia of Mexican favorites.

Hitting it out of the Stadium

Grab breakfast at **The Good Egg** (see Travelwise), where low-choles-
terol items share billing with waffles, pancakes, omelets, frittatas, and
creative adaptations of such Mexican classics as *huevos rancheros*.

Then, to experience the Phoenix Open—one of the biggest events
of the PGA Tour—from the players' point of view, tackle the **Stadium
Course** of the **Tournament Players Club of Scottsdale** *(17020 N.
Hayden Rd. 480-585-3939. www.tpc.com/daily/scottsdale/index.html)*.
Designed by Tom Weiskopf and Robert Trent Jones protégé Jay Mor-
rish, the 7,089-yard Stadium course is tucked among the bouldered
McDowell Mountains. The layout bristles with native flora that dig-
nify the term "rough": ironwood, hackberry, cactus, brittlebush,
cholla, jojoba, and creosote. Even if you hit the ball straight down
every fairway, you'll see plenty of wildlife as well: rabbits, quail, bats,
swallows, woodpeckers, hummingbirds, roadrunners, and coyotes.

For an upscale 19th hole, watch the sunset over French cuisine
at **Mary Elaine's** (see Travelwise) in Scottsdale. The restaurant is part
of **The Phoenician** *(480-941-8200 or 800-888-8234. www.thephoene
cian.com)*, a five-star resort set amid 250 acres of starkly beautiful
terrain at the base of Camelback Mountain. Best of all, the Phoenician features 27 championship holes on three golf courses named for
the surrounding landscape: **Oasis, Canyon,** and **Desert.**

—*Mark Miller*

Teeing off on the 11th hole of the Monument Course at Troon North

Travelwise

GETTING THERE

To reach the Biltmore from the Phoenix airport (15 miles; 25 minutes), exit onto 24th St. and head north. Turn right on Missouri Ave., which leads to the Biltmore driveway.

GENERAL INFORMATION

Contact the **Greater Phoenix Convention & Visitors Bureau** (400 E. Van Buren St., Ste. 600, Phoenix 85004. 602-254-6500 or 877-225-5749. www.phoenixcvb.com); **Scottsdale Convention & Visitors Bureau** (480-945-8481 or 800-782-1117. www.scottsdale cvb.com); or **City of Phoenix Golf Courses** (www.ci.phoenix.az.us/SPORTS/golf.html).

SEASONS

Comfortable year-round. Spring and fall are temperate; summer temperatures frequently exceed 100°F; late summer brings rain.

ANNUAL EVENT

Phoenix Open Golf Tournament (last full week of Jan., Scottsdale. 602-870-4431. www.phoenixopen.com) PGA golfers shoot four rounds as 500,000 look on.

GOLFING

Cave Creek Golf Course (15202 N. 19th Ave., Phoenix. 602-866-8076) Foothills and mountains create a pleasing backdrop to this challenging 6,290-yard, par 72 course.

Encanto 18 Golf Course (2745 N. 15th Ave., Phoenix. 602-253-3963) Palms and salt cedar trees grace this 1935 municipal course (6,167 yards, par 70). Wide, level fairways and few hazards favor the average golfer.

There's a nice restaurant named Mulligan's.

Papago Golf Course (5595 E. Moreland St., Phoenix. 602-275-8428) The massive red Papago Buttes frame tree-lined fairways on the city's prettiest course. Despite doglegs, these 6,590 yards will not overwhelm most golfers.

Sheraton San Marcos (100 N. Dakota St., Chandler. 602-968-3358) Arizona's oldest grass links golf course, opened in 1928, evokes midwestern courses because it was designed before awareness of local water limits cut turf acreage. Eucalyptus, willow, palms, and salt cedar provide ample shade.

LODGING

Hermosa Inn (5532 N. Palo Cristi Rd., Paradise Valley. 602-955-8614 or 800-241-1210. www.hermosainn.com. $$$) Having grown to 35 luxury casitas from a hand-built 1930s adobe studio, the inn offers swimming, tennis, and a hacienda-style restaurant (**Lon's**) serving contemporary American fare.

DINING

Aunt Chilada's (7777 South Pointe Pkwy. 602-431-6470) See p. 246.

First Watch (4422 N. 75th St. 480-941-8464) See p. 246.

The Good Egg (6149 N. Scottsdale Rd. 480-991-5416) See p. 247.

Mary Elaine's (6000 E. Camelback Rd. 480-423-2444. Closed Sun.-Mon.) See p. 247.

Mrs. White's Golden Rule Café (808 E. Jefferson St., Phoenix. 602-262-9256. Mon.-Fri. 11 a.m.-5 p.m. $$) This popular downtown landmark serves Southern-style plate lunches, notably "smothered" chicken.

Los Picos (1542 W. University Dr., Mesa. 480-833-4711. Breakfast, lunch, & dinner Sat.-Sun.; lunch & dinner Mon. & Wed.-Fri.; closed Tues. $) A family eatery specializing in seafood from Mexico's Pacific coast.

T. Cook's (Royal Palms Hotel, 5200 E. Camelback Rd. 602-808-0766) See p. 246.

Vincent Guerithault on Camelback (3930 E. Camelback Rd. 602-224-0225. Closed for lunch Sat.-Sun., closed Sun.-Mon. June-Sept. $$$) Southwestern ingredients meet classic French cuisine with exceptional results.

The Mild Wild West
Cowboy comforts on guest ranches

THE OLD WEST TOOK ITS FINAL BOW in Arizona, the last mainland territory to join the Union (on Valentine's Day in 1912). The most appealing aspects of that era, however—a rural gentility, a love of horses, the peace of small towns and wide-open spaces—live on at Arizona's guest ranches and historic hamlets.

Phoenix to Wickenburg

Phoenix retains few vestiges of its youth, but territorial flavors linger nearby in the former gold-mining town of **Wickenburg** *(Chamber of Commerce, 216 N. Frontier St. 928-684-5479. www.wickenburgchamber.com)*. Make this your weekend base.

En route from Phoenix to Wickenburg, visit the 90-acre **Pioneer Arizona Living History Village** *(3901 W. Pioneer Rd., exit 225 off I-17. 623-465-1052. www.pioneer-arizona.com. Wed.-Sun.; adm. fee)*. This collection of about 30 historical buildings, 27 miles north of downtown, includes an opera house, a bank, a chapel, and (of course) a saloon. Grab lunch in the rustic **Pioneer Café** *(623-465-0683)*.

Take Ariz. 74 west to Wickenburg *(Carefree Hwy. exit from I-17S)* through a desert garden of brittlebush, lupine, scorpion weed, Mexican poppies, and saguaro cactus. Turnouts are few, so pull well off the road if you want to stroll in the Sonoran Desert.

To the west, hard by the Bradshaw Mountains, lies Wickenburg, named for the German-American miner whose gold strike prompted the town's establishment in 1863. Park downtown on Tegner or Apache Street, where you'll find galleries, restaurants, Western shops, and antique dealers. Use the chamber of commerce's free walking-tour map to find many of Wickenburg's 23 sites on the National Register of Historic Places, including the city hall and jail on Yavapai Street. The building with the horse atop it houses **Ben's Saddlery** *(174 N. Tegner St. 928-684-2683)*, one of the few Arizona shops that still handcrafts its own saddles and boots. Break in your new pair with a one-block stroll to **Chaparral Ice Cream & Bakery** *(45 N. Tegner St. 928-684-3252)*, which makes what it serves.

After lunch at the friendly **Cowboy Café** (see Travelwise), walk to

NOT TO BE MISSED

- The desert by starlight
- Floating in a blue pool in the afternoon, watching clouds sail overhead
- The silence that shrouds once booming Vulture Mine • Desert sunsets seen from horseback

the **Desert Caballeros Western Museum** *(21 N. Frontier St. 928-684-2272. www.westernmuseum.org. Adm. fee),* known for works by Albert Bierstadt, George Catlin, Thomas Moran, Frederic Remington, and Charles Russell. Downstairs it's the year 1915 in the **Early Arizona Street Scene and Period Rooms**.

If you're booked into a ranch, you should return to the spread come evening; most operate on the American plan, so they'll expect you for meals. Luxurious **Rancho de los Caballeros** (see Travelwise) grew from a modest operation started in 1948 into a deluxe resort with an 18-hole course that *Golf Digest* ranks among Arizona's top five. Like most ranches, it offers daily trail rides.

You can learn to rope cattle from a horse at **Merv Griffin's Wickenburg Inn** (see Travelwise). Go for a swim when you arrive, then dress for the genteel dinners that are a tradition of guest-ranch life.

Around Wickenburg

If you're not bunking at a ranch, start your day with brunch at **The March Hare** (see Travelwise) in a charming early 1900s home.

From town, take a half-hour drive *(US 60 W for 2.5 miles, then Vulture Mine Rd. S for 12 miles)* to reach Henry Wickenburg's abandoned **Vulture Mine** *(928-684-5479. Closed Aug. and Mon.-Fri. June-July; adm. fee).* The Vulture yielded billions in gold, bankrolling Arizona's growth, but it's been a ghost town since 1942. Today its many relics include an assay office, stamp mill, and miners' lodgings.

Most ranches reserve trail rides for guests, but a trusty steed can be yours south of town at **Trails West Horseback Adventures** *(51000 US 60, Milepost 113. 928-684-2600. www.ridethewest.com. Closed June-Oct.).* Guided desert ambles last one hour to all day. If you've never ridden, this makes a superb introduction to the "cowboy's office."

If, like the thoroughly modern cowpoke in the 1936 Johnny Mercer song "I'm an Old Cowhand," you'd rather ride the range in a Ford V-8, head for **BC Jeep Tours** *(56558 Rancho Casitas Rd. 928-684-7901).* Summer trips depart in early morning and evening—prime wildlife-watching times.

Some evening excursions include cookouts. If yours does not, reserve a table at **Charley's Steak House** (see Travelwise).

Prescott & Jerome

Get an early start on the 59-mile drive up Ariz. 89 through **Prescott National Forest** to Arizona's former territorial capital, **Prescott** *(Chamber of Commerce, 117 W. Goodwin St. 928-445-2000 or 800-266-7534. www.prescott.org).* If you leave before breakfast, turn right on Gurley as soon as you enter Prescott for brunch at **The Hassayampa Inn** (see Travelwise), a three-story redbrick hotel dating from 1927.

Head next for the rustic 1927 **Sharlot Hall Museum** *(415 W. Gurley St. 928-445-3122. www.sharlot.org. Adm. fee).* Antique buildings recount Prescott's history; you can also stroll a quartet of gardens. The spare furnishings in the **Governor's Mansion,** built of rough pine in 1864, prove that pioneer life afforded scant luxury, even to the highly placed. The fancier **Frémont House** and **Bashford House** rose a decade later, when timber booms established Prescott's elite.

From Prescott, follow Ariz. 89 north 7 miles to the **Phippen Museum** *(4701 Ariz. 89 N. 928-778-1385. Closed Tues.; adm. fee),* where paintings, drawings, and bronzes commemorate artist George Phippen. His favorite subjects: cowboys and daily life in the Old West.

Backtrack to Ariz. 89A and head east 27 miles to once notorious **Jerome** *(Chamber of Commerce, 310 Hull Ave. 928-634-2900. jerome chamber.com).* In the 1880s, Jerome notched itself into the side of Cleopatra Hill, which harbored a mother lode of copper. Thousands labored mightily here, then played just as hard in the saloons and brothels of Jerome—"the wickedest town in the West," according to one Eastern newspaper. After mining ended in the 1950s, Jerome's population sank to 50. Low rents and splendid scenery drew a bohemian crowd that turned the town into a creative colony in the 1960s. Today the old Hotel Jerome houses the **Jerome Artists Cooperative Gallery** *(502 Main St. 928-639-4276),* where you can peruse (and purchase) the work of some 40 local artisans.

After viewing the photos in the Jerome Historical Society's **Mine Museum** *(Main St. and Jerome Ave. 928-634-5477. Adm. fee),* follow its walking-tour map to ferret out Jerome's most fascinating archi-

On horseback through the hills near Prescott

tecture. Then, from the switchback above town, take Perkinsville Road northwest 1 mile to **Gold King Mine** *(928-634-0053. Adm. fee).* Opened in 1890, the mine went bust in 1914. Staffers re-create the past by firing up the old sawmill.

For a speedy return to Wickenburg, head southeast 9 miles on Ariz. 89A to a right on Ariz. 260/279 to I-17 S, then take Ariz. 74 west.

—Mark Miller

Travelwise

GETTING THERE
Wickenburg is 54 miles NW of Phoenix. The Prescott-Jerome loop is 220 miles round-trip.

GENERAL INFORMATION
Contact **Wickenburg Tourism** *(216 N. Frontier St., Wickenburg 85390. 928-684-5479. www.outwickenburgway.com)* or the **Arizona Dude Ranch Association** *(P.O. Box 603, Cortaro, AZ 85652. No phone. www.azdra.com).*

ANNUAL EVENT
Cowboy Poetry Gathering *(1st weekend in Dec. Del E. Webb Center for the Performing Arts, 1090 S. Vulture Mine Rd. 928-684-*

5479) Poems, songs, and readings by notables celebrate the cowpunching life.

LODGING
Best Western Rancho Grande *(293 E. Wickenburg Way, Wickenburg. 928-684-5445. www.bwranchogrande.com. $)* A comfortable alternative to out-of-town guest ranches.

Kay El Bar Guest Ranch *(N of Wickenburg via Rincon Rd. 928-684-7593 or 800-684-7583. www.kayelbar.com. Closed May–mid-Oct. $$)* Adobe rooms, cottages, and casitas on a working cattle ranch founded in 1909.

Merv Griffin's Wickenburg Inn *(34801 N Ariz. 89, Wickenburg. 928-684-7811 or 800-942-5362. www.uswelcome.com/arizona /mervgri.htm)* See p. 250.

Rancho de los Caballeros *(1551 S. Vulture Mine Rd., Wickenburg. 928-684-5484 or 800-684-5030. www.sunc.com. Oct.-May)* See p. 250.

DINING
Anita's Cocina *(57 N. Valentine, Wickenburg. 928-684-5777. $)* Classic Mexican dishes in a friendly family restaurant.

Charley's Steak House *(1187 W. Wickenburg Way. 928-684-2413. Closed Sun.-Mon. and summer)* See p. 250.

Cowboy Café *(686 N. Tegner St. 928-684-2807)* See p. 249.

Hassayampa Inn *(122 E. Gurley St. 928-778-9434 or 800 322-1927. www.hassayampainn .com)* See p. 250.

The March Hare *(170 W. Wickenburg Way. 928-684-0223. Tues.-Sat.)* See p. 250.

Rancho de los Caballeros *(1551 S. Vulture Mine Rd., Wickenburg. 928-684-5484. No credit cards. $$)* A popular guest ranch. Welcomes nonguests for dinner by reservation.

Pittsburgh

Rubbing Elbows with Robber Barons 254

Laurel Highlands 258

Exterior of Fallingwater, Frank Lloyd Wright's 1935 masterpiece on Bear Run, Pennsylvania

Rubbing Elbows with Robber Barons
At play in posh Pittsburgh

THE FACE OF PITTSBURGH TODAY reflects its industrial past. Beginning in the mid-1800s, the area's deposits of coal and iron ore put the city at the epicenter of three flourishing industries: steel, iron, and glass. Trying to outdo one another as builders and benefactors, steel and coal barons such as Andrew Carnegie and Henry Clay Frick made Pittsburgh a rich and vital city by 1920. Gone are the smokestacks and black soot that came with the growth, thanks to two major clean-ups. Remaining are the finer gifts these industrialists left behind: innovative architecture, stately homes, and fine museums.

Downtown & Oakland

Start your weekend by checking into the **Omni William Penn Hotel** (see Travelwise) in downtown Pittsburgh, aka the "Golden Triangle." Commissioned by Henry Frick in 1916 and renovated several times over the years, the redbrick hotel retains its lush, Old World charm.

Orient yourself with a stroll around downtown. The Penn stands beside two impressive buildings financed by Frick, Andrew Carnegie's chief rival. Skyscrapers at the time, Frick's 11- and 20-story structures were designed to block sunlight from reaching Carnegie's headquarters nearby. The Flemish Gothic roof of the 1915 **Union Trust Building** (*2 Mellon Center*) bristles with ornate spires. One block south is the 1901 **Frick Building.** A 1913 street leveling stranded the structure's marbled, gilded lobby 12 feet above ground level. Today the original lobby remains overhead, acting as a mezzanine. Downtown Pittsburgh's other architectural intrigues can be discovered on a walking tour, held weekly in summer by the Pittsburgh History and Landmarks Foundation (*412-471-5808. www.phlf.org. Fee for tour*).

Head east 3 miles to **Oakland** to visit two of the four world-famous **Carnegie Museums of Pittsburgh** (the other two are located

NOT TO BE MISSED

● Polka music on 620 AM ● Grand Ballroom of the William Penn Hotel ● Lawrence Welk's bubble machine at Pittsburgh Regional History Museum

Modern Pittsburgh merits closer scrutiny.

on the North Side). Treasures housed in the **Carnegie Museum of Art** *(4400 Forbes Ave. 412-622-3131. www.carnegiemuseums.org. Closed Mon. Sept.-June; adm. fee)* include the fruits of Carnegie's efforts to locate "the Old Masters of tomorrow"—that is, new artistic talent—as well as rare architectural castings from around the globe. Within the same building is the **Carnegie Museum of Natural History,** where dinosaur skeletons share space with Egyptian mummies and a collection of live insects. The Oakland site also comprises the **Carnegie Library of Pittsburgh** *(412-622-3114. www.clpgh.org)*—largest of the 2,800 libraries that Carnegie set up nationwide—and the sumptuous **Music Hall.**

The 537-foot Gothic tower across Forbes Avenue is the University of Pittsburgh's **Cathedral of Learning**—the tallest schoolhouse this side of Moscow. The cathedral is home to the popular and appealing **Nationality Classrooms** *(Cathedral of Learning, University of Pittsburgh. 412-624-6000. Adm. fee);* these working classrooms offer cultural snapshots of 26 countries from various centuries.

Next to the Cathedral of Learning is an attractive neo-Gothic structure, the **Heinz Memorial Chapel** *(5th and Bellfield Aves. 412-624-4157. www.discover.pitt.edu/chapel. Closed Sat.),* financed in the 1930s by the Heinz family (of ketchup fame). At 73 feet, its transept windows are among the world's tallest stained-glass panels.

Just across the Schenley Park Bridge, past the Carnegie Museum, is the **Phipps Conservatory and Botanical Gardens** *(1 Schenley Park. 412-622-6914. www.phipps.conservatory.org. Closed Mon.; adm fee)*. Built in 1893 by steel millionaire Henry Phipps, the conservatory houses thousands of plants—from tropical orchids to Japanese bonsai—for the serious botanist and casual fern-gazer alike.

Come nightfall, myriad diversions beckon. Pittsburgh's downtown "cultural district" features the **Pittsburgh Symphony Heinz Hall** *(600 Penn Ave. 412-392-4900. www.pittsburghsymphony.org. Tours by appt.)*, home to the Pittsburgh Symphony Orchestra. There's also the **Benedum Center** *(719 Liberty Ave. 412-456-2600. www.steelnet.com /pct)*, the city's opera and ballet hall. A third option is to drive or take one of the two funiculars *(412-442-4000)* that run from West Carson Street to the top of **Mount Washington** (south of the Monongahela River) for a meal in a restaurant along aptly named Grandview Avenue, with the city glittering hundreds of feet below.

Let's do The Strip

Do as the locals do and head for **The Strip,** a mile-long section of restored factories along the Allegheny River about a mile from downtown. Here fresh produce and prepared foods of all sorts are sold in a bustling market atmosphere along Smallman Street and Penn Avenue. The activity reaches its frenetic peak on Saturday mornings.

A few blocks south is the excellent **Senator John Heinz Pittsburgh Regional History Center** *(1212 Smallman St. 412-454-6000. Adm. fee)*. Among the many well-designed exhibits is "Heinz 57," which chronicles the life and legacy of Pittsburgh success story (and America's favorite condiment-maker) Henry J. Heinz.

To reach **Clayton**—Henry Clay Frick's beautifully restored family homestead—take Penn Avenue east a couple of miles past Oakland to the **Frick Art & Historical Center** *(7227 Reynolds St. 412-371-0600. www.frickart.org. Closed Mon.; adm. fee for Clayton tours only, reservations required for tours)*. More than 90 percent of the furnishings and objets d'art on display in the lavishly decorated turn-of-the-20th-century house are period pieces owned by the Frick family.

Also on the grounds of the Clayton estate is the **Frick Art Museum.** Inside you'll find an intimate selection of European and Asian art. The **Car and Carriage Museum** showcases Frick's top-of-the-line early automobiles and grand horse-drawn carriages.

For a refined afternoon break from all that history and art, go a few miles west on Fifth Avenue to the restored 1886 mansion at **Sunnyledge** (see Travelwise). A formal tea is served each day from 3 to 5 p.m. amid the rich oak paneling of this upscale hotel and restaurant.

To cap off the day, head back to The Strip: By night it transforms itself into one of the liveliest restaurant and dance club districts in Pittsburgh. Or have a classic pasta meal in **Bloomfield,** Pittsburgh's Little Italy, up Liberty Avenue about 2 miles from downtown.

From soup cans to science

Across the Allegheny River lies Pittsburgh's North Side, a district that holds two outstanding contemporary galleries—the latest additions to the growing family of Carnegie Institute Museums. Start with a visit to the **Andy Warhol Museum** *(117 Sandusky St. 412-237-8300. www.warhol.org. Closed Mon.-Tues.; adm. fee)*, an eight-story tribute to the iconoclastic pop artist, who lived in Pittsburgh and graduated from Schenley High School and the Carnegie Institute before moving to New York. For an intriguing look at the man's eclectic life and work, begin on the top floor and work your way down.

Change gears and head west about a mile to the **Carnegie Science Center** *(1 Allegheny Ave. 412-237-3400. Adm. fee)*. This hands-on, interactive science museum features wind tunnels, infra-red cameras, and other devices to captivate the kinetically inclined. A fun adjunct to the science center lies just across the street: Try throwing strikes from a regulation pitcher's mound at the **UPMC SportsWorks.** There are 70 sports-oriented exhibits here; don't leave town before you've tried your hand at a few.   —*Lawrence M. Porges*

Travelwise

GENERAL INFORMATION
The **Greater Pittsburgh Convention & Visitors Bureau** *(425 6th Ave. 412-281-7711 or 800-359-0758. www.visitpittsburgh.com)* has brochures on walking tours and other activities. The **Port Authority Downtown Service Center** *(534 Smithfield St. 412-442-2000)* sells passes and provides schedules for the city's extensive public transportation system.

SEASONS
Though Pittsburgh's climate is fairly moderate, its winters can be cold and snowy. Arts festivals take place during the summer.

LODGING
Omni William Penn Hotel *(530 William Penn Pl. 412-281-7100. www.omnihotels.com. $$)* This grande dame of city accommodations occasionally has low weekend rates.

Renaissance Pittsburgh Hotel *(107 6h St. 412-562-1200 or 800-468-3571. www .renaissancehotels.com. $$)* The Fulton Building, built in 1906 by steel magnate Henry Phipps, has been renovated to create this 300-room luxury hotel.

Sunnyledge *(5124 5th Ave. 412-683-5014.*

$$-$$$) Each of the eight rooms in this restored Victorian mansion is luxuriously—and uniquely—decorated.

DINING
Del's *(4428 Liberty Ave., Bloomfield. 412-683-1448. $-$$)* A friendly staple of the Pittsburgh scene since 1949, Del's serves generous portions of fine Italian food.

The Church Brew Works *(3525 Liberty Ave. 412-688-8200. www.ChurchBrew.com. $$)* Housed in a decommissioned 1902 church, this cavernous brew pub features creative American fare washed down by home-made beers.

Monterrey Bay Seafood Grotto *(1411 Grandview Ave. 412-481-4414)* Diners flock to this top-notch seafood restaurant both for its 20 varieties of fresh fish nightly and for the view it offers of the city from high atop Mount Washington.

Primanti Brothers *(18th and Smallman Sts. 412-263-2142. $)* A Pittsburgh landmark since 1933. Features giant sandwiches stuffed impossibly high with meat and fixings—including, somewhat unexpectedly, French fries.

Laurel Highlands
History & hiking in the heartland

THOUGH NAMED FOR THE MOUNTAIN LAUREL, this woodsy region southeast of Pittsburgh is defined by water, not flora: Trickling rivulets join mountain streams to create frothy white water that can wreak destruction on the land or debouch into broad, placid rivers. At Ohiopyle State Park, waterways that once shaped the steel and coal industries now provide recreation.

Johnstown area
In 1889 some 30,000 people lived on the valley floor amid the riverside factories of **Johnstown,** Pennsylvania—an industrial boomtown and the world's biggest producer of steel. Upstream from this crowded and polluted city, wealthy Pittsburgh industrialists such as Andrew

The Youghiogheny River loops around fall foliage in Ohiopyle State Park.

Carnegie, Henry Clay Frick, and Andrew Mellon had constructed a resort on a man-made lake above the Little Conemaugh River.

On May 31 of that year, rising waters from a heavy rainstorm overwhelmed the leaky earthen mound that was the South Fork Dam. When the dam gave way, the 2-mile-long lake disgorged 20 million tons of water into the ravine below. Less than an hour later, a 60-foot-high wave moving 40 miles per hour scoured Johnstown off the map, killing 2,209 people.

At the **Johnstown Flood National Memorial** *(733 Lake Rd., St. Michael. 814-495-4643. Adm. fee)*, a story-and-a-half diorama of the advancing flood wave—complete with railcar, barn roof, and a like-ness of 16-year-old Victor Heiser—dominates the visitor center. At listening stations the 90-year-old Heiser recounts surfing a barn roof through the roiling water and carnage; a movie re-creates the terror of the flood. Outside you can stand on a boardwalk atop the remains of the dam, surveying the empty lake bed and the gorge that chan-neled the raging tide to Johnstown.

Follow Pa. 869 toward US 219. Along the way, pause at the **South Abutment dam site** in the small town of **St. Michael** to ponder the structure that failed—and tax your imagination conjuring the sheer volume of water that would be needed to fill the valley before you.

Having seen the source of the flood, take US 219 south to Johnstown, where the **Johnstown Flood Museum** *(304 Washington St. 814-539-1889. Adm. fee)* continues the story. The museum's Oscar-winning documentary, *The Johnstown Flood*, recounts the sequence of events. Period photos show survivors amid the destruction.

A few blocks west of the museum, the short rail line known as the **Johnstown Incline Plane** *(711 Edgehill Dr. 814-536-1816. Adm. fee)* rises from the confluence of the Little Conemaugh and Stony Creek Rivers, scaling a grade of 70 degrees (thanks to counterbalanced weights) and giving a bird's-eye view of the flood's path. The Cambria Steel Company built the incline plane in 1890 as an escape to higher ground during floods. In 1936 the device lifted more than 4,000 people to safety. It proved its worth again—this time in reverse—when six flood control dams burst during a July 1977 flood: The plane lowered rescue workers and boats to the rising waters.

Follow the Stony Creek River a mile north of the flood museum to the **Heritage Discovery Center** *(Broad St. and 7th Ave. 814-539-1889 or 888-222-1889. Adm. fee),* which spotlights the southern and eastern European immigrants who populated the rebuilt Johnstown in 1910. Interactive exhibits bring to life eight immigrant characters and re-create the sights and sounds of coal mines and a steel mill.

Ohiopyle region

Drive south to **Ohiopyle State Park** *(724-329-8591)* and you will experience the scenery that drew Carnegie and his cronies to the Laurel Highlands. Comprising wooded valleys, steep crests, and a river with the tongue-twisting name of Youghiogheny, the park's 19,116 acres offer something for everyone.

The main attraction is the 14-mile stretch of the "Yawk" (as the river is known to familiars) and its 900-foot-deep gorge, which bring thousands of canoeists, kayakers, and rafters here each year. To wet a paddle or watch the fun, head for the town of **Ohiopyle.** The name—a Native American word for "frothy water"—describes the wide falls in the center of the village. Below the falls, the lower Yough enters a horseshoe-shaped caldron of Class III and IV rapids so popular with white-water fans that the park requires boaters to reserve a starting time *(fee on weekends).* Several concessionaires offer white-water rafting trips.

If you don't relish a white-knuckle descent of the gorge, nearly 80 miles of hiking and biking paths lace the woods. Take the bridge from the old train-depot visitor center to the **Ferncliff Natural Area**

NOT TO BE MISSED

● **Diorama at Johnstown Flood National Memorial** ● **Frank Lloyd Wright's futuristic Fallingwater** ● **Award-winning film at Johnstown Flood Museum** ● **Peaceful Ferncliff Trail in Ohiopyle State Park**

across the river, then set out on the bosky **Ferncliff Trail** for a 1.7-mile walk among rhododendrons and wildflowers. Or follow the 3-mile **Meadow Run Trail** along mountain streams, passing the 30-foot-high bridal veil of **Cucumber Falls.** After your hike, refuel and relax at **The Finjan** *(US 40, Farmington. 724-329-7767),* a gourmet coffee shop and bookstore a few miles south of the park.

You're not alone if the scenery spurs you to call this region home. In 1935, the family of Pittsburgh department-store owner Edgar Kaufmann commissioned architect Frank Lloyd Wright to design a weekend home beside a favorite waterfall a few miles north of the park. Wright surprised them by building his signature **Fallingwater** *(Pa. 381. 724-329-8501. Mid-March–mid-Nov. Tues.-Sun., weekends mid-Nov.–Dec. and 1st 2 weeks of March; adm. fee)* directly over a cascade on Bear Run. Wright's radical, cantilevered design—descending rectangles of native stone and glass—mimics the ledges of the waterfall and blends the building into the scenery.

Ligonier area

Begin your day northeast of Ohiopyle along US 30 in **Ligonier** *(Ligonier Valley Chamber of Commerce 724-238-4200).* The pretty, small-town Main Street seems to celebrate the 1950s: no Wal-Marts here. A church, arts and crafts shops, and cafés ring the town green, known as "the Diamond." From May through August, townsfolk and visitors gather around a Victorian bandstand for Sunday evening concerts.

A few blocks from the green, **Fort Ligonier stockade** *(US 30 and Pa. 711. 724-238-9701. May-Oct.; adm. fee)* harks back to the colonial struggle for control of the Ohio and Mississippi Rivers. First built by the British in 1758, this faithful reconstruction introduces you to a soldier's life during the French and Indian War (1754-1763). The fort's stone-fronted museum houses artifacts recovered from the site.

Next, head west about 15 miles on US 30 to Greensburg for a circuit of the **Westmoreland Museum of American Art** *(221 N. Main St. 724-837-1500. Wed.-Sun.; donation).* Grouped by topic rather than period, the exhibits trace the evolution of American art by comparing differing treatments of similar subjects. Here you'll find works by such standouts as Mary Cassatt, Winslow Homer, and John Singer Sargent. The collected Laurel Highlands landscapes contrast starkly with canvases capturing the region's steel and coal industry.

Continue your cultural odyssey in Jennerstown, where an 1805 gristmill now plays host to the **Mountain Playhouse** *(7690 Somerset Pike/Pa. 985. 814-629-9201. Tues.-Sun. June–mid-Aug., Wed.-Sun. Sept.-Oct.; adm. fee).* The theater company stages traditional summer stock in a pastoral setting, including the streamside **Green Gables Restaurant** *(814-629-9201. Closed Mon. June-Oct.; closed Mon.-Fri. rest of year).* Green Gables rents rooms as well.

—*Sean M. Groom*

Travelwise

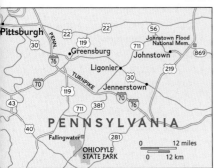

GETTING THERE

Located in southwest Pennsylvania north of the Maryland-West Virginia border, the Laurel Highlands are roughly bounded by the Monongahela River to the west and US 219 to the east. From Pittsburgh, head east on I-376 to US 22. Drive 40 miles east to Pa. 56, then follow it south to Johnstown.

GENERAL INFORMATION

Laurel Highlands Visitors Bureau *(120 E. Main St., Ligonier 15658. 724-238-5661 or 800-333-5661. www.laurelhighlands.org)*

SEASONS

Year-round. Spring through fall is best for hiking and river activities. Fall foliage usually peaks in mid-October. Skiing and snowshoeing opportunities in winter.

ANNUAL EVENTS

Ligonier Highland Games *(Ligonier, Sept. 412-851-9900)* Scottish music and fun.

National Road Festival *(Uniontown area, May. 724-437-7913)* Music, food, and storytelling along 90 miles of the National Road, including a wagon train.

Pennsylvania Maple Festival *(Meyerdale, March. 814-634-0213)* Tours of historic Maple Manor, bluegrass bands, and an old-time sugar camp.

MORE THINGS TO SEE & DO

Kentuck Knob *(Ohiopyle Chalk Hill Rd., Ohiopyle. 724-329-1901. Closed Mon.; adm. fee)* Guided tours of Frank Lloyd Wright's 1956 Usonian house on a ridge above the Youghiogheny River gorge.

Rafting Several concessionaires offer rafting trips and rentals on the Youghiogheny River. Contact Ohiopyle State Park *(724-329-8591)*.

Skiing There are three ski resorts in the area, plus dozens of miles of cross-country ski trails. Contact the Laurel Highland Visitors Bureau for information.

Westmoreland Heritage Railroad *(1 Depot St., Youngwood. 724-925-6543. Fare)* Tour the Laurel Highlands on a 1940s train.

West Overton Museums *(Pa. 819, Scottdale. 724-887-7910. May-Oct.; adm. fee)* The state's only intact pre-Civil War village offers tours of a distillery, an 1838 homestead, and the birthplace of Henry Clay Frick.

LODGING

Glades Pike Inn *(2684 Glades Pike Rd., 6 miles W of Somerset. 814-443-4978. $)* This B&B offers 19th-century charm in a redbrick building that was formerly a stagecoach stop.

Historic Stone Restaurant & Country Inn *(US 40, Farmington. 724-329-8876. $-$$)* The sturdy, native-stone facade of this B&B and restaurant reflects its origins as an 1822 inn on the National Road. Rooms in the original structure feature Victorian antiques; a newer wing offers modern decor.

Nemacolin Woodlands *(US 40, Farmington. 724-329-8555 or 800-422-2736. $$-$$$)* This full-service spa and resort pampers guests amid luxurious surroundings. Restaurants run the gamut from French cuisine to seafood to hearty American fare.

DINING

Chez Gerard *(Business US 40, Hopwood. 724-437-9001. $$$)* An authentic French restaurant known for its selection of cheeses.

Foggy Mountain Lodge *(Old Distillery Rd., Stahlstown. 724-593-1000 or 877-364-4968)* The restaurant *($$)* offers fine American cuisine; steaks are a specialty. There are also 12 guest rooms *($-$$)* on the 120-acre compound.

Lenora's *(207 S. Liberty St., Perryopolis. 724-736-2509. $$$)* Attention to detail and excellent cuisine distinguish this Victorian-style restaurant, where the chef often makes time to greet each guest.

Portland & Seattle

Garden Delights 264

Seaside Oregon 268

Columbia River Gorge 273

On the Volcano Trail 277

Mill Town Memories 281

Orcas Island 285

Pure Pacific Northwest 289

Hikers amble near Puget Sound.

Garden Delights
Portland's pretty public spaces

A BEVY OF FAMOUS GARDENS in Portland provides the kind of serenity that soothes the soul and nurtures the spirit. There's nothing more relaxing and rejuvenating than spending a weekend exploring these living treasures, each one a masterpiece of form and color. As diverse as the Willamette Valley landscape and the people who settled it, Portland's gardens range in style from classical Chinese and traditional Japanese to landscaped river bluffs, native woodlands, and single-species show-offs.

Downtown & Washington Park

Start your garden tour in Chinatown, where the **Portland Classical Chinese Garden** *(N.W. 3rd and Everett Sts. 503-228-8131. www.port landchinesegarden.org. Adm. fee)* opened in 2000. Covering an entire city block, the walled garden is modeled after the private garden retreats of Imperial Court officials during the Ming dynasty (A.D. 1368-1644). Every detail of this uniquely urban garden is filled with rich cultural and symbolic meaning. The garden unfolds with frequent surprising vistas as you make your way down covered walkways, winding past a lake and over bridges, through a landscape of fantastically shaped rocks, trees, shrubs, screens, and ornate pavilions. Most of the plants you see—ginger, banana trees, ginkgoes, and the "Three Friends of Winter" (a pine tree, clump of bamboo, and plum tree, often depicted together in Chinese paintings and poetry)—are indigenous to China. You can stroll through this magical garden on your own, but a guided tour will illuminate the fascinating details.

NOT TO BE MISSED

● **Tea in the Classical Chinese Garden**
● **The Japanese Garden's Flat Garden** ● **Magnolia Walk at Elk Rock Garden**
● **Frank Lloyd Wright's Usonian house in the Oregon Garden**

From Portland's newest garden you can drive, take a bus, or walk the approximately 2 miles to its oldest, the renowned **Washington Park International Rose Test Garden** *(400 S.W. Kingston Ave. 503-823-3636)*. This is most definitely a place to stop and smell the roses. Established in 1917, it's the nation's oldest continuously operating public rose test garden and one of 26 official testing gardens for the All-American Rose Selections. Offering spectacular proof that Portland

Strolling Pond Garden, at Portland's Japanese Garden

deserves its nickname, City of Roses, you'll marvel at some 8,000 roses representing about 525 species, all grown on two broad terraces with views of the city and Mount Hood. The roses are at their fragrant peak in June, when Portland hosts its Rose Festival extravaganza, but you'll be able to appreciate the blooms throughout summer and early fall.

The All-American razzle-dazzle of the rose garden is offset by the serene, contemplative beauty of the nearby **Japanese Garden** (*611 S.W. Kingston Ave. 503-223-1321. www.japanesegarden.com. Adm. fee*). A traditional Japanese gate marks the entrance to this 5.5-acre refuge, acclaimed as one of the most authentic Japanese gardens outside of Japan. You can wander on your own, but taking one of the guided tours will shed light on the subtle intricacies of its design. Five different garden styles are seamlessly integrated by stone paths and steps. Along the way you'll pass carefully placed stones and lanterns, meticulous plantings, and carefully contrived viewpoints. The Japanese notion of "borrowed scenery" becomes apparent as you walk through the **Strolling Pond Garden,** where a waterfall, a koi pond, and a wooden bridge zigzagging through iris beds seem natural extensions of the hillside with its towering conifers. In the **Tea Garden,** be sure to take a peek at the ceremonial teahouse, built in Japan using pegs instead of nails. Then make your way down the stone steps in the **Natural Garden,** where ferns, trees, and shrubs grow to the murmuring accompaniment of hillside streams, to the Zen-inspired **Dry Landscape Garden.** Instead of plants, the "dry garden" utilizes stones that are raked to create a quiet, meditative mood.

Greater Portland area

Make your first stop **Leach Botanical Garden** *(6704 S.E. 122nd Ave. 503-823-9503. Closed Mon.)*, which emphasizes plants native to the Pacific Northwest. Before you start wandering the tempting array of trails, stop at the visitor center—the former home of botanist Lilla Leach—for a map of the grounds. For three decades, starting in the 1920s, Lilla and her husband spent their summers plant-hunting in nearby mountains. One of her discoveries, a small rhododendron-type plant, was named *Kalmiopsis leachiana* in her honor. In the 1940s the Leaches devoted themselves to their woodland garden, which was willed to the city in the 1980s. The garden today encompasses some 16 acres with more than 2,000 plant species and cultivars. Wander at will; you'll find dozens of camellias, viburnums, hollies, wildflowers, and groundcovers.

Closer to downtown, between Reed College and the Eastmoreland golf course, sprawls the **Crystal Springs Rhododendron Garden** *(S.E. 28th Ave., 1 block N of Woodstock Ave. 503-771-8386. Open daily; adm. fee March–Labor Day Thurs.-Mon.)*. The Portland chapter of the American Rhododendron Society established this seven-acre gem in 1950 to showcase the Northwest's favorite flowering shrubs. Time your visit from April through June, when the 2,500 rhododendrons and companion azaleas burst into a spectacular display of color.

After viewing the "rhodies," wend your way west to the **Elk Rock Garden of the Bishop's Close** *(11800 S.W. Military Ln. 503-636-5613)*. One of Portland's outstanding private gardens, Elk Rock was created over many decades by Peter Kerr, a Scotsman who came to Portland in 1888 and prospered as a grain merchant. His celebrated English-style garden spreads around his manor house, completed in 1916. House and garden were eventually given to the Episcopal Bishop of Oregon with the stipulation that the garden be opened to the public. As you stroll through, pay particular attention to the trees: Kerr was one of the first gardeners in the Northwest to make use of natives such as Douglas-fir and giant sequoia. If you're visiting in May or June, don't miss the blooming **Magnolia Walk.** In the barer months of December and January you can feast your eyes on the yellow blossoms of winter-flowering witch hazels and smell the heady scents of winter-blooming viburnums. At any time of year you'll get a marvelous view of the Willamette River and Elk Rock Island by following the trail along the cliff beyond the South Lawn out to the scenic overlook known as The Point.

—*Donald S. Olson*

Travelwise

GETTING THERE
The gardens in this weekend escape are within a 5-mile radius of downtown Portland, the beginning point of the garden tour.

GENERAL INFORMATION
Contact the **Portland Oregon Visitors Association** (Info. Ctr., 701 S.W. 6th Ave., Ste. 1, Portland, OR 97204. 503-275-8355 or 877-678-5263. www.travelportland.com) and **Portland Parks & Recreation** (1120 S.W. 5th Ave., Ste. 1302, Portland, OR 97204. 503-823-7529. www.parks.ci.portland.or.us).

SEASONS
The peak blooming season for Portland gardens is staggered between April and July, but they are worth visiting any time of year.

ANNUAL EVENT
Portland Rose Festival (June, various sites in Portland. 503-227-2681) A month-long celebration of the rose, featuring more than 60 events including boat races, music, and an all-floral parade.

MORE THINGS TO SEE & DO
Joy Creek Nursery (20300 N.W. Watson Rd., Scappoose. 503-543-7474) Located about 18 miles west of Portland off US 30, Joy Creek is one of the area's best nurseries for high-quality, hard-to-find outdoor plants.
Oregon Garden (879 W. Main St., Silverton, off I-5, about 50 miles S of Portland. 503-874-8100. www.oregongarden.org. Adm. fee) This brand-new and still evolving botanical garden, which will eventually grow to some 240 acres, is a living tribute to Oregon's rich diversity of wild and cultivated plants. Make a point to wander through the ancient white-oak forest, where you'll see trees 150 to 400 years old, and be sure to visit the Bosque, a central plaza where 40 planter boxes, each containing a single white ash tree, are set among reflecting ponds. Another must-see is the **Frank Lloyd Wright Usonian house,** dating from 1964 and moved here in 2001.
Portland Nursery (5050 S.E. Stark St., Portland. 503-231-5050) If you're looking for garden plants, shrubs, trees, ornaments, or tools, this southeast Portland nursery is one of the best places to shop.

Schreiner's Iris Gardens (3625 Quinaby Rd. N.E., Portland. From Portland take I-5 S to Brooks exit, then W on Brooklake Rd., S on River Rd., and E on Quinaby. 503-393-3232 or 800-525-2367. Viewing area open mid-May–early June) You'll be astonished at the sheer variety of irises, available in virtually every color of the rainbow, at this famous iris farm near Salem.

LODGING
Heron Haus (2545 N.W. Westover Rd., Portland. 503-274-1846. www.heronhaus.com. $$) One of the special delights of this Tudor-style B&B, dating from 1904 and located close to Forest Park (the largest urban wilderness in the U.S.), is a hidden orchard. Six rooms.
MacMaster House (1041 S.W. Vista, Portland. 503-223-7362 or 800-774-9523. www.macmaster.com. $-$$) This antique-filled 1895 mansion is within walking distance of the rose garden and Japanese Garden in Washington Park. Six rooms.
Portland's White House (1914 N.E. 22nd Ave., Portland. 503-287-7131 or 800-272-7131. www.portlandswhitehouse.com. $-$$) The rose-festooned decks in back of this elegant federal-style mansion cum B&B make an idyllic spot for warm-weather breakfasts and afternoon refreshments. Nine rooms.

DINING
Basta's Trattoria (410 N.W. 21st Ave., Portland. 503-274-1572. Dinner daily, lunch Tues.-Fri. $$-$$$) In warm weather you can enjoy authentic Italian cooking in Basta's charming terrazzo-style outdoor dining area.
L'Auberge (2601 N.W. Vaughn St. 503-223-3302. Closed Mon. $$$) Dine alfresco in an urban garden setting at this long-established French restaurant.
Silver Grille (206 E. Main St., Silverton. 503-873-4035. Dinner only Wed.-Sun. $$$) This contemporary bistro near the Oregon Garden emphasizes products of the Willamette Valley in its French-influenced cooking.
Wildwood (1221 N.W. 21st Ave., Portland. 503-248-9663. $$$) This perennial Portland favorite with outdoor seating specializes in fresh Pacific Northwest cuisine.

Seaside Oregon
A drive on the wild side

WITH ITS CRASHING SURF, towering headlands, and seal-studded coves, Oregon's central and northern coast is a wild wonder to behold. Whether hiking through a rain forest high above the Pacific or strolling a stretch of white-sand beach sprinkled with sand dollars, you'll find that the uncrowded Oregon coast lets you get up close and personal with nature on a very grand scale. This getaway meanders north along US 101 between Newport and Astoria, exploring intriguing coastal hamlets, cozy beachfront inns, great seafood restaurants, and a host of sight-seeing possibilities.

Newport to Depoe Bay

You'll probably hear seals barking—a sure sign that you've arrived at the Oregon coast—as you stroll along the picturesque Bay Front in **Newport.** This lively fishing town on Yaquina Bay is home to the **Oregon Coast Aquarium** (*2820 S.E. Ferry Slip Rd. 541-867-3474. www.aquarium.org. Adm. fee),* which provides a marvelous introduction to the diverse creatures and ecosystems you'll be seeing along the Pacific. Walk underwater in the clear, 200-foot tunnel snaking through ocean habitats with sharks, rays, and thousands of other fish swimming all around you, then take a gander at the special tanks for graceful jellies, sea horses, and dozens of other deep-dwelling denizens. Seals, sea lions, sea otters, and seabirds have their own outdoor habitats. From the aquarium, a short nature trail winds along the Yaquina Bay estuary to **Hatfield Marine Science Visitor Center** (*2030 S. Marine Science Dr. 541-867-0271. www.hmsc.orst.edu. Closed Tues.-Wed. Oct.–Mem. Day),* where hands-on exhibits let you discover the work of marine-science researchers and ocean explorers.

At **Yaquina Head Outstanding Natural Area** *(adm. fee),* 3 miles north of Newport off US 101, the gleaming white column of Oregon's tallest lighthouse presides over a scene of rugged offshore islands teeming with murres, oystercatchers, cormorants, puffins, guillemots, and gulls. Harbor seals laze on rocky ledges and slide into the wave-tossed sea. You can explore Yaquina Head's unusual cobble-covered beach and take a guided tour of the historic lighthouse, completed in 1873. In the **visitor center** *(541-574-3100)* you'll learn more about ships, seabirds, marine life, and human history on the headland.

Yaquina Head and its historic lighthouse

Crashing breakers send geyserlike sprays called "spouting horns" over the seawall at **Depoe Bay,** an oceanside hamlet about 12 miles north of Newport. Here, from the world's smallest year-round navigable harbor, **whale-watching excursion boats** run by Tradewinds *(E side of US 101, Depoe Bay. 541-765-2345 or 800-445-8730. www.tradewindscharters.com. Fare)* chug out to view gray whales as they pass up and down the coast on their winter *(Dec.-Feb.)* and spring *(mid-March–May)* migrations. Some of the 30-ton behemoths remain along the Oregon coast throughout the entire summer and can be viewed from the coastal headlands around Depoe Bay.

Depoe Bay to Cannon Beach

Heading north from Depoe Bay, US 101 soon passes through a piece of **Siletz Bay National Wildlife Refuge,** a diverse estuarine habitat that includes marshes, mudflats, and forestland. The refuge is just south of **Lincoln City,** a popular and populous coast town that sprawls along US 101. Continue north to **Pacific City,** where you'll find one of the best walking beaches in Oregon at **Robert Straub State Park** *(W of main intersection, Pacific City. 503-842-3182 or 800-551-6949).* Chances are you'll have its miles of sand and dunes all to yourself.

Leave US 101 just north of Pacific City and enjoy the spectacular ocean views along the 39-mile scenic byway called the **Three Capes Scenic Drive.** The three capes—Cape Kiwanda, Cape Lookout, and Cape Meares—are majestic coastal headlands, and to fully appreciate their grandeur you need to do a little exploring on foot. A relatively easy 2.5-mile round-trip trail at **Cape Lookout State Park** *(503-842-4981. Adm. fee)* winds high above the sea, through old-growth rain forest with moss-draped Sitka spruce and western hemlock, to breathtaking views at the cape's end.

The scenic drive continues inland, through lushly green coastal valleys dotted with grazing herds of Holsteins, Jerseys, and Guernseys, to rejoin US 101 at **Tillamook,** headquarters for Oregon's dairy industry. You might want to sample the famous cheese and ice cream and take the short, self-guided tour at the **Tillamook County Creamery Association Visitor Center** *(4175 US 101 N., Tillamook. 503-815-1300),* the state's largest cheese factory.

Spend your second night in an oceanfront hotel or cozy inn at **Cannon Beach** *(Chamber of Commerce, 207 N. Spruce. 503-436-2623. www.cannonbeach.org),* a charming beach town named for a piece of wrecked ship with three cannon that washed ashore in 1846. Dozens of intriguing shops, galleries, and restaurants line Hemlock, the main street. For a romantic dinner, try

NOT TO BE MISSED

- Sea otters at Oregon Coast Aquarium
- Oceanside hot-tubbing at Channel House at Depoe Bay • Oysters at Bay House in Lincoln City
- Hiking Cape Lookout

JP's (see Travelwise), with its superlative wine list, and marvelous Continental-style food, including sumptuous seafood chowder, rich Chicken Cordon Bleu, and sublime desserts. The intimate, candelit **Bistro** (see Travelwise) serves fresh seafood, including grilled salmon and seafood stew.

Cannon Beach to Astoria

After a leisurely breakfast take a morning stroll on **Cannon Beach.** Haystack Rock, a gigantic sea stack, rears up from the edge of what is possibly the most popular beach on the coast, filled with joggers, kite flyers, beach buggies, and dog walkers. Then head north about 19 miles on US 101 to **Fort Clatsop National Memorial** *(92343 Fort Clatsop Rd., Warrenton. 503-861-2471. www.nps.gov/focl. Adm. fee).* Re-created close to its original site is the log stockade used as winter headquarters by Lewis and Clark and the Corps of Discovery during the winter of 1805-06. The **visitor center** is packed with information about the momentous Lewis and Clark expedition, which observes its bicentennial from 2003 to 2006.

From Fort Clatsop continue northwest to nearby **Fort Stevens State Park** *(Fort Stevens Hwy., Hammond. 503-861-2000. Adm. fee),* where you can visit another historic coastal fort, this one erected during the Civil War to guard the mouth of the Columbia River. The park's long, sandy beach offers a perfect opportunity for one last beach walk. The century-old wreck of the *Peter Iredale*, its iron ribs sticking up from the sand, is a stark reminder that mariners of yore referred to this treacherous section of the Pacific near the Columbia Bar as the "graveyard of the Pacific."

Astoria, just 10 miles east of Fort Stevens, was founded in 1811 as a fur-trading post by John Jacob Astor. Located at the mouth of the Columbia River, it grew to become a prominent port, cannery, and logging town. Grandest of the town's many Victorian-era residences is **Flavel House** *(441 8th St., Astoria. 503-325-2203. Adm. fee),* an ornate mansion completed in 1885 for a prosperous sea captain.

Friday through Sunday you can take a restored riverfront trolley *(503-325-6311)* to and from several locations along the river. Be sure to get off for the **Columbia River Maritime Museum** *(1792 Marine Dr. Astoria. 503-325-2323. Adm. fee)* to view historical fishing boats, Coast Guard rescue craft, nautical artifacts, and displays about shipwrecks, lighthouses, and fishing. A unique floating lighthouse designed to serve as a navigational aid to ships in the treacherous waters off the Columbia Bar is a part of the museum. Before heading back to Portland on US 30, drive to the park at the top of **Coxcomb Hill** *(16th St. 1 mile S)* and climb to the observation deck of the **Astoria Column** *(503-325-2963)* for one last memorable view of the magnificent Oregon coast.

—Donald S. Olson

Travelwise

GETTING THERE

This drive follows the coast for 135 miles between Newport and Astoria, all on or near US 101. Newport is 130 miles (3-4 hours) southwest of Portland via I-5 (fastest) or Ore. 99 west (most scenic) to Corvallis, then west on US 20. From Astoria, it's 95 miles (2 hours) back to Portland via US 30.

GENERAL INFORMATION

Contact the **Oregon Tourism Commission** *(775 Summer St. N.E. Salem, OR 07301 800-547-7842. www.traveloregon.com)* or **Oregon State Parks** *(800-551-6949. www.oregonstateparks.org).*

LODGING

Cannon Beach Hotel Lodgings *(1116 S. Hemlock, Cannon Beach. 503-436-1392 or 800-238-4107. www.cannonbeach hotel.com. $-$$)* Lodging at three small, charming inns in the heart of Cannon Beach. 26 rooms total.

Channel House *(35 Ellingson St., Depoe Bay. 541-765-2140 or 800-447-2140. www.cha nnelhouse.com. $$-$$$)* A luxuriously roman-

tic inn with private hot tub overlooking the sea.

Surfsand Resort *(Hemlock and Gower Sts., Cannon Beach. 503-436-2274 or 800-547-6100. www.surfsand.com. $$)* Family-friendly oceanside resort featuring sea-facing balcony units, some with kitchens. 86 rooms.

Tolovana Inn *(3400 S. Hemlock St., Cannon Beach. 503-436-2211 or 800-333-8890. www.tolovanainn.com. $$)* Oceanfront resort offering studios and roomy suites with kitchens; indoor pool, sauna, hot tub, on-site masseur. 175 rooms.

DINING

Bay House *(5911 S.W. Hwy. 101, Lincoln City. 541-996-3222. Closed Sun.-Tues. in winter. $$$)* One of the coast's finest restaurants, serving wonderfully fresh and inventive food, including delectable pan-fried Pacific oysters.

Bistro *(263 N. Hemlock St., Cannon Beach. 503-436-2661. $$$)* Seafood. See p. 271.

Cannery Café *(1 6th St., Astoria. 503-325-8642. $$-$$$)* A former cannery converted into a riverside café, this eatery serves up good bouillabaise, clam chowder, and grilled halibut.

Canyon Way Restaurant & Bookstore *(1216 S.W. Canyon Way, off Bay Front, Newport. 541-265-8319. Restaurant closed Sun.-Mon. $$)* Stop at the deli for take-out sandwiches or dine in the restaurant, featuring fresh pan-fried cod and Dungeness crab cakes.

Columbian Café *(1114 Marine Dr., Astoria. 503-325-2233. $$)* Small, funky, and usually jammed, this Astoria favorite offers vegetarian-oriented lunches and seafood pastas.

Grain & Sand Bakery *(1064 S. Hemlock St., Cannon Beach. 503-436-0120. June-Oct. Thurs.-Mon., Nov.-May Fri.-Mon. $)* Friendly neighborhood gathering place good for latte or pot of exotic tea, and homemade baked goods.

JP's *(116 S. Hemlock St., Cannon Beach. 503-436-0908. Dinner only; closed Sun., 3 weeks in Dec. $$$)* Continental menu. See p. 271.

Sea Hag *(58 E. Hwy. 101, Depoe Bay. 541-765-2734. $$-$$$)* Specialties at this long-established seafood restaurant include thick clam chowder, local oysters, shrimp croissants.

Columbia River Gorge
In the footsteps of history

THE LONGEST NAVIGABLE WATERWAY west of the Rockies, the Columbia River for centuries has served as a vital transportation route, traveled by Chinook in cedar dugout canoes, the epochal expedition of Meriwether Lewis and William Clark, and thousands of weary Oregon pioneers. This getaway follows the same route taken by those historic voyagers, through the furrowed desert canyons and high basalt cliffs of the majestic Columbia River Gorge, alongside the Great River of the West.

Western gorge

A dozen miles east of Portland, I-84 crosses the Sandy River and enters the **Columbia River Gorge National Scenic Area** *(541-386-2333)*, where the suburban snarl of outlet malls and truck stops suddenly gives way to evergreens and the stately Columbia itself.

As you travel east, the valley soon narrows and deepens, with rock walls rising up from river's edge. At Corbett, follow Corbett Hill Road as it switchbacks up the bluff to the **Historic Columbia River Highway.** Railroad lawyer Sam Hill and engineer Samuel C. Lancaster championed the construction of this scenic road over steep bluffs and through hammer-hard basalt.

Construction began in 1913, but modern highways eventually eclipsed the road. Fortunately, several stretches like this one have been restored for auto travel; others are open to hikers and bikers. Follow the historic highway east to the **Vista House** *(Crown Point State Scenic Corridor. 503-695-2261. Closed Nov.-Feb.)*, a stone monument built in 1916 to commemorate Oregon pioneers. Sitting atop Crown Point 733 feet above the river, it offers 360-degree views of the gorge.

Eastward, the road drifts down the mountainside into a ferny oasis, where one waterfall after another sluices through the conifers. Trumping them all is **Multnomah Falls,** a plume of water hurling 620 feet off a basalt ledge, the nation's second highest waterfall. Stop at the 1920s **Multnomah Falls Lodge** (see Travelwise) for a bite to eat and information on trails. It's an easy walk to the historic **Benson Footbridge** that spans the falls.

NOT TO BE MISSED

- Scoping out the salmon at Bonneville Dam's fish-viewing window
- Mount Hood at sunset
- Juicy red Bartlett pears from Hood River Valley fruit stands

Hydroelectric dams tamed the wild Columbia of Lewis and Clark's day. **Bonneville Dam** buried what the explorers called the Great Shute, a 7-mile-long series of falls and rapids just upstream. Long a vibrant Chinook village and busy portage, today it is called **Cascade Locks,** where the stern-wheeler *Columbia Gorge (541-374-8427. www.sternwheeler.com. June-Sept.; fare)* churns up and down the now placid river on sight-seeing cruises.

Hood River area

With the gorge serving as a natural wind tunnel, the sleepy town of **Hood River** was reborn in the 1980s as one of the world's top windsurfing destinations. Today all manner of sports enthusiasts flock to this lively community of 5,800. Weekenders from Portland and European tourists alike frequent the sports stores, gift shops, and restaurants that fill the turn-of-the-century storefronts along Oak Street.

Windsurfers move up and down the Columbia depending on conditions, but you can often find them launching from a spot near the Spring Creek Fish Hatchery on the Washington shore *(4 miles W of Hood River Bridge on Wash. 14)*. Pick a high-wind day, sit on the rocks, and watch some of the finest sailors in the world practice loops (forward somersaults) and other tricks.

Cherry, pear, and apple trees—and increasingly, vineyards—crosshatch the lush **Hood River Valley,** which stretches from the Hood

Windsurfing through the Columbia River Gorge

River south toward Mount Hood. At the Hood River County Chamber of Commerce *(405 Portway Ave. 541-386-2000)*, pick up a map for the **Fruit Loop,** a scenic route that winds through the valley's orchards.

As Ore. 35 approaches **Parkdale,** snowy **Mount Hood** fills the windshield. Stop at the Forest Service Hood River Ranger Station *(6780 Ore. 35, Parkdale. 541-352-6002)* for maps and hiking suggestions; a web of trails spins off Ore. 35 as you continue toward the mountain. Try **Tamanawas Falls,** a 3.8-mile round-trip along a splashing creek to an amphitheater of rock and a 100-foot falls, or the 6-mile (one way) **East Fork Trail,** slaloming alongside the milky glacial waters of the East Fork Hood River. A Northwest Forest Pass available at the ranger station and at area businesses is required at many trailheads. At the town's east end begins the **Twin Tunnels Trail,** a 5-mile stretch of the Historic Columbia River Highway that's been paved for biking, hiking, and other nonmotorized use *(fee)*.

Eastern gorge

Meriwether Lewis described in 1806 the stark, high-desert landscape of the eastern gorge: "The mountains through which the river passes…are high, broken, rocky…and in many places exhibit very romantic seenes."

Experience the bold drama of this land at the 231-acre **Tom McCall Preserve** *(5 miles E of Hood River. Take I-84 exit at Mosier and follow Scenic Loop signs 7 miles up Historic Columbia River Hwy. to Rowena Crest Viewpoint)*. Footpaths weave through grasslands to **Rowena Crest,** a rocky promontory bordered by sheer basalt cliffs at the edge of the gorge. A surprising diversity of plants and animals thrive in this seemingly barren land of golden grasses and dusty plateaus, with notably bountiful spring wildflowers.

Lewis and Clark camped several nights farther east near **The Dalles,** today the largest city in the sparsely populated eastern gorge. Waterfalls near here (now inundated by The Dalles Dam) challenged their expedition and, later, the weary Oregon Trail pioneers. The Dalles became a busy gathering point for travelers as they readied for a treacherous trip down the river or around Mount Hood. A series of colorful **murals** along Second and Federal Streets depict The Dalles's lively 19th-century history. The Dalles Area Chamber of Commerce (see Travelwise) offers guided walking tours of the historic commercial district. Stop for lunch at the **Baldwin Saloon** (see Travelwise) for seafood, sandwiches, and burgers in a well-preserved 1876 saloon.

The Dalles is also home to the superb **Columbia Gorge Discovery Center** and **Wasco County Historical Museum** *(5000 Discovery Dr. 541-296-8600. www.gorgediscovery.org)*. Interactive exhibits focus on the geology and biology of the gorge, indigenous Native American cultures, and the settlement of European emigrants.

East of The Dalles, the **Lower Deschutes River** unfurls like a silver ribbon through a desert canyon of gray-green sagebrush. A gravel bike path traces the river's north shore, part of it an old wagon road. A 4.2-mile hiking trail loops along the river's edge, then switchbacks up the canyon and crosses lush Ferry Spring. You'll find trailheads for both at the **Deschutes River State Recreation Area,** where the Deschutes empties into the Columbia. Upstream at Maupin *(US 197 S from The Dalles),* sign up for a **rafting trip** with CJ Lodge B&B *(541-395-2404)* for a rollicking white-water ride—a taste of how Lewis and Clark traveled 200 years ago. —*Tina Lassen*

Travelwise

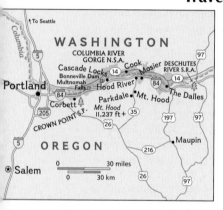

GETTING THERE
The Columbia River Gorge National Scenic Area begins just east of Portland and extends to the Deschutes River, 80 miles upstream. Most of the sites and activities included in this getaway can be found along or near I-84, which parallels the Columbia's southern shore.

GENERAL INFORMATION
Contact the **Hood River County Chamber of Commerce** *(405 Portway Ave., Hood River, OR 97031. 541-386-2000 or 800-366-3530. www.hoodriver.org)* or **The Dalles Area Chamber of Commerce** *(404 W. 2nd St., The Dalles, OR 97058. 541-296-2231 or 800-255-3385. www.thedalleschamber.com).*

SEASONS
Summer and fall are your best bets for dry, sunny weather. Rain is common on the gorge's west end, with clearer skies farther east.

MORE THINGS TO SEE & DO
Windsurfing Lessons, rentals, sales at Big Winds *(207 Front St., Hood River. 541-386-6086).*

LODGING
Beryl House B&B *(4079 Barrett Dr., Hood River. 541-386-5568. www.berylhouse.com. $)* 1906 farmhouse near town tucked among the orchards with mountain views. 4 rooms.
Best Western Hood River Inn *(1108 E. Marina Way, Hood River. 541-386-2200 or 800-828-7873. www.hoodriverinn.com. $-$$)* On the Columbia, with kid-pleasing amenities such as an indoor pool. 149 rooms.
Hood River Hotel *(102 Oak Ave., Hood River. 541-386-1900 or 800-386-1859. www.hoodriverhotel.com. $-$$)* Turn-of-the-20th-century European charm. 41 rooms.

DINING
Baldwin Saloon *(205 Court St., The Dalles. 541-296-5666)* Seafood, burgers. See p. 275.
Brian's Pourhouse *(606 Oak St., Hood River. 541-387-4344. $$$)* Fresh, inventive Pacific Northwest fare.
McMenamins Edgefield *(2126 S.W. Halsey St., Troutdale. 503-669-8610)* On the grounds of a 1911 "county poor farm," the Black Rabbit Restaurant *($$$)* offers fine dining, the Power Station Pub soups and sandwiches *($$).* Brewey and winery onsite as well.
Multnomah Falls Lodge *(5000 Historic Columbia River Hwy., Bridal Veil. 503-695-2376. www.multnomahfallslodge.com. $$$)* See p. 273.
Sixth Street Bistro *(6th St. at Cascade St., Hood River. 541-386-5737. $$$)* Good Pacific Northwest cuisine.

On the Volcano Trail

Mount St. Helens & other legacies of a restless Earth

FROM ANCIENT MAGMA FLOWS to 20th-century eruptions, volcanoes have sculptured and resculptured the Pacific Northwest's dramatic topography. This weekend getaway steers you northeast from Portland into southern Washington, down sinewy forest roads that link together a trio of peaks and delve into a world of lava beds, canyons, and caves. Some of the sights are well known, others less so—but all showcase these volcanic wonders in our midst.

Along the Columbia River

Northeast of the Portland area, the Columbia River chisels through 4,000-foot-high cliffs of basalt, wrinkled and shattered by ancient faults. Follow Wash. 14 east as it squeezes between the cliffs and the Columbia's north bank, into the heart of the 80-mile-long **Columbia River Gorge National Scenic Area** *(541-386-2333)*.

Two miles east of Skamania off Wash. 14, **Beacon Rock State Park** *(509-427-8265)* is named for an 848-foot ancient volcano core. Scale the mile-long hodgepodge of steps and paths to the rocky spire summit. Views of the Columbia River Gorge fill the horizon.

A few miles east in Stevenson, the **Columbia Gorge Interpretive Center** *(990 S.W. Rock Creek Dr. 509-427-8211 or 800-991-2338. Adm. fee)* offers insight into the area's geology and cultural history, with films, Native American artifacts, and a three-story-high replica of a fish wheel, used in the 19th century to harvest the Columbia's bountiful salmon.

Follow Wash. 14 farther east to Cook, then the Cook-Underwood Road north 7 miles to the small town of Willard. From here, Forest Road 66 slaloms along the east edge of the **Big Lava Bed,** a 500-foot-deep remnant of a primeval lava flow. Though tucked deep in fir forest, the terrain remains barren, with pumice boulders and shallow pits carpeted in spongy pine needles. Carry a compass; it's easy to lose your bearings in this lunar landscape.

The third highest and second most voluminous of the Cascade

NOT TO BE MISSED

● **Picking huckleberries in Gifford Pinchot National Forest** ● **The Truman Trail's view into Mount St. Helens's gaping mouth** ● **Friday night seafood buffet at Skamania Lodge**

volcanoes, 12,276-foot **Mount Adams** (see Travelwise) towers above the foothills to the northeast. Without the dramatic pyramid summit that characterizes many volcanoes, the humpbacked mountain became known as the "forgotten giant"—misidentified by Lewis and Clark, shortchanged by cartographers (who understated its elevation by 3,000 feet for decades!), and still overlooked by many outdoor enthusiasts. Rangers can suggeset dozens of trails and viewpoints.

One of the best ways to take in the mountain's awesome beauty is to hike to the top of **Sleeping Beauty,** a nearby rocky promontory. The 1.4-mile trek brings you face to face with Adams's glaciated west face. *(To find trailhead from FR 66, follow signs to Trout Lake, then head NW on FR 88, 8810, and 40. Contact Gifford Pinchot N.F., 360-891-5000).*

Mount St. Helens

On May 18, 1980, Mount St. Helens uncorked its fury. A lateral blast from deep within the Earth shattered its north face, pulverized its top 1,300 feet, and triggered 1,600-degree pyroclastic flows, instantly rearranging more than 200 square miles of landscape. Today, 110,000-acre **Mount St. Helens National Volcanic Monument** *(360-247-3900)* protects the truncated mountain and its scarred surroundings. Access is from the west, south, or east via three dead-end roads. Most people approach from the west, where five visitor centers contain exhibits; at one, the **Johnson Ridge Observatory,** you can peer into the crater. For even more dramatic looks at the eruption's effects, plan on spending some time on the south and east sides.

The south side's most popular attraction predates the 1980 eruption by some 1,900 years. Bring a coat, sturdy shoes, and a strong flashlight to explore **Ape Cave,** a 2.4-mile-long underground lava tube formed by the flowing lava of an ancient eruption. *(From Lewis River Campground, follow FR 90 W to FR 83 N and FR 8803 W.)*

Back on Forest Road 83, continue north 7 miles to **Lahar Viewpoint,** a barren floodplain created in 1980 by the mud-and-ash river, or lahar, unleashed by a torrent of instant glacial meltwater. Proceed another mile to road's end to explore **Lava Canyon,** where Muddy Creek tumbles through a tight slot of slick basalt. The 1.3-mile loop trail clambers up and down ladders and across a suspension bridge.

Windy Ridge Drive (FR 99) leads up Mount St. Helens's east flank into the "blast zone," where the eruption's force toppled century-old firs like toothpicks. *(Backtrack on FR 83 and FR 90; go N 30 miles on FR 25, then W 16 miles on FR 99.)* The road ends at **Windy Ridge,** 4 miles from Mount St. Helens's gaping crater. Log-jammed **Spirit Lake** sprawls off to the north and west. Beyond the gate, follow the 9-mile-long (one way) **Truman Trail** onto an otherwordly pumice plain.

You could easily while away another day or two at Mount St. Helens, especially if you want to explore its west-side visitor centers and trails. But it's tough to resist the pull of **Mount Rainier National**

Spring splendor at Mount Rainier National Park

Park *(360-569-2211), less than a two-hour's drive north. (From jct. of FR 99 and 25, go N 20 miles on FR 25 to Randle, then W 18 miles on US 12. For Mount Rainier, go N 17 miles on Wash. 7 and E 13 miles on Wash. 706 to Nisqually park entrance. To reach the W side of Mount St. Helens, continue W from Randle on US 12, then S on I-5 to Wash. 505 or 504 exit.)*

Mount Rainier National Park

The undisputed king of the Cascade volcanoes, **Mount Rainier** wears its crown well. Washington's highest peak at 14,411 feet, it dominates the skyline throughout western Washington and stands visible deep into Oregon. Native Americans called it *Tahoma*—"great snowy mountain"—befitting a peak with more than 35 square miles of glaciers.

Seven miles from the Nisqually entrance, **Longmire** is named for pioneer James Longmire, who discovered thermal springs percolating through this meadow in 1883. The lodge and baths he built drew the area's first tourists and eventually generated support for a national park. Hike the 0.5-mile **Trail of the Shadows** through a high canopy of fir and hemlock, circling Longmire's meadow and passing "Iron Mike," a ferrous spring that tints the mossy rock a vivid orange.

One of the Northwest's greatest treks, the **Wonderland Trail** winds past Longmire, part of its 93-mile circuit around Rainier. Hugging the mountainside at about 5,000 feet, the trail skirts alpine meadows, high-mountain lakes, and glaciers.

From Longmire, follow the 12-mile corkscrew road to…**Paradise.**

This postcard-perfect valley lives up to the hyperbole especially in July and August, when wildflowers bloom. But it can seem less than heavenly on summer weekends, when throngs crowd area trails and the excellent exhibits of the **Henry M. Jackson Memorial Visitor Center** *(June–Sept. daily, weekends rest of year).* Get an early start and consider a weekday visit. Better yet, hike a 6-mile stretch of the Wonderland Trail. You'll pass 168-foot-high Narada Falls before emerging in the valley. And that's truly the best way to reach Paradise.

It's 168 miles back to Portland via Wash. 706 and 7, US 12, and I-5.

—Tina Lassen

Travelwise

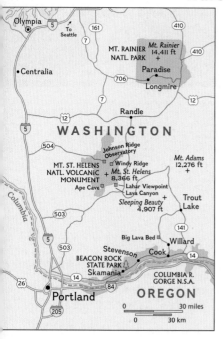

GETTING THERE

This weekend in southwest Washington begins at the Gifford Pinchot National Forest Headquarters in Vancouver, Wash., on the north side of the Portland metro area. Buy a forest map and a Northwest Forest Pass *(fee)*, required at many trailheads. Then return south on I-205 to Wash. 14 and head east.

GENERAL INFORMATION

Contact the **Gifford Pinchot National Forest**

(10600 N.E. 51st Circle, Vancouver, WA 98682. 360-891-5000. www.fs.fed.us/gpnf); **Mount Adams Ranger District** *(2455 Hwy. 141, Trout Lake, WA 98650. 509-395-3400);* **Mount St. Helens Visitor Center** *(3029 Spirit Lake Hwy., Castle Rock, WA 98611. 360-274-2100); or* **Mount Rainier National Park** *(Tahoma Woods, Star Route, Ashford, WA 98304. 360-569-2211. www.nps.gov/mora).*

SEASONS

Best months to visit are June through September. Wildflowers usually peak in early August, and autumn colors usually peak in late September. Snow closes many Forest Service and Park Service roads November to late May.

LODGING & DINING

Blue Heron Inn *(2846 Spirit Lake Hwy., Castle Rock. 360-274-9595 or 800-959-4049. www. blueheroninn.com. $$)* Simple, clean accommodations with views of Mount St. Helens; seven rooms, breakfast and dinner served family style.

Mount Rainier National Park *(360-569-2275. www.guestservices.com/rainier. $)* Several history-drenched lodges within the national park boundaries are prime lodging options. Closest to the park entrance is **National Park Inn** in Longmire, open all year. **Paradise Inn** lies farther up the mountain, open mid-May until the end of September. Both inns have excellent on-site dining rooms.

Skamania Lodge *(1131 Skamania Way, Stevenson. 509-427-7700 or 800-221-7117. www.dolce.com. $$)* Elegant rustic lodge with huge fieldstone fireplaces, spa facilities, 195 rooms.

Mill Town Memories
Puget Sound's towering trees
& Victorian villages

THE VAST, VIRGIN FORESTS of central Puget Sound were a siren call to 19th-century lumber barons and woodsmen. The sawmills are quiet now, but interesting reminders of the era when timber was king can still be discovered in small communities that dot the water's edge from Bainbridge Island to the Olympic Peninsula.

Bainbridge Island

Your getaway begins at Pier 52 *(801 Alaskan Way)* in downtown Seattle, where you'll drive your vehicle into a Washington State ferry for the 35-minute trip to Bainbridge Island. As the boat slips away from the mainland, head up to one of the observation decks for spectacular views of the Seattle skyline and the islands and peninsulas clustered in Puget Sound, with the Olympic Mountains gleaming behind.

Winslow, where you'll disembark, is the largest community on **Bainbridge Island,** a peaceful, 26-square-mile island directly west of Seattle. Timber companies arrived in the 1850s because the island's trees grew so straight they could be used as masts for sailing ships. From mills at Port Madison and Port Blakely (which had the world's largest sawmill), cedar, fir, and hemlock were shipped all over the globe. The patchwork of trees you see today along the water's edge, in parks, and beside the roads is third growth.

Thanks to the wealth generated by their logging operations, the families of timber barons could live in princely splendor, as you'll see at the **Bloedel Reserve** *(7571 N.E. Dolphin Dr., 7 miles N of Winslow off Wash. 305. 206-842-7631. www.bloedel reserve.org. Closed Mon.-Tues.; adm. fee, reservations required).* Save at least two hours to explore this magnificent 150-acre estate. From the gatehouse, where you can obtain a map, you're free to wander at your own pace. The main path meanders through meadows and second-growth woodlands with stands of hemlock, cedar, and Douglas-fir to a series of superbly maintained formal gardens. Swans glide through picturesque ponds and bald eagles survey Puget Sound from snags high above the water. The dignified French Country

NOT TO BE MISSED

● **Wandering through the gardens at Bloedel Reserve** ● **The little beach at Point No Point Lighthouse** ● **Strolling around Port Townsend's neighborhoods**

mansion that now serves as a visitor center was the home of the Bloedel family, who bought the estate in the 1950s. On your way back to the gatehouse you'll pass through the sublime Japanese Garden and the extraordinary Moss Garden.

From the Bloedel Reserve backtrack to Wash. 305 and continue west. When you cross Agate Pass Bridge you've arrived on the **Kitsap Peninsula,** 400 square miles in size and surrounded by 236 miles of saltwater shoreline. Though Kitsap County has developed rapidly over the last decade, stands of giant trees still line the highways and there's a scenic vista at every bend of the craggy coastline.

From Wash. 305 turn north on Wash. 307 and east on Wash. 104 into **Kingston.** This small, old-fashioned town, which serves as a landing for ferries to and from Edmonds *(N of Seattle)*, also makes a good lunch stop. Try **Main Street Ale House** (see Travelwise), where you can sit on the waterside deck and enjoy such offerings as pan-fried oysters, fish tacos, and blackened salmon sandwiches.

Then follow Hansville Road north through a mixed forest of shaggy cedars, tall Douglas-firs, lacy hemlocks, and gray-barked alders. Near **Hansville,** at the peninsula's northern end, the road dips and a shimmering vista of Puget Sound appears. A 1-mile spur road from Hansville leads to **Point No Point Lighthouse.** The squat lighthouse, at the end of a sandy spit jutting into Admiralty Inlet, has been flashing since 1879. Surf fishermen cast for salmon along the driftwood-strewn beach.

Return to Wash. 104 and follow the road as it curves north to **Port Gamble,** a remarkably preserved company town founded in 1853 by A. J. Pope and William Talbot. The site was chosen for its deep-water harbor and seemingly endless supplies of fir, cedar, and hemlock. The Pope & Talbot lumber mill here, which got its start by supplying timber to the rapidly growing San Francisco area, was the oldest continuously operating sawmill in North America until its 1995 closing.

Port Gamble was built to look like the founders' hometown of East Machias, Maine. Driving or walking along its neat-as-a-pin streets, you'll see remarkable examples of 19th-century wood-frame houses—from simple cottages to ornate mansions dripping with gingerbread trim. Be sure to stop at the **Port Gamble General Store** *(1 Rainier Ave. 360-297-7636)*, a wonderful three-story emporium built in 1916. The first floor functions as a general store with a deli counter in back, while the **Of Sea and Shore Museum,** displaying an enormous collection of shells from Puget Sound and around the world, occupies the second- and third-floor balconies. Around back, on the ground floor, you'll find the charming **Port Gamble Historic Museum** *(360-297-8074. Closed Dec.-Feb.; adm. fee)*, featuring several period rooms. A saw-filing room from the early 1900s displays the equipment required to keep the mill's enormous saws sharp.

Cycling among Northwest giants

Olympic Peninsula

Crossing the Hood Canal Bridge west of Port Gamble, you enter
the **Olympic Peninsula.** Take the Wash. 19 turnoff from Wash. 104
and follow it northwest. You pass the golf course and marina towns of
Port Ludlow and **Port Hadlock** and, in a few miles, hook up with
Wash. 20, which takes you into **Port Townsend.**

 Back during the lumber heyday, this Victorian seaport town was
queen of the Puget Sound region. Founded in 1851, it served as a
major commercial hub and port of entry for tens of thousands of
immigrants and adventurers in the newly opened lands of the Pacific
Northwest. With its amazing architectural legacy and heart-stopping
views of Admiralty Inlet, the Cascades, and the Olympic Mountains,
Port Townsend is an alluring place to stop for the the night. **James
House** (see Travelwise), a Victorian mansion the size of a small hotel,
offers roomy and atmospheric accommodations overlooking Port
Townsend Bay and the mountains. Stop at the **Port Townsend Visitor Information Center** (*2437 E. Sims Way. 888-365-6978 or 360-385-*

2722. *www.ptguide.com)* for other suggestions, as well as a self-guided walking/driving tour map that highlights dozens of the town's historic buildings.

When you're ready to return to Seattle, take Wash. 20 south to Wash. 104 and follow that east to Kingston, where a 30-minute ferry ride brings you back to Edmonds.   *—Donald S. Olson*

Travelwise

GETTING THERE
Puget Sound's lumber towns are located west of Seattle; total mileage is 130 miles by car and ferry. It's 50 miles from Winslow to Port Townsend, 95 using secondary roads and backtracking. Port Townsend lies 40 miles from Kingston.

GENERAL INFORMATION
Contact the **Bainbridge Island Chamber of Commerce and Visitor Center** *(590 Winslow Way E., Winslow, WA 98110. 206-842-3700. www.bainbridgechamber.com)* or **Washington State Ferries** *(206-464-6400 or 888-808-7977. www.wsdot.wa.gov/ferries).*

MORE THINGS TO SEE & DO
Biking Rentals available at the **BI Cycle Shop** *(195 Winslow Way, Winslow. 206-842-6413).*
Sea kayaking For rentals and tours of Port Townsend Bay call PT Outdoors *(1017B Water St., Port Townsend. 888-754-8598).*
Whale-watching P.S. Express *(431 Water St.,*

Port Townsend. 360-385-5288. pugetsoundex press.com)* offers one-day excursions.

LODGING
Ann Starrett Mansion *(744 Clay St., Port Townsend. 360-385-3205 or 800-321-0644. www.starrettmansion.com. $$-$$$)* Enormous 1889 mansion, now an 11-room B&B.
Fūrin-Oka Futon & Breakfast *(12580 Vista Dr. N.E., Bainbridge Island. 206-842-4916. www.futonandbreakfast.com. $$)* Traditional Japanese guest house in a Japanese garden.
James House *(1238 Washington St., Port Townsend. 360-379-5551 or 800-385-1238. www.jameshouse.com. $$-$$$)* See p. 283.
Palace Hotel *(1004 Water St., Port Townsend. 360-385-0773 or 800-962-0741. www.oly mpus.net/palace. $-$$)* Beautifully restored redbrick Victorian hotel with 17 rooms.

DINING
Lonny's *(2330 Washington St., Port Townsend. 360-385-0700. Closed Tues. Oct.-June. $$$)* Upscale restaurant specializing in char-grilled Northwest seafood and pasta.
Main Street Ale House *(11225 State Hwy. 104, Kingston. 360-297-0440. Lunch $, dinner $$$)* Seafood specialties. See p. 282.
Osamu *(1208 Water St., Port Townsend. 360-379-4000. $$)* Japanese restaurant serving great sushi, grilled or alder-smoked seafood.
Salal Café *(634 Water St., Port Townsend. 360-385-6532. $$)* Cheerful and unpretentious, perfect for a hearty breakfast or lunch.
Silverwater Café *(237 Taylor St., Port Townsend. 360-385-6448. $$)* Waterfront restaurant with good all-around selection.
Wild Coho *(1044 Lawrence St., Port Townsend. 360-379-1030. Dinner Wed.-Sun. $$$)* Fine uptown restaurant serving only 30 people a night; "Northwest-centric" menu.

Orcas Island
Kayaking among whales & other idyllic pursuits

THE SAN JUANS, A MAGIC ARCHIPELAGO of rocks, islets, and islands lying in the watery embrace of Puget Sound northwest of Seattle, are home to whales, bald eagles, and a few thousand humans who think they've found paradise on Earth. Of the four main islands accessible to visitors, Orcas Island casts the strongest spell, as you'll discover on this three-day getaway.

Getting to paradise

Some people fly in on seaplanes; others cruise over in their yachts or sailboats. But the majority of visitors to Orcas Island arrive by ferry from **Anacortes,** about 85 miles north of Seattle. Just past Mount Vernon, turn off I-5 and head west for 20 miles on US 20 to the well-marked ferry terminal. Be sure to check a current Washington State ferry schedule *(206-464-6400 or 888-808-7977 in Washington and British Columbia. www.wsdot.wa.gov/ferries)* before you arrive. Many visitors park their cars on the mainland and head over to the island with their bikes, or they rent bikes once they arrive.

Sight-seeing begins as soon as the ferry heads out into Rosario Strait and slips into Harney Channel between Blakely Island to the north and Decatur Island to the south. Carved out by glaciers, the rock-rimmed, evergreen-clad San Juans rise gently from the silvery blue waters. So many birds nest and breed here that 84 islands have been designated as the **San Juan Islands National Wildlife Refuge** *(206-753-9467).*

After an hour's ride, the ferry docks at **Orcas Village,** one of three population centers on 59-square-mile Orcas Island. With a general store, a hotel, and rental shops for sea kayaks and bicycles, the village mostly caters to ferry traffic. As you drive or bicycle north on Orcas Road, the island's charms become immediately apparent. Roads twist and turn through a hilly, compact landscape of forest and pasturelands where water shimmers around every bend and 2,407-foot Mount Constitution rises to the east. You won't find a stoplight anywhere on the island.

NOT TO BE MISSED

● **Riding the ferry from Anacortes to Orcas Island** ● **Wandering through the mansion at Rosario Resort** ● **The view from the observation tower atop Mount Constitution**

Orcas Road brings you to Main Street in **Eastsound,** the island's largest town. It sits at the head of East Sound, a long fjordlike inlet that cleaves Orcas Island almost in two. With its gleaming white Victorian church standing beside a tranquil bay dotted with miniscule islands, Eastsound is a photo op waiting to happen. The town is busiest on Saturdays May through September, when a farmers' market is held in the Village Square and visitors pour in to rent bicycles and kayaks.

At some point during your stay, visit the **Orcas Island Historical Museum** *(North Beach Rd. 360-376-4849. June-Sept. Tues.-Sun., call for schedule).* Six one-room homesteader log cabins from the 1880s to 1890s were joined together to create this intriguing time capsule of island life. **Darvill's Bookstore** *(Main St. 360-376-2135),* with a tiny coffee bar in back, is a wonderful place to browse. The delightfully old-fashioned **Comet Café** (see Travelwise) is one of the friendliest places to stop for breakfast, lunch, or a fresh-baked pastry.

In July and August it's imperative that you book your getaway lodging before you arrive on Orcas Island. There are inns, bed-and-breakfasts, campsites, and two upscale resorts, which fill up quickly. **Rosario Resort & Spa** in Eastsound (see Travelwise), with a marina and landing strip for seaplanes, has long been the island's premiere destination. A magnificent 54-room mansion, completed in the early 1900s for shipbuilder and Seattle mayor Robert Moran, serves as the resort's centerpiece. The house is a must-see, even if you're not

Sea kayakers near Rosario Resort, Orcas Island

staying at the resort. Time your visit for the 5 p.m. show in the **Music Room,** when resident pianist Christopher plays the 1,972-pipe Aeolian organ and relates Moran's remarkable story. Afterward, have a cocktail in Moran's former dining room or dinner in the **Compass Room,** a romantic spot for gourmet dining.

Another option is to stay on the island's southwest side at **Deer Harbor Marina,** busy with yachts, tall-masted schooners, and excursion boats. Idyllic cabins overlook one of the island's prettiest spots at the **Resort at Deer Harbor** (see Travelwise). In summer the resort operates an on-site restaurant, or, year-round, you can walk up the road to eat at the **Deer Harbor Inn** (see Travelwise), specializing in steaks and seafood.

Island explorations

On your second day you might want to go on a wildlife-viewing expedition, rent a kayak and paddle around the island's coves, or hike up Mount Constitution. On a long summer's day you could do all three.

The San Juans are famous for their orcas, and **whale-watching excursions** are a top draw. Three orca pods totaling about 80 individuals are frequently sighted in the summer when they follow schools of migrating salmon close to shore. In the wildlife-rich waters you might also spot minke and gray whales, dolphins, seals, and sea lions.

Of the 300 bird species that have been sighted in the San Juans, the bald eagles are the most spectacular. You can often spot them perched on snags near the shoreline or soaring over a bay or cove. The island's diverse habitats also support cormorants, ospreys, hawks, owls, turkey vultures, great blue herons, and wild turkeys. Easily paddled and steadier than canoes, kayaks allow you to skim close to shore and view birds and other wildlife from the water.

Olga, on the island's southeastern shore, is a favorite destination for bicyclists and those exploring by car. There's not much more to Olga than a general store, but scenic **Olga Road** from Eastsound passes through a thickly wooded section of 5,252-acre **Moran State Park** (see Travelwise), a favorite hiking spot, with 30 miles of trails. Two easy walks circle two of the park's freshwater lakes, **Cascade Lake** and **Mountain Lake.**

Whatever you do, don't miss a visit to the park's observation tower atop **Mount Constitution,** the highest point in the San Juans. A marked turnoff from Olga Road winds up to the stone tower, where a stunning eagle's-eye view awaits: Almost the entire San Juan archipelago is laid out below you. It's a view you'll carry with you when you drive back onto the ferry to the mainland. If, that is, you can tear yourself away from the spell of Orcas Island.

—*Donald S. Olson*

Travelwise

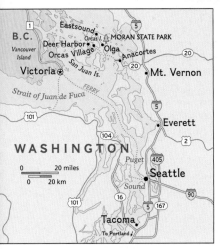

GETTING THERE

It's 85 miles (90 minutes) from Seattle north to Anacortes; the ferry ride to Orcas Island takes another hour. Kenmore Air *(425-486-1257 or 800-543-9595)* has daily flights to Orcas Island from Seattle's Lake Union. On the island, a circuit from Orcas Village to Eastsound to Olga and back again, with a detour to the top of Mount Constitution, is less than 60 miles.

GENERAL INFORMATION

Contact the **Chamber of Commerce** *(N. Beach Rd., Eastsound, WA 98245. 360-376-2273. www.orcasisland.org)* and **Moran State Park** *(Olga Rd. www.parks.wa.gov).* Also, log on to *www.islandcam.com* and *www.san juanweb.com.*

MORE THINGS TO SEE & DO

Arts & crafts Crow Valley Pottery *(2274 Orcas Rd., Eastsound. 360-376-4260 or 800-684-4267)* sells pottery made from local clays.

Biking Rentals at Boardwalk on the Water *(Orcas Village. 360-376-2971),* Marina Bicycle Rental *(Deer Harbor Marina. 360-376-3037),* and Wildlife Cycles *(N. Beach Rd., Eastsound. 360-376-4708).*

Kayaking For guided wildlife-watching tours contact Osprey Tours *(Eastsound. 360-376-3677. www.fidalgo.net/~kayak/)* or Orcas Outdoors Inc. *(Orcas Village. 360-376-4611. www.orcasoutdoors.com).* Shearwater Adven-

tures *(Deer Harbor Marina. 360-376-4699)* and West Beach Kayaks *(W. Beach Resort, Eastsound. 360-376-2240 or 877-937-8224)* rent kayaks and offer guided excursions.

Whale-watching Among the many outfitters are Whale Spirit Adventures *(W. Sound County Dock. 360-376-5052 or 800-376-8018)* and Deer Harbor Charters *(Deer Harbor Marina. 360-376-5989 or 800-544-5758).*

LODGING

Inn at Ship Bay *(326 Olga Rd., Eastsound. 360-376-3933. www.innatshipbay.com. $$-$$$)* The waterfront guest rooms in this 11-room shipshape inn have fireplaces and balconies.

Inn at the Market *(86 Pine St., Seattle. 206-443-3600 or 800-446-4484. www.innatth emarket.com. $$-$$$)* A great place to start your trip if you're traveling to Orcas Island from outside Seattle. 70 rooms.

Old Trout B&B *(5272 Orcas Rd., Eastsound. 360-376-7474. www.oldtroutinn.com. $$)* Situated on a trout pond, this small inn has three suites and a cottage.

Resort at Deer Harbor *(31 Jack and Jill Ln., Deer Harbor. 360-376-4420 or 888-376-4480. www.deerharbor.com. $$-$$$)* See p. 287.

Rosario Resort & Spa *(1400 Rosario Rd., Eastsound. 360-376-2222 or 800-562-8820. www.rosarioresort.com. $$$)* See pp. 286-87.

DINING

Bilbo's Festivo *(310 A St., Eastsound. 360-376-4728. Dinner daily; lunch also in summer. $$)* Mexican cuisine.

Christina's *(Porter Bldg., Main St., Eastsound. 360-376-4904. Dinner only; closed Tues.-Wed. $$$)* Innovative, ever changing menu; one of the best restaurants in the San Juans.

Comet Café *(N. Beach Rd., Eastsound. 360-376-4220. Closed Sun.)* See p. 286.

Compass Room *(Rosario Resort & Spa. 360-376-2222 or 800-562-8820)* Romantic dining. See p. 287.

Deer Harbor Inn *(Deer Harbor. 360-376-1040. Dinner only. $$$)* See p. 287.

Vern's Bayside *(Main St., Eastsound. 360-376-2231. Breakfast, lunch, dinner. $$)* Waterside eatery with outdoor patio and plain home cooking.

Pure Pacific Northwest
*Wandering the tide-tugged
coastline north of Seattle*

IF YOU'RE LOOKING FOR a quintessential slice of the Pacific Northwest, you'll find it in Skagit and Whatcom Counties just north of Seattle. Tucked in between the majestic North Cascades and a glimmering network of bays and islands, the area between La Conner and Bellingham is full of unhurried country roads and scenic surprises. With their historic towns, sophisticated museums, charming B&Bs, and out-of-this-world seafood restaurants, the two counties offer all the ingredients for a perfect two-day getaway.

Skagit Valley
In the **Skagit Valley,** just an hour north of Seattle, fields of tulips bloom in the shadow of snowcapped mountains, and saltwater laps at the edges of verdant farmland. Profiting from the valley's mild climate, evenly distributed rainfall, and rich soil, the tulips peak in mid-March through April, attracting flower lovers from around the world.

Take the Wash. 534 exit off I-5 and follow it into **La Conner,** in the heart of the valley. Founded in 1869, the idyllic town of some 750 residents spreads along the southern portion of the Swinomish Channel. It's something of a fishing village, farming center, and artists colony rolled into one. Before exploring, you might want to pick up a map at the La Conner Chamber of Commerce *(413 Morris St., La Conner. 360-466-4778 or 888-642-9284. www.laconnerchamber.com).*

Head up the hill to the **Skagit County Historical Museum** *(501 S. 4th St., La Conner. 360-466-3365. Closed Mon.; adm. fee).* Located on a high ridge, the museum provides a panoramic valley view. After seeing the museum's collections of Native American and pioneer artifacts, stroll down to the **La Conner Quilt Museum** *(703 S. 2nd St., La Conner. 360-466-4288. www.laconnerquilts.com. Closed Mon.-Tues.; adm fee),* housed in the historic Gaches Mansion, built in 1891. If quilts aren't your thing, it's fun to poke around the

NOT TO BE MISSED

● **The tulip fields around La Conner** ● **La Conner's Museum of Northwest Art** ● **Dining at the Oyster Bar on Chuckanut Drive**

restored Victorian Tudor mansion with its turn-of-the-20th-century furnishings.

La Conner's reputation as an artists colony began back in the late 1930s, when Morris Graves, Mark Tobey, Guy Anderson, and Kenneth Callahan—artists now considered the nucleus of the Northwest school—settled in the vicinity. Their quietly powerful works, often influenced by the area's moist, milky, maritime light and the mysteriously shifting contours of land and sea, are displayed in the **Museum of Northwest Art** (*121 S. 1st St. 360-466-4446. www.museumofnwart .org. Closed Mon.; adm. fee*). This small, sophisticated museum is unique in that it exhibits, collects, and preserves the art of the region.

Along First Street, La Conner's commercial center, you'll find plenty of upscale shops, several good restaurants, and seasonal stands selling smoked salmon. **Calico Cupboard Café & Bakery** (see Travelwise) is known for its cinnamon rolls and delectable pastries.

Part of the pleasure of this getaway is to experience the ever shifting transitions between land and water. As you head north along the La Conner-Whitney Road and Bayview-Edison Road toward Edison, the vast, treeless expanse of the Skagit Valley spreads out as far as the eye can see, watched over by snowcapped Mount Baker and the North Cascades. There are plenty of back roads to explore, where you can visit farms selling apples and berries as well as oysters and shellfish.

With its sheltered waterways, open fields, and upland forests, the valley is one of North America's great wintering bird migration areas. From November to February flocks of tundra swans and snow geese dot the bare fields, and bald eagles are so plentiful that the valley hosts a **Bald Eagle Festival** (*www.skagiteagle.com*) in early February.

No one has ever given an official name to the jigsaw puzzle of bays, islands, and channels that characterize this tide-washed coastline, but it's sometimes referred to as the Salish Sea. The mix of fresh- and saltwater habitats is considered so ecologically important for birds, fish, and other wildlife that **Padilla Bay** has been designated a National Estuarine Research Reserve. Exhibits at the reserve's **Breazeale Interpretive Center** (*10441 Bayview-Edison Rd., Mt. Vernon. 360-428-1558. Closed Mon.-Tues.*) focus on local wildlife and ecology. You can bird-watch from the reserve's nearby observation deck (*closed Mon.-Tues.*).

Chuckanut Drive

As you leave the flatlands of the Skagit Valley and enter Whatcom County, the coastal scenery undergoes a dramatic change. Near the tiny hamlet of Edison, Bayview-Edison Road joins Wash. 237, which jogs east to connect with Chuckanut Drive (US 11). The 10-mile coastal stretch of **Chuckanut Drive,** Washington's first scenic road, winds along the rocky shoulder of conifer-clad Chuckanut Mountain, high above Samish Bay. Viewpoints along this curving, two-lane road

Tulips paint Skagit Valley red (and yellow, purple, and pink) in spring.

offer panoramas of the San Juan Islands rising blue-green in the distance. For a closer look at the Puget Sound shoreline, turn off at **Larrabee State Park** *(245 Chuckanut Dr. 360-676-2093)* and take the short path down to the pebbly, driftwood-strewn beaches.

Chuckanut Drive is locally famous for its seafood restaurants. One of the best places to dine is the **Oyster Bar** (see Travelwise), perched in the trees with fabulous views of Samish Bay. The restaurant has been serving fresh local oysters since the 1930s.

Chuckanut Drive continues all the way to **Fairhaven,** once a town in its own right but now a southern suburb of Bellingham. Many of the redbrick commercial buildings downtown date from the 1880s.

Bellingham, overlooking Bellingham Bay, is a pretty and pleasant place. If you drive up into the city's residential section, along Utter and West Holly Streets, you'll see a fine collection of turn-of-the-20th-century houses. Have a look at the fine collections of Northwest art and historical artifacts displayed in the Whatcom Museum of History & Art *(121 Prospect St. 360-676-6981. Closed Mon.).* Then head up Sehome Hill to the forested campus of **Western**

Washington University *(Visitor Information Center, S. College Dr. 360-650-3424. Closed weekends)*, which boasts a magnificent collection of outdoor sculptures, including major works by Richard Serra and Isamo Noguchi. From the university, Arboretum Drive winds up to an observation tower with stunning views of Bellingham Bay and the North Cascades. —*Donald S. Olson*

Travelwise

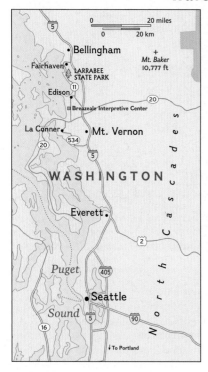

GETTING THERE
The entire getaway is 200 miles round-trip from Seattle. La Conner, the first stop, is about 70 miles north of Seattle, off I-5.

GENERAL INFORMATION
Contact **Bellingham/Whatcom County Convention & Visitors Bureau** *(904 Potter St., Bellingham, WA 98226 360-671-3990. www.bellingham.org).*

ANNUAL EVENT
Skagit Valley Tulip Festival *(360-428-5959. tulipfestival.org. Mid-March–April)* The tulip fields cover a 15-mile radius, and events are scattered throughout.

LODGING
Alice Bay Bed & Breakfast *(11794 Scott Rd., Bow. 360-766-6396 or 800-652-0223. www.alicebay.com. $-$$)* Birders love this peaceful, one-suite retreat on Samish Island.

Hotel Bellwether *(1 Bellwether Way, Bellingham. 877-411-1200 or 360-392-3100. www.hotelbellwether.com. $$-$$$)* Luxury 68-room hotel overlooking its own marina, Bellingham Bay, and the San Juans.

Kristy's Cottage *(3056 Chuckanut Dr., Bow. 360-766-6868. www.chuckanutmanor.com. $$)* Cozy, antique-filled hideaway overlooking Samish Bay.

Skagit Bay Hideaway B&B *(17430 Goldenview Ave., La Conner. 888-466-2262 or 360-466-2262. www.skagitbay.com. $$-$$$)* Two-suite guest house nestled in fir trees and overlooking Skagit Bay; treetop deck.

DINING
Calico Cupboard Café & Bakery *(720 S. 1st St., La Conner. 360-466-4451. $)* Mouthwatering pastries. See p. 290.

Chuckanut Manor *(3056 Chuckanut Dr., Bow. 360-766-6191. $$)* Popular dining spot famous for its Friday night seafood smorgasbord and views of Samish Bay.

La Conner Pub *(702 1st St., La Conner. 360-466-9932. $$)* Fish and chips on the water.

La Conner Seafood & Prime Rib House *(614 S. 1st St., La Conner. 360-466-4014 $$-$$$)* An award-winning waterfront restaurant where everything is prepared from scratch.

Oyster Bar *(2578 Chuckanut Dr., Bow. 360-766-6185. Dinner only. $$$)* See p. 291.

Oyster Creek Inn *(2190 Chuckanut Dr., Bow. 360-766-6179. $$$)* Long-established seafood restaurant on Chuckanut Drive.

St. Louis

Mark Twain Country 294

Missouri Rhineland 298

A farmer plows his field with Belgian horses near Hermann, Missouri.

Mark Twain Country
Life on the Mississippi & beyond

MUCH HAS CHANGED along the Mississippi River since the mid-19th century, when a boy named Sam Clemens prowled the waterfront in Hannibal, Missouri, watching steamboats come and go. But the broad brown river still glides past hills and farms, the same river that inspired the grown-up Sam—then calling himself Mark Twain—to write such classics as *Adventures of Huckleberry Finn* and *Life on the Mississippi.* Explore Mark Twain country to see the tiny cabin where Sam Clemens was born, the house where he grew up, and the town that nurtured one of America's most important literary voices.

Hannibal: America's hometown

Hannibal's downtown sits on low ground between hills to the north and south, its Main Street just a short stroll from the Mississippi of Mark Twain's books. To begin your literary adventure, your first stop should be the **Mark Twain Boyhood Home** *(208 Hill St. 573-221-9010. www.marktwainmuseum.org. Adm. fee).* Museum displays include artifacts and photos from early days in Hannibal, one of Twain's famous white suits, and a typewriter on which he wrote some of his books. In the **Boyhood Home,** restored to its mid-19th-century appearance, you'll see the upstairs bedroom where Sam Clemens and his brother Henry slept and the parlor where Mrs. Clemens entertained friends.

Also part of the museum complex is the **Grant's Drug Store/Pilaster House,** full of antique medical devices and drugs; the Clemens family lived upstairs for a time while Judge Clemens (Sam's father) held court at the Justice of the Peace Office. Two blocks away on Main Street is the **New Mark Twain Museum** *(120 N. Main St.),* with interactive exhibits and audio interpretations of scenes from Twain's novels, a re-creation of a riverboat pilothouse overlooking the Mississippi, and 15 original Norman Rockwell paintings used as illustrations in special editions of Twain's books.

After your museum visit, walk east on Hill Street to pay your

---

NOT TO BE MISSED

- The Mississippi from Riverview Park in Hannibal ● Rockcliffe Mansion's woodwork
- Sleeping in Mark Twain's bedroom at Garth Woodside Mansion

Fishing for catfish during Tom Sawyer Days, Hannibal

respects to the mighty Mississippi at Hannibal's riverboat landing, with its walking path along the river. If it's lunchtime, nearby **Lula-Belle's** (see Travelwise) serves a varied menu in a 1917 building that operated as a brothel for nearly 40 years.

For an easy overview of Mark Twain's Hannibal, take a narrated tour on the **Hannibal Trolley** *(220 N. Main St. 573-221-1161. Closed Nov.-March; fare)* or **Twainland Express Sightseeing Tours** *(400 N. 3rd St. 573-221-5593. Closed Nov.-April; fare)*, which visit many local attractions. One of the highlights is **Mark Twain Cave** *(1 mile S of town on Mo. 79. 573-221-1656. Adm. fee)*, the model for the cave so prominently featured in *The Adventures of Tom Sawyer*. Mazelike passages wind through limestone past intricately eroded rocks and decades of signatures—including that of the outlaw Jesse James, who visited here in 1879.

It's well worth a stop at the **Rockcliffe Mansion** *(1000 Bird. 573-221-4140. Adm. fee)* to see the ornate woodwork and Tiffany lamps of this 28,600-square-foot house, built in 1900 by a local lumberman. Mark Twain spoke from the broad staircase when he visited Hannibal for the last time, in 1902.

In the north part of town, **Riverview Park** *(off Harrison Hill Rd.)* offers tremendous sunset panoramas of the Mississippi River from the tall bluff where stands a **Mark Twain statue,** looking out over the waterway that shaped his life.

At the end of the day, your lodging can continue the Twain theme: Set on 36 acres south of town, **Garth Woodside Mansion Bed and Breakfast** (see Travelwise) was built in 1871 by a wealthy business-man who had been a boyhood friend of Mark Twain's. The famous writer stayed in what he called this "spacious and beautiful house" when he visited Hannibal. Antiques original to the Garth family, an impressive staircase, and hiking trails on the grounds are among the mansion's enticing features.

Beyond Hannibal

Several studios are part of the **Provenance Project** *(800-525-6632. www.provenanceproject.org),* an association of artists and artisans located along 45 miles of Mo. 79, from Hannibal south to Clarksville. Including painters, sculptors, jewelry designers, weavers, and others, the project recruits creative people to relocate along the river as part of a synergistic plan aiding artists and the communities where they live. The reward for travelers is a chance to browse a number of galleries of varied works. Brochures listing studio locations and hours are available at tourist offices, banks, libraries, and the galleries themselves. In Hannibal don't miss **Ayers Pottery** *(308 N. 3rd St. 573-221-6960)* to see beautifully glazed bowls, cups, and other stoneware.

Then drive south on Mo. 79 about 40 miles to **Louisiana,** with its striking, historic storefronts along the highway and Georgia Street. Among the studios here, be sure to visit **Louisiana Purchase** *(317 Georgia St. 573-754-6574. Closed Sun.-Mon.),* with works in stained glass by David Nagy, and **Reflections of Missouri Gallery** *(107 S. 9th St. 573-754-6634),* featuring John Stoeckley's watercolor and pen-and-ink depictions of regional scenes.

Continue south to **Clarksville,** with its attractive downtown on the Mississippi River. Take some time to relax on the riverbank, as barges filled with grain and goods chug up- and downstream. Then see jew-elry and tableware at **ASL Pewter** *(114 Howard St. 573-242-3770. Stu-dio tours Sat.-Sun. and by appt.)* and ironwork at **D.A. Rinedollar Blacksmith Shop** *(117 N. 2nd St. 573-242-3323. Open by appt.).*

From Clarksville, return to Louisiana and drive west on US 54, Mo. 154, and Mo. 107 about 50 miles to see another important Mark Twain site. Although the author grew up in Hannibal, he was born in a rented two-room cabin in what he called the "almost invisible village of **Florida.**" A red granite monument marks the original location of that tiny home, which has been moved a quarter mile and preserved within a modern museum at **Mark Twain Birthplace State Historic Site** (*Cty. Rd. U, off Mo. 107. 573-565-3449. Adm. fee*). The museum displays personal items and furniture that belonged to the writer-humorist, as well as manuscripts and printer's proofs of some of his books. You'll gain insight into how a man from such humble beginnings used his magical touch with words to speak for the common people, and become beloved the world over.

—*Mel White*

Travelwise

GETTING THERE
Hannibal is about 100 miles north of St. Louis via US 61.

GENERAL INFORMATION
Contact the **Hannibal Convention & Visitors Bureau** (*505 N. 3rd St., Hannibal, MO 63401. 573-221-2477 or 866-263-4825. www.VisitHannibal.com*).

SEASONS
Spring through fall is the best time to visit.

ANNUAL EVENTS
Autumn Historic Folklife Festival (*3rd weekend in Oct., downtown Hannibal. 573-221-6545*) Craftspeople demonstrate 19th-century lifestyles along town streets.

National Tom Sawyer Days (*Several days around July 4, various sites in Hannibal. 573-221-2477 or 866-263-4825. www.VisitHannibal.com*) This popular celebration includes fence-painting and frog-jumping contests.

MORE THINGS TO SEE & DO
Optical Science Center and Museum (*214 N. Main St., Hannibal. 573-221-2020. Closed Oct.-April; adm. fee*) Optical illusions, light shows, antique eyeglasses entertain visitors.

Riverboat Mark Twain (*Hannibal riverfront. 573-221-3222. www.marktwainriverboat.com. Closed Dec.-March; fare*) Sight-seeing cruises, plus jazz trips on the river.

LODGING
Belle's River Heritage Collection (*111 Bird, Hannibal. 573-221-6662 or 800-882-4890. www.lulabelles.com. $-$$*) Bed-and-breakfast accommodations in a variety of settings in and around Hannibal, from a small house to rooms on Main Street downtown.

Garth Woodside Mansion Bed and Breakfast (*11069 New London Rd., Hannibal. 573-221-2789 or 888-427-8409. www.GarthMansion.com. $$-$$$*) A former Twain haunt. See p. 296.

Sixth Street Guest Haus (*407 N. 6th St., Hannibal. 573-248-0082. www.sixthstreetguesthaus.com. $$*) Five upscale apartments with kitchens in an 1870 house.

DINING
LulaBelle's (*111 Bird, Hannibal. 573-221-6662. $$*) A popular lunchtime spot. See p. 295.

Riverview Café (*1 mile S of Hannibal on Mo. 79 at Sawyer's Creek. 573-221-8292. Closed Jan.-March. $$*) A Mississippi vista highlights this restaurant featuring American-style food.

TJ's Supper Club (*Mo. 36 and Munger Ln., Hannibal. 573-221-5551. $$*) Prime rib is the specialty at this favorite local restaurant and lounge.

Missouri Rhineland
Wine tasting along the Missouri River

THE GREEN HILLS AND ROLLING FARMLAND along the lower Missouri River seem at first like a typical midwestern landscape—but the country west of St. Louis holds a savory surprise. Nearly a dozen wineries cluster within just a couple of hours' drive here, offering travelers a weekend escape as flavorful as it is scenic and historical. The vineyards, and several quaint riverside towns, are in part the legacy of German immigrants who moved to this area in the mid-

German-style Hermann

19th century, bringing with them Old World traditions that still echo along the tall bluffs of the Missouri.

Hermann

The pretty town of **Hermann** ranks as the best known of all the "German" communities along the Missouri River and makes a fine starting point for your explorations. The town's first settlers, arriving in 1836, were from Philadelphia. Fearing that their European heritage was being diluted in that Eastern city, they aimed to preserve their way of life in a new colony on the American frontier. Hermann still has streets named Mozart, Goethe, and Gutenberg, and it maintains much of its Old World flavor—in architecture, food, and, of course, wine.

To learn about German immigration and its highly important influence in Missouri, visit **Deutschheim State Historic Site** *(107-109 W. 2nd St. 573-486-2200. www.mostateparks.com/deutschheim*

.htm. Adm. fee), where tours through two 1840s houses interpret fascinating aspects of state and local history and customs. The Pommer-Gentner House illustrates the lifestyle of an upper-class but unostentatious family, while the Strehly House depicts a more modest household, complete with original family items.

The **Historic Hermann Museum** *(4th and Schiller Sts. 573-486-2017. Closed Thurs. and Oct.-April; adm. fee)* presents exhibits in an 1871 school building full of furniture, toys, locally made pottery, artifacts from riverboat days, and countless other items from the town's past. The picturesque town clock atop the old school has kept time since 1891.

Hermann's wineries rank among the town's major attractions, and the best known and most historic may be **Stone Hill Winery** *(1100 Stone Hill Hwy. 573-486-2221. www.stonehillwinery.com)*. Among the country's largest wine producers in the late 19th century, Stone Hill, like other wineries, was shut down during Prohibition, its vaulted cellars used for growing mushrooms. Revived in 1965, it again offers award-winning wines, including a fine red Norton. The winery's **Vintage Restaurant** (see Travelwise), set in a renovated carriage house, is among Hermann's finest dining spots.

Move on to sample the wines of **Hermannhof Winery** *(330 E. 1st St. 573-486-5959. www.hermannhof.com)* in the firm's imposing brick downtown building. As is the case at many wineries, Hermannhof sells locally made cheese, bread, and sausage for an impromptu picnic, perhaps along the Missouri riverbank just a short stroll away.

Thus fortified, follow First Street (Mo. 100) 2 miles southwest of town to the **Adam Puchta Winery** *(1947 Frene Creek Rd. 573-486-5596)*, the oldest winery in Missouri still under its original family ownership. The sixth generation of Puchtas is producing wine in this quiet setting on the bank of Frene Creek.

Along the river

The next day, you may feel the need for some exercise. If so, head north over the Missouri River on Mo. 19 to **Katy Trail State Park** *(800-334-6946. www.katytrailstatepark.com)*, a 225-mile hiking-biking route that follows the converted railbed of the Missouri-Kansas-Texas Railroad (the "Katy" line). Small towns and inns along the way offer the chance for overnight trips. Check with tourism organizations for lists of bike rental shops and shuttle services. Many local trail enthusiasts consider the 16-mile segment from McKittrick (the nearest trailhead to Hermann) to Treloar among the Katy's most scenic.

NOT TO BE MISSED

● A glass of good Norton from Stone Hill or Hermannhof ● Walking the Katy Trail near McKittrick ● The homey feeling of Hermann's Strehly House

● The one-block downtown of New Haven, 13 miles east of Hermann

Then spend a leisurely afternoon rambling along the Missouri River east of Hermann, on Mo. 100. At New Haven, visit **Röbller Vineyard** *(275 Röbller Vineyard Rd. 573-237-3986),* known for its Norton reds, before continuing to **Washington,** a river town with German-influenced brick storefronts lining its downtown streets. Washington grew up around a ferry landing on the Missouri. Today, **Rennick Riverfront Park** is a pleasant place to sit and watch the river roll by.

Front, Elm, and Main Streets are where you'll find most of Washington's antique shops, under the massive tower of the 1866 St. Francis Borgia Catholic Church. Stop at the **Gary R. Lucy Gallery** *(Main and Elm Sts. 636-239-6337)* to see this artist's river-themed historical paintings. Exhibits at the **Washington Historical Society Museum** *(4th and Market Sts. 636-239-0280. Closed Mon. and Jan.-Feb.)* include artifacts of the Missouri Meerschaum Company, which has been making corncob pipes in Washington for more than a century (Mark Twain preferred them); the J. B. Busch Brewery, established here in 1854 by a member of the famous Busch family of St. Louis; and Franz Schwarzer, a Washington zithermaker whose instruments were famous worldwide at the end of the 19th century.

Missouri's wine road

From Washington, cross the Missouri River on the Mo. 47 bridge and go east on Mo. 94. This winding, rolling highway has been designated Missouri's Weinstrasse, or "wine road," in honor of the number of wineries along the route. The first you'll reach, at the tiny town of Dutzow, is **Blumenhof Vineyards** *(Mo. 94. 636-433-2245. www.blumenhof.com),* which offers wine tasting, spacious grounds for picnicking, and an access point to the Katy Trail.

Continue east to the village of **Augusta,** center of the nation's first officially designated wine district. It's easy to spend a few hours in antique shops and artists' studios here before moving on to **Mount Pleasant Winery** *(5634 High St. 636-482-4419. www.mountpleasant.com),* where you can tour old stone cellars and, of course, sample a few more reds and whites. At **Augusta Winery** *(High and Jackson Sts. 636-228-4301. www.augustawinery.com),* try the Seyval Blanc, a fine dry white, or the dry red Chambourcin. **Montelle Winery** *(1.5 miles E of Augusta on Mo. 94. 636-228-4464. www.montelle.com)* sits on a high bluff with a fine view of forested ridges, farms, and the Missouri River below. Tables on the terrace offer a superb setting for a picnic.

Ten miles east of Augusta, drive west on Mo. F to reach the **Daniel Boone Home** *(1868 Mo. F, Defiance. 636-798-2005. Closed Dec.-Feb.; adm. fee).* Boone helped his son build this four-story house of locally quarried limestone between 1803 and 1810. Guided tours take in the life and times of the legendary frontiersman, who died here in 1820.
—*Mel White*

Travelwise

GETTING THERE
To reach Hermann from St. Louis, take I-70 west about 50 miles and drive south on Mo. 19 for 15 miles.

GENERAL INFORMATION
Contact the **Hermann Visitor Information Center** *(312 Market St., Hermann, MO 65041. 573-486-2744 or 800-932-8687. www.hermannmo.com);* the **Washington Area Visitor Center** *(301 W. Front St., Washington, MO 63090. 636-239-7575 or 888-792-7466. www.washmo.org);* or the **Greater Augusta Chamber of Commerce** *(P.O. Box 51, Augusta, MO 63332. 636-228-4005. www.augusta-missouri.com).*

SEASONS
Spring and fall are the best times to visit for moderate temperatures and for seasonal festivals. Some attractions close in winter.

ANNUAL EVENTS
Art Fair and Winefest *(3rd weekend in May, Rennick Riverfront Park, Washington. 888-792-7466)* Music, wine tasting, and art show.

Maifest *(3rd weekend in May, various sites in Hermann. 573-486-3596 or 800-932-8687)* Dating from 1952, this German-themed festival includes Maypole dances and carnival rides.

Octoberfest *(Oct. weekends, various sites in Hermann. 573-486-2744 or 800-932-8687. www.hermannmo.com)* Museum tours, special winery events, and German food and music.

Wurstfest *(4th weekend in March, various sites in Hermann. 573-486-2744 or 800-932-8687. www.hermannmo.com)* Sausage is the star of this celebration, which includes music

and a dachshund competition.

MORE THINGS TO SEE & DO
Shaw Nature Reserve *(Mo. 100, Gray Summit. 636-451-3512. www.mobot.org. Closed Sun.; adm. fee)* Twelve miles east of Washington, this 2,400-acre natural area offers hiking trails, tallgrass prairie, and wildflower gardens.

Swiss Meat and Sausage Company *(2056 Mo. 19, 12 miles S of Hermann. 573-486-2086)* A celebrated source of fine family-made sausage, hams, and other meats.

LODGING
Birk's Gasthaus *(700 Goethe St., Hermann. 573-486-2911. www.birksgasthaus.com. $)* Nine rooms in an ornate 1886 house.

Captain Wohlt Inn *(123 E. 3rd St., Hermann. 573-486-3357. $-$$)* Three suites and five rooms near Hermann's historic district.

Market Street Bed and Breakfast *(210 Market St., Hermann. 573-486-5597. $)* Beautiful woodwork highlights this Victorian inn on Hermann's major thoroughfare. Three rooms.

Schwegmann House Bed and Breakfast *(438 W. Front St., Washington. 636-239-5025. www.schwegmannhouse.com. $$)* This 1861 brick house facing the river offers nine antique-filled rooms.

Weirick Estate Bed and Breakfast *(716 W. Main St., Washington. 636-239-4469. $)* Three guest rooms in an 1879 Victorian house overlooking the Missouri River.

DINING
American Bounty *(430 W. Front St., Washington. 636-390-2150. Closed Mon.-Tues. $$)* Innovative soups and beef and seafood dishes.

Elijah McLean's *(600 W. Front St., Washington. 636-239-9463. $$)* Popular American-style restaurant in an 1839 Georgian house overlooking the river.

Simon's on the Waterfront *(4 Schiller St., Hermann. 573-486-2030. Closed Mon.-Tues. $-$$)* The menu ranges from barbecue and Cajun dishes to German specialties.

Vintage Restaurant *(573-486-3479. Closed winter. $$)* Fine dining. See p. 300.

Wild Grapevine *(4th and Market Sts., Hermann. 573-486-8463. Closed Sun.-Mon. $$)* Traditional German dishes and sausages.

Salt Lake City

Powder Paradise   304

Jurassic Journeys   308

Bear River Range   312

Going cross-country, Utah

Powder Paradise
Skiing the Wasatch Range

AS MUCH OF THE WORLD LEARNED during the 2002 Winter Olympic Games, Salt Lake City is a snow-sports paradise, with *ten* ski resorts located fewer than 60 miles from Salt Lake City. This getaway has you sampling two or three of them. The weekend is ideal for those who dream of making turns surrounded only by fellow skiers: Neither Alta nor Deer Valley permits snowboarders, yet neighboring resorts welcome them.

Alta

The mining-settlement-turned-ski-town of **Alta** sits at the head of Little Cottonwood Canyon. One of a handful of overnight options here is the 57-room **Alta Lodge** (see Travelwise), located at the base of the **Alta Ski Area** *(801-359-1078. www.alta.com)*. Walk gingerly down the long flights of stairs to the lodge, where management strives to foster camaraderie in the tradition of ski inns of yore. You might find yourself chatting with octogenarian Bill Levitt, Alta's mayor of the last three decades. Levitt, who purchased the Alta Lodge in 1959, says his primary operational duty today is "to walk around and look worried."

Some would call Alta anachronistic, but Mayor Levitt declares that Alta is "not the past, but the future" of skiing. Indeed, for many skiers a visit to Alta is a pilgrimage; some never leave, sincerely believing heaven couldn't be better. Jump onto the Wildcat lift or the Collins lift to access expert and intermediate terrain on the resort's "front side." For more novice-friendly terrain, go to the Albion Base and board either the Albion or Sunnyside lift. If you're of at least intermediate ability, don't miss riding the Supreme lift to Point Supreme for astonishing views of the ski area, the surrounding mountains, and the broad Heber Valley to the east.

Alta is best known for its fearless-expert terrain of steep chutes and gullies; but it is evenly divided between novice, intermediate, and expert terrain, all often buried under fresh, feather-light powder that's around 5 percent water and 95 percent air—little wonder skiing through it feels like flying!

Schussing down the Wasatch Range

Enjoy lunch at **Alf's Restaurant,** located mid-mountain at the base of the Cecret (a "secret" spelling that's a legacy of the silver-mining days) and Sugarloaf lifts. The building's exterior could use an old-fashioned makeover, but inside are black-and-white photos, along with a large display of classic wooden skis, that capture the essence of the ski area.

If you purchased a dual-area ticket providing access to the lifts of both Alta and neighboring **Snowbird Ski and Summer Resort** *(801-933-2222. www.snowbird.com),* whose modern ambience makes it rather like Alta's polar opposite, you can now take the Sugarloaf detachable quad to the Sugarloaf Saddle and drop into Snowbird's Mineral Basin. Snowbird is absolutely immense, with open ridges, rocky crags, and steep, avalanche-prone slopes, lending a dramatic, European Alps feel to the resort.

Park City

Located on the eastern side of the Wasatch Range, **Park City** was a crumbling, dying mining town as recently as the early 1960s. During the last few decades it has experienced a huge boom, thanks largely to the bounty of white gold that falls from the skies and now attracts thousands of skiers and snowboarders each year.

Rest your legs before another session of hammering the downhills by exploring Park City's colorful downtown district. Begin at the upper end of Main Street, where you can attempt to devour one of the deliciously huge omelettes served at **Morning Ray Café** (see

Travelwise). Then waddle uncomfortably down the street and poke your nose into a few of the unique boutiques inhabiting the town's old buildings. Most were built after a devastating fire in 1898, but quite a few wear plaques declaring that they were built before the conflagration.

Next, drive north toward I-80 and turn into the **Utah Olympic Park** *(435-658-4200. Adm. fee).* To experience your own Olympic thrill, take a wild and exhilarating ride *(fee)* down the bobsled track on which a few new records were set during the 2002 Winter Olympic Games. The Joe Quinney Winter Sports Center houses the **Alf Engen Ski Museum** *(801-328-0389. www.engenmuseum.org).* A film and exhibits highlight the storied history of skiing in Utah, up to and including the 2002 Winter Games. That history also includes the life of the ski-industry pioneer whose name the museum wears.

On the way back to town, try classic or skate skiing at the **White Pine Cross Country Ski Area** *(Park Ave./Utah 224. 435-615-5858. www.whitepinetouring.com. Trail fee, rentals and lessons available),* where more than 10 miles of groomed trails radiate over a flat to rolling countryside. If you'd like to try something different, there's no shortage of other options: Consider an over-snow tour with **Park City Snowmobile Adventures** *(435-645-7256);* a puppy-powered excursion through Wasatch Mountain State Park with **Wild Dog Mushing Company** *(435-671-0900);* or drift-busting on horseback with **Wind in Your Hair Riding** *(435-649-4795).*

But let's not forget the slopes. Three major ski areas surround Park City: **The Canyons** *(435-649-5400 or 888-226-9667. www.thecanyons.com),* **Park City Mountain Resort** *(435-649-8111 or 888-222-7275. www.parkcitymountain.com),* and **Deer Valley Resort** *(435-649-1000 or 800-424-3337. www.deervalley.com).*

Renowned for its uncompromising attention to detail, Deer Valley, which hosted several events of the 2002 Winter Olympic Games, is perennially rated by the ski press as one of the top resorts in the country. It doesn't hurt, either, that the director of skiing is Stein Eriksen, the legendary Olympic gold and silver medalist at the 1952 Oslo games.

There's plenty for every level of skier on Deer Valley's four peaks. (Deer Valley caters strictly to skiers; snowboarders are welcome, but their boards are not.) A good way to get your bearings is to join a **Mountain Host Tour** *(see trail map for meeting times and places).* Intermediates will want to try some of the runs striping Flagstaff Mountain, such as the twisting, giggle-inducing Sidewinder. While known primarily for its ultra-buffed, groomed runs, the resort hides plenty of powder stashes—witness the bowls and chutes dropping away from the ridge joining Flagstaff Mountain and Empire Canyon —as well as heavily moguled runs for skiers with pistons for knees.

—*Michael McCoy*

Travelwise

GETTING THERE

Alta is southeast of Salt Lake City via I-215 and Utah 210; Park City is east of the city via I-80 and Utah 224.

GENERAL INFORMATION

Contact the **Park City Visitor Information Center** *(750 Kearns Blvd., Park City, UT 84060. 435-658-4541. www.parkcityinfo.com).*

SEASONS

Depending on snowfall, the ski season can run late November through mid-April. The best skiing is typically February and March, when the resorts have good snow bases.

ANNUAL EVENT

Sundance Film Festival *(Jan., Park City, Salt Lake City, and Sundance Resort. www.sundance.org)* Robert Redford's Sundance Institute sponsors this screening of feature-length independent films and shorts.

OTHER SKI AREAS
Alpine skiing:

Brighton Ski Resort *(801-532-4731 or 800-873-5512. www.skibrighton.com)* In Big Cottonwood Canyon on the west slope of the Wasatch. Family-friendly.

Snowbasin Ski Resort *(801-620-1000. www.snowbasin.com)* Situated outside Ogden, this skiing paradise lies farther afield than the Park City area resorts. It hosted the 2002 Olympic downhill and super-G events.

Solitude Mountain Resort *(801-534-1400. www.skisolitude.com)* Also up Big Cottonwood Canyon. Intermediate and advanced skiers will love the terrain.

Nordic skiing:

Soldier Hollow *(18 miles S of Park City in Wasatch Mountain State Park. 435-654-1791. Adm. fee)* Offers about 16 miles of cross-country trails.

LODGING

Alta Lodge *(801-742-3500 or 800-707-2582. www.altalodge.com. $$-$$$)* Quintessential ski lodge. See p. 304.

The Châteaux at Silver Lake *(Deer Valley. 435-658-9500. www.chateaux-deervalley .com. $$-$$$)* High prices are matched by exceedingly lofty standards. Its mid-mountain

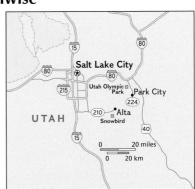

location can't be beat.

Cliff Lodge *(Entry 4 of Snowbird. 801-742-2222 or 800-453-3000. www.snowbird.com. $$-$$$)* A beautiful, bunkerlike maze that includes a couple of private clubs, as liquor-serving establishments are classified in Utah.

Hampton Inn *(10690 S. Holiday Park Dr., Sandy. 801-571-0800. www.hamptoninn .com. $)* Located about 15 miles from Alta, this national-chain hotel is close to several restaurants.

Holiday Inn Express Hotel & Suites *(1501 W. Ute Blvd., Park City. 435-658-1600. www.utahhospitality.com. $$)* This national-chain hotel features a fitness center, hot tub, pool, and covered parking. Shuttles available during ski season.

DINING

Main Street Pizza & Noodle *(530 Main St., Park City. 435-645-8878. $-$$)* Pizzas, pastas, sandwiches, and stir-fries.

Mariposa *(Deer Valley's Silver Lake Village, 435-645-6715. Closed Mon. $$$)* Intimate restaurant with an award-winning menu. Try a sampler of a half dozen dishes.

Morning Ray/Evening Star Café *(268 Main St., Park City. 435-649-5686. $-$$)* Open in the morning as the Morning Ray, in the evening as the Evening Star. See pp. 305-306.

Steak Pit *(Level 1, Snowbird Center. 801-742-2222. $$-$$$)* Fresh seafood and juicy steaks; Snowbird's oldest dining establishment.

Jurassic Journeys
Down & dirty with Utah's dinosaurs

FOR 150 MILLION YEARS, beginning in the Triassic and continuing through the Jurassic and Cretaceous periods, dinosaurs roamed the land. Their day came to a sudden end some 65 million years ago, probably after a giant asteroid crashed into the Earth. The "terrible lizards" are gone, but not forgotten, as the fossil records they left behind attest—including those in the high, painted deserts of northeastern Utah.

Alpine & the Wasatch Range

Stop first at the **North American Museum of Ancient Life** (*20 miles S of Salt Lake City off I-15, Alpine/Highland exit. 801-766-5000 or 888-672-6040. www.dinosaurpoint.com. Closed Sun., and Mon. in winter; adm. fee*) in the Thanksgiving Point amusement complex. The self-described "largest dinosaur museum in the world" does a superlative job of combining the science of dinosaurs with the undeniable entertainment factor of the ancient beasts. Among the dozens of highlights are a fossil lab with technicians at work, displays dedicated to the excavations at Como Bluff, Wyoming, and an immense, 110-foot-long *Supersaurus* specimen from outside Delta, Colorado. At the Erosion Table, get your hands wet and sandy while fashioning a river system. And in the large Sunset Quarry, excavate into deep sand to uncover simulated fossil bones.

Next, drive north to where you exited I-15, and take Utah 92 east. The ensuing **Alpine Loop Scenic Backway** shoots through the jaws of American Fork Canyon, then winds up and over the Wasatch Range. It's a spectacular drive, but sections of the road are narrow, steep, and serpentine enough to make the drive not advisable for those averse to heights and/or exposure.

After about 10 miles you'll reach **Timpanogos Cave National Monument** (*801-756-5238. www.nps.gov/tica*). At the visitor center you can sign up for a ranger-led tour (*fee*) through three interconnected caves bejeweled in helictites, stalactites, and cave popcorn. To reach the cave entrance, you need to hike a strenuous, 1.5-mile trail

---

NOT TO BE MISSED

- **Star Tunnel, North American Museum of Ancient Life** ● **Lehi Roller Mills Oatmeal at Sundance** ● **Josie Bassett's homestead, Dinosaur National Monument** ● **Red-tailed hawks soaring over the Uinta Basin**

Exposed fossils at Dinosaur Quarry, Dinosaur National Monument

that gains over 1,000 feet of elevation; on it you will walk from Precambrian rocks over a billion years old to younger rocks of the Mississippian epoch. These limestones, in which the caves were created along a fault zone through the dissolving action of groundwater, are "only" 330 million years old—but that still makes them more than twice as old as the Jurassic-age rocks of the Morrison formation, the most common source of dinosaur fossils in the region.

Consider overnighting up the road at Robert Redford's **Sundance** (see Travelwise), nestled in the afternoon shadow of Mount Timpanogos, the crown of the Wasatch Range. The resort blends admirably into its natural setting, with attractive cottages tucked creekside into woods near the base of the ski mountain. Sundance attracts an eclectic clientele that can range from mountaineering types to artists and actors. In the large library of lender videotapes, dig up a classic movie such as *Jurassic Park* to keep the dino momentum going.

Vernal

After sleeping in, or perhaps mountain biking on the trails at Sundance *(rentals available),* drive 18 miles into Heber City and turn east onto US 40. Sixteen miles later you'll encounter the **Daniels Summit Lodge** (see Travelwise), sitting atop its namesake 8,000-foot-high mountain pass. The resort's **Lodgepole Grill** (see Travelwise), with its Wild West decor and tasty food, makes a good lunch stop.

From there, descend from the timber and lush, high-country meadows onto an arid desert plateau, where the stratification of colorful sediments is apparent whether layer-cake flat or magnificently twisted and folded. Soon you'll enter the Utah tourism region aptly known as Dinosaurland. The theme climaxes in **Vernal,** 128 miles from Heber City, where dinosaur depictions and references run rampant. Head 10 miles northeast of town to the brilliantly exposed Navajo sandstone of **Red Fleet State Park** *(435-789-4432),* where you can investigate a 200-million-year-old dinosaur trackway.

Back in Vernal, wander over to the excellent **Utah Field House of Natural History State Park** *(235 E. Main St. 435-789-3799).* The museum features exhibits on the natural history and human prehistory of the region, and on the 2.7-billion-year geologic record of the Uinta Mountains, the largest east-west trending range in the contiguous 48 states. Standing outside, in re-created natural habitats, are life-size models of dinosaurs—including the fierce, carnivorous Utahraptor. The Northeastern Utah Visitor Center *(435-789-7894)* is housed in the same building as the museum.

Dinosaur National Monument

To track down **Dinosaur National Monument** *(435-789-2115. www .nps.gov/dino. Adm. fee),* go 12 miles southeast from Vernal on US 40, then turn north on Utah 149. You'll course through an area of rugged landscape possessing enough scenic attributes to justify a visit even if it held no dinosaur fossils. It does, of course, yet the monument's 330 square miles, the majority of which lie in Colorado, also contain canyon oases, long stretches of the Green and Yampa Rivers, and some of the least disturbed high-desert landscapes in the West.

The **Quarry Visitor Center** protects one of the most important paleontological discoveries in world history. First investigated in 1909 by Earl Douglass of Pittsburgh's Carnegie Museum, the Morrison sandstone of this hogback ridge has yielded several complete fossil skeletons and thousands of bones, representing nearly a dozen species of dinosaurs—including *Diplodocus, Stegosaurus,* and *Allosaurus*—along with fossil remains of other creatures that lived here 150 million years ago, such as turtles and crocodiles. More than 1,500 fossil bones are exposed, still partially embedded in the rock wall.

The **Tour of the Tilted Rocks** scenic drive follows Cub Creek Road. You'll see Native American pictographs and petroglyphs, a prairie-dog town, and some unforgettable vistas. Juniper trees grow along the base of angled rocks, which are backed by much larger outcrops, some of them appearing like rows of giant, back-slanting sharks' teeth. Take time at the site of **Josie Bassett's cabin** at the turnaround 12 miles out to inspect one of the intriguing box canyons where the solitary pioneer kept her cattle. Consider hiking the 2-mile **Desert Voices Nature Trail** *(trailhead at Split Mountain Campground)* later in the day, after the temperature has cooled and the chances of spotting wildlife are greater.

Flaming Gorge-Uintas Scenic Byway

Return to Salt Lake City via the **Flaming Gorge-Uintas Scenic Byway;** you'll have a hard time keeping your eyes on the road. It heads north from Vernal on US 191, then skirts the southern border of Flaming Gorge National Recreation Area on Utah 44. More than a dozen "Wildlife Through the Ages" waysides, along with four designated nature trails, interpret the past and present habitats and wildlife of this spectacular outback. Keep an eye out for current residents such as bighorn sheep, pronghorn, and elk. The distance from Vernal to Manila, the northern terminus of the byway, is about 65 miles. From there, return to Salt Lake City by driving 57 miles northwest to Fort Bridger, Wyoming, then 115 miles west on I-80.   —*Michael McCoy*

·····························

Travelwise

GETTING THERE
From Salt Lake City, this 425-mile route heads south and loops counterclockwise through northeast Utah and southwest Wyoming.

GENERAL INFORMATION
Contact the **Dinosaurland Travel Board** *(55 E. Main St., Vernal, UT 84078. 435-789-6932 or 800-477-5558. www.dinoland.com).*

SEASONS
Summer is the most popular time to visit; September and October offer more solitude and terrific fall colors. The high road over the Wasatch Range is not open in winter.

ANNUAL EVENT
Dinosaur Roundup Rodeo *(2nd week in July, Vernal. 800-421-9635)* Competitions among bull riders, barrel racers, team ropers, and young mutton busters, as well as a parade, cowboy dances, and concerts.

MORE THINGS TO SEE & DO
Fort Bridger State Historic Site *(Fort Bridger, WY. 307-782-3842. Adm. fee)* A reconstruction of Jim Bridger's 1843 trading post that served mountain men, Indians, pioneers, Pony Express riders, and frontier soldiers; a rock wall raised during the Mormon occupation of the 1850s; and renovated structures remaining from the military years, which began in 1857.

LODGING
Best Western Dinosaur Inn *(251 E. Main St., Vernal. 435-789-2660. www.bestwestern .com. $-$$)* A 60-room hotel located close to

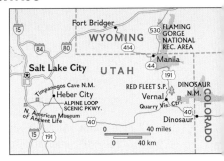

the Utah Field House of Natural History and downtown restaurants.

Daniels Summit Lodge *(US 40 at Daniels Pass. 435-548-2300 or 800-519-9969. www.danielssummit.com. $-$$)* A beautiful retreat with 48 rooms. See p. 309.

Landmark Inn *(288 E. 100 South, Vernal. 435-781-1800. www.landmark-inn.com. $-$$)* Quaint, quiet 10-room bed-and-breakfast occupying a former Baptist church.

Sundance *(off Utah 92. 801-225-4107. www.sundanceresort.com. $$$)* See p. 309.

DINING
Curry Manor *(corner of Vernal Ave. and 200 South, Vernal. 435-789-2289. Closed Sun. $$-$$$)* Fine dining in a venerable two-story brick house.

Lodgepole Grill *(Daniels Summit Lodge, US 40 at Daniels Pass. 435-548-2300. $-$$$)* Country-style food, including baby back ribs and hamburgers. See p. 309.

Bear River Range
In the shadow of
mountain peaks & pioneers

THE SPIRIT OF THE OLD WEST endures in this region, which played a prominent role during the beaver-trapping years of the 1820s and the subsequent days of westward migration on the Oregon Trail. From the attractive city of Logan, a name deriving from mountain man Ephraim Logan, who first visited the Cache Valley in 1824, you'll climb alongside the dancing waters of the Logan River, then descend to beautiful Bear Lake and north into Idaho. Along the way you'll gain appreciation for the land and its people.

Cache Valley

Logan boasts delightfully earthy stores and boutiques in its historic downtown, in close proximity to the magnificent **Logan Tabernacle** *(100 N. Main St.)* and **Logan Temple** *(100 N. 200 East. Closed to non-Mormons)*. For an afternoon of living history lessons, drive 6 miles southwest on US 89/91 to the 160-acre grounds of the **American West Heritage Center** *(435-245-6050. www .americanwestcenter.org. Closed Labor Day–Mem. Day, and Sun.; adm. fee)*. The Jensen Historical Farm, where you can milk a cow, represents the era from 1880 to 1917; in the Pioneer Area, displays and docents bring alive the period of 1845 to 1870.

Before the pioneer era, mountain men and fur traders ruled the area. Along the Blacksmith Fork River near present-day Nibley is the site of the **July 1826 Cache Valley rendezvous.** Hundreds of Native Americans and trappers, both free and conscripted, gathered for two weeks of trading, gaming, and general carousing. It was one in a series of annual rendezvous held at various locations in the central and northern Rockies during the fur-trading era. The 1826 rendezvous was attended by such notable mountain men as Jim Bridger, Jedediah Smith, and James P. Beckwourth, who wrote, "the unpacking of the medicine water contributed not a little to the heightening of our festivities."

NOT TO BE MISSED

● **Mule deer bounding up the steep hillsides of the Bear River Range** ● **A hearty cup of coffee at Caffe Ibis Coffee Roasting Co., Logan** ● **Bicycling the Spring Hollow Trail at Stokes Nature Center**

Logan Canyon

After breakfast, head north on US 89. You'll climb onto the bench holding the Utah State University campus, then come to the Forest Service's Logan Ranger District Visitor Center *(1500 E. Hwy. 89. 435-755-3620).* Continuing east on the **Logan Canyon Scenic Byway,** you'll quickly enter the mouth of the canyon, whose confines once provided food and shelter for Shoshone, and in later times yielded timber for a burgeoning Cache Valley population; today Logan Canyon serves as a premier getaway for outdoors enthusiasts.

One mile from the Forest Service office, park and walk half a mile upstream to the Stokes Nature Center *(435-755-3239. www.logan nature.org).* Watch for American dippers wading and swimming in the Logan River, which at this elevation is more like a mountain stream. Then continue driving up the road, which mimics every meander in the river as it twists beneath lofty walls of fractured limestone, embellished at their bases with bursts of pine and juniper.

Turn right after about 15 miles on Forest Road 007 *(gravel)* to detour to **Old Ephraim's Grave,** resting site of the last known and allegedly largest ever grizzly bear in these parts. He was killed in 1923 and the monument reportedly stands as tall as he did. Backtrack to US 89, but stop about 1.5 miles before reaching the road to hike the **Temple Fork Sawmill Trail.** It meanders along Temple Fork Creek for several miles to the site of an 1877 sawmill. The lumber used for constructing much of early-day Logan was milled here.

Back on US 89, things soon open up, with dry, south-facing slopes clad in sagebrush and willow thickets lining the stream's course.

Bear Lake & beyond

From the 7,800-foot crest of the **Bear River Range,** begin dropping toward **Bear Lake,** whose blue-green waters shimmer 8 miles west to east and 20 miles south to north. The fur-traders' rendezvous of both 1827 and 1828 took place on the south shore of the big lake, but today the area is more heralded for its berries than its beaver population. So, on reaching **Garden City** at 38 miles, swing into a café and order a round of the settlement's best known product: milk shakes made with luscious, locally grown raspberries.

Continue north on US 89 along the western shore of Bear Lake, eventually curving east into Montpelier, Idaho. Visit the **National Oregon/California Trail Center** *(jct. of US 89 and US 30. 208-847-3800. www.oregontrailcenter.org. Adm. fee).* It resides at the site of the Clover Creek Encampment, where mid-19th-century migrants rested for the next leg of their arduous journeys westward. The center's displays convey life on the trail.

You can enjoy an outstanding prime-rib dinner for a shockingly low, small-town price at **Butch Cassidy's Restaurant & Saloon** (see Travelwise). The outlaw reference dates from August 13, 1896, when

Robert Leroy Parker, aka Butch Cassidy, and a pair of partners robbed the youthful Bank of Montpelier.

For the return trip to Logan, follow Idaho 36 west to Preston. The Bear River Massacre took place just northwest of town. On January 29, 1863, one of the darkest days in American history, some 300 Northern Shoshone men, women, and children were slaughtered by volunteers of Col. Patrick E. Conner's Third California Infantry. Continue south on US 91. Just before reentering Utah you'll pass through **Franklin,** the first town settled in Idaho—although at the time it was thought to be in Utah, and was in fact incorporated in 1869 by that state's legislature. A survey three years later revealed the error. The town stands as an excellent example of an early Mormon settlement; some wonderful old buildings line its main street.

—*Michael McCoy*

Travelwise

GETTING THERE
Logan is 80 miles north of Salt Lake City via I-15 and US 89/91.

GENERAL INFORMATION
Contact the **Cache Valley Tourist Council** *(160 N. Main St., Logan, UT 84321. 435-752-2161 or 800-882-4433. www.tourcachevalley.com).*

ANNUAL EVENT
Festival of the American West *(late July–early Aug., Logan. 435-245-6050 or 800-225-3378)* Western music, cowboy poetry, Indian and mountain-man encampments, and more.

LODGING
Best Western Clover Creek Inn *(243 N. 4th St., Montpelier, ID. 208-847-1782. www .bestwestern.com. $-$$)* Nice motel across from Butch Cassidy's Restaurant & Saloon.

Bluebird Inn *(423 Hwy. 89, Fish Haven, ID. 208-945-2571 or 800-797-6448. www.the bluebirdinn.com. Closed Nov.–Mem. Day. $$)* Situated a half mile north of the Utah border on a hill above Bear Lake. Each of the five rooms features a fireplace and separate bath.

Providence Inn B&B *(10 S. Main St., Providence. 435-752-3432 or 800-480-4943. www.providenceinn.com. $$-$$$)* Seventeen unique and lavishly appointed rooms in a mansionlike, 1926 addition to the Old Rock Church, which dates back to 1871.

DINING
Butch Cassidy's Restaurant & Saloon *(230 N. 4th St., Montpelier, ID. 208-847-3501. $-$$)* Prime rib is the specialty of the house. Serves breakfast, lunch, and dinner. See p. 313.

Callaway's Too *(2 N. Main St., Providence. 435-753-8637. Evenings only. Closed Sun.)* A deli and gourmet shop offering pastas, seafood, and breads.

Harbor Village Restaurant *(785 N. Bear Lake Blvd., Garden City. 435-946-3448. $-$$)* This restaurant overlooks the turquoise waters of Bear Lake; it specializes in steak cuts.

Zanavoo Restaurant *(4888 E. Hwy. 89, Logan. 435-752-0085. $-$$)* Gorgeous setting just east of Second Dam. Prime rib, steaks, and seafood.

San Francisco

City of Views 316

Russian River Wineries 320

Monterey Bay 325

Gold Rush Days 329

Bay view from North Beach, San Francisco

City of Views
Seeing San Francisco from
on high & down low

BUILT ON A HILLY PENINSULA flanked by sea cliffs, San Francisco offers fantastic views in every direction. Some vantages are ideal for picnics or hikes, some lend themselves to sketching or quiet contemplation, and others are ideal for sipping a cocktail and watching the sun set over the Pacific. Don't forget your camera on this encounter with one of America's most beautiful cities.

Views by land

Start your quest for great views in **North Beach,** San Francisco's old Italian neighborhood. Crowning Telegraph Hill, **Coit Tower** *(end of Lombard St.)* offers a splendid, maplike perspective that encompasses the bay. Take the elevator *(fee)* to the top, 210 feet up. Back on the main floor, WPA murals depict working life in 1930s California. Then walk down to **Jack Early Park** *(Grant Ave. bet. Francisco and Chestnut Sts.),* a postage-stamp-size platform that even many locals don't know about. It's well worth the 64 steps up to a sweeping maritime view extending from bridge (Golden Gate) to bridge (Bay).

Across Columbus Avenue and up on Russian Hill, the painting-lined hallway of the **San Francisco Art Institute** *(800 Chestnut St. 415-771-7020. Closed Sun.)* leads to a broad concrete deck and another stunning backdrop of city and bay. It's a lovely spot for an informal lunch; the **SFAI Café** sells sandwiches and daily specials at art student prices. (Before you leave, be sure to check out SFAI's Diego Rivera Gallery, featuring a two-story mural Rivera painted in 1931.)

Or hop in a car and take your lunch to **China Beach** *(end of Seacliff Ave., off El Camino del Mar at 27th Ave.),* where a postcard scene of the Golden Gate Bridge awaits. Watch freighters from Asia head toward Oakland as pelicans and seagulls soar overhead. The swimming is safe but chilly.

For a different perspective, drive north across the Golden Gate Bridge to the **Marin Headlands.** Several turnouts along Conzelman

NOT TO BE MISSED

- Ferry ride to Sausalito at dusk
- Picnic at China Beach or Angel Island
- The 360-degree revolving view at Equinox Restaurant
- City Lights Bookstore on Columbus Ave. in North Beach

Soaking in a famous scene from the Marin Headlands

Road offer dramatic vantage points from *above* the famous orange-red bridge that spans the entrance to San Francisco Bay. Below, the blue-gray Pacific changes hues with the season and the tides.

Follow US 101 north to the Calif. 1 exit; turn left at the second stoplight, which is Calif. 1, and head west to Panoramic Highway, where you turn right. This road takes you to Muir Woods, Stinson Beach—and one of the best short hikes around, atop **Mount Tamalpais** *(415-388-2070).* Drive into the Mount Tamalpais State Park on Pantoll Road, turn right onto East Ridgecrest Boulevard, and drive 5 miles to the East Peak. The 360-degree view from the **Verna Dunshee Loop** takes in the entire Bay Area.

For another stunning walk, head back across the Golden Gate and head for **Sutro Heights Park,** at the western end of Geary Boulevard. At the Merrie Way parking lot, you'll find a trailhead for the **Coastal Trail** *(451-556-8642).* Framed by eucalyptus trees and Monterey pines, the path ambles along San Francisco's dramatic shoreline all the way to the Golden Gate Bridge, a distance of about 3.5 miles. In just a mile, you'll reach the most spectacular part: **Lands End** and its perspective on the Farallon Islands, the Marin Headlands, and the Golden Gate.

Just in time for sunset, settle into a window table inside the **Phineas T. Barnacle Bar** at the **Cliff House** *(1090 Point Lobos Ave. 415-386-3330. Bar closed for renovation),* sip an Irish coffee, and soak in the full grandeur of the glowing colors over Seal Rocks and the Pacific.

If you'd rather watch the sun set on the city itself, return downtown to the legendary **Top of the Mark,** a tradition San Franciscoans and tourists alike have followed since 1939. Or try **The View Lounge,** which sits high atop the Marriott Hotel. One of the city's most famous venues for a romantic dinner is the **Carnelian Room,** 52 floors above the Financial District, offering a 360-degree panorama of the sparkling city far below. Hold off on dessert and move to the **Equinox Restaurant,** which revolves 360 degrees each hour, offering a subtly shifting spectacle, and watch the full moon rise above San Francisco Bay.

Several hotels atop Nob Hill feature jaw-dropping panoramas: the **Fairmont Hotel,** where luxury suites take in Twin Peaks, Alcatraz, and Grace Cathedral, and more affordable rooms overlook Union Square; the **Huntington Hotel,** where all 100 rooms and 35 suites have park or city views; and the **Mark Hopkins Inter-Continental Hotel.** (See Travelwise for all.)

Views by water

Head to Pier 41 for a day on the water. The **Blue & Gold Fleet Ferries** *(415-773-1188 or 415-705-5555. www.blueandgoldfleet.com)* depart from here for your choice of excursions to Angel Island, Alcatraz, or Sausalito.

It's a 20-minute ride to the 750-acre **Angel Island State Park** *(415-435-1915. www.angelisland.com),* a woodsy oasis in the middle of the bay. You can hike, mountain bike (bring your own or rent one), picnic, take a sea kayak tour, and camp (reservations required). Hike to the top of **Mount Livermore** for an unobstructed 360-degree view of the entire Bay Area; on a clear day you can count five bridges: Golden Gate, Bay, Richmond-San Rafael, San Mateo, and Dumbarton.

Ferries to **Alcatraz Island** *(415-705-5555)* leave Pier 41 for the 15-minute ride to the infamous prison, now a popular historic site. Take a guided tour of the former home of "Scarface" Al Capone, "Machine Gun" Kelly, and Robert "Birdman" Stroud. Evening "Alcatraz After Hours" visits are often available.

On clear evenings, the **Sausalito Ferry** affords a charming look at San Francisco's glittering profile; from the debarkation point, it's an easy walk to the **Water Street Grill** (see Travelwise) for cocktails, live music, and dinner.

Just when you think you've seen San Francisco in every way possible, a different dining experience awaits at **Forbes Island** (see Travelwise). Board the pontoon boat at Pier 39's "H" Dock for the short ride past the famous sea lions to this man-made island. It features live palm trees, a sandy beach, a waterfall, and a 40-foot lighthouse with circular viewing platform. Inspired by Jules Verne's *20,000 Leagues Under the Sea,* the dining room sits underwater, studded with portholes. —*Barbara Alexandra Szerlip*

Travelwise

GETTING THERE
San Francisco is such a diverse city—topographically, ethnically, culturally—that it's easy to forget that it's only 47 square miles or so. This compactness, coupled with a logical grid of streets and avenues, makes getting around fairly easy. Many viewpoints can be reached by public transportation, including BART *(415-989-2278)* and Muni buses *(415-673-6864)*.

GENERAL INFORMATION
Contact the **San Francisco Convention & Visitors Bureau/Information Center** *(900 Market St., San Francisco, CA 94102. 415-391-2000. www.sfvisitor.org).*

SEASONS
Regardless of the season, it's always a good idea to dress in layers; fog often rolls in during the day. Winter is often wet and blustery.

MORE THINGS TO SEE & DO
Fort Point Pier *(bet. Fisherman's Wharf and Fort Point)* Alcatraz and Angel Islands, the Palace of Fine Arts (designed for the 1915 Panama-Pacific Exposition), and the manicured Marina District compose the view from the pier. For a dramatic perspective of the Golden Gate Bridge's underbelly, climb nearby **Fort Point's** granite spiral staircases to the upper tiers.

Treasure Island *(I-80 E across Bay Bridge to Treasure Island/Yerba Buena Island exit, proceed to main gate)* This 400-acre man-made island was formerly home to the famous China Clippers. Gorgeous views of San Francisco's skyline, plus the two distinct sections of the Bay Bridge—a suspension structure on the San Francisco side to the west, a cantilever-truss design to the east.

Twin Peaks *(lower Market St. past Castro to Twin Peaks Blvd., turn right, follow road uphill)* On clear days, Christmas Tree Point offers a panorama that stretches from Mount Diablo in the East Bay to Mount Tam.

Whale-watching The Oceanic Society *(415-474-3385. www.oceanic-society.org)* offers eight-hour whale-watching cruises to the Farallon Islands—weekends June through November for blues and humpbacks, December through April for grays. These waters also are home to porpoises, dolphins, sea lions, seals, and a quarter of a million seabirds. Tours depart from the Yacht Harbor, adjacent to the Fort Mason Center.

LODGING
Fairmont Hotel *(950 Mason St., Nob Hill. 415-772-5000 or 800-527-4727. www.fairmont.com. $$$)* See p. 318.

Huntington Hotel *(1075 California St., Nob Hill. 415-474-5400 or 800-227-4683. www.huntingtonhotel.com. $$$)* See p. 318.

Mark Hopkins Inter-Continental Hotel *(1 Nob Hill. 415-392-3434. $$$)* See p. 318.

Seal Rock Inn *(545 Point Lobos Ave. at 48th Ave., at end of Geary Blvd. 415-752-8000 or 888-732-5762. www.sealrockinn.com. $$)* An unpretentious, off-the-beaten-track motel whose every room looks out on the Pacific.

Washington Square Inn *(1660 Stockton St. 415-981-4220. $$-$$$)* Cozy North Beach inn with European charm and most rooms facing Washington Park. 15 rooms.

Westin St. Francis *(335 Powell St. 415-397-7000. $$$)* A 1904 grande dame in a great location on Union Square; tower rooms have better views but less charm. 1,192 rooms.

COCKTAILS WITH A VIEW
Carnelian Room *(Bank of America bldg., 555 California St. 415-433-7500. $$$)* 52 floors up. See p. 318.

Top of the Mark *(Mark Hopkins hotel, 1 Nob Hill, 19th fl. 415-616-6916. $$-$$$)* Sunset cocktails, light dinners, and weekend brunch. Live music on most nights. See p. 318.

The View Lounge *(Marriott Hotel, 55 4th St., 39th fl. 415-442-6127. $$-$$$)* Cocktails and light snacks. See p. 318.

DINING
Equinox Restaurant *(Hyatt Regency's rooftop, 5 Embarcadero Center. 415-291-6580. $$$)* See p. 318.

Forbes Island *(afloat between Piers 39 and 41. 415-951-4900. www.forbesisland.com. Closed Mon.-Tues. $$$)* See p. 318.

Greens *(Fort Mason, Bldg. A. 415-771-6222. $$-$$$)* Vegetarian restaurant built by Zen carpenters, with dramatic views.

Water Street Grill *(660 Bridgeway, Sausalito. 415-332-8512. $$-$$$)* See p. 318.

Russian River Wineries
Wine tasting among the redwoods

A COUPLE OF VALLEYS WEST of Napa Valley hides a surprisingly unknown land of grapevines, redwood trees, and picturesque villages, perfectly sited along the banks of the jade-hued Russian River. More than 130 vineyards and wineries thrive in this hilly, fog-shrouded niche about an hour's drive north of San Francisco—many of them well-known names, including Korbel, many just tiny little places producing only 3,000 cases a year. But everywhere you go you'll find friendly, welcoming people, proud of their region's beauty and the quality of their wines, giving you the sense that you've stumbled across Napa Valley of yore.

Healdsburg & the Dry Creek Valley

A good place to begin your visit is tiny, trendy **Healdsburg,** settled in the mid-1800s by farmers and gold miners on the fringes of the Dry Creek and Russian River Valleys. Its small, Spanish-style plaza, dating from 1857 and edged with upscale boutiques, spas, galleries, and wine-tasting bars, is experiencing a renaissance, alerting you to the fact that things won't always be so quiet here. Making noise in the foodie world is the divine **Dry Creek Kitchen** (see Travelwise), brainchild of nationally renowned chef Charlie Palmer. An ever changing menu, described as classic European with a fresh American take, combines the freshest of local ingredients: pan-seared Sonoma foie gras, for instance, or pomegranate-molasses-glazed liberty duck. The restaurant occupies the 55-room **Hotel Healdsburg** (see Travelwise), a modern deco extravaganza of luxury.

After lunch, take a driving or biking tour on uncrowded country lanes north of town in the **Dry Creek Valley,** its narrow vale and tawny hills striped with vineyard after vineyard. Grapes have been grown here for more than a century, producing award-winning Zinfandels, Cabernet Sauvignons, Pinot Noirs, and Chardonnays. A good loop entails driving north on Healdsburg Avenue to Lytton Springs Road and turning

NOT TO BE MISSED

- **Evening concerts on Healdsburg Square**
- **Dry Creek Kitchen's to-die-for pan-roasted salmon**
- **Counting stars from Ridenhour Ranch's hot tub**
- **Standing beneath Armstrong's sky-scraping redwoods**

Russian River vines

left to Dry Creek Road, which runs along the eastern side of Dry Creek Valley. Turn right to Yoakim Bridge Road, then left to West Dry Creek Road, which edges the valley's western side. If you go south to Mill Street you can loop back to town.

Everywhere you go, you pass winery after winery—your choice of where to stop. Favorites include the **Simi Winery** *(16275 Healdsburg Ave. 707-433-6981 or 800-746-4880. www.simiwinery.com),* founded in 1876 by two Italian brothers who originally came to California for the gold rush. An interesting aside is the fact that the winery was bequeathed to one of their daughters in 1904, who negotiated it through Prohibition, the Depression, and male chauvinism. Near the octagonal tasting room stands a redwood-shaded picnic area—an inviting place to pause for a snack. Also watch for **Pedroncelli Winery** *(1220 Canyon Rd. 707-857-3531 or 800-836-3894),* founded in 1927, making it the oldest continual family-run winery in the Dry Creek Valley; it's known best for its Zinfandels. At the **Raymond Burr Vineyards** *(8339 W. Dry Creek Rd. 707-433-4365 or 888-900-0024. www.raymondburrvineyards.com),* two of the Perry Mason actor's Emmys are on display. With the small winery's perfect location on a hill, facilitating excellent drainage (and wonderful views), Cabernet Sauvignon is the big award-winner here.

South to Guerneville & the Russian River Valley

The next day, head south out of Healdsburg along Westside Road into the heart of the Russian River Valley. This region is the centerpiece of Sonoma Valley's most notable wine appellations for Chardonnay and Pinot Noir, and wineries line the road one after another. Among them, **Rabbit Ridge Winery** *(3291 Westside Rd. 707-431-7128. www.rabbitridgewinery.com),* one of California's top Zinfandel producers, has one of the region's loveliest settings: The terrace looks out over a placid green pond and dark, timbered hills. Next door, at redwood-shaded **Belvedere** *(4035 Westside Rd. 707-431-4442. www.belvederewinery.com),* sip a glass of Chardonnay, Pinot Noir, or Zinfandel as you stroll through the aroma garden, comparing its taste to specific flowers, berries, and herbs. A little farther south, **Hop Kiln Winery** *(6050 Westside Rd. 707-433-6491. www.hopkilnwinery.com)* is housed in a 1905 three-towered hops-drying barn that once supplied San Francisco breweries. In the wood-paneled tasting room, sample the award-winning Zinfandels, as well as the unique A Thousand Flowers blend.

The wineries disappear farther south as Westside Road twists through wild, oak-covered hills. Eventually you come to River Road, where a right turn brings you alongside the Russian River to **Guerneville,** an old logging town and resort area with eclectic, easygoing charm. Craft shops and a few galleries cluster along Main Street, and you can tour the baronial estate of **Korbel Champagne Cellars**

(13250 River Rd. 707-824-7000), occupying a historic ivy-covered building among the redwoods. Established in 1882 by three brothers, Korbel was the region's first significant winery, and it remains the area's largest winemaking facility. Tours are one of the most complete in the business; don't miss the old-style European gardens.

The main reason why people have been coming to Guerneville since the 1920s is to rejuvenate beside the **Russian River,** which twists for some 100 miles between the Mayacamas Mountains in Mendocino County to the Pacific Ocean. The area offers redwood-shaded hiking trails, gravelly beaches ideal for putting in a canoe, and a slow-moving current that beckons on hot, lazy days. Prime sunbathing spots include **Monte Rio's** beach *(park beneath bridge)* and **Johnson's Beach** *(16241 Beach St., Guerneville. 707-869-2022)*. Canoe, kayak, and paddleboat rentals are available at both.

Another popular activity is hiking at nearby **Armstrong Redwoods State Reserve** *(17000 Armstrong Woods Rd., Guerneville. 707-869-2015)*, a 875-acre reverence-inducing stand of old-growth redwoods towering above the mossy, ferny forest floor. Among the easy paths, the **Pioneer Trail** winds past the Parson Jones Tree, at 310 feet the park's tallest tree. For something a little more strenuous, try the trails that lead into the backcountry of the adjacent **Austin Creek State Recreation Area** *(707-869-2015)*.

Many people enjoy staying in rustic cabins along the river, but if you're in want of luxury, try the **Applewood Inn & Restaurant** (see Travelwise), a mission revival–style lodging surrounded by vineyards and redwoods. The restaurant features a sophisticated California Provençale menu, with organic, innovative food.

South of Guerneville

South of Guerneville, the land becomes more developed as you edge closer to the populous Bay Area. There are, however, a couple of hidden spots to seek out before leaving the region. **Iron Horse Vineyards** *(9786 Ross Station Rd., Sebastopol. 707-887-1507. www.ironhorsevineyards.com)* offers one of the prettiest settings around, with its barn-red winery set amid rolling hills. One of the area's best places for lunch is **Topolos at Russian River Vineyards** (see Travelwise), where you sit *en plein air* in the shade of grape arbors; the Greek-influenced menu reflects the owners' heritage. The winery is known for its Zinfandels, but in the tasting room also be sure to try its unusual Alicante Bouschet varietal (all grown organically).

If you wander south along Calif. 116 back to US 101, you'll pass through **Sebastopol,** in the heart of apple country. A down-to-earth enclave with revolutionary-thought bookstores and tie-dye everywhere, the town is also a great shopping stop: Seek out **Milk & Honey** and **Copperfield's Books and Music,** both on North Main Street. —*Barbara A. Noe*

Travelwise

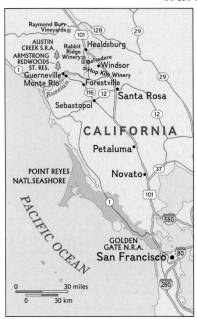

GETTING THERE

Healdsburg lies 75 miles north of San Francisco via US 101, which runs like a spine through the Russian River region.

GENERAL INFORMATION

Contact the **Russian River Wine Road Association** (707-433-4335. www.wineroad.com); the **Russian River Chamber of Commerce & Visitor Center** (16209 1st St., Guerneville, CA 95446. 707-869-3577 or 800-253-8800. www.russian river.com); and the **Healdsburg Chamber of Commerce & Visitors Bureau** (217 Healdsburg Ave., Healdsburg, CA 95448. 707-433-6935 or 800-648-9922. www.healdsburg.org).

SEASONS

Spring brings mustard flowers and budding vineyards. Summer days are long and lazy, perfect for reviving along the river. The harvest and crush of grapes traditionally starts in early Sept.

ANNUAL EVENT

Jazz on the River (Sept., Guerneville. 510-655-9471) Float on the river while listening to jazz.

MORE THINGS TO SEE & DO

Biking For bike rentals, self-guided tours, or design-your-own adventure, Spoke Folk Cyclery (201 Center St., Healdsburg. 707-433-7171) is the place to go.

Canoeing & kayaking For rentals and shuttle service: Burke's Canoe Trips (River Rd., 1 mile N of Forestville. 707-887-1222. www.burkes canoetrips.com) or W.C. Bob Trowbridge Canoe Trips (13840 Old Redwood Hwy., Healdsburg. 707-433-7247 or 800-640-1386).

Duncans Mills This Victorian lumber town's wood-frame buildings have been resurrected as galleries, craft shops, and restaurants.

Monte Rio Center point of this tiny town, known for its swimming beach, is a quonset-hut movie theater with murals depicting community history.

Occidental The little hamlet is famous for its dueling Italian restaurants and fun shops.

LODGING & DINING

Applewood Inn & Restaurant (13555 Hwy. 116. 707-869-9093 or 800-555-8509. www.applewoodinn.com. $$-$$$ lodging; $$$ dinner) 19 rooms or suites; California Provençale menu in the restaurant. See p. 323.

Cape Fear (25191 Main St., Duncans Mills. 707-865-9246. $$) A fun, down-to-earth place with seafood, salads, and innovative entrées.

Dry Creek Kitchen (317 Healdsburg Ave., Healdsburg. 707-431-0330. $$$) Gourmet dining. See p. 320.

Grape Leaf Inn (539 Johnson St., Healdsburg. 707-433-8140. www.grapeleafinn.com. $$-$$$) Victorian B&B with 12 guest rooms.

Hotel Healdsburg (25 Matheson St., Healdsburg. 707-431-2800 or 800-889-7188. www.hotelhealdsburg.com. $$$) 55 guest rooms. Spa, pool, country gardens. See p. 320.

Ridenhour Ranch House (12850 River Rd. 707-887-1033 or 888-877-4466. www.riden hourranchhouseinn.com. $$) Constructed of redwood in 1906, the friendly inn has 8 guest rooms. Outdoor hot tub.

Topolos at Russian River Vineyards (5700 Gravenstein Hwy. N., Forestville. 707-887-1575 or 800-TOPOLOS. www.Topolos.com. $$) Greek menu. See p. 323.

Monterey Bay
Call of the wild coast

MUCH OF THE MONTEREY BAY coastline still looks as it did when seafaring Spaniards first arrived in the 16th century. The very un-pacific Pacific, its waters rife with sea lions, seals, and other marine life, as well as surfers, breaks against miles of granite. This weekend explores various aspects of the bay, from the funky surfer town of Santa Cruz to the old Spanish city of Monterey, with chances to get out onto, or into, the water along the way.

Santa Cruz

A seaside destination since the 1880s, **Santa Cruz** is a university town known for its surfers, eccentrics, and left-wing politics. Focal point is the **Santa Cruz Beach Boardwalk** *(831-426-7433. www.beachboard walk.com)*, an old-time amusement park edging a mile-long beach; it boasts more than 30 rides, including the 1911 Looff Carousel and the Giant Dipper, one of the world's oldest wooden roller coasters. For lunch, indulge in locally grown French-fried artichoke hearts, followed by saltwater taffy or a caramel apple from **Marini's on the Boardwalk** (est. 1915). Down on the beach, several volleyball games are usually in progress, and ocean swimming is popular in summer.

Surfers have revered the waves off the Santa Cruz coastline for more than a hundred years. One primo spot to watch hotdoggers is **Steamer Lane,** near Lighthouse Point north of the boardwalk; it's said to be the birthplace of the wetsuit (a surfer began oiling his clothes to ward off the water's chill). Nearby, the quaint **Surfing Museum** *(Mark Abbott Lighthouse, W. Cliff Dr. 831-420-6289. www.santacruzparksandrec.com. Wed.-Mon. p.m.)* provides insight into the wave-riding skill.

Farther north, **Natural Bridges State Park** *(2531 W. Cliff Dr. 831-423-4609)* features butterfly-encrusted trees (thousands of monarchs winter here Oct.-Feb.) and some of the state's best tide pools. A couple of trails wind through the park, including the **Butterfly Trail** and the **Forest Nature Trail.**

For dinner, head back to the Municipal Wharf, where half a dozen restaurants feature fare from local nets. A favorite is **Sea Cloud**

NOT TO BE MISSED

- View from atop Santa Cruz Beach Boardwalk Ferris wheel ● Paddling Elkhorn Slough in search of wildlife ● Watching sea otters frolic at Monterey Bay Aquarium

Restaurant & Social Club (see Travelwise), whose upstairs bay windows offer a terrific sunset-over-the-ocean view.

Out on the bay

No perspective of Santa Cruz is complete without spending time afloat. As far as the eye can see, these waters are part of the **Monterey Bay National Marine Sanctuary** *(831-647-4201)*, one of the world's richest marine environments; it's home to sea otters, sea lions, harbor seals, pelicans, dolphins, and whales. The sanctuary runs along a quarter of the California coastline, from Cambria to just north of the Golden Gate Bridge. Its diverse habitats include wave-washed beaches, kelp forests, and the Monterey Submarine Canyon, which descends 2 miles into the oceanic abyss, twice as deep as the Grand Canyon.

Get out on the water several different ways. Rent a kayak from Kayak Connection *(Santa Cruz Harbor. 831-479-1121. www.kayak connection.com)*, which also offers sunset and moonlight paddles. Or set sail on the **Chardonnay II** *(831-423-1213. www.chardonnay.com)*, a 70-foot-long sailboat whose range of excursions include a brewmaster cruise, a sunset sail, and a Wednesday evening regatta. If you prefer fishing, Stagnaro's Sportfishing *(on wharf. 831-427-2334. www.stagnaros.com)* will take you to the best spots for salmon, rock cod, halibut, or snapper.

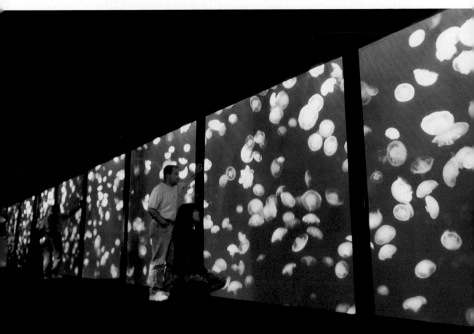

Moon jellies at the Monterey Bay Aquarium

Side trip to Elkhorn Slough & Salinas

Thirty miles south of Santa Cruz, just off Calif. 1 in Moss Landing, sprawls **Elkhorn Slough National Estuarine Research Reserve** *(831-728-2822)*. These 1,400 acres of salt marsh and tidal flats are home to more than 200 species of birds. Spend the morning cruising the slough on a 27-foot pontoon boat *(Elkhorn Slough Safari 831-633-5555)*, or get eye level with sea otters and striped jellyfish on a naturalist tour *(Monterey Bay Kayaks, 831-373-5357 or 800-649-5357)*.

Hikers and bikers should check out the **Monterey Bay Coastal Trail** *(831-372-3196)*, which winds from Elkhorn Slough past the **Salinas River Wildlife Refuge** to Fort Ord and Point Lobos.

It's a 15-minute drive from Moss Landing to **Salinas**—via Calif. 1 and 183, then follow signs—in the heart of John Steinbeck country. The 37,000-square-foot **National Steinbeck Center** *(1 Main St. 831-775-4720)* is an elegant tribute to the Nobel Prize–winning author, who set many of his stories in Monterey, Salinas, and other nearby spots. Nearby **Steinbeck House** *(132 Central Ave. 831-424-2735)* was the novelist's childhood home.

Monterey

Monterey has perched on Monterey Bay's southern edge since the 1700s, when Spaniards established a mission here. After Mexico acquired independence from Spain in 1821, the settlement blossomed into a thriving port, with goods passing through from all over the world. This history is recounted at the **Monterey State Historic Park** *(831-649-2118)*, where you can tour the **Custom House** (California's oldest government building) and other historical buildings. Here, too, is the **Maritime Museum of Monterey** *(831-373-2469. Closed Mon.; adm. fee)*, with sextants, model ships, and other relics related to the city's maritime past.

Across the way, **Fisherman's Wharf,** built in 1846 and still a working pier, is a festive array of seafood restaurants and shops; many whale-watching and fishing trips leave from here as well.

Monterey may be most famous for the **Monterey Bay Aquarium** *(886 Cannery Row. 831-648-4888. www.montereybayaquarium.org)*, where you'll discover more than 250,000 creatures and plants native to the waters just outside its door. Don't miss the three-story-high kelp forest (it grows 8 inches a day!), where a diver feeds the vast array of fish at 11:30 a.m. and 4 p.m. daily. Other must-sees include the Marine Mammals Gallery, the Deep Reefs, and the dramatic new "Artful Jellies" exhibit, which combines live jellyfish displays with ocean-related contemporary art.

In the evening, stroll along **Cannery Row,** overlooking the bay. Once home to sardine factories, immortalized by John Steinbeck in his book *Cannery Row,* the eight-block waterfront stretch has been gussied up with shops and restaurants. —*Barbara Alexandra Szerlip*

Travelwise

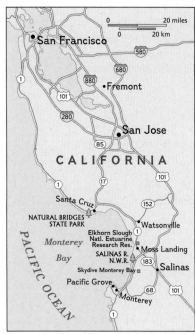

Whale-watching Monterey Bay Whale Watch *(Sam's Fishing Fleet, Fisherman's Wharf, Monterey. 831-375-4658. www.gowhales.com)* offers a variety of trips in search of migrating grays, blues, orcas, and humpbacks.

LODGING

Babbling Brook Inn *(1025 Laurel St., Santa Cruz. 831-427-2437 or 800-866-1131. www.babblingbrookinn.com. $$-$$$)* A secluded B&B with waterfall and seven Impressionist and Postimpressionist rooms.

Darling House *(314 W. Cliff Dr., Santa Cruz. 831-458-1958. www.darlinghouse.com. $$-$$$)* A 1910 marvel by William Weeks.

Green Gables Inn *(301 Ocean View Blvd., Pacific Grove. 831-375-2095 or 800-722-1774. www.foursisters.com. $$-$$$)* 11 rooms, overlooking the water.

Merritt House Inn *(386 Pacific St., near wharf, Monterey. 831-646-9686 or 800-541-5599. www.merritthouseinn.com. $$-$$$)* Built as a private residence in 1830, the inn has 25 rooms and 3 adobe suites, all with fireplaces.

Seven Gables Inn *(555 Ocean View Blvd. 831-372-4341. www.pginns.com. $$-$$$)* Romantic 1886 Victorian mansion, 14 rooms.

DINING

Beach Street Café *(399 Beach St., Santa Cruz. 831-426-7621. $)* Sandwiches and salads, and one of the world's largest collections of Maxfield Parrish (1870-1966) prints.

Paradiso Trattoria *(654 Cannery Row, Monterey. 831-375-4155. $$)* Views of seals and otters accompany your eggplant cannelloni or fire-roasted Ahi.

Phil's Fish Market & Eatery *(7600 Sandholdt Rd., Moss Landing. 831-633-2152. $)* A popular local lunch spot.

Sardine Factory *(701 Wave St., Cannery Row, Monterey. 831-373-3775. $$$)* A local favorite since 1968. Try the signature abalone bisque.

Sea Cloud Restaurant & Social Club *(49-B Municipal Wharf, Santa Cruz. 831-458-9393. $$)* See p. 325.

Spado's *(66 W. Alisal St., Salinas. 831-424-4139. $$)* Owned by the same Sicilian family for three generations. The parmesan-encrusted lamb shanks over polenta are a favorite.

GETTING THERE

Santa Cruz is about 70 miles south of San Francisco via US 101 and Calif. 17. Or take curving Calif. 1, with its spectacular, coast-hugging views of the Pacific.

GENERAL INFORMATION

Contact the **Santa Cruz County Conference & Visitors Council** *(1211 Ocean St., Santa Cruz, CA 95060. 831-425-1234 or 800-833-3494. www.santacruzca.org)* or the **Monterey County Convention & Visitors Bureau** *(401 Camino El Estero, Monterey, CA 93942. 831-649-1770 or 877-MONTEREY. www.montereyinfo.org)*.

SEASONS

Summer fog can hamper visibility for travelers. The beaches are busiest May through Nov.

MORE THINGS TO SEE & DO

Horseback riding Early-bird and sunset rides on the beach and bluffs are offered by Seahorse and Friendly Acres Ranch *(Calif. 1, Half Moon Bay. 650-726-2362)*.

Gold Rush Days
Treasures of the Sierra foothills

THE DISCOVERY OF GOLD on the South Fork American River in 1848 changed California from a remote farming outpost to a magnetic destination. By 1850, the golden Sierra Nevada foothills had 100,000 new residents, all with big dreams of cashing in on the Mother Lode. Despite the fact that the gold rush predated the Civil War and came and went within a decade, many of the towns, lavish Victorian houses, and mining camps survive today.

Placerville & Coloma

First it was called Dry Diggins, after three men pulled $20,000 in gold up out of a dry gulch. Then Hangtown, as local vigilantes tended to hand out "pine tree justice." Finally, in 1854, California's (then) third largest city became **Placerville.**

Several local businesses, from bakeries to tattoo parlors, prefer the town's more colorful handle. **Hangman's Tree** *(305 Main St. 530-622-3878)* is a popular bar and historic landmark. Just look for the life-size dummy hanging by its neck above the window. Hangtown Fry (an oyster and bacon omelette supposedly invented when a lucky prospector demanded the most expensive ingredients available) is still served at **Hangtown Grill** (see Travelwise).

Main Street is Placerville's center. Notable gold rush–era buildings along its length include the three-story **Cary House** *(300 Main St.),* known for its iron shutters, and the stone-and-brick **Fountain and Tallman Soda Works** *(524 Main St.),* home to the Fountain and Tallman Museum *(530-626-0773. Fri.-Sun. p.m.).* **Placerville Hardware Store** *(441 Main St.)* has been going strong since 1852; rope is still measured in 100-foot lengths by running it from the front door to the back rooms. If you like antiques, you'll find half a dozen shops and collectives with Main Street addresses within two blocks of each other.

Enjoy English high tea at **Tea in the Garden** *(366 Main St. 530-626-4946).* Be sure to stop by the **Placerville Coffee House & Pub** *(594 Main St. 530-642-8481),* where you can walk through a

---

NOT TO BE MISSED

- White-water rafting on the American River
- Spending the night in a vintage Victorian B&B
- A leisurely autumn drive through Apple Hill's orchards ● Ordering a Hangtown Fry at Hangtown Grill, Placerville

150-foot-long mining shaft dating from 1849 to 1859 at the back. A mile north of downtown is the 61-acre **Gold Bug Park & Mine** *(Bedford Ave. 530-642-5207. www.goldbug.org)*, great for picnics, hiking, or gold panning. Built in 1888, it's the state's only city-owned gold mine.

In autumn or early winter, consider a drive through **Apple Hill** *(530-644-7692. www.applehill.com)*, a collection of more than 40 orchards, farms, and ranches north of US 50. You can purchase just about anything made from apples, including cider donuts and apple cheesecake, or harvest 17 different varieties of the fruit yourself.

Coloma lies 8 miles north of Placerville on Calif. 49. Encompassing about 85 percent of the town, the 290-acre **Marshall Gold Discovery State Historical Park** *(Calif. 49. 530-622-3470. www.parks .ca.gov)* is a favorite with hikers and gold-history enthusiasts. Visit the reconstructed **Sutter's Mill,** where gold was first discovered on January 24, 1848, a living history blacksmith shop, a restored 19th-century schoolhouse, the Wah Hop Chinese General Store & Bank, and other period buildings.

The area is also home to several American River rafting companies, including **Whitewater Connection** *(530-622-6446 or 800-336-7238. www.whitewaterconnection.com)* and **Adventure Connection** *(530-626-7865 or 800-556-6060. www.raftcalifornia.com)*. Guided trips are offered between April and early October.

Auburn & Grass Valley

From Coloma, it's a 17-mile drive along scenic, winding Calif. 49, past horse, cattle, and sheep ranches, to the town of **Auburn,** lorded over

Looking for nuggets at the Marshall Gold Discovery State Historical Park

by the enormous gold-digger statue. The **Placer County Museum** *(101 Maple St. 530-889-6500)*, located inside the 1898 County Courthouse, houses exhibits ranging from Native American basketry to gold nuggets and early telegraphs.

Then head for nearby **Old Town.** Many of the original wooden buildings in this historic district were lost to fires, then replaced with brick structures that incorporate everything from Queen Anne and beaux arts to Greek Revival styles. Guided walking tours are offered the first Saturday of every month by the county museum *(530-889-6500)*, or pick up a self-guided map at the tiny post office—the oldest continually operated post office (1849) in the West. **The Hook & Ladder Firehouse** *(Commercial St. at Lincoln Way)* is home to the oldest volunteer fire department this side of Boston (1852). **Awful Annie's** (see Travelwise) is a good place for breakfast or lunch. **Bootleggers Tavern & Grill** (see Travelwise), the back half of which was Auburn's original City Hall, offers elegant dinner entrées.

For an interesting twist on gold rush history, continue north 24 more miles on Calif. 49 to **Grass Valley.** Because much of the area's gold lay in quartz veins hundreds of feet below the surface, the requisite drilling, blasting, and pumping required men willing to work in precarious dark tunnels. That's how Grass Valley came to be settled by tin miners from Cornwall, England, hoping for a better life.

Traditional Cornish pasties, stuffed with an array of meats, vegetables, or apples, make an inexpensive meal. You'll find them at **Marshall's Pasties** *(203 Mill St. 530-272-2844)* and **Cousin Jack Pasties** *(corner of S. Auburn and Main Sts. 530-272-9230)*.

Adding to the town's colorful past is the fact that European femme fatale Lola Montez owned a home at **248 Mill Street** (it's now the Chamber of Commerce). A former intimate of King Ludwig I of Bavaria, Montez was often seen walking on local hillsides with her pet bear, Major, and assorted monkeys. Also worth a visit is the 700-acre **Empire Mine State Historic Park** *(10791 E. Empire St. 530-273-8522)*. One of the state's largest and richest mines, its network of tunnels running beneath the town can be seen on a guided tour.   —*Barbara Alexandra Szerlip*

Travelwise

GETTING THERE

Gold country is located east of San Francisco in the Sierra Nevada foothills. The 130-mile drive from San Francisco to Placerville, via I-80 and US 50, takes about two hours. Calif. 49 (aka the Mother Lode or Golden Chain Highway) is the main north-south artery, connecting Nevada City (north) to Jamestown (south).

GENERAL INFORMATION

Contact the **El Dorado County Chamber of Commerce** *(542 Main St., Placerville, CA 95667. 530-621-5885 or 800-457-6279. www.eldoradocounty.org);* the **Auburn Chamber of Commerce** *(601 Lincoln Way, Auburn, CA 95603. 530-885-5616. www.auburnchamber.net);* or the **Grass Valley and Nevada**

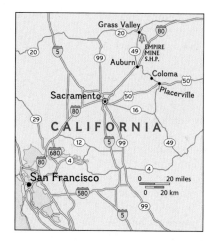

County Chamber of Commerce (248 Mill St., Grass Valley, CA 95945. 530-273-4667 or 800-655-4667. www.gvncchamber.org).

SEASONS

The region is lovely year-round, with fall and spring offering the best chances to beat the crowds and find good weather. Summer can be hot. In winter, heavy snows sometimes cause traffic problems. Call Caltrans (800-427-7623 in CA) ahead of time for road conditions.

ANNUAL EVENTS

Cornish Christmas (Fri. p.m. Thanksgiving-Christmas, downtown Grass Valley. Contact chamber at 530-273-4667) Booths sell food, crafts, and clothing, street musicians perform in Victorian garb, and stores stay open late.

Historic County Inns Christmas Tour (1st weekend in Dec., Placerville. 877-262-4667. www.goldcountrylodging.com. Fee) A self-guided tour of Victorian B&Bs, lodges, and country homes in and around Placerville.

MORE THINGS TO SEE & DO

Gold Country Wine Tours (888-560-2564. www.goldcountrywinetours.com) Excursions to Sierra foothill wineries. To visit Placerville area wineries on your own, visit www.eldo radowines.org for a listing; many have tasting rooms.

Southern Gold Country If you enjoyed this foray into Gold Country's northern half, consider a return visit to towns in the south, including **Murphys** and **Angels Camp,** as well

as nearby **Columbia State Historic Park** (Parrott's Ferry Rd., off Calif. 49, 4 miles N of Sonora. 209-532-0150 or 209-532-4301).

LODGING

Chichester-McKee House (800 Spring St., Placerville. 530-626-1882 or 800-831-4008. www.innlover.com. $$) A gorgeous Victorian B&B with four rooms. It was the first house in town to boast indoor plumbing.

Coloma Country Inn (345 High St., Coloma. 530-622-6919. www.colomacountryinn.com. $-$$) Dating from 1852 and located within Marshall Gold Discovery State Park, the inn has a pond, gardens, and carriage house. Six rooms.

Elam Biggs B&B (220 Colfax Ave., Grass Valley. 530-477-0906. $-$$) A rose-covered picket fence surrounds this 1892 Queen Anne Victorian B&B. Five rooms.

Placerville KOA Campground (6 miles W of Placerville off US 50, 4655 Rock Barn Rd., Shingle Springs. 530-676-2267 or 800-562-4197) The 18-plus-acre site includes complete hookups, tent sites, and hot showers.

Power's Mansion Inn (164 Cleveland Ave., Auburn. 530-885-1166. www.vfr.net/~po erinn. $-$$) This ornate 1898 Victorian offers 15 rooms.

DINING

Awful Annie's (160 Sacramento St., Auburn. 530-888-9857. Closed dinner. $) Omelettes and sandwiches. See p. 331.

Bootleggers Tavern & Grill (210 Washington St., Auburn. 530-889-2229. $$-$$$) Steak, seafood, pasta, chicken. See p. 331.

Café Luna (451 Main St., Placerville. 530-642-8669. $$$) Where the locals go for lunch and dinner. California nouveau cuisine.

Hangtown Grill (423 Main St., Placerville. 530-626-4431. $$) Steaks, ribs, and more. See p. 329.

Railroad Café (111 W. Main St., Grass Valley. 530-274-2233. Dinner Fri.-Sat. only) Enjoy breakfast ($) as toy train cars circle on tracks suspended overhead; burgers and such for lunch ($) and dinner ($$).

Shanghai Restaurant & Bar (289 Washington St., Auburn. 530-885-9446. $$) In business since 1896, Shanghai serves Chinese food on what was the site of the American Hotel (built 1851), one of the gold rush's oldest hostelries.

Washington, D.C.

Around the Chesapeake 334

Blue Ridge Ramble 338

Presidential Palaces 342

Chesapeake Bay Maritime Museum, St. Michaels, Maryland

Around the Chesapeake
A weekend on the bay

YOU DON'T HAVE TO DRIVE all the way to the ocean for a maritime weekend. On the Chesapeake Bay—the country's largest estuary —there are sunrises with waterbirds, fresh tidal breezes, fishing boats in coves, and long views of water and sky. A visit to Annapolis, St. Michaels, and Solomons Island uncovers a wealth of history, tucked-away fishing hamlets, no-frills crab shacks, museums of local culture, and bed-and-breakfasts you'll want to return to.

Annapolis

About an hour east of Washington, the brick-street port of Annapolis sits on the mouth of the Severn River, just off the bay. For historic interest and scenic appeal, this town is hard to beat. The nation's capital for a brief period in the early 1780s, Annapolis harbors more than 50 buildings predating the Revolutionary War, and hundreds more from the 19th century. The **Maryland State House** (*State Circle. 410-974-3400*) contains the Old Senate Chamber where the Treaty of Paris was ratified in 1784, officially ending the Revolutionary War.

It's a short walk to the **U.S. Naval Academy** (*visitor center at King George and Randall Sts. 410-263-6933*), home to 4,000 midshipmen and a gorgeous chapel that holds the crypt of naval hero John Paul Jones. At noon, watch the midshipmen form up in front of Bancroft Hall and march in to lunch.

For your lunch, walk over to the **City Dock** and dine at any one of the many good places serving seafood, including the 1750 **Middleton Tavern** (see Travelwise). Afterward, take a stroll around the dock; breathe in the briny air and listen to the sailboat halyards clanging against their masts. To see how the town looked in the 18th century, check out the waterfront model in the **Victualling Warehouse** (*77 Main St. 410-268-5576*), an early 1700s food-storage building now operating as a gift shop run by the Historic Annapolis Foundation.

The dock is also the place to join a cruise into Annapolis Harbor and the Severn River: **Watermark Cruises** (*410-268-7601*) runs 40- and 90-minute tours that give you a waterside view of the town,

NOT TO BE MISSED

- Eating steamed Maryland blue crabs waterside ● City Dock, Annapolis ● A narrated cruise out of St. Michaels ● Touch tank at the Calvert Marine Museum

Bustling Main Street, Annapolis

the Naval Academy, Thomas Point Lighthouse, and the nearby bridges. Or go wind-powered aboard the *Woodwind* *(410-263-7837)*, a 74-foot schooner; help hoist the sails on an informative two-hour cruise. The golden glow across the water on a sunset cruise is especially memorable.

For a real roll-up-your-sleeves waterfront dining experience, head to **Cantler's Riverside Inn** (see Travelwise) on Mill Creek; crack your own crabs on tables covered with brown paper, dip the meat in vinegar and/or butter, and savor the taste of the Chesapeake.

St. Michaels

Motor across the **Chesapeake Bay Bridge,** enjoying spectacular bay views, then drive south and west onto the clawlike peninsula that holds the fishing village of St. Michaels. St. Michaels was a shipbuilding center during the Revolutionary War; in the War of 1812, the town fooled the British (so the story goes) by hanging lanterns in trees and on ship masts, causing the enemy to overshoot the town.

Though its importance as a port diminished after the completion of the Bay Bridge in 1951, St. Michaels stayed busy with agricultural and seafood processing. Today, tourism and yachting are the main industries, catering to visitors seeking charm and character.

Spend some time at the **Chesapeake Bay Maritime Museum** *(Mill St. 410-745-2916. www.cbmm.org. Adm. fee)*, where you'll learn about bay history and how millions of bushels of crabs, oysters, and clams journey every year from the bay to the table. Spread over 18 acres, the museum holds ship models, decoys, skipjacks and other boats, and a restored 1879 lighthouse. In the Waterman's Wharf area try your hand at baiting a crab pot or tonging for oysters; the walk-on skipjacks and pilothouse offer a close-up look at authentic engines, navigation instruments, and weather-forecasting equipment.

If you've worked up an appetite, walk across the street to the **Crab Claw** (see Travelwise) for good seafood, or head over to Talbot Street for a wide selection of restaurants and shops, many of the latter specializing in nautical items.

On a visit to a bay town, it's hard to resist getting out on the water. With the gulls wheeling and calling and a fresh breeze up, that vast body of water beckons. Give in to your impulses: Sign up for a one- or two-hour narrated **cruise** *(Patriot Cruises 410-745-3100)* aboard the 65-foot *Patriot;* you'll learn about local history and waterfowl.

For an unusual cruise, drive 15 miles to the end of the peninsula and take an oystering skipjack out from **Tilghman Island.** The *Rebecca T. Ruark (410-886-2176. Seasonal)* is one of the few working sail-powered oystering crafts remaining on the bay; a cruise with a waterman in this shallow-draft vessel will give you a feel for the life of the bay like nothing else you'll likely find on a weekend visit.

Solomons Island

Fifty-five miles south of Annapolis, Solomons Island offers another classic Chesapeake experience. Located on the point where the Patuxent River slides into the Chesapeake, low-key Solomons Island is a natural haven for boaters and vacationers.

The **Calvert Marine Museum** *(Solomons Island Rd. 410-326-2042. www.calvertmarinemuseum.com. Adm. fee)* does an excellent job presenting the area's natural and cultural history. Fossil sharks, sea turtles, and giant seabirds take you way back into prehistory, while aquariums hold aquatic plants and animals found in the area today—don't miss the oyster reef and its strange blennys that appear to be trapped in empty shells. The museum runs hour-long cruises around the inner harbor on the 1899 bugeye **William B. Tennison** *(410-326-2042. May-Oct. Wed.-Sun.; fee).*

Just south of the museum, you cross onto the actual island. Park by the boardwalk and take a stroll along the wide Patuxent. Waterbirds wing overhead, and sailboats glide far out on the river.

As you head back to Washington, stop at **Calvert Cliffs State Park** *(6 miles N of Solomons on Md. 2/4. 301-888-1410).* The cliffs have been closed because of erosion, but stroll the 2-mile trail to the beach and hunt for fossilized sharks' teeth. Along the way, look for herons and ducks among the spatterdock in the marsh.

—*John M. Thompson*

Travelwise

GETTING THERE

Annapolis is 35 miles east of Washington, D.C., via US 50/301. St. Michaels lies 53 miles southeast of Annapolis via US 50 and Md. 33; Solomons Island is south via Md. 2.

GENERAL INFORMATION

Contact the **Annapolis and Anne Arundel County Conference & Visitors Bureau** *(26 West St., Annapolis, MD 21401. 410-280-0445. www.visit-annapolis.org)* or the **Talbot County Office of Tourism** *(11 N. Washington St., Easton, MD 21601. 410-770-8000. www.talbotcounty.md).*

SEASONS

Summer is high season, when bay activities offer relief from the heat. Late fall is prime oyster season. Winters are chilly and damp.

ANNUAL EVENTS

Commissioning Week *(mid-May, U.S. Naval Academy, Annapolis. 410-263-6933)* Dress parades and precision-flying demonstrations by the Blue Angels.

Maryland Renaissance Festival *(late Aug.– late Oct., Annapolis. 410-266-7304 or 800-296-7304. Adm. fee)* Food, crafts, jousting, and musical entertainment.

MORE THINGS TO SEE & DO

Fishing Marinas in Chesapeake Beach and Solomons Island have several charter boat operators. Bluefish, trout, rockfish, and flounder are the typical catches. The online Chesapeake Bay Boating Guide *(www.thebayguide.com)* provides a listing of charter operators.

LODGING

Maryland Inn *(58 State Circle, Annapolis. 410-263-2641 or 800-847-8882. $$-$$$)* The 1772 hostelry features 44 elegant guest rooms and fine dining.

Parsonage Inn *(210 N. Talbot St., St. Michaels. 410-745-5519. $$)* An eight-room bed-and-breakfast in an 1883 Victorian house.

William Page Inn *(8 Martin St., Annapolis. 410-626-1506. $$-$$$)* A restored 1908 five-room bed-and-breakfast in the heart of town.

DINING

Bistro St. Michaels *(403 S. Talbot St., St. Michaels. 410-745-9111. Closed Tues.-*

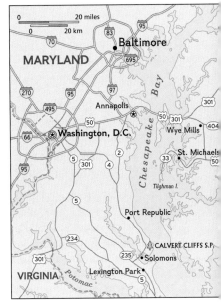

Wed. $$$) Eastern Shore classics with a decidedly French influence; entrées include grilled rockfish and beef tenderloin.

Buddy's Crabs & Ribs *(100 Main St., Annapolis. 410-626-1100. $$$)* Fun eatery with raw bar and view of dock area.

Cantler's Riverside Inn *(end of Forest Beach Rd., off US 50, St. Margarets Rd. exit. Annapolis. 410-757-1311. $$-$$$)* Steamed hardshell crabs. See p. 335.

Crab Claw *(156 Mill St., St. Michaels. 410-745-2900. Seasonal. $$-$$$)* Steamed Maryland blue crabs, oysters, seafood, and Delmarva fried chicken. Indoor and outdoor dining. See p. 336.

Middleton Tavern *(Randall and Pinkney Sts., Annapolis. 410-263-3323. $$)* In operation since 1750, the tavern offers an oyster bar, steaks, seafood, and more. See p. 334.

Rod 'N' Reel *(Md. 261 and Mears Ave., Chesapeake Beach. 410-257-2735. $$)* This popular spot offers classic Maryland crab cakes, soft-shell crabs, oysters, and fresh fish, with views of the marina and bay.

Blue Ridge Ramble
Vineyards & views

IN VIRGINIA, WHERE THOMAS JEFFERSON planted his first vines in 1774, winemaking goes hand in hand with America's past. This getaway takes you down idyllic back roads to country wineries and along Skyline Drive to see the glories of the Blue Ridge. You'll saunter through historic small towns and glimpse the fields, fences, and manor houses of Virginia's hunt country, which, like the making of fine wine, epitomize the state's tradition of elegant living.

Middleburg & environs

About an hour west from Washington, just as the foothills of the Blue Ridge loom into view, US 50 narrows and enters Middleburg, where winemaking and Thoroughbred horses are the dominant interests. Middleburg's main street is lined with high-end shops full of boots and saddles, your dream armoire, and acres of tweedy clothing. Stop at the **Piedmont Gourmet** *(23 E. Washington St. 540-687-6833)* and pick up bread, cheese, and pâté for your picnic on the lawn at nearby **Piedmont Vineyards** *(Plains Rd./Va. 626. 540-687-5528. www.piedmontwines.com).* Turn left at the intersection of US 50 and Va. 626, where you'll spot one of the grape-cluster signs that direct travelers to the nearest winery. At Piedmont, claim a picnic table on the mansion lawn and order up a bottle of the opulent Special Reserve Chardonnay, called "world-class" by renowned wine expert Robert Parker.

After lunch follow Va. 626 south to Va. 55 west and on to Markham, where a right on Leeds Manor Road (Va. 688) takes you to the hillside chalet of **Naked Mountain Vineyard** *(540-364-1609. www.nakedmtn.com. March-Dec. Wed.-Sun., weekends Jan.-Feb.)* for a tasting of Bob Harper's award-winning Chardonnays and Rieslings.

Continuing west on Va. 55, a left turn on Harrels Corner Road (Va. 638) leads to **Linden Vineyards** *(540-364-1997. www.lindenvineyards.com. April-Nov. Wed.-Sun., weekends Dec.-March),* one of Virginia's leading wineries. Take a glass of the spicy Hardscrabble red onto the deck and gaze out over the orchard where owners Jim and

NOT TO BE MISSED

- A wine tasting at Linden Vineyards
- Seeing the fall foliage along Skyline Drive
- A performance at Staunton's Blackfriars Playhouse
- Millwood's Black Penny Antiques

Linden Vineyards, Virginia

Peggy Law grow historic varieties of apples, including Thomas Jefferson's favorite, the aromatic Esopus Spitzenburg.

From Linden, follow Happy Creek Road (Va. 624) north along the banks of the Shenandoah River, where you can get out for a close look at a stream that shaped American history, first as our western frontier, then as the scene of innumerable Civil War cavalry clashes, including the one at nearby Cool Spring. Proceed to **Millwood,** a semiabandoned Virginia Brigadoon with a quintessential country store and excellent antique shopping.

After Millwood, take US 340 south to White Post and **L'Auberge Provençale** (see Travelwise), a romantic French country inn that has somehow mysteriously materialized here in the Virginia Piedmont. L'Auberge lives up to its name in rooms with brightly tiled fireplaces, rustic French antiques, and four-poster beds, and in the kitchen, where owner-chef Alain Borel produces Provençale favorites, including mussels and smoked rabbit, accompanied by a selection of French and American (including Virginia) wines.

Winchester & Staunton

Before continuing south, head north on US 340 to Winchester. Stroll through the town's eclectic and well-preserved historic district for a crash course in American architectural history including George Washington's 1755-56 military office. Pick up a map for your self-guided tour at the welcome center *(2 N. Cameron St. 540-722-6367).*

Back in the car, head south on US 340 to **Shenandoah National**

Park *(540-999-3500. www.nps.gov/shen)* and the renowned **Skyline Drive.** Motor 105 miles south through the park's spectacular dense forests and mountain meadows bursting with wildflowers. Plenty of places along the way allow you to gaze out over the Shenandoah Valley. **Limberlost Trail** at Milepost 43 is just the place to take a short hike through groves of hemlocks.

Turn west on US 250 to visit Staunton (pronounced STAN-ton hereabouts), an intact and flourishing Victorian town. Walking-tour maps are available at the visitor center *(New Street parking garage. 540-332-3971).* And don't miss the **Woodrow Wilson Birthplace and Museum** *(18-24 N. Coalter St. 540-885-0897. www.woodrowwilson .org. Adm. fee)* for a look at the antebellum home where the 28th President was born and a collection of lively exhibits depicting his life and years of public service. Vintage auto buffs will find nirvana when they see Wilson's mint-condition 1919 Pierce-Arrow limousine.

Consider overnighting and dining at the **Belle Grae Inn** (see Travelwise), an enclave of several Victorian houses offering both rooms and suites. Saturday night in Staunton means Shakespeare, so ask the inn to get your tickets for the **Blackfriars Playhouse** *(10 S. Market St. 540-885-5588. www.shenandoahshakespeare.com)* to see a troupe that is winning international acclaim for its performances.

Monticello wine district

Driving east from Staunton on US 250 you'll soon enter Virginia's historic Monticello wine district, the birthplace of American wine. Turn north at the village of Crozet, to follow Va. 810, a secluded back road. More grape-cluster signs will point you to two small wineries. At the first, **White Hall Vineyards** *(434-823-8615. www.whitehallvineyards.com. Closed Mon.-Tues. and mid-Dec.–Feb.),* you'll want to sample the Cabernet Franc, an award-winning, sumptuous red with rich fruit flavors. Farther along Va. 810, you'll be directed to **Stone Mountain Vineyards** *(434-990-9463. www.stonemountainvineyards.com. Closed Mon.-Fri. and Jan.-Feb.),* the ultimate country winery, with an excellent Cabernet Sauvignon and a knockout view from the deck.

Turn east on US 33; follow the grape-cluster signs to **Barboursville Vineyards and Historic Ruins** *(540-832-3824. www.barboursvillewine.com).* The ruins are the remains of the plantation house (ca 1822) designed for Governor James Barbour by his friend Thomas Jefferson. Barboursville's wine, however, is far from ruinous, especially the opulent Barbera Reserve. And, since Barboursville is owned by Italian wine interests, your lunch at its restaurant, **Palladio** (see Travelwise) will be strictly *alla Italiana.* Before heading back to Washington, stop off at **Horton Cellars** *(540-832-7440. www.hvwine .com),* on US 33 in Gordonsville, for a taste of their internationally renowned Viognier and Dionysius, Horton's blockbuster red.

—*Bill Whitman*

Travelwise

GETTING THERE
Middleburg is 45 miles west of Washington, D.C., on US 50.

GENERAL INFORMATION
Contact the **Winchester-Frederick County Visitor Center** *(1360 Pleasant Valley Rd., Winchester, VA 22601. 540-662-4135 or 800-662-1360. www.visitwinchesterva.com)* or the **Staunton Convention & Visitors Bureau** *(P.O. Box 58, Staunton, VA 24402. 540-332-3865. www.stauntonva.org).* Call **Virginia's Wine Marketing Program** *(800-828-4637. www.virginiawines.org)* for their excellent guide to the state's wineries.

SEASONS
Year-round. Fall brings the grape harvest and spectacular leaf-peeping along Skyline Drive.

ANNUAL EVENTS
Autumn Explosion and Barrel Tasting at Barboursville Vineyards *(Oct. 540-832-3824. www.barboursvillewine.com. Adm.fee)*

Virginia Wineries Festival *(Aug., Great Meadow, The Plains. 800-277-2675. www .vintagevirginia.com. Adm. fee)* A tasting of the state's vintages.

MORE THINGS TO SEE & DO
Belle Grove Plantation *(US 11, Middletown. 540-869-2028. www.bellegrove.org. Closed Nov.-March; adm.fee)* An 18th-century house with working farm, thriving crafts center.

Frontier Culture Museum *(US 250, Staunton. 540-332-7850. www.frontier.state.va.us. Adm. fee)* Working farms representing 17th-century England, 18th-century Germany and Ireland, and 19th-century America demonstrate how the Shenandoah Valley's culture was molded by immigrant settlers.

Oatlands Plantation *(US 15, 6 miles S of Leesburg. 703-777-3174. www.oatlands.org. Closed Jan.-March; adm fee)* A grand Virginia estate with 1804 manor house furnished in antiques; exquisite historical garden.

LODGING
Belle Grae Inn *(515 W. Frederick St., Staunton. 540-886-5151 or 888-541-5151. www .valleyva.com/bellegrae. $$-$$$)* See p. 340.

Fuller House Inn *(220 W. Boscawen St.,*

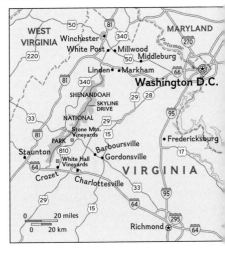

Winchester. 540-722-3976 or 877-722-3976. *$$)* This three-room Greek Revival bed-and-breakfast dates from the late 18th century.

L'Auberge Provençale *(US 340, White Post. 540-837-1375 or 800-638-1702. www .laubergeprovencale.com. $$. Restaurant closed Mon.-Tues.)* See p. 339.

Sampson Eagon Inn *(238 E. Beverley St., Staunton. 540-886-8200 or 800-597-9722. www.eagoninn.com. $$)* An elegant antebellum mansion with five guest rooms.

Wayside Inn *(7783 Main St., Middletown. 540-869-1797 or 877-869-1797. www.along thewayside.com. $$)* Welcoming travelers since 1797; 22 rooms furnished in periods ranging from early American to Victorian.

DINING
Beverley Restaurant *(12 E. Beverley St., Staunton. 540-886-4317. Closed Sun. $)* Known for its southern home cooking, especially its great pies and breads.

Cork Street Tavern *(8 W. Cork St., Winchester. 540-667-3777. $$$)* A popular local hangout famous for its ribs and steaks.

Depot Grille *(42 Middlebrook Ave., Staunton. 540-885-7332. $$$)* Steaks and seafood in the town's 1902 train station.

Palladio *(Barboursville Vineyards. 540-832-7848. Closed Mon.-Tues. $$)* See p. 340.

Presidential Palaces
Private homes of public figures

FROM THE ARCHITECTURAL PIZZAZZ of Thomas Jefferson's Monticello to the bucolic simplicity of James Monroe's Ash Lawn–Highland, the homes of the Presidents reflect the personalities of their owners. Since the Presidents are endlessly fascinating, why not take a weekend to tour their homes? Between Washington, D.C., and Charlottesville, Virginia, you can visit six presidential houses and enjoy a leisurely drive through Virginia's glorious piedmont countryside.

The White House & Woodrow Wilson House

Start with a visit to the home of every U.S. President since John Adams. The most visited historic home in America, the **White House** *(1600 Pennsylvania Ave., N.W., Washington D.C. 202-456-7041. www.whitehouse.gov. Closed Sun.-Mon.)* was taking shape during George Washington's Presidency, but it wasn't until 1801—near the end of Adams's term—that it was ready for occupancy. Since then, the house has been expanded, renovated, and redecorated many times, each President adding his own personal touch. The two biggest renovations came after the British burned it in 1814 and during a major structural overhaul in the late 1940s (Truman had to live across the street for four years).

NOT TO BE MISSED

- **The Potomac River view from Mount Vernon**
- **Springtime dogwood blossoms in Charlottesville**
- **Summer operas at Ash Lawn-Highland**
- **Flower-bordered walk on Monticello's west lawn**

To tour the house during high season *(mid-March–Labor Day)*, you need a free, timed ticket, available at the visitor center *(SE corner of 15th and E Sts.)* starting at 7:30 a.m. for that day only. The walk-through of the house takes anywhere from 20 minutes to 1.5 hours. You enter several rooms used for entertaining dignitaries, including the tremendous **East Room** and the oval-shaped **Blue Room** with its Monroe furniture.

To see where the 28th President lived for the last three years of his life, head over to the **Woodrow Wilson House** *(2340 S St., N.W., Washington D.C. 202-387-4062. www.woodrow wilsonhouse.org. Closed Mon.; adm. fee).* The only President with a Ph.D., the scholarly Wilson (1856-1924) moved to this dignified brick town house after seeing the country through World War I.

Mount Vernon's riverside facade

High ceilings and fancy plasterwork give distinction to the dining room, drawing room, library, and solarium. The furnishings were moved directly from the White House after his two terms. Though neither he nor his wife, Edith, were big collectors, the furniture here reflects Wilson's refined yet unpretentious tastes. On his nightstand, notice the Bible on which he took the oath of office; also in the bedroom hangs a portrait that reminded him of his first wife, Ellen.

Mount Vernon & Montpelier

With relatively light crowds, mornings are a good time to call upon George Washington's (1732–1799) **Mount Vernon,** the second most visited home in the country *(S end of G.W. Memorial Pkwy., Mt. Vernon. 703-780-2000. www.mountvernon.org. Adm. fee).* The palatial Potomac River estate is a monument both to the father of the country and to southern aristocracy. Some 500 of the plantation's original 8,000 acres remain, giving you ample room to explore the landscape that Washington knew. The house is furnished with original and period antiques: In the study, for instance, are Washington's globe, telescope, and 884-volume library. The master bedroom on the second floor holds the four-poster bed in which he died.

The quickest way from here to your next site is to head south on I-95, then exit at Fredericksburg and take Va. 3 and 20 to Orange, for a total of about 75 miles. After the interstate, it's pleasant to drive through the rolling hills of rural Virginia.

James Madison's home lies a few miles south of town. The "father of the U.S. Constitution," Madison (1751–1836) lived at **Montpelier** *(Va. 20. 540-672-2728. www.montpelier.org. Adm. fee)*, a mansion built by his father in 1760. Many rooms are bare of furnishings; the emphasis instead is on architecture. Unplastered walls offer a fascinating look at 18th-century construction techniques. In 1900 the du Pont family bought the house and more than doubled its size to 55 rooms. A few rooms have been kept the way the du Ponts left them: James Madison's mother's bedroom is a jazzy chrome-and-mirror lounge, with a glass mantelpiece and checkerboard floor—every bit as shocking in a historic house now as it was in the 1930s. Don't miss the formal gardens, the Madison and slave cemeteries, and a 1.5-mile trail through a forest of tulip poplars and oaks.

Monticello & Ash Lawn–Highland

Continue south on Va. 20 to Charlottesville. Head over to the **Monticello Visitor Center** *(I-64 and Va. 20. 434-977-1783)* to view the excellent exhibits and film before proceeding up the "little mountain" to Thomas Jefferson's **Monticello** *(Va. 53. 434-984-9822. www.monticello.org. Adm. fee)*, his architectural masterpiece. Of all the houses you visit this weekend, this is one you simply can't miss; in fact, it's the only house in the United States on UNESCO's World Heritage List of international treasures. "All my wishes end," wrote Jefferson (1743–1826), "where I hope my days will end, at Monticello."

The multitalented third President combined aesthetics and imagination in this graceful neoclassic house: A dome, octagonal rooms, skylights, alcove beds, dumbwaiter, and heat-saving double doors are a few of the flourishes you find throughout that reflect Jefferson's wide-ranging intellect. Even during his time, the entrance hall with its archaeological displays was intended as a museum.

Jefferson once described the Presidency as a "splendid misery and a daily loss of friends." Luckily, he was able to enjoy Monticello for 17 years after his Presidency. He could visit his friend James Monroe (1758–1831) at nearby **Ash Lawn–Highland** *(2.5 miles S of Monticello via Va. 53 and 795. 434-293-9539. Adm. fee)*. It was Jefferson who urged Monroe to move to the neighborhood. Though many Monticello visitors pass on Ash Lawn, they miss a chance to compare the lifestyles of the two country gentlemen. More rustic than Monticello, the fourth President's home still retains the feel of a working plantation. Peacocks strut through boxwood gardens, cows graze in pastures, lambs bleat in their pens, and the smell of wood smoke often permeates the air.

For lunch, stop just down the hill from Monticello at **Michie Tavern** (see Travelwise), a 1784 hostelry. In spring, arrive early to beat crowds and load your pewter plate with fried chicken, stewed tomatoes, black-eyed peas, and corn bread.

Down in **Charlottesville**, you might want to walk around the University of Virginia, which Jefferson designed as an "academical village." He modeled the 1826 Rotunda on Rome's Pantheon; the south side affords a sweeping view of the lawn, flanked by colonnades and pavilions. —*John M. Thompson*

Travelwise

GETTING THERE
Charlottesville lies 2.5 hours southwest of Washington, D.C., via US 29 or I-95 and Va. 3 and 20.

GENERAL INFORMATION
In Washington, visit or call the **Visitor Information Center** *(1300 Pennsylvania Ave., N.W. 202-328-4748. Closed Sun.)* or the **Washington, D.C., Convention & Tourism Corp.** *(1212 New York Ave., N.W. 202-789-7007. www.washington.org).* In Charlottesville, contact the **Charlottesville Regional Chamber of Commerce** *(500 E. Market St., Charlottesville, VA 22902. 434-295-3141).*

SEASONS
Spring is lovely in both Washington and Charlottesville; winter is the least crowded time. Summers can be hot and muggy.

ANNUAL EVENTS
Ash Lawn–Highland Summer Music Festival *(June-Aug.)* Operas alfresco.

Montpelier Hunt Races *(1st Sat. of Nov. 540-672-0027)* Steeplechase racing and Jack Russell terrier races at Madison's Montpelier.

Mount Vernon by Candlelight *(late Nov.–mid-Dec. Fri.-Sun.)* Visitors are treated to hot cider, cookies, and caroling; tours include the normally off-limits third floor.

LODGING
200 South Street Inn *(200 South St., Charlottesville. 434-979-0200 or 800-964-7008. $$)* Situated near the downtown pedestrian mall, this inviting inn created from two historic houses features 19 rooms and 2 suites.

Silver Thatch Inn *(3001 Hollymead Dr., Charlottesville. 434-978-4686 or 800-261-0720. $$)* A 1780 farmhouse has seven rooms furnished with period antiques.

Tabard Inn *(1739 N St., N.W., Washington, D.C. 202-785-1277. $$$)* Overstuffed Victo-

rian charmer with 40 rooms.

Willow Grove Inn *(14079 Plantation Way, 1 mile N of Orange. 540-672-5982 or 800-949-1778. $$$, inc. breakfast and dinner)* 1778 plantation house on 37 acres; ten antique-filled rooms and suites.

DINING
Bizou *(119 Main St. W., Charlottesville. 434-977-1818. $$)* The French chef at this eatery always comes up with palate-pleasing entrées.

Iron Gate Inn *(1734 N St., N.W., Washington, D.C. 202-737-1370. $$)* Delicious Mediterranean-inspired cuisine in a lovely setting.

Michie Tavern *(0.5 mile W of Monticello on Va. 53. 434-977-1234. $$)* Southern cuisine typical of the 18th century. See p. 344.

Old Mill Room *(Boar's Head Inn, US 250, 1 mile W of Charlottesville. 434-972-2230. $$$)* A refined Virginia establishment featuring southern-influenced menus; dark woods and a crackling fire add atmosphere.

Pizzeria Paradiso *(2029 P St., N.W., Washington, D.C. 202-223-1245. $$)* Small, very popular restaurant offering the best pizza in town. Try the Atomica.

Illustrations Credits

cover, Michael Melford; 1, Bob Krist; 2-3, Paul Harris/stone/Getty Images; 4, Bob Krist; 9, Kevin Fleming/CORBIS; 11, Franz-Marc Frei/CORBIS; 15, Raymond Gehman/CORBIS; 19, Jim Zuckerman/CORBIS; 21, Mark E. Gibson/CORBIS; 24-25, Richard Cummins/CORBIS; 31, Farrell Grehan/CORBIS; 34, James P. Blair/CORBIS; 39, Phil Schermeister; 42, Michael T. Sedam/CORBIS; 45, Richard A. Cooke/CORBIS; 47, Tom Nebbia/CORBIS; 53, Kelly Culpepper/TRANSPARENCIES, Inc.; 55, Randy Faris/CORBIS; 57, Stephen Simpson/FPG/Getty Images; 61, Jason Lindsey/perceptivevisions.com; 66, Jonathan Nourok/stone/Getty Images; 71, Bill Luster; 73, Raymond Gehman; 75, Steven L. Raymer/NG Image Collection; 78-79, Glen Allison/stone/Getty Images; 83, Michael S. Lewis/CORBIS; 85, Tony Demin/Network Aspen; 89, David Hiser/Network Aspen; 93, Nicholas DeVore III/Network Aspen; 97, Scott Barrow; 99, Scott Barrow; 105, Cheryl Hogue/BRITSTOCK; 107, Andrea Wells/stone/Getty Images; 109, David G. Houser/Houserstock; 114, Randall Hyman; 119, Joseph McNally/Image Bank/Getty Images; 121, Phil Schermeister/Network Aspen; 123, Bill Luster; 128, Dave G. Houser/CORBIS; 131, Luc Beziat/stone/Getty Images; 133, Jeffrey Aaronson/Network Aspen; 137, Phil Schermeister; 139, Robert Yager/stone/Getty Images; 143, Rich Reid/Colors of Nature; 149, Rick Doyle/CORBIS; 152, Chuck Place/Place Stock Photography; 155, Phil Schermeister/Network Aspen; 159, Joel Sartore/www.joelsartore.com; 161, Jerry Driendl/FPG/Getty Images; 166-167, Bob Krist/CORBIS; 170, Thomas Mangelsen/ Minden Pictures; 173, Tom Bean; 175, Richard Hamilton Smith; 179, Hiroyuki Matsumoto/stone/Getty Images; 181, Kim Steele/PhotoDisc/Getty Images; 185, Chip Clark; 189, Jim Richardson/CORBIS; 192, Gail Mooney; 197, Matt Bradley; 199, Adam Jones/Danita Delimont, Agent; 201, Bob Krist/stone/Getty Images; 206, Wolfgang Kaehler/CORBIS; 211, Philip Gould/CORBIS; 213, Catherine Karnow; 215, Jake Rajs; 219, Carol Kitman; 222, Rich Pomerantz; 225, William A. Bake/Image Bank/Getty Images; 227, Kelly/Mooney Photography/CORBIS; 233, Bob Krist; 236, Alan & Linda Detrick; 239, David Muench/CORBIS; 241, Tom Bean; 247, Tony Roberts/CORBIS; 251, Kerrick James; 253, Richard A. Cooke/CORBIS; 255, Richard Bickel/CORBIS; 258-259, Richard A. Cooke/CORBIS; 263, Richard Olsenius/NG Image Collection; 265, Wolfgang Kaehler/CORBIS; 269, Phil Schermeister/Network Aspen; 274, Scott Barrow; 279, David Muench/CORBIS; 283, Neil Rabinowitz/CORBIS; 286, Joel W. Rogers/CORBIS; 291, Neil Rabinowitz /CORBIS; 293, Randall Hyman; 295, Buddy Mays/CORBIS; 298-299, Randall Hyman; 303, Howie Garber/Image Bank/Getty Images; 305, Richard Price/FPG/Getty Images; 309, George H. H. Huey; 315, Catherine Karnow; 317, Catherine Karnow; 321, David Sanger/Danita Delimont, Agent; 326, Monterey Bay Aquarium/Randy Wilder; 330, Phil Schermeister; 333, Scott Barrow; 335, Scott Suchman /Danita Delimont, Agent; 339, Kenneth Garrett; 343, John Skowronski; backcover, Catherine Karnow (top); Luc Beziat/stone/ Getty Images (bottom).

Index

A

Acadian Cultural Center,
Lafayette, La. 209
Acadian Memorial, St. Mart-
inville, La. 210
Adams, Mount, Wash. 277–278,
280
Admiral Nimitz Museum S.H.S.,
Tex. 119–120
Alamo, San Antonio, Tex. 113
Alcatraz Island, San Francisco,
Calif. 318
Alta, Utah 304–305, 307
American Cave Museum and
Hidden River Cave, Horse
Cave, Ky. 184
American Clock & Watch
Museum, Bristol, Conn.
222–223
American Jazz Museum, Kansas
City, Mo. 122–123
Amherstburg, Ont. 105–106
Amicalola Falls S.P., Ga. 17
Anahuac N.W.R., Tex. 111
Andy Warhol Museum,
Pittsburgh, Pa. 257
Angel Island S.P., Calif. 318
Ann, Cape, Mass. 26–27, 28
Annapolis, Md. 334–335, 337
Anza-Borrego Desert S.P., Calif.
154–156, 158
Appalachian Trail, U.S. 16
Apple Hill, Calif. 330
Aquarium of the Pacific, Long
Beach, Calif. 147
Arabia Steamboat Museum,
Kansas City, Mo. 124
Arcola, Ill. 62
Arizona Biltmore Resort and Spa,
Phoenix, Ariz. 245–246
Arlington, Vt. 34, 36
Armstrong Redwoods State
Reserve, Guerneville,
Calif. 323
Arrowhead, Lenox, Mass. 39
Art Deco Welcome Center, Miami
Beach, Fla. 160
Arthur, Ill. 62–63, 64
Ash Lawn-Highland, near Monti-
cello, Va. 344, 345
Asheville, N.C. 46–48, 50, 52, 54
Ashton Villa, Galveston, Tex. 110
Astoria, Oreg. 271
Atchafalaya Basin, La. 211–212
Athens, Ga. 10–11, 13
Auburn, Calif. 331
Auburn, Ind. 66–67, 68
Auburn Hills, Mich. 101–102

Augusta, Mo. 301, 302
Aurora, Ind. 75–76
Avalon, Calif. 148, 149–150

B

Bahia Honda S.P., Fla. 167–168
Bailey-Matthews Shell Museum,
Sanibel Island, Fla. 169
Bainbridge Island, Wash.
281–282, 284
Bandera, Tex. 117–118, 119, 120
Barboursville Vineyards and
Historic Ruins, Va. 340
Barnacle S.H.S., Fla. 162
Baton Rouge, La. 207
Beacon Rock S.P., Wash. 277
Beale Street, Memphis, Tenn.
192–193
Bear Lake, Utah 313
Beauregard-Keyes House, New
Orleans, La. 203
Belle Isle, Mich. 104
Bellingham, Wash. 291–292
Bennington, Vt. 33–34, 36
Berkshires (mountains), Mass.
37–40
Betsy Ross House, Philadelphia,
Pa. 227
Beverly Hills, Calif. 141
Big Cypress National Preserve,
Fla. 171–172
Biltmore Estate, Asheville, N.C.
46–48, 50
Biltmore Hotel, Coral Gables, Fla.
163
Bingham-Waggoner Estate, Inde-
pendence, Mo. 129
Bishop's Palace, Galveston, Tex.
110
Blackstone River and Canal
Heritage S.P., Mass. 21–22
Blackstone River Valley, Mass.-R.
I. 20–23
Blanchard Springs Caverns, Ark.
196–197
Blanchard Springs Recreation
Area, Ark. 197–198
Bloedel Reserve, Bainbridge
Island, Wash. 281–282
Blowing Rock, N.C. 51, 54
Bluebird Café, Nashville, Tenn.
181–182
Boone, N.C. 51
Borrego Palm Canyon, Calif.
154–155
Boulder, Colo. 86–87, 89–90, 91
Bourbon Street, New Orleans, La.
203
Bowling Green, Ky. 186
Bowman's Hill Wildflower
Preserve, Pa. 234
Boyce Thompson Arboretum S.P.,

Ariz. 242
Brandywine Valley, Del.-Pa.
235–238
Branford, Conn. 43
Brasstown, N.C. 53, 54
Brasstown Bald, Ga. 16
Breaux Bridge, La. 210, 212
Brevard, N.C. 52
Bristol, Conn. 222–223
Brown County, Ind. 69–71, 72
Brown County S.P., Ind. 70
Bucks County, Pa. 231–234
Buena Vista, Colo. 94, 96
Buffalo National River, Ark. 196

C

Cabbage Key, Fla. 171
Cajun Village, Sorrento, La. 207
Calvert Cliffs S.P., Md. 336
Calvert Marine Musuem,
Solomons Island, Md. 336
Cannon Beach, Oreg. 270
Captiva Island, Fla. 170
Carnegie Museums of Pittsburgh,
Pittsburgh, Pa. 254–255
Carnegie Science Center,
Pittsburgh, Pa. 257
Carpinteria, Calif. 142, 144–145,
146
Carpinteria Bluffs Nature
Preserve, Carpinteria, Calif.
144–145
Casa Navarro S.H.S., San
Antonio, Tex. 115
Cayo Costa S.P., Fla. 171
Chadds Ford, Pa. 237–238
Champaign, Ill. 62, 64
Charles H. Wright Museum of
African-American History,
Detroit, Mich. 103–104
Charlottesville, Va. 345
Chattahoochee N.F., Ga. 16, 17,
18
Cherokee, N.C. 53
Chesapeake Bay, and region
334–337
Chesapeake Bay Maritime
Museum, St. Michaels, Md.
335–336
Chesterwood (estate), Mass. 38
Chicago, Ill. 55–59
Chickasaw Village, Miss. 189
Christian C. Sanderson Museum,
Chadds Ford, Pa. 237
Chuckanut Drive, Wash. 290–292
Cincinnati, Ohio 73–75, 77
Clarksville, Mo. 296
Clayton (mansion), Pittsburgh,
Pa. 256
Clermont (mansion), N.Y. 216
Clinton's Soda Fountain, Inde-
pendence, Mo. 129

Cliveden, Philadelphia, Pa. 229
Coconut Grove, Fla. 162–163, 164
Coloma, Calif. 330
Columbia, Tenn. 187–188
Columbia River and Basin, Canada-U.S. 273–276
Columbia River Gorge National Scenic Area, Oreg. 273, 277
Columbia River Maritime Museum, Astoria, Oreg. 271
Constitution, Mount, Wash. 287
Coral Gables, Fla. 163, 164
Coronado, Calif. 151
Country Club Plaza, Kansas City, Mo. 125
Country Music Hall of Fame and Museum, Nashville, Tenn. 180
Covington, Ky. 74
Cradle of Forestry in America N.H.S., N.C. 49
Crane Point Hammock, Fla. 165–166
Crystal Springs Rhodendron Garden, Portland, Oreg. 266

D

Dahlonega, Ga. 14, 16, 17–18
The Dalles, Oreg. 275, 276
Danville, Ill. 63, 64
Danville, Ky. 80
Dearborn, Mich. 100–101
Deer Valley Resort, Utah 306
Del Mar, Calif. 152–153
Delaware Art Museum, Wilmington, Del. 236
Denver, Colo. 83–85, 87, 90, 91
Depoe Bay, Oreg. 270
Deschutes River State Recreation Area, Oreg. 276
Desert Botanical Garden, Phoenix, Ariz. 240, 244
Destrehan Plantation, Destrehan, La. 205
Detroit, Mich. 98–99, 102, 103–104, 106
Detroit Historical Museum, Detroit, Mich. 99
Detroit Institute of Arts, Detroit, Mich. 98
Deutschheim S.H.S., Mo. 299–300
Diamond Caverns, Ky. 185
Dillsboro, N.C. 53
Dinosaur N.M., Colo.-Utah 310
Dinosaur Ridge National Natural Landmark Visitor Center, Colo. 89
Dolphin Research Center, Fla. 166
Donaldsonville, La. 206, 208
Dorset, Vt. 35
Doylestown, Pa. 231–232, 234

Dry Creek Valley, Calif. 320, 322

E

Eastsound, Wash. 286–287
Eatonton, Ga. 11–12, 13
1859 Jail, Marshal's Home, and Museum, Independence, Mo. 129
Elbert, Mount, Colo. 93–94
Eleanor Roosevelt N.H.S., N.Y. 216
Elk Rock Garden of the Bishop's Close, Portland, Oreg. 266
Elkhorn Slough National Estuarine Research Reserve, Moss Landing, Calif. 327
Etowah River, Ga. 17
Eunice, La. 211

F

Fair Lane (estate), Dearborn, Mich. 100–101
Fallingwater, Pa. 261
First USA Riverfront Arts Center, Wilmington, Del. 236–237
Flaming Gorge-Uintas Scenic Byway, Utah 311
Fonthill, Doylestown, Pa. 231
Fort Clatsop National Memorial, Oreg. 271
Fort Collins, Colo. 85–86, 87
Fort Ligonier stockade, Ligonier, Pa. 261
Fort Stevens S.P., Oreg. 271
Franklin D. Roosevelt N.H.S., N.Y. 215–216
Fredericksburg, Tex. 119–120
Fremont Street Experience, Las Vegas, Nev. 135
French Quarter, New Orleans, La. 200, 202–203
Frick Art & Historical Center, Pittsburgh, Pa. 256

G

Galveston, Tex. 108–112
Galveston Island S.P., Tex. 111
Garden District, New Orleans, La. 203
Gaylord Opryland Resort and Convention Center, Nashville, Tenn. 182–183
Genoa, Wis. 177
Gloucester, Mass. 26–27, 28
Golden, Colo. 88, 91
Golden Gate Bridge, San Francisco, Calif. 316, 317
Graceland, Memphis, Tenn. 193–194
Grand Ole Opry, Nashville, Tenn. 180–181, 182–183
Grand Opera House, Wilmington, Del. 237

Grass Valley, Calif. 331–332
Great River Bluffs S.P., Minn. 176
Great River State Trail, Wis. 178
Greenport, N.Y. 219
Greensburg, Pa. 261
Greylock, Mount, Mass. 39–40
Groton, Conn. 41–42
Guerneville, Calif. 322–323
Guilford, Conn. 43

H

Hagley Museum and Library, Wilmington, Del. 235
Hannibal, Mo. 294–296, 297
Harrisville, N. H. 30
Harry S. Truman N.H.S., Mo. 130
Hassayampa River Preserve, Ariz. 243
Healdsburg, Calif. 320, 324
Henry Ford Museum and Greenfield Village, Dearborn, Mich. 100
Heritage Discovery Center, Johnstown, Pa. 260
Hermann, Mo. 299–300, 302
The Hermitage, Nashville, Tenn. 182
High Island, Tex. 111
Highlands, N.C. 52
Hildene (mansion), Vt. 35, 36
Hill Country State Natural Area, Tex. 118
Hollywood, Calif. 138–141
Hollywood Boulevard, Los Angeles, Calif. 138–140
Hood, Mount, Oreg. 275
Hood River, Oreg. 274–275, 276
Horse Cave, Ky. 184
Hotel Del Coronado, Coronado, Calif. 151, 153
Houmas House Plantation and Gardens, Darrow, La. 207
Hudson River and Valley, N. Y. 214–217

I

Independence, Mo. 129–130
Independence Hall, Philadelphia, Pa. 226
Independence N.H.P., Philadelphia, Pa. 226–227
Indianapolis, Ind. 65–66, 68
Institute of Texan Cultures, San Antonio, Tex. 114

J

Jaffrey, N. H. 29
James A. Michener Art Museum, Doylestown, Pa. 232
James K. Polk Home, Columbia, Tenn. 187–188
Japanese Garden, Portland, Oreg. 265–266

Jean Lafitte National Historical Park and Preserve, La. 209
Jennerstown, Pa. 261
Jerome, Ariz. 251–252
Jesse James Farm and Museum, Kearney, Mo. 128
Jesse James Home, St. Joseph, Mo. 128
J.N. "Ding" Darling N.W.R., Fla. 170–171
John Tarrant Kenney Hitchcock Museum, Riverton, Conn. 223
Johnstown, Pa. 258–259, 260
Johnstown Flood Museum, Johnstown, Pa. 260
Johnstown Flood National Memorial, St. Michael, Pa. 259
Johnstown Incline Plane, Johnstown, Pa. 260
Joshua Tree N.P., Calif. 156–157

K

Kansas City, Mo. 122–126
Katy Trail S.P., Mo. 300–301
Kearney, Mo. 128
Keeneland Race Course, Ky. 80
Kemper Museum of Contemporary Art, Kansas City, Mo. 125
Kennett Square, Pa. 237–238
Kent, Conn. 221–222
Kent Falls S.P., Conn. 222
Kentucky Down Under, near Horse Cave, Ky. 184
Kentucky Horse Park, Ky. 78–79
Kerrville, Tex. 119, 120
Kickapoo State Recreation Area, Ill. 63
Kingston, Wash. 282
Kitsap Peninsula, Wash. 282
Kokomo, Ind. 67
Korbel Champagne Cellars, Guerneville, Calif. 322–323
Kykuit, N.Y. 215, 217

L

La Conner, Wash. 289–290, 292
La Crosse, Wis. 177
La Jolla, Calif. 151–152, 153
La Villita, San Antonio, Tex. 115
Labrot & Graham distillery, Versailles, Ky. 80
Lafayette, La. 209–210, 212
Lake Waramaug S.P., Conn. 221
Lambertville, N.J. 233
Las Vegas, Nev. 131–136
L'Auberge Provençale, White Post, Va. 339, 341
Laura: A Creole Plantation, Vacherie, La. 205
Laurel Highlands, Pa. 258–262

Lawrence, Mass. 22–23
Lawrence Heritage S.P., Mass. 22–23
Lawrenceburg, Ind. 75, 77
Leach Botanical Garden, Portland, Oreg. 266
Leadville, Colo. 92–93, 96
Len Foote Hike Inn, Ga. 17, 18
Lenox, Mass. 38, 39, 40
Lexington, Ky. 78, 82
Ligonier, Pa. 261, 262
Litchfield, Conn. 223–224
Litchfield History Museum, Litchfield, Conn. 224
Lock Museum of America, Terryville, Conn. 222
Logan, Utah 312, 314
Logan Canyon, Utah 313
Long Beach, Calif. 147–148, 150
Longfellow-Evangeline S.H.S., La. 210
Longwood Gardens, Kennett Square, Pa. 237
Los Angeles, Calif. 141
Lost Maples State Natural Area, Tex. 118–119
Lost River Cave, Bowling Green, Ky. 186
Louisiana, Mo. 296
Louisiana State Museum, New Orleans, La. 201
Louisiana State University Rural Life Museum, Baton Rouge, La. 207
Lowell, Mass 22
Lowell N.H.P., Lowell, Mass. 22
Lyndhurst, Sunnyside, N.Y. 214

M

Macon, Ga. 12, 13
Madison, Conn. 43
Madison, Ga. 11, 13
Mammoth Cave N.P., Ky. 184–185
Manchester, Vt. 34–35, 36
Marathon, Fla. 165, 168
Marblehead, Mass. 26
Mark Twain Birthplace S.H.S., Mo. 297
Mark Twain Boyhood Home, Hannibal, Mo. 294
Market Square, San Antonio, Tex. 115
Marshall Gold Discovery S.H.P., Coloma, Calif. 330
Martin, Lake, La. 212
Mashomack Preserve, Shelter Island, N.Y. 220
Meadow Brook Hall, Rochester, Mich. 101
Medina, Tex. 118
Memphis, Tenn. 191–194
Memphis Rock 'n' Soul Museum,

Memphis, Tenn. 191
Mercer Museum, Doylestown, Pa. 232
Miami, Fla. 164
Miami Beach, Fla. 160–162
Middle Keys, Fla. 165–168
Middleburg, Va. 338, 341
Midgeville, Ga. 12
Midway, Ky. 79–80
Milledgeville, Ga. 13
Mission Beach, Calif. 151
Monadnock S.P., N. H. 30–31
Monterey, Calif. 327, 328
Monterey Bay Aquarium, Monterey, Calif. 327
Monterey Bay National Marine Sanctuary, Calif. 326
Montgomery Place, Annandale-on-Hudson, N.Y. 216, 217
Monticello, Ill. 62
Monticello, Va. 340, 344
Montpelier, Idaho 313–314
Montpelier (mansion), Va. 344, 345
Monument Mountain, Mass. 37
Moody Gardens, Galveston, Tex. 110
Moody Mansion, Galveston, Tex. 110
Moon Walk, New Orleans, La. 200
Moravian Pottery and Tile Works, Doylestown, Pa. 231–232
Morrison, Colo. 91
Moss Landing, Calif. 327
The Mount, Lenox, Mass. 38–39
Mount Mitchell S.P., N.C. 49–50
Mount Rainier N.P., Wash. 278–280
Mount St. Helens National Volcanic Monument, Wash. 278, 280
Mount Tamalpais S.P., Calif. 317
Mount Vernon, Va. 343, 345
Mountain Playhouse, Jennerstown, Pa. 261
Mountain View, Ark. 195, 196, 198
Multnomah Falls, Oreg. 273
Museum of Northwest Art, La Conner, Wash. 290
Museums at 18th and Vine, Kansas City, Mo. 122–124
Music Row, Nashville, Tenn. 182
Mutual Musicians Foundation, Kansas City, Mo. 125–126
Mystic, Conn. 41, 44
Mystic Seaport, Mystic, Conn. 41

N

Nashville, Ind. 69–71, 72
Nashville, Tenn. 180–183
Nassau Inn, Princeton, N.J.

228–229, 230
Natchez Trace Parkway, Miss.-Tenn. 187–190
National Center for Atmospheric Research, Boulder, Colo. 90
National Civil Rights Museum, Memphis, Tenn. 193
National Eagle Center, Wabasha, Minn. 176
National Earthquake Information Center, Golden, Colo. 88
National Frontier Trails Center, Independence, Mo. 129
National Steinbeck Center, Salinas, Calif. 327
Natural Bridges S.P., Calif. 325
N.C. Wyeth House and Studio, Chadds Ford, Pa. 237
Negro Leagues Baseball Museum, Kansas City, Mo. 123–124
Nelson-Atkins Museum of Art, Kansas City, Mo. 125
Nemours Mansion and Garden, Wilmington, Del. 235
New Hope, Pa. 232
New Iberia, La. 210–211, 212
New London, Conn. 42–43
New Orleans, La. 200–204
Newport, Oreg. 268
Norman Rockwell Museum, near Stockbridge, Mass. 38
North American Museum of Ancient Life, near Salt Lake City, Utah 308
North Beach, San Francisco, Calif. 316
North Carolina Arboretum, near Asheville, N.C. 48
North Fork, Long Island, N.Y. 218–219, 220
North Tarrytown, N.Y. 214–215
Nottoway Plantation, White Castle, La. 207

O

Oak Alley, Vacherie, La. 205
Oak Park, Ill. 57–58
Ocmulgee N.M., Macon, Ga. 12
Ohio River, U.S.: riverboats 74–75
Ohiopyle S.P., Pa. 260–261
Ojai, Calif. 142–144, 145, 146
Ojai Valley Inn & Spa, Ojai, Calif. 144, 146
Olana S.H.S., N.Y. 216
Old Barracks Museum, Trenton, N.J. 228
Old U.S. Mint, New Orleans, La. 202
Olga, Wash. 287
Olympic Peninsula, Wash. 283–284
Ontario, Canada 106

Opry House, Nashville, Tenn. 182–183
Opryland, USA 182
Orcas Island, Wash. 285–288
Orcas Island Historical Museum, Eastsound, Wash. 286
Orcas Village, Wash. 285
Orchid Farm, Carpinteria, Calif. 146
Oregon Coast Aquarium, Newport, Oreg. 268
Orient, N.Y. 219
Orient Beach S.P., N.Y. 219
Ozark Folk Center S.P., Ark. 195–196
Ozark Plateau, Ark.-Mo. 195–198

P

Padilla Bay National Estuarine Research Reserve, Mt. Vernon, Wash. 290
Palm Springs, Calif. 157, 158
Paramount Studios, Los Angeles, Calif. 140
Park City, Utah 305–306, 307
Pawtucket, R. I. 20
Peabody Essex Museum, Salem, Mass. 25–26
Peabody Hotel, Memphis, Tenn. 194
Pearl S. Buck Historic Site, Perkasie, Pa. 232
Penland School of Crafts and the Penland Gallery, near Spruce Pine, N.C. 52
Pepin, Lake, Minn. 175
Perryville, Ky. 80–81
Perryville Battlefield S.H.S., Ky. 81
Peter Wentz Farmstead, Worcester, Pa. 229, 230
Peterborough, N. H. 29–30, 31, 32
Pharr Mounds, Miss. 188–189
Philadelphia, Pa. 226–228, 229, 230
Philipsburg Manor, North Tarrytown, N.Y. 214–215, 217
Phippen Museum, near Prescott, Ariz. 251
Phipps Conservatory and Botanical Gardens, Pittsburgh, Pa. 255–256
Phoenix, Ariz. 240, 244, 245, 248
Piedmont Vineyards, Va. 338
Pigeon Key, Fla. 167
Pioneer Living History Museum, Ariz. 249
Pisgah N.F., N.C. 48–49
Pittsburgh, Pa. 254–257
Placerville, Calif. 329–330
Pony Express Museum, St. Joseph, Mo. 127–128
Port Gamble, Wash. 282

Port Townsend, Wash. 283–284
Portland, Oreg. 264–267
Portland Classical Chinese Garden, Portland, Oreg. 264
Prairie Acadian Cultural Center, Eunice, La. 211
Prescott, Ariz. 250–251
Princeton, Mount, Colo. 94–95
Princeton, N.J. 228–229
Princeton Battlefield S.P., N.J. 228
Princeton University 228
Provenance Project, Mo. 296

Q

Queen Mary (ocean liner) 148, 150

R

Rainier, Mount, Wash. 279
Red Rocks Park, Colo. 89
Red Wing, Minn. 174–175, 178
Renaissance Center, Detroit, Mich. 98
Rhinebeck, N.Y. 216
Rising Sun, Ind. 76
River Road African American Museum and Gallery, La. 207
River Walk, San Antonio, Tex. 114
Riverton, Conn. 223
Robert Allertown Park, Monticello, Ill. 60, 62
Rockome Gardens, Ill. 63
Rockport, Mass. 27
Rosario Resort & Spa, Eastsound, Wash. 286–287, 288
Rush Historic District, Buffalo National River, Ark. 196
Russian River and Valley, Calif. 322, 323, 324
Ryman Auditorium, Nashville, Tenn. 180–181

S

St. Charles Streetcar, New Orleans, La. 203
St. Helens, Mount, Wash. 278
St. Joseph, Mo. 127–128, 130
St. Joseph Museum, St. Joseph, Mo. 127
St. Martinville, La. 210
St. Michael, Pa. 259–260
St. Michaels, Md. 335–336
Salem, Mass. 24–26, 28
Salida, Colo. 95, 96
Salinas, Calif. 327
San Antonio, Tex. 113–116
San Antonio Missions N.H.P., Tex. 113–114
San Antonio Museum of Art, San Antonio, Tex. 115–116
San Francisco, Calif. 316–319
San Francisco Art Institute, San Francisco, Calif. 316

San Juan Islands, Wash. 285–288
Sanctuary Golf Course at West-
world, Scottsdale, Ariz. 246
Sanibel Island, Fla. 169–172
Sanibel-Captiva Conservation
Foundation's Nature Center,
Sanibel Island, Fla. 169
Santa Catalina Island, Calif.
148–150
Santa Cruz, Calif. 325–326, 328
Santa Cruz Beach Boardwalk,
Santa Cruz, Calif. 325
Scottsdale, Ariz. 246, 248
Seattle, Wash. 281
Sebastopol, Calif. 323
Second Baptist Church of
Detroit, Detroit, Mich. 104
Seven-Mile Bridge, Fla. 166–167
Shadows-on-the-Teche, New
Iberia, La. 210–211
Shaker Village of Pleasant Hill,
Ky. 81, 82
Sharlot Hall Museum, Prescott,
Ariz. 250–251
Shelter Island, N.Y. 219–220
Shenandoah N.P., Va. 339–340
Simi Winery, Healdsburg, Calif.
322
Skagit Valley, Wash. 289–290
Slater Mill Historic Site, R. I. 20
Sleepy Hollow, N.Y. 214–215
Sloane-Stanley Museum, near
Kent, Conn. 222
Snowbird Ski and Summer
Resort, Utah 305
Solomons Island, Md. 336
Sorrento, La. 207, 208
South Beach area, Miami Beach,
Fla. 160–162
South Bend, Ind. 67
South Mountain Park, Phoenix,
Ariz. 240, 244
Southern Vermont Arts Center,
Manchester, Vt. 35
Spa Ojai, Ojai, Calif. 144
Space Center Houston, Houston,
Tex. 108
Spanish Governor's Palace, San
Antonio, Tex. 115
Staatsburgh, N.Y. 216
Staunton, Va. 340, 341
Stax Museum of American Soul
Music, near Memphis, Tenn.
193
Stockbridge, Mass. 37–38
Stone Hill Winery, Hermann, Mo.
300
Stonington, Conn. 41
Stony Creek, Conn. 43
The Strip, Las Vegas, Nev. 132–135
Sun Studio, Memphis, Tenn.
191–192

Sunnyside, Tarrytown, N.Y. 214,
217
Sutro Heights Park, San Francisco, Calif. 317
Swanzey, N. H. 32

T
T. Cook's, Phoenix, Ariz. 246, 248
Taliesin West, Scottsdale, Ariz.
246
Tanglewood, Lenox, Mass. 38, 40
Tapping Reeve House and Law
School, Litchfield, Conn.
223–224
Tarpon Bay Beach, Sanibel Island,
Fla. 170
Tarrytown, N.Y. 214
T.C. Steele S.H.S., Ind. 70
Tempe, Ariz. 242
Terryville, Conn. 222
Tezcuco Plantation Home, La.
207
Tillamook, Oreg. 270
Timpanogos Cave N.M., Utah
308–309
Toccoa River, Ga. 17
Tom McCall Preserve, Oreg. 275
Torrey Pines State Reserve, Calif.
152
Tournament Players Club of
Scottsdale, Scottsdale, Ariz.
247
Trempealeau N.W.R., Wis.
176–177
Trenton, N.J. 228
Truman Presidential Museum
and Library, Independence,
Mo. 129–130
Tubman African American
Museum, Macon, Ga. 12
Two Harbors, Calif. 149

U
Underground Railroad 103–106
Union Station, Kansas City, Mo.
124
University of Georgia 10
University of Pittsburgh 255
Urbana, Ill. 62
U.S. Coast Guard Academy, New
London, Conn. 42
U.S. Naval Academy, Annapolis,
Md. 334
U.S. Naval Submarine Base, Gro-
ton, Conn. 41–42
Utah Field House of Natural His-
tory S.P., Vernal, Utah 310
Utah Olympic Park, Park City,
Utah 306

V
Valley Forge N.H.P., Pa. 229
Van Cortlandt Manor, Croton-

on-Hudson, N.Y. 215, 217
Vanderbilt Mansion N.H.S., N.Y.
216
Venetian Pool, Coral Gables, Fla.
163
Vermilionville, La. 209
Vernal, Utah 310
Versailles, Ky. 79–80
Vevay, Ind. 76, 77
Vizcaya (villa), Coconut Grove,
Fla. 162
Vogel S.P., Ga. 16

W
Walter P. Chrysler Museum,
Auburn Hills, Mich. 101–102
Waltham, Mass. 22
Waramaug, Lake, Conn. 221
Wasco County Historical
Museum, The Dalles, Oreg.
275
Washington, D.C. 345
Washington, Mo. 301, 302
Washington Crossing Historic
Park, Washington Crossing,
Pa. 228
Washington Crossing S.P., N.J.
228
Washington Historical Society
Museum, Washington, Mo.
301
Washington Park International
Rose Test Garden, Portland,
Oreg. 264–265
Western Washington University
291–292
Westmoreland Museum of Amer-
ican Art, Greensburg, Pa. 261
Weston, Vt. 35
White House, Washington, D.C.
342
Wickenburg, Ariz. 249–250, 252
Wilmington, Del. 235–237
Winchester, Va. 339
Windsor, Ont. 104–105
Winona, Minn. 176
Winslow, Wash. 281
Winterthur Museum, Garden and
Library, Wilmington, Del.
235–236
Wolfsonian Florida International
University, Miami Beach, Fla.
161
Woodrow Wilson Birthplace and
Museum, Staunton, Va. 340
Woodrow Wilson House, Wash-
ington, D.C. 342–343
Woonsocket, R. I. 20–21

Y
Yaquina Head Outstanding
Natural Area, near Newport,
Oreg. 268

National Geographic Guide to Weekend Getaways

Published by the National Geographic Society

John M. Fahey, Jr., *President and Chief Executive Officer*

Gilbert M. Grosvenor, *Chairman of the Board*

Nina D. Hoffman, *Executive Vice President*

Prepared by the Book Division

Kevin Mulroy, *Vice President and Editor-in-Chief*

Charles Kogod, *Illustrations Director*

Marianne R. Koszorus, *Design Director*

Elizabeth L. Newhouse, *Director of Travel Books*

Staff for this Book

Barbara A. Noe, *Editor*

Cinda Rose, *Art Director*

Joan Wolbier, *Designer*

Melissa G. Ryan, *Illustrations Editor*

Allan Fallow, Jane Sunderland, *Text Editors*

Jerry Camarillo Dunn. Jr., Sean M. Groom, Ann Jones, Tina Lassen, Mark Miller, Haas H. Mroue, Michael McCoy, Barbara A. Noe, Donald S. Olson, Lawrence M. Porges, Jeff Sypeck, Barbara Alexander Szerlip, John M. Thompson, Mel White, Bill Whitman, *Writers*

Caroline Hickey, Jane Sunderland, Michelle Harris, Victoria Garrett Jones, Amy R. Mack, *Researchers*

Carl Mehler, *Director of Maps*

Nicholas P. Rosenbach, The M Company, *Map Research and Production*

Lise Sajewski, *Editorial Consultant*

R. Gary Colbert, *Production Director*

Richard S. Wain, *Production Project Manager*

Sharon Kocsis Berry, *Illustrations Assistant*

Connie Binder, *Indexer*

Carolinda E. Averitt, *Contributor*

Manufacturing and Quality Control

Christopher A. Liedel, *Chief Financial Officer*

Phillip L. Schlosser, *Managing Director*

John T. Dunn, *Technical Director*

One of the world's largest nonprofit scientific and educational organizations, the National Geographic Society was founded in 1888 "for the increase and diffusion of geographic knowledge." Fulfilling this mission, the Society educates and inspires millions every day through its magazines, books, television programs, videos, maps and atlases, research grants, the National Geographic Bee, teacher workshops, and innovative classroom materials. The Society is supported through membership dues, charitable gifts, and income from the sale of its educational products. This support is vital to National Geographic's mission to increase global understanding and promote conservation of our planet through exploration, research, and education.

For more information, please call 1-800-NGS LINE (647-5463) or write to the following address:

National Geographic Society
1145 17th Street, N.W.
Washington, D.C. 20036-4688
U.S.A.

Visit the Society's Web site at www.nationalgeographic.com.

Library of Congress Cataloging-in-Publication Data

Guide to weekend getaways : 74 mini vacations across America
  p. cm.
Edited by Barbara A. Noe
Includes index.
ISBN 0-7922-6862-8 (pbk.)   ISBN 0-7922-6943-8 (dlx.)
  1. United States--Tours. I. Noe, Barbara A. II. National Geographic Society (U.S.)
(U.S.)

E158 .G953 2002
917.304'93--dc21   2002069314